SELL
& RE-SELL
YOUR
PHOTOS

ROHN ENGH

Writer's
Digest
Books

Cincinnati, Ohio

Library of Congress Cataloging in Publication Data

Engh, Rohn.
    Sell and re-sell your photos.
    Bibliography: p.
    Includes index.
    1. Photographs—Marketing. I. Title.
TR690.E53   770'.68'8   81-1872
ISBN 0-89879-288-6   AACR2

Book design by Barron Krody.

I'd like to dedicate this book to my parents, Mr. and Mrs. Lynn A. Engh ("Muzzie and Coolie"). My dad inspired me to believe that anything is possible in life if you "Keep in a good frame of mind." My mother showed me how to enjoy my blessings twofold by sharing them with others.

. . . To my two boys, Danny and Jim (both are pictured in this book; that's Danny on the cover), for constantly reminding me that most problems can be solved if you meet them with childlike freshness and clarity of vision.

. . . And to my wife, Jeri, for the common sense, good humor, and love that keep our family on a straight course.

I'd like also to acknowledge Jeri's wonderful help on this book. For eleven months we watched the seasons change as we toiled over the manuscript. Not only did she bring her professional writing expertise to the project, she is my severest critic and my best friend.

Sincere thanks also go to Robert Cavallo and Lou Jacobs, Jr., for their knowledgeable aid with the copyright section, to David Strickler for his help on the model-release section, to Milwaukee attorney-author Ellen Kozak for fine-tuning the copyright section, to Bill Pursche for his valuable contributions to the computer chapter, and to Julian Block, Jerry Kleinberg, Bill Knight and David Klinger for their expertise on the taxes section.

There are many others whose influence or example through the years have helped make this book possible. The best way I can express my appreciation is to pass what I have learned on to you.

Rohn Engh
Pine Lake Farm
Osceola, Wisconsin

TABLE
OF
CONTENTS

INTRODUCTION
Exciting opportunities at your doorstep. The system:
eight elements.   **1**

1. The Wide World of Possibilities   5

The buyers are waiting. Trends in the marketplace. 20,000 photographs a day. A wide-open door. Find the market, then create. You, the stock photographer. The "theme" markets. Prime markets: books and magazines. Secondary markets. Third-choice markets. You supply the pictures—they'll supply the checks.

2. What Pictures Sell and Resell?   19

The difference between a good picture and a good *marketable* picture. Pictures. Good marketable pictures. No-risk marketing. The Rohn Engh principle for producing a marketable picture every time. The principle. Evoke a mood. Using the principle. Photos that you can *read into*. The missing link: 4 illustrations that show why the $P+B+S+I$ formula works. On target and off target: 10 photo illustrations that miss the mark, and why. You are an important resource to photobuyers. A gallery of stock photos.

3. Finding Your Corner of the Market   49

First, find yourself. Photographically . . . who am I? Your PMS/A (personal photographic marketing strength/areas). Track A. Track B. The majors and the minors. How to use the reference guides and directories. Using your local interlibrary loan service. Chart your course . . . build a personalized market list. Setting up your list. The specialization strategy.

Keeping on top with newsletters. Track A: The boulevard of broken dreams. For sale or for soul? How to find your PMS/A. How to narrow down your market list. Publisher's buying power guide.

4. Getting Started 73

Seize the day. A dozen reasons why I can't! The four-weekend action plan to launch your photo-marketing enterprise.

5. Producing a Marketable Product 79

Some basic questions answered. What film should I use? Black-and-white. Color. Black-and-white: What makes a marketable print? How extensive should tonal gradation be? What size should I print and what paper should I use? Should I rely on color to black-and-white conversion? How do I make sure my color will sell? The most commonly asked questions about color. Is 5247 film useful for the stock photographer? Cut your photo costs.

6. Taking and Making Photo Illustrations 93

Do you take or make them? Danger ahead: trite pictures. An example. How do I manage the models? Control the conversation. Relax your models. Should you pay your models? Other model sources. And what about model releases? Dealing with officials. Special effects. The dramatic-lighting formula. Notes on the taking and making of photo illustrations in this book.

7. The Fine Art of Dealing with Photobuyers 111

Getting to know them. The reliability factor. The photobuyer connection. Should you visit a photobuyer? Should you write? Should you telephone? Get on the available-photographers list. Sample marketing categories form letter. Selling the same picture over and over again. Sell and re-sell your photos. Photocopying your photographs. The central art file. The permanent-file system. The pirates.

8. Pricing Your Pictures 125

Master your marketing system first. Sell and re-sell. The price range. Base camp: Inside editorial use. Pricing guide one. Which range for you? Using the pricing system: What to charge. Payment for other uses. Pricing guide two. Within the price range, should you charge the high end or the low end? Second use of your pictures. Pricing guide for photo re-use. State your fee. Pricing the service photo. The lowest fee possible: nothing.

9. Managing Your Mail-Marketing Operation   141

Our postal service—a bargain for the photo illustrator. Preparing your stock photos for market. Sending black-and-whites. Print multiple copies. Sending transparencies. Identify your prints and transparencies. Captions. Packaging: The key to looking like a pro. How to send your submissions. Writing the cover letter. First-class stationery. Deadlines: a necessary evil. Unsolicited submissions. The magic query letter. Seasonal trends in photobuying. Should you deal with foreign markets? What are the heavy purchasing months? How long do photobuyers hold your pictures? Using postcards to relieve the agony. A holding fee—should you charge one? Sales tax—do I need to charge it? When can you expect payment? How safe are your pictures in the hands of an editor? Lost, stolen, or strayed? Your recourse for lost pictures. How much compensation should you expect? Liability notices. A twenty-four-point checklist to success.

10. If You Don't Sell Yourself, Who Will?   171

Promoting your photography, how to blow your own horn. Talent can take you just so far. Look like a pro even if you don't feel like one yet. Your personal trademark. Your letterhead. Envelopes. Business cards. Build a mailing list. Mailers—they pay for themselves. Brochures. Postcards. Catalogs. The phone. Credit lines and tearsheets—part of the sale. Show yourself off. Trade shows. Speaking engagements. Radio and TV interviews. Press releases. Promotional news features. Advertising. Reassess your promotional effectiveness. Postscript. Portfolios. Exhibitions. Salons. Contests. Decor photography. Greeting cards, calendars, and posters. Some final self-promotion suggestions.

11. Assignments   193

An extra dimension for the stock photographer. Negotiating your fee. He who speaks first . . . Expenses. Extra mileage from assignments. A sample expense form. The stringer. Self-assignments—where do you start? Speculation. Take a free vacation. Who buys travel pictures? What does the travel photobuyer really need? What about postcards? Making the contact. A typical assignment query letter. Sample shotgun (after-the-trip) query letter. A sampling of "hot sellers."

12. Stock Photo Agencies and Decor Photography   213

Outlets for Track A. Prepare to share your profit. Agencies: a plus with limitations. How to find the right agency. Researching the agencies. How to contact a stock photo agency. The PhotoDataBank and Compu/Pix/ Rental. The timely stock agencies. Possible problems in dealing with stock agencies. Contracts. Conflicts. Delays. Do you need a personal rep? Start your own mini-agency. The individual agency. The co-op agency. Decor photography: Another outlet for your standards. Single sales. Multiple sales. What makes a marketable decor photograph? What to charge. Black-and-white or color? Size. Production. How to make your decor photography more salable. Frames. Promotion. Leasing. More information on decor photography.

13. Keeping Records: Knowing Where Everything Is   235

The lazy person's way to extra sales—knowing what is selling. File it! How to avoid excessive recordkeeping. Knowing how to put your finger on it: cataloging your black-and-whites and transparencies. Black-and-white. What files will you need in your photo-marketing operation? Transparencies. A cross-referencing system for retrieving your pictures. Here's how to do it. Protecting your files. Everything has its place.

14. Working Smart   247

The success habit: Following through. Setting goals. Getting organized. Time your goals. Is it easy? A Survival Secret. Think small. Don't misdirect your work. Your PMS/A—the heart of working smart. You manage the business—not the other way around. A self-evaluation guide. How to measure your sales strengths. Your success scorecard. Pictures just aren't selling? A ledger to assess your sales strengths. The five reasons for rejection. A potpourri of additional aids in working smart. Remember the law of 125. Let magazine articles teach you. Insurance. Toll-free numbers. Grants, loans, scholarships, fellowships, and aids.

15. Rights and Regulations   263

Copyright. Copyright infringement. Group registration. How to contact the copyright office. Interpreting the law. Be wary of dates. Laying claim to your picture. Stamps to protect your prints. Some drawbacks of the new law. A remedy. Q & A forum on copyright. Work for hire. Which usage rights do you sell? Read the fine print. Forms to protect your rights. Legal help. Model releases. Freedom of the press. The sponsor is the winner. You will rarely need a model release for editorial use. Model releases—when must you get them? Oral releases. Can we save them both? The right of privacy and our First Amendment rights. Sample model release. Sample guardian's consent (for model release). A turning point. "Fruity" question.

16. Your Stock Photo Business: A Mini Tax Shelter   295

The great rebate. The system to beat the system. A government incentive to start up your business. Your stock photography business deductions.

Office-in-the-home. Home. Auto use. Travel expenses. Entertainment. Advertising/promotion. Photo-related items. Printing. Business education, self-improvement, memberships. Office and supplies. Extra deductions. Depreciation. The "S" corporation. Additional tax avoidances.

17. Computers 307

Makes life easier? What is a computer? Which computer to buy? Cataloging and retrieving your pictures. Telecommunications: Getting in touch. Captions. Word processing. Spread sheets. Graphics. Where to from here?

Appendix A. Third-Choice Markets 329

Paper product companies: postcards, calendars, greeting cards, posters. Puzzles, placemats, gift wraps. Commercial accounts: ad agencies, graphic design studios, record covers. AV: filmstrips, motion pictures, video discs. Business and industry. Fashion. Product photography. Newspapers. Government agencies. Art photography.

Appendix B. Choosing Your Equipment 335

Big camera or little camera? Your accessories.

Appendix C. Spotting Your Black-and-Whites 338

Appendix D. The Darkroom 339

Developing and printing: Do it yourself or farm it out? Darkroom equipment. To develop film. To print. Combine the options.

Appendix E. Tips for Nonwriters 342

Bibliography 344

Books on selling your pictures. The business side. Legal questions and the photographer. Newsletters for photojournalists and writers with a camera. Special reports. Seminars and workshops. Additional workshop sources. Associations. Directories that will list your stock photography.

Index 352

Introduction

Exciting Opportunities at Your Doorstep

Will a Rolls-Royce be sitting in your driveway if you follow the principles set forth in this book? Maybe not. But then again, maybe two of them will. Or maybe a moped will. In other words, you'll reach whatever goals you set for yourself. That's the exciting part about all this: whatever your goals, you have complete control over whether they come to fruition. Success or failure in publishing your pictures is not determined by the wave of some mysterious wand out there in the marketplace. If you've got the know-how, you determine how far and how fast you go. This book will give you that know-how.

In more than twenty-five years of selling photographs, I've refined a marketing system that works for me today better than ever, and is working for scores of other stock photographers who have learned the system in my seminars and through my market newsletters. Hundreds of letters in my files attest to the efficacy of the system, testimony from photographers who are publishing their pictures (and depositing checks) with regularity.

The components of the system are simple—but the process isn't easy. It takes effort, energy, and perhaps some unlearning of initial misconceptions—but that's all that's required, and there are compensations:

Live anywhere. No need to live in the canyons of Manhattan or downtown Chicago to be close to the markets. They're as close as your mailbox. You can work entirely by mail, entirely at home, and still score in the wide world of markets open to you. Whether your headquarters is a high mountaintop cabin in Wyoming or a high-rise in Hartford, the markets will actually come to you through this system.

Pick your hours. You can arrange your own schedule and enjoy the flexibility of being independent. You can work at your stock photography full time or part time.

Be your own boss. Photobuyers don't care whether you're an amateur or a pro, a housewife or a parachutist. They're concerned about the quality of your picture and whether it meets their current needs.

Take paid vacations. You can pay for your trips through assignments you initiate or by judicious picture taking and picture placing, all described in my system. If you enjoy travel, you'll find your situation can become one of having to pick and choose among all the trip opportunities open to you.

Earn more money. You will sell the same photo over and over again. You'll choose from hundreds of good-paying markets you never knew existed, and you'll enjoy working with them because they're in your interest areas.

See your pictures in print. You'll be seeing your credit line in national circulation, sharing insights and your views of life in all its beauty, humor, discord, poignancy, delight, tragedy, and fascination. Sometimes your picture will make a tangible social contribution, sometimes it'll be business-as-usual. But it will all be deeply satisfying, with the gratification that comes from starting with a clear piece of film and creating something entirely your own.

The System: Eight Elements

There are eight elements in my marketing system that I'll explore with you in detail in the course of this book:

1. I touched on this one above: You market your photos by **mail**. No need to pound the pavements with a portfolio.

2. You distinguish between *service* photography and *stock* photography (photo illustration). The service photographer markets his *services*—on schedules that meet the time requirements of ad agencies, businesses, wedding parties, portrait clients. The stock photographer takes and markets his *pictures*—on his own timetable, selling primarily to books, magazines, and publishing companies of all kinds all over the country. My marketing system addresses the stock photographer.

3. You distinguish between good pictures and good *marketable* pictures. The former are the excellent scenics, wildflowers, sunsets, silhouettes of birds in flight, scenic shots of the lake, pet pictures. These are A-1 pictures, but in spite of the fact we see them everywhere in the marketplace (on greeting cards, record covers, posters, travel brochures, maga-

zine ads), they're terribly difficult (they can cost you money) to market yourself. I'll tell you why later in the book. You learn how to place these pictures in the right stock photo agencies, who *can* market them for you, for now-and-then supplementary income. For regular income you sell good *marketable* pictures: photo illustrations. You continue to take pictures in your interest areas, but you learn how to turn a picture into a highly marketable shot, for sale to book and magazine publishers.

4. You find your **PMS/A**—your **personal photographic marketing strength/areas**—and specialize. Knowing how to do this will give you invaluable insight and irresistible momentum. To my knowledge, it is treated nowhere else in the photographic literature.

5. You determine *your* **Market List,** coordinated with your PMS/A. You don't sell your pictures before you understand how to market them. Selling happens naturally, after you do your marketing homework.

6. You look like a **pro** with your photo-identification methods, your stationery, labels, packaging, your cover and query letters, and your product.

7. You focus on only a **corner** of the market pie. Not the whole pie. You specialize.

8. You find the market **first**, then create for that market, not the reverse.

You may find this book quite different from what you initially expected. Many books on photography glamorize market possibilities for the serious amateur or new professional; I have tried to present an honest overview. I am a working stock photographer, and as publisher of three photo-marketing newsletters, I deal daily with the realities of the photography marketplace.

My goal in this book is to give you the tools to be able to sell consistently to markets you enjoy working with.

The new markets you discover will surprise you with their photography budgets of $10,000, $30,000, and $70,000 a month (a month, not a year). "Are these markets in New York and L.A.?" you might ask. No. Times have changed. New York, Chicago, and L.A. markets are still the top markets for service photographers, but publishing markets for the stock photographer abound all over the country.

This book will help you tap these markets, and you'll discover the real excitement, the genuine exhilaration, of the venturesome process of producing your pictures and sharing them through publication.

The sky is the limit. Where you go with your photography is up to you.

Onward. With today's dramatic increase in the use of photography, as well as in the number of new markets and special-interest magazines and books, the challenges and satisfactions in the field of stock photography have never been greater. You can be part of them.

1.
The
Wide World
of
Possibilities

The Buyers
Are Waiting

You've probably turned to a photograph in a book or magazine and said, "I can take a better picture than that."

You are probably right . . . and not only from the point of view of quality or subject matter. Often a photo you see published in a magazine or book doesn't really belong there. When the deadline arrived, it was used by the photo editor because it was there, not because it was the perfect photograph.

Photobuyers would gladly use *your* photographs, if they knew you existed, and if you'd supply them with the pictures they *need*, when they need them. The buyers are literally waiting for you, and there are thousands of them. This book is going to show you how to locate the markets that are, this moment, looking to buy pictures from someone like you, with your special know-how, and your camera talent. This book is also going to show you a no-risk method for determining what photobuyers need, and how to avoid wasting shoe leather, postage, and energy with markets that don't offer any future for your kind of photography. You'll earn the price of this book in one week through the postage or phone bills it will save you.

If you're a newcomer to the field of photo marketing, you'll be surprised to learn you can start at the top. I know many who have done so, and I did, myself. I sold my first picture to the *Saturday Evening Post*. Many of my pictures have sold to *Reader's Digest, Parents, U.S. News & World Report, People, Redbook*, and others. But let me interrupt here to say I soon discovered that if I wanted to sell *consistently* to the top magazines, I would have to travel continually and make my headquarters in a population center a good deal larger than Osceola, Wisconsin.

There are at least 10,000 picture markets today. I figured that if I subtracted the top-paying newsstand magazines, numbering about 100, that left 9,900 for me to explore. I learned that most of these markets were as close as my mailbox, and that many of them were actually eager for my photographs. Most important, I could sell to these markets on my own timetable and live wherever I wanted to.

Trends in the Marketplace

Back in 1960 when I began marketing my pictures, there were very few persons with the title "photo editor." The art director or an editor at a publishing house doubled as the person who selected pictures, and the process often was hurried, at the last moment, whenever the book or magazine text was finalized. Pictures in those days frequently served simply to fill white space or to support a subject with documentation.

During recent decades, our society has become increasingly visually oriented, to the point of a veritable explosion in the use of visuals. People today are more prone to be viewers than readers. Reading material is more and more capsulized (witness the proliferation of condensed books and specialized newsletters). People rely less on the printed word and more on pictorial images for entertainment and instruction. Textbooks have more pictures and larger type. Illustrated seminars and instructional slide programs are the preferred tools for education throughout industry, and of course TV is conditioning all of us to visuals every day.

Words and printed messages aren't going out of style, but a look in any direction today shows us that photography is one of the most prominent means of interpreting and disseminating information.

If you've grown up in the TV era, the switch to increased picture use is probably not apparent to you. The publishing industry, however, is greatly aware of it. New positions have been created in publishing houses—photo editor, photo researcher, photo acquisition director—positions that never existed in the past. Revolutionary machinery has been developed to handle and reproduce pictures. Publishers produce millions of dollars worth of books, periodicals, and audiovisual materials every year. The photographs used in these products often make the difference between a successful venture and a failure. An editor isn't kidding when he says, "I need your picture."

The breadth of the marketplace this book will introduce you to may come as a surprise. For example, some publishing houses spend as much as $10,000 to $80,000 a month on photography. Some of those thousands could regularly be yours, if you learn sound methods for marketing your pictures.

As I mentioned earlier, you can start at the top. It's not impossible. But making a full-time activity of selling to the top markets requires a specific lifestyle and work style. You need to examine your total goal plan and make some major decisions before you launch out after the biggies. Only a handful break into that small group of top pros who enjoy regular assignments from the top markets. And most of those top pros pay their dues for years before they get to where their phone rings regularly.

Too often, the newcomer to any field believes the top is the only place it's at. The actor or the musician rushes to Hollywood to make it big. We all know how the story ends. Out of thousands, only a few are chosen. We also know they are *not* chosen on the basis of talent alone. Being at the right place at the right time is usually the key. The parallel holds true in photography. Good photographers are everywhere—just check the Yellow Pages. As with actors and musicians (or artists, dancers, writers), talent is only one of the prerequisites.

But if you are serious about your photography and are willing to look beyond the top, you'll discover a wide, wide world of possibilities out there for you. There are markets and markets—and yet more markets. You *will* get your pictures published, consistently, with excellent monetary return, and with the inner satisfaction that comes from putting your pictures out where others can enjoy them. You can accomplish this if you apply the principles I outline in this book. Your pictures will be at the right place at the right time, and your name will be on the checks sent out regularly by the picture buyers you identify as *your* target markets.

20,000 Photographs a Day

As you read this page, at least 20,000 photographs are being bought for publication in this country at fees of $20, $35, $50, $75, $100 for black-and-white and often twice as much for color. I'm not talking about ad agencies or general newsstand-circulation magazines. They're the closed markets, already tied up by staff photographers or established pros.

I'm referring to the little-known wide-open markets that produce books, magazines, and related printed products. Such publishing houses have proliferated all over the country in the last three decades. Opportunities for selling photographs to the expanding publishing industry have never been greater. Some publishing companies are located in small towns, but that's no indicator of their photography budgets, which can range, as I've said, from $10,000 to $80,000 per *month*.

A Wide-Open Door

These publishers are in constant need of photographs. Many publishing companies produce up to three dozen different magazines or periodicals, plus related publications such as bulletins, books, curriculum materials, brochures, filmstrips, and reports. Staffs of the larger publishing houses have scores of projects in the fire at one time, all of them needing photographs. As soon as a company, large or small, completes a publishing project or current issue, it is searching for photographs for the next project on the layout board.

Textbook publishers are in fierce competition with each other to nail down contracts with colleges and universities, technical institutes, school boards, and associations, to produce millions of dollars of photo-illustrated educational materials.

Regional and special-interest magazines number in the thousands. While many general-interest magazines have been struggling or folding, regional and special-interest magazines (open markets for the stock photographer) have been on the rise, and new ones continue to appear on the publishing scene. With the enormous amount of information available in any field or on any subject in today's world, our culture has become one of specialization. Increasingly, magazines and books reflect this emphasis, focusing on self-education and specific areas of interest, whether business, the professions, recreation, or leisure. This translates into still more markets for the stock photographer.

Another major marketplace is the hundreds of denominational publishing houses that produce scores of magazines, books, periodicals, curriculum materials, filmstrips, posters, and bulletins. Some of these companies employ twenty or more editors who are voraciously eager for photos for all their publishing projects. Very few of these are what you might think of as religious. Their photography budgets are high because their sales volume is high.

As I mentioned earlier, there are nearly 10,000 markets open to the stock photographer today. (That's apart from the about 100 top magazines such as *National Geographic* and *Sports Illustrated*.) These are 10,000 open markets, accessible to both the part-timer and full-timer. Photobuyers in these markets are constantly revising, updating, putting together new layouts, new issues, new editions, new publication projects.

If you compare the per-picture rate paid by these markets against that paid by the 100 top magazines, or against the $500 per picture that an advertising photographer receives for commercial use of his picture, there's a big difference. But that's misleading. Unless you number yourself among the relative handful of well-known veteran service photographers who sell to the top magazines (many have staff photographers in any case), this is sweepstakes marketing—a sometime thing. The same goes for top commercial assignments. When you score, it's for a healthy dollar, but how frequently can you count on it? Commercial accounts and the top magazines often require all rights (they ask you to sign a "work-for-hire" agreement) to your photos, as well.

In contrast, as a stock photographer selling (renting) your photos for editorial use, you can circulate hundreds of pictures to publishing houses for consideration, each picture making from $20 to $200 at every sale. You don't have to worry about the beck-and-call mobility and time-deadline requirements of top magazine assignments, or the frazzle of commercial assignments, and you can sell the same pictures over and over again.

You can do this from your own home, wherever you live. For the past twenty years I've operated successfully out of a 100-acre farm in rural Wisconsin and can attest that more and more photographers are doing the same thing from such diverse headquarters as a quiet side street in Kansas City, an A-frame in Boulder, an apartment in Albany.

When you master the photo-marketing system outlined in this book, you'll know how to select your markets from the vast numbers of possibilities and then tap them for consistent, dependable sales. If you're like most of us, you'll find that your range of markets includes some that are good starting points (easy to break into but pay modestly); some that are good showcases for you (prestigious publications in your special-interest areas that may pay little but offer a good name to include in your list of credits, or good visibility to other photobuyers); many that will be regular customers for modest but steady return; and many that will be regular well-paying customers.

Find the Market, Then Create

Many photographers who are successful today say their careers surged forward when they realized that they were conducting the business side of their endeavors exactly backwards. They had been creating first, then trying to find markets for the photos they produced. This system can work to a certain extent (and everyone gets lucky now and then), but it doesn't make for consistent, predictable sales. It's another form of sweepstakes marketing. Here's the secret to guaranteed sales: Find the market first.

This isn't to say that you pick just any market and create for it. I mean search out markets that appeal to you as a person and a photographer—markets you would love to deal with and create for.

Finding your corner of the marketplace (see Chapter 3) is going to be like prospecting. It's going to take some digging, but the nuggets you discover are going to be worth the effort.

You, the Stock Photographer

After you become familiar with the photo-marketing system described in this book, you'll find that you can wear two hats in photography.

One hat is that of the stock photographer, the other the service photographer. What's the difference?

The *service photographer* markets his *services* on schedules that meet the time requirements of his clients: ad agencies, businesses, wedding parties, portrait clients, and PR, publicity, and audiovisual accounts. The service photographer usually finds he needs several different kinds of cameras, a myriad of lenses and accessories, and frequently a well-equipped studio.

The *stock photographer* markets *stock photographs* (*photo illustrations*), which he takes and sells on his own timetable, selling almost exclusively to publishers of books, magazines, and related publications. The stock photographer can operate with only one camera and three lenses, though he's better off with two cameras (see Appendix B). The extensive equipment and studio of the service photographer aren't necessary.

A photographer can be either a service photographer or a stock photographer, or both. The marketing system in this book, however, *addresses the stock photographer.* The demand for photo illustrations in the publishing world has increased dramatically in the last decade. So have the photography budgets of publishing houses. And so has the need for stock photographers—the photographers who can supply on-target photo illustrations to the highly specialized magazine and book industries.

The "Theme" Markets

The primary markets for photo illustration are the publishing companies located in every corner of the country, and the magazines and books they produce. I've already touched on some major categories—educational, regional, special interest, and denominational. Now we'll take a look at each market in detail.

Remember that publishing houses specialize. If in your research you come across a magazine that's new to you in one of your fields of interest, you'll often discover that the magazine's publishing house produces several additional magazines, usually related or on the same theme. If your photo-marketing strengths include that theme, you've discovered one of your top markets.

Prime Markets

1. Magazines
2. Books

Secondary Markets

1. Stock photo agencies
2. Decor photography outlets

Third-Choice Markets

1. Paper product companies (calendars, greeting cards, posters, postcards, etc.)

2. Commercial accounts (ad agencies, PR firms, record companies, audiovisual houses, graphic design studios, etc.)

3. Newspapers, government agencies, and art photography sales

You'll find a full discussion of third-choice and secondary markets later in this book, so I'll say just a word about them here.

The third-choice markets range in marketing potential from "possible" to "not possible" for the stock photographer. In Appendix A, I outline what to expect at these markets and what the requisites are for making sales in them.

The secondary markets, stock photo agencies and decor photography, are discussed in detail in Chapter 12. Stock agencies aren't markets in the usual sense; they're middlemen who can market your photo illustrations for you. Decor photography (sometimes called photo decor, or wall decor) involves selling large photos (16x20-inch to wall-size) that can be used as wall art in homes, businesses, and public buildings.

Both the agency and decor areas offer sales opportunities to the stock photographer and can be important to your operation, but just how important may be different from what you initially assume. Agency sales can be successful when you place the right categories of pictures in the right agencies (not necessarily the most prestigious), and this takes some homework. Likewise, the decor route has its assets and its liabilities. Chapter 12 gives you the know-how to approach agencies and decor photography with a chance for elation rather than frustration.

Now to the prime markets for the stock photographer, magazines and books (see Tables 1-1 and 1-2).

Magazines

You can determine a range for the photo budget of a magazine by asking yourself this question: "Whose dollars support the magazine?" If the magazine runs on advertising support, the photography budget is usually high. In the case of an industry magazine, if a company underwrites it, the photography budget is also usually high. The photo budget is in the middle range if an organization or association supports the magazine, or if subscriptions alone support it. Many magazines operate with a combination of advertising and subscription revenue, making for healthy photo budgets. Magazines with no advertising, subscription, or industry/ association support can be expected to have low photography budgets. In Chapter 3, I'll show you how to be selective in choosing your magazine markets.

Budget, of course, should not be the sole factor you use in determining what markets to work with. Often it's actually easier to sell ten pictures at $75 each to a medium-budget publication than one picture at $750 to one of the top-paying magazines. You can use the budget question to good advantage, though, in determining how healthy a magazine is, and

Magazine Markets

Category	Description	How they use photographs	Examples
Special interest (avoca-tion)	Focus on a specific subject area, aimed at a specific target audience such as travelers or amateur athletes who are either activists or armchair enthusiasts. Sold at newsstands, by subscription, or free. Advertising-supported. Good markets when they match your PMS/A. Pay is excellent.	To illustrate articles, how-to features, photo essays, covers; to establish a mood.	*Organic Gardening* *Happy Wanderer* *Ski Canada Magazine* *Official Karate* *Hot Rod Magazine* *Elementary Electronics* *Horse and Horseman* *Diver Magazine* *Popular Photography* *Writer's Digest*
Trade (vocation)	Address a specific professional audience, such as farmers, electricians, computer programmers, pilots, wholesalers. Not sold at newsstands. Advertising-supported. If your PMS/A includes technical knowledge, this will be a rewarding market. Pay is excellent.	To illustrate technical articles, how-to features, covers, photo essays, and industry news.	*Industrial Photography* *Magazine Age* *The Ohio Farmer* *Wings* *Solar Age Magazine* *Weeds, Trees, and Turf*
Business	Industry-produced (internal and external) as a medium to reach both employees and the general public. Not sold at newsstands. Usually free. Editors expect a solid knowledge of their field of interest. Pay is excellent.	To illustrate articles, covers, photo essays, industry trends; to establish a mood.	*Ford Times* (Ford Motor Co.) *Aramco World* (Middle East oil industry) *Friends* (Chevrolet) *Inland* (Inland Steel Co.)
Denomi-national	Numerous denominational magazines, newspapers, bulletins, and curriculum	To illustrate articles, photo essays, news	*Lutheran Standard* *U.S. Catholic*

Table 1-1. Magazine markets.

	materials on a wide variety of topics. Distributed by subscription or given away free to membership. Pay is medium to low but volume purchasing is high.	items, photo stories, covers; to establish a mood.	*Marriage and*
			    Family Living
			Living With
			    Children
			Alive

Assoc-iations, organiza-tions	Published for members of organizations and clubs. News and events, plus general-interest articles. Not sold at newsstands. By subscription. Supported sometimes by dues and by advertising. Audience is usually specialized. Pay is mediocre.	To illustrate articles, covers, news items, photo essays; to establish a mood.	*Elks Magazine*
			Kiwanis
			    Magazine
			National 4-H
			    News
			Scouting
			    Magazine
			The Rotarian

Local	Audience is usually a local metropolitan area. Feature stories, articles, and pix of local interest. Advertising-supported. Subscription, newsstand. Pay is low, but exposure is valuable.	To illustrate articles, covers, news items, photo stories; to establish a mood.	*Chicago*
			Charlotte
			    Magazine
			Phoenix Living
			Westchester
			    Magazine
			Los Angeles
			    Magazine
			Sunday
			    newspaper
			    magazine
			    sections

State and regional	Audience is statewide or encompasses several states. Feature stories, articles, and pictures of regional interest. Sold at newsstands and by subscription. Pay is usually low, but volume makes up for it.	To illustrate articles, covers, news items, photo stories and essays; to establish a mood.	*Rhode Islander*
			    Magazine
			South Carolina
			    Magazine
			Northwest
			    Magazine
			Arizona
			    Highways
			Sunset
			    Magazines
			Minneapolis-
			    St. Paul

News services	Timely features and news pictures produced by staff,	To illustrate articles, news	Enterprise Science

Table 1-1. (cont.)

	stringers, and freelancers. They can use pictures of your area. Pay is low.	items, covers; to establish a mood.	Service Black Press Service King Features Syndicate
General newsstand	General, national interest, and large circulation (see Appendix A). These magazines are supported by advertising and subscription and appeal to a broad segment of the population (e.g., women, sports enthusiasts, etc.). These are third-choice markets for you because they assign most of their photo needs to staff photographers, well-known veteran stock photographers, or stock photo agencies.		Redbook Good Housekeeping Money People National Geographic Sports Illustrated Reader's Digest Esquire

Book Markets

Category	Description	How they use photographs	Examples	Rating in terms of numbers of photo illustrations purchased
Encyclopedias and dictionaries	Multivolume and single volume. Some contain a broad range of information, others cover specific topics such as medicine, wood-working. Foreign-language editions. Children's versions.	To illustrate articles, section heads, updates, revisions, supplements.	Britannica World Book, Inc. Handyman's Van Nostrand's Scientific The Illustrated Computer Dictionary Science Dictionary of the Plant World	C
Textbooks	Textbooks range from brief paperbacks to multivolume	To illustrate chapter heads,	Ginn Scott, Foresman	A

Table 1-1 (cont.); and *Table 1-2.* Book markets.

	hardcover series. Used in schools, associations, churches, businesses. All subjects (e.g., biology, math, history, special ed.). Foreign-language editions.	covers, technical articles, revisions, supplements; to establish moods.	Silver Burdett Houghton- Mifflin D. C. Heath
Church curric- ulum	Sunday school course books, Bible study materials, adult education, confirmation texts, family living and inspirational books.	To illustrate articles, chapter heads, updates, photo essays; to establish moods.	United Methodist Church American Baptist **B** Church Episcopal Church
Consumer trade	Sold in bookstores, in supermarkets, by mail order, and through book clubs. Range from coffee-table books to bestsellers to vest-pocket references. General and specialized hardcover and paperback. Specialized subject areas range from photographic to popular science to poetry.	To illustrate chapters, jackets, covers; chapter heads, section heads; how-to photo essays, updates.	*The American* *Wilderness* *The Entrepre-* *neurial* *Woman* *How to Buy a* *Condominium* *Great Trails* **D** *of the West* *American* *Wildflowers* *Photography* *and the* *Art of* *Seeing*

Table 1-2. (cont.)

thus how stable a market it might be for you. Chapter 8 will show you how to determine the photo budget and the price you should ask for your photos.

Books

Approximately 40,000 books are published in this country every year. Books are produced by publishers who orchestrate the complete package: assigning manuscripts, editing, graphics, printing, promotion, and distribution. When you deal with a book publisher, ask these questions: "How well-known is the publishing company?" "How long have they been in business?" "How wide is the market appeal of the book in question?" The photography budget is usually high if the book has a broad potential audience and the publishing company is well established. Fledgling book publishers, small presses, and limited-audience publishers rarely pay high fees. Again, however, this is primarily to orient yourself—I am not suggesting your targets should be only the high-paying markets. Selling a small publisher one-hundred pictures at a bulk rate of $25 each makes good sense. In Chapter 3, I'll show you how to find your target book markets; Chapters 7 and 11 will tell you more about sales to book publishers.

You Supply the Pictures—They'll Supply the Checks

The prime markets pay stock photographers millions of dollars a year to get the pictures they need. Sounds promising for the photographer, and it is, but wait—the key word above is *need*.

Whether you plan on grossing $50 or $50,000 in sales each year with your photography, don't ever forget that photobuyers purchase only pictures they need, not pictures they like. If you supply the *right* pictures to them, they'll buy. I've heard dozens of photographers over the years complain that their pictures weren't selling. When I examined their selling techniques, it was easy to see why: They were putting excellent photographs in front of the wrong buyers. A photobuyer may think your pictures are beautiful, but he won't purchase them unless they fit the publication's specific requirements. A photo editor is like any other consumer: If he thinks he *needs* it, he'll buy it. Chapters 2 and 3 will show you how to determine what the photobuyer's needs are and how to fill them.

Will your models cooperate with you? The boys in the picture above were happy to drive their bikes in a figure-8 between two telephone poles I designated.

The Family of Children featured this picture. I started with two scenes: children playing a game, and a cemetery in winter. Put the two together and you have a new picture.

2.
What Pictures Sell and Resell?

The Difference Between a Good Picture and a Good Marketable Picture

What kind of a picture can you be sure will sell for you—consistently? And what kind of picture will disappoint you—consistently?

You may be surprised at the answers to these two questions. The heart of the matter is that one type is a good picture, and the other is a good *marketable* picture. The surprise is that good pictures seem like they ought to be marketable, because we see them everywhere, looking at us from billboards, magazine covers, brochures, advertisements, greeting cards. These good pictures are the lovely scenics, the beautiful flower close-ups, the sunsets and dramatic silhouettes—those excellent Kodak-ad shots and contest winners. These photos could also be called *standard excellent pictures*.

"But why do they consistently ring up *no sale* when I try to market them?" you ask. Because the ad agencies, graphic design studios, and top magazines who use these standard excellent shots don't *need* them; 99 percent of the time their photobuyers have hundreds, indeed thousands, of these beauties at their fingertips—in inventory, at their favorite local stock photo agencies, or available from the list of service photographers they've long worked with and know are reliable. Ninety-nine percent of the pictures you see published in newsstand magazines or in calendars, brochures, or posters are obtained from one of those two sources: stock photo agencies or top established pros.

The established pro usually has a better supply of standard excellent pictures than the average photographer or serious amateur, even though the latter may have been photographing for years. Pros have work schedules and assignments that afford them hundreds of opportunities to supplement their stock files. The pros can shoot more easily and less expensively because an assignment already has them in an out-of-the-way, timely, or exotic location, and they can piggyback stock-file photos on their original assignment. Getting the same shots could cost you a great deal in travel and operations expense. And buyers of these photos don't turn to a photographer with a limited stock file who's unknown to them and has no track record when they want a good picture.

The best place for your standard excellent photos, then, is in a major stock agency. This, too, is a form of sweepstakes marketing. But chances are that even amid the tough competition in the agencies, you'll realize a sale now and then as a nice tributary to the main river of your sales.

I realize there are a dozen books on the market that report that you can sell the standard excellent picture to buyers. There are also books that assert that you can write the blockbuster novel, write a top-forty hit song, or make a hit record that sells a million copies. I don't doubt that the authors of these books have hit the jackpot themselves or know someone who has. But you open yourself up to two disadvantages when you attempt to appeal to the common denominator of the public's taste:

1. First of all, the romance and appeal of stock photography soon fades after you've snapped an angle of the Washington monument or a sunset in Monterey Bay for the twentieth time, or a standard symbol of power (ocean waves), hope (sunlight streaming through rolling dark clouds), and so on.

The original exhilaration of stock photography diminishes when you realize you are following someone else's tracks; when you know others have the identical pictures in their files that you do. On the one hand, it can be money in the bank when you hike in to get the standard shot of the *Maroon Bells* in Colorado, but it's disheartening to discover tripod marks or chewing gum wrappers in a spot where you had thought you were experiencing a moment of discovery. Eventually, you come back to your starting point and say, "There must be more to stock photography than this."

If you were to continue to snap these exquisite clichés as your standard stock in trade, what would you have after two or three decades? Would a publisher aggressively seek you out to publish an anthology of your work? Not if your photos were cookie-cutter versions of standard subject matter, making you indistinguishable from hordes of other stock photographers.

2. The second disadvantage is economic. The law of supply and demand indicates that it's dangerous to count on consistent sales to the markets who buy the standard excellents. The market is so flooded with these pictures that the idea that your particular versions would hit every time or most of the time enters the realm of high optimism—admirable, perhaps, but not too practical.

Pictures

Can you read into these pictures? Do they evoke a mood? When they were first made in the thirties, few photobuyers considered them blockbusters. Instead, picture buyers at the time were probably purchasing the standard decorative pictures of the day. Today, the pictures below (illustrations 2-1 and 2-2) endure and are included in anthologies. Are you aiming your stock photography activities at pictures that will endure?

Illustration 2-1.

Illustration 2-2.

Have I discouraged you? If you have an unquenchable desire to make this category of stock photography your career, by all means persevere and aim to join the small group of top pros. But if you feel you've been spinning your wheels and getting frustrated in your photo-marketing efforts, this chapter is going to be worth the price of this book many times over, because it will blueprint for you the kinds of pictures you *can* start selling—*today*.

Good Marketable Pictures

What, then, are the good *marketable* pictures that will be the mainstay of your photo-marketing success? These pictures are the consistent marketing bets—the photos you can count on to be dependable sellers. These photos have buyers with ample purchasing budgets eager to purchase them, right away and over and over.

No-Risk Marketing

These good *marketable* pictures are the ones photobuyers *need*. Let the pictures in the magazines and informational books in your local library be your guide. These editorial (nonadvertising, or noncommercial) pictures show ordinary people laughing, thinking, enjoying, crying, helping each other, working, building things or tearing them down, playing, sharing. The world moves on and on, and our books and magazines are our chronicle. About 20,000 such photo illustrations are published every day, and more than 140,000 appear every week. They are pictures of all the things people do at all ages and in all stations of life. These pictures are often in black-and-white, and they're what editors need constantly. These are good *marketable* photo illustrations—the bestsellers. They may not sell for $750 apiece, but if you plan your marketing system wisely, you can easily sell ten for $75 each.

To clarify the difference in your chances of selling these good *marketable* pictures compared with standard excellent pictures, consider the Boston Marathon. Out of hundreds and hundreds of dedicated runners, there's only one winner. The trophy goes to the pro who practices day in and day out, who makes running a full-time occupation. Anyone can get lucky, so I can't deny that you might win the Boston Marathon—that is, you might score with one of your standard excellent pictures in a national magazine. But the odds weigh heavily against you.

The first step, then, toward consistent success in marketing your photographs is to get out of the marathon and start running your own race. The marathon is crowded with fine photographers, all of them shooting pictures that everyone else is shooting. Newcomers usually enter the photo-marketing marathon because of an erroneous concept of what photobuyers want (need), and thus an erroneous concept of what they, as stock photographers, should supply them with.

I once asked a photobuyer, "Why do newcomers always submit standard excellent pictures, instead of on-target, marketable pictures?" His answer: "I think the photography industry itself is partly at fault. Their multimillion-dollar instructional materials, their ads, their slide programs are always aimed at how to take the *good* picture. Photographers believe they have reached professional status if they can duplicate that kind of picture."

Well-meaning advice from professional stock photographers themselves sometimes adds to this misconception. In their books, seminars, or conversations, successful stock photographers sometimes tend to forget how many years of dues-paying they went through before they could sell standard excellents consistently. Successful people in any field—medicine, theater, professional sports, photography—often hand out advice based on the opportunities open to them at their current status. They fail to put themselves in the shoes of a newcomer who has yet to establish a track record.

In running your own race, you'll be up against competition, too, but it's manageable competition. As you'll discover in Chapter 3, you'll be targeting your pictures to specific markets and taking good *marketable* pictures built around your particular mix of interests, access, and expertise.

The Rohn Engh Principle
for Producing a Marketable Picture Every Time

The secret to producing good marketable stock photos can be discovered in the markets themselves—the books, magazines, periodicals, brochures, ads, and other materials that are produced by the publishing industry every day.

Use this test: Tear pages of photographs from magazines, periodicals, booklets, etc., and spread them out on your living room floor. Now place copies of your own black-and-whites or color prints* on the floor, or project your color slides. Do a self-critique. Do you see a disparity in content and appearance between the published photos and your own? If so, how could you improve your pictures? If your pictures blend in, matching the quality of the published photos, you'll be leaps ahead of the competition.

Next, give yourself a quick course in how to take marketable illustrations: select any of the published photo illustrations, and then go out and take photographs as similar to them as you can set up, using a Polaroid camera to give yourself fast, on-the-spot checks on how you can improve your picture quality.

Am I suggesting that you copy someone else's work? Yes, and if they will admit it, pros will tell you that's how they originally learned many of the nuances of good photography. But the word *copy* is a no-no in the creative world. (Unfortunately, purists place undue derogatory emphasis on the word.) If, because of conditioning, the word *copy* doesn't go down well for you, try *duplicate*.

When you check the content and style of published photo illustrations, you'll find they consistently feature a reasonably close-up view

---

*Transparencies (slides) are generally used for publication. Only 10 percent of the publishing industry accepts color prints for publication.

and a bold, posterlike design. Magazine covers are good examples of stock photography.

A stock photo is successful when the viewer can *read* into it. It should evoke a mood. The viewer's desire to see what's going on requires a close look. The viewer shouldn't have to study the picture to perceive what it's trying to say, so a medium or close-up view works best. Bring the main subject or person in close. Most newcomers to stock photography improve their pictures 100 percent when they move toward their subject for a tighter composition.

Like the background, the composition of your pictures should be simple and uncluttered. Strive for a clean and posterlike design, a picture that conveys its reason for being at one glance.

Try not to think of yourself as a "photographer" but instead as a graphic designer who happens to use photography as his medium.

The Principle

This four-step principle is guaranteed to produce marketable photo illustrations every time.

$$P = B + P + S + I$$

PICTURE equals BACKGROUND plus PERSON(S) plus SYMBOL plus INVOLVEMENT.

Most of the successful stock photos you come across in your research will contain these elements. There are always exceptions to the rule, and we'll go into some of those after we explore the formula in detail. And, of course, as we learned in aesthetics, all works of art have both *form* and *content*. You are able to learn how to produce the format of a painting, poem, or photograph. But producing the *content*, the spirit, is another matter. This talent is unique to you.

Step 1: Background. Choose it wisely. Too often a photographer doesn't fully notice the background until he sees his developed pictures. The background you choose can often make the difference between a sale and no sale. For example, if you are photographing a pilot, don't just snap a picture by a corner of the hangar that could be any building. Search the airport area for a background that says *aviation*. Similarly, an office shot could include a desk or typewriter to set the scene. Or a stock brokerage could show a computer screen flashing prices in the background.

These background clues should be noticeable, but not obtrusive, and the picture should not be cluttered with other objects. The background is crucial to how successfully your picture makes a single statement. Your illustration is more dramatic and more marketable if it expresses a single idea—and does it with economy. As you plan your stock photo, ask yourself, "What can I eliminate in this composition while still retaining my central theme?"

Evoke a Mood

Your central theme doesn't always have to be describable in words; it can be a mood you wish to convey—a feeling that, if expressed with simplicity, actually lends itself to a variety of interpretations by different viewers. By eliminating unnecessary distractions, you guide the viewer to a strong response to your photograph. A clean, simple background is usually available to you. Remember, you have 360 degrees to work with. Maneuver your camera position until the background is uncluttered.

Employ your knowledge of design, color, composition, and chiaroscuro (the play of darks against lights and vice versa). If the pilot is wearing a light uniform, shift your camera angle to include a dark mass behind him for contrast. If he is wearing a dark uniform, choose a light background. This technique will give your stock photos a three-dimensional quality.

Think "cover." Leave space near the top of your composition for a logo. Editors complain to us here at PhotoSource International that most pictures are submitted in a horizontal format. A vertical format lends itself best to book and magazine covers, and many page layouts as well.

Step 2. Person(s). Now that you have a suitable background, maneuver yourself or your models (in some cases, you'll have to do the maneuvering because the models won't or can't move for you) so that background and models are in the most effective juxtaposition. The models themselves must be interesting-looking and/or appealing. Choose them, when possible, with an eye to their photogenics.**

If your picture will be used for commercial purposes—such as advertising, promotion, endorsement—you will want a model release (signed consent to be photographed) from your models. For pictures that will be used for editorial purposes, such as in textbooks, magazines, encyclopedias, or newspapers, a model release in most cases is not necessary. (See Chapters 6 and 15 for more on models and model releases.)

Your photos are illustrations, not posed portraits, so the people in them must be engrossed in doing or observing something. We are all people watchers, and stock photos are always more interesting when the people in them are genuinely involved in some activity.

Remember: You are making a picture, not taking one. The only thing you should take is your time.

Step 3. Symbol. In stock photography, anything that brings a certain idea to mind is a symbol. Symbols are everywhere in our visually orient-

---

**Model = any person in your picture. Neighbors, relatives, politicians, celebrities, schoolteachers, lifeguards, policewomen, groups of children at a playground, groups of adults at a town meeting—all are defined in our terms as models. I'm not talking about professional models.

ed world. They are used effectively as logos or trademarks in business, for example. In a stock photo, a symbol can be anything from a fishing pole to a tractor to a stethoscope. In the case of the pilot, his uniform, his cap, an airplane, a propeller, a wind sock, are all symbols. Including an appropriate symbol will make your illustration more effective. Use your object symbols as you would a road sign—to tell your viewers where you are. However, be careful that your symbol is not so large or obvious that it overpowers the rest of your photo; symbols are most effective when they are used subtly. Avoid the temptation to use such mundane symbols as a pitchfork for a farmer, a sombrero for a Mexican musician, or a net for an Italian fisherman. The goal is to clue in your viewer to what is going on, but not knock him over the head with it. Let him experience some discovery as he looks at your picture. Next time you are perusing pictures in a magazine or book, watch for the "road signs" and note how and how often symbols are used in stock photos.

Step 4. Involvement. The people in your picture should be the subject of the picture (showing enjoyment, unhappiness, fear, etc.); or they should be interacting, helping each other, working with something, playing with something, etc.; or they should be absorbed in watching or contemplating some object, scene, or activity. Marketable photo illustrations have an involvement, a dynamism, about them that's distinct from the portrait or scenic quality of standard excellent pictures.

Using the Principle

The principle gives you the necessary ingredients. As with all recipes, that's just a starter. There can be variations, and final results are in the hands of the chef.

Photos That You Can *Read Into*

Illustrations 2-3 through 2-8 show the formula at work. In this first picture (illustration 2-3), the principle is used to suggest a story. When I took this photograph, I was driving a back road in West Virginia. The dilapidated shed, the lighting on the Appalachian foothills, the shadows, the lonely road, all seemed to suggest rural poverty. I asked my traveling companion to walk along the road and hang his head down. For the symbol I gave him a suitcase. It introduces an element of involvement and spurs the viewer to think—to feel that the man is leaving home or is returning. Either interpretation gives rise to feelings about the photograph and its subject, with resultant interest. This picture was taken in the sixties and is no longer in my contemporary file. Yet I have sold it twice in the last year from my historical file.

The principle *can* work if some of the elements are missing. In this mountain scene (illustration 2-4), symbol and involvement, per se, are lacking. Yet the picture is still successful because, in this case, the back-

Illustration 2-3.

Illustration 2-4.

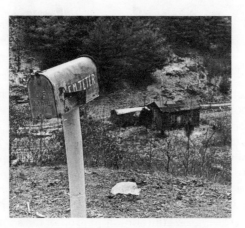

Illustration 2-5.

ground doubles as the symbol. The background is a panorama the person is obviously involved in, enraptured by, as he sits quietly as part of the stillness of the scene. Without the person, the photo would have failed as a marketable picture. The photo moves from the standard excellent scenic category to the good marketable category because of the predominant position and emphasis (with backlighting) given to the person. The picture says *involvement* or *contemplation*, in contrast to pictures that say *pretty scene* and include a person placed in the photo as a minor element for orientation.

Again, here is a variation on the principle that nevertheless works as a marketable stock photo. In this case, the person is missing (illustration 2-5). In most cases, stock photos need people, but as in this instance, not always. The symbol here is the mailbox; involvement is with the modest cabin in the background, achieved by the juxtaposition of the two. The picture gives the desired feeling of poverty and isolation, heightened by the arduous climb to the mailbox, the link to the rest of society. As long as a picture without people *implies* people, as this one does, you come out with a marketable stock photo.

Illustration 2-6.   **Illustration 2-7.**

In illustration 2-6, I wanted to use light poles disappearing into the fog to create a mood, and I knew my picture would be more salable if it had people in it. But people can *detract* from a feeling of a picture if they're just stuck into the composition. Having the older boy take the younger by the hand as they headed down their path along the lampposts added the right touch of naturalness and involvement. This picture has sold twenty-seven times so far.

Rather than overstate, let simplicity transmit the mood you wish to convey. In illustration 2-7, the contemplation of the soon-to-be graduate is captured in profile, almost cameo, against the smooth expanse of the

Illustration 2-8.   **Illustration 2-9.**

wall in a school hallway. In this case, a clean background was chosen in order to focus attention on the symbol—the graduation cap and tassel. The person is involved with the symbol by its effect on her demeanor, causing her to be in deep reflection.

Symbols can underscore what your photograph is attempting to portray. On location where you are photographing, you will often find such symbols as flags, plaques, maps, and posters. Once you position your model for lighting, nondistracting background, etc., you can add dimension to your photograph by placing appropriate symbols into the background. Without the visual aid of the sign in illustration 2-8, this photograph would be explained only by a caption. The sign on the wall authentically orients the viewer to the girl's job interview.

Involvement in your photo illustrations sometimes means actual work for your models. Why is illustration 2-9 so successful?

B = Background is uncluttered and lends itself to storyline.
P = Person is included in storyline.
S = Symbol (shovel) serves to emphasize activity.
I = Involvement is real.

You can manufacture a mood by coming in the back door. While doing a story at a university, I was struck by the starkness of an examination room. The folding chairs, lined up in sterile rows, symbolized the loneliness and isolation that students can experience at a large university. I asked a young man who was accompanying me to sit in one of the chairs in the middle of my composition and to lean forward and look at his shoes. The picture (page 92) gets the idea across, and he was spared the self-consciousness or awkwardness of having to come up with a facial expression for the mood I wanted to portray.

The Missing Link

Meaningful pictures happen when you take an active hand in your composition. A snowy birdhouse hanging from a frosty limb on a December morning is picturesque. But when you add a young mother and her little boy (the people), a new dimension evolves. For this photograph (illustration 2-10) you may have supposed the photographer snapped a picture of a young mother and son who happened upon a snow-covered birdhouse. The process was actually in reverse. I happened upon the birdhouse, and then sought out my models as an interesting contrast to the stark frozen beauty. Try to think of your photography in these terms—*in reverse*. Find your background first, then the other elements: people, symbol, involvement. The resulting photo illustrations will be more marketable.

Illustrations 2-11 through 2-14 show how, with the elements in slightly different alignment, or with one or another principle element missing, illustration 2-10 wouldn't make it as a good marketable picture.

Illustration 2-10.

1. Background distracting or inappropriate (Illustration 2-11).
2. People missing (Illustration 2-12).
3. Symbol missing (Illustration 2-13).
4. No involvement with symbol (Illustration 2-14).

Illustration 2-11.   **Illustration 2-12.**

Illustration 2-13.

Illustration 2-14.

On Target and Off Target

Illustrations 2-15 through 2-24 were taken by photography students. They are close to being good marketable pictures, and some are better than others, but they all need alterations to make the grade.

Illustration 2-15. *Move in close. Your audience needs to see what's going on. The photographer wasted half his frame in this case. This picture improves when we eliminate everything but the essentials.*

Illustration 2-16. *The background is clean and uncluttered, the involvement factor is high—but the camera angle is off. We want to see more of the fountain, more facial expression.*

Illustration 2-17. Again, this picture needs that "right" expression. The idea here is good—but the photographer lost a chance for a good marketable picture by not shooting enough film (shoot ten to one) to have a selection that includes the best expression from the best angle. The lighting on the little girl's face is not flattering, but remember, stock photography is not portraiture. Your primary aim is to capture expression and mood.

Illustration 2-18. This stock photo expresses a mood or an emotion. It has the potential to be highly marketable because it lends itself to the many themes treated in books and magazines. Expression and position of the model could be improved. The man's nervous hands are incongruous with his contemplative face. On these shots, you need to shoot ten or twelve to capture that "just right" expression. Ask the model to continue to move slightly after each exposure. Then choose the "right picture" when you examine your contact sheet.

Illustration 2-19. Stock photos that are successful follow the $P = B + P + S + I$ principle. The photographer should have moved to the left or right so as to include a meaningful background. The cup could serve as a symbol, but involvement with the cup (such as pouring coffee into it or drinking from it) would have made the picture more marketable. This picture is a portrait, or a documentary picture, but it is not a good stock photo.

Illustration 2-20. Stock photography can leave much to the imagination. This picture is successful because the person's face is not in full view. Thus, it is not a portrait; it conveys a mood. This picture could be used many ways: articles on loneliness, meditation, boy-girl relationships, education. You'll be surprised at the uses photobuyers find for your pictures. The background is relatively uncluttered and nondistracting, which helps to emphasize the center of interest. This photo gets eight points out of ten as a good marketable picture.

Illustration 2-21. *This is a typical amateur picture, "The Character Study." (We all have at least ten of these in our files.) This type of photograph is very difficult to market—there are millions of them available to photobuyers because everybody takes these pictures. It's a portrait, with no involvement, no symbol, no dynamism, no action in the photograph. Include any of these, and it becomes a marketable picture.*

Illustration 2-22. *A slice of life is what photobuyers like to see in your stock photos. This could be a good nuts-and-bolts picture with good marketing potential. But the photographer failed to answer several questions for us: Does the fellow like what he's doing? Does he hate it? Is this task easy? Is it difficult? The picture, because of poor body position, is too static. Again, if the photographer had shot ten to one, she would have gotten at least one frame where the model's expression revealed his feelings about what he's doing.*

Illustration 2-23. *Use your knowledge of optics and composition to get the best stock photo out of every situation. Making a three-quarter view out of this one and using a telephoto lens would improve it 100 percent. You are not making a portrait of the two young women, so it is excusable to feature one face more than the other in your composition.*

Illustration 2-24. *This picture is marketable, but it borders on being too clever, too cutesy. It's also old hat. Clichés are a fact of life in the stock photo business—but handle them with care and use them sparingly. On the other hand, don't go to the other extreme and be obscure.*

You Are an Important Resource to Photobuyers

This, then, is what marketable stock photography is all about. These are the kinds of good marketable pictures that allow you to run your own race.

To restate the problem with standard excellent shots: While you might hit a calendar or cover with one of these now and then, to depend on this type of shot for consistent sales is a mistake. Every buyer has hundreds of this kind of shot in inventory. Or he gets buried in them if he puts out a request for them. *National Geographic*, for example, will not let us run a listing in our *Photobulletin* asking for a photo of a bald eagle. They know they would be deluged with bald eagles. The editors know they could shout out the window and fifty photographers would respond with bald eagle photos. But you will find plenty of *National Geographic* listings for people interacting with the environment, or for wildlife from specific parts of the world.

For every one of those "good pictures" that finally hits, you'll sell hundreds of good *marketable* pictures. One sunset at the beach *might* finally sell for a nice $500, but you won't sell it again for three years or five years. Meanwhile, one picture of a boy chasing a bubble will sell scores of times—and bring more return in the long run. The latter is a good marketable stock photo. And you'll have twenty, thirty, forty more of these, selling at the same pace, for every sunset in your supply.

Don't rely on wishful thinking. A few stock photographers do get lucky, but by and large, those who are on top, and who stay there, are those who have recognized the overwhelming odds in the marathon route and have switched over to what I call "Track B" in the next chapter. There's competition in that race, too, but it's manageable enough to keep you healthily striving for excellence.

Whether you sell and resell your pictures is not up to the photobuyers, but to you, the stock photographer. You control whether you sell or don't sell—by controlling the content of your pictures.

When you are out on your next photographing excursion, keep two guidelines in mind:

1. Shoot discriminately. Treat each piece of film you expose as a finished product that will one day be on a photobuyer's desk.

2. As you prepare to take a shot, ask yourself, "Is it marketable?" (One photographer I know taped this question to the back of her camera.) I am not suggesting that you get involved in areas of photography that don't appeal to you. As I explain in the next chapter, you have assets, photographically, that are individual to you. In the course of this book, I'll show you how to match your photographic interests with the needs of buyers who are on the lookout for the kind of pictures you can easily supply. For example, if you live in New Mexico, there's a lot of picture taking and selling to be done that a person in Michigan can't do. And your geo-

graphic location is only one advantage you have over other photographers. You may be into sailing or raising hunting dogs. You may be an armchair geologist. Your hobbies and interests, and your knowledge and your career field, are assets. So, I say to persons new in the field of photomarketing, "You *can* position yourself where the competition is manageable." With your own PMS/A (personal photographic marketing strength/areas), which we'll learn to identify in the next chapter, you can be an important resource to buyers who are, right now, waiting for your pictures.

Your aim is to sell the greatest number of pictures with the least amount of lost motion (i.e., unsuccessful submissions). Why take risks? Photomarketing is a business. Once you know the difference between a good picture and a good *marketable* picture, your sales will start to soar.

The photo illustration has four essential elements: A meaningful background, people, a symbol, and involvement. Sometimes you happen upon all four spontaneously; other times you have to plan them out and pull them together yourself. This classic photo, "Rescue from a Washout," by western photographer Bill Ellzey of Telluride, Colorado, illustrates the results of the latter, or "previsualization," as Ellzey calls it. He located one of the few remaining wooden windmills in his region, set up his tripod and coached his two cowboy cousins into lifting a three-day-old calf from the draw. Nature cooperated with a sudden snow flurry. So did the horses when they responded to his cousin's whistle (as directed by Ellzey). It took twenty-two shots to get that just-right picture. Back at the ranch, Ellzey and his frozen cousins thawed out (and baby calf happily returned to Mother). The picture continues to be a hot seller.

A GALLERY OF STOCK PHOTOS

Stock photos and stock photographers come from all walks of life. Here is a selection of pictures that have had repeat sales and a glimpse at the people who produced them.

I asked fellow stock photographers to send me samples of stock photos that produce continual revenue for them. All of these photographers zero in on their own PMS/A and supply their own corner of the market.

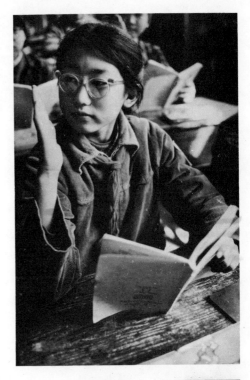

"My specialty is travel photography, and I have flown nearly four million miles and visited eighty-six countries. Currently, my stock files contain 350,000 images on a wide variety of subjects. My wife and I market these directly to advertising agencies, magazines, newspapers, textbooks, and PR firms. We also market through picture agencies."

Carl Purcell
Alexandria, Virginia

"I am a full-time photo illustrator, in my twenty-fifth year of happy work. My pictures are used in magazines, books, posters, greeting cards, and advertising. I often illustrate articles on religion, education, and family relations. I have a writer-friend who often works with me. I have built up a large clientele and am able to sell my inspirational scenics as well as a variety of subjects."

Jini Dellaccio
Sequim, Washington

"I've been involved with photography for the past twenty years, mostly as a photo-journalist working on assignment for national magazines. My strongest images are of people—a subject I never tire of. I find I'm able to sell and resell these photos to book publishers and magazines through my own mini-stock-photo agency. This photo is especially popular, as it combines the beautiful facial expression of the little girl with a large open area for publishers to use for type."

Rick Smolan,
New York, New York

"Having been a professional photographer for ten years I strongly feel that the secret to selling and re-selling is to maintain a strong stock file and to be professional and dedicated in one's marketing. Follow up every lead, contact photobuyers, send out stock lists and be always alert to any possibility that opens up new avenues of potential income. While much of my photography is travel-oriented I also cover journalism and in my New York studio specialize in theatrical portraiture for the performing arts. Much of my repeat sales in travel photography are, of course, in color.

Lee Snider/Photo Images
New York, New York

"I got started as a photo illustrator with a sale to a local evening paper while still a schoolboy back in 1948. Most of my photography career has been as a service photographer, but speculative submissions of pictures and photo/text packages are an increasingly important part of my income. I see concentration on writing and stock photography as the next stage of my career. I find that pictures of the people in the countries I visit are my best stock photo sellers such as this sponge vendor in Athens."

Dennis Mansell
Braintree Essex, England

"After twenty years as a service photographer/reporter for a newspaper, I became a full-time freelance stock photographer fourteen years ago. I enjoy the freedom from assignments. I offer thousands of good stock photos to magazine and book publishers; my specialty is the human-interest people picture, in basic contexts of home, school, and church."

David S. Strickler
Newville, Pennsylvania

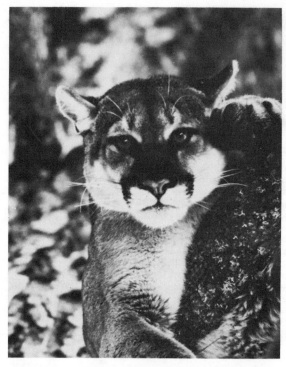

"I'm a STOCK photographer. I now shoot mostly on speculation. In a recent San Francisco workshop I was asked to recount the preceding 6 months. The process of looking back was both pleasant and a bit surprising. I had worked in Thailand, in Oregon (a wild horse round-up), in the Grand Canyon (225 miles of white water), at Joshua Tree National Monument, in Indonesia (5 weeks via motorcycle), I had photographed California Desert Bighorn, and the Canadian Rockies, plus Vancouver B.C. (pre Expo). Our family income is admittedly modest, but my wife and I think of ourselves as rich."

Ron Sanford
Gridley, California

"Although my main income is derived from assignment photography in the field of recreation and leisure-time activities for national advertising accounts, stock photography has always been a very important part of my total income. The most successful photos are those of people doing things. Several of my color photos have enjoyed remarkable sales records. This photo has been sold, by both my agents and myself, over forty-two times in the last ten years."

Burton McNeely
Land O' Lakes, Florida

"I've been a service photographer for seventeen years. A couple of years ago I discovered that a lot of material I had shot with 35mm on assignment could be sold as single stock pictures. I have found a good market for my pictures of people and kids in all kinds of activities. It doesn't take long to get on a publisher's good side if you keep sending him the kind of pictures he needs."

Jack Hamilton
Milwaukee, WI

"I began to query editors for their stock photo needs nine years ago. Since then, I've sold hundreds of photos as a part-time freelancer. I sell both black-and-white and color to publishers of magazines, books, calendars and greeting cards. I love to work for myself! Each sale moves me closer to my goal of going full-time.

The shot illustrated (my wife and son) is my best seller in black-and-white. I think that it sells repeatedly because it illustrates so many concepts, e.g., love, caring, education. The fact that good minority photos are scarce is also a factor. My advice to freelancers: Find a specialty and become known for it; and subscribe to Photomarket!"

Jim Bradshaw
Washington, DC

"Besides photography, I also dabble in carpentry, farm work, and other odd jobs, especially if they include travel. Thus, my photography covers the gamut of human-interest subjects. I have been doing stock photography since 1972 and recently set up my own mini-stock-photo agency, marketing photos for a number of other professional photographers as well. Over 150 different publishers have used my photos in their magazines and books. This one has sold thirty four times so far—illustrating Christmas, adventure, etc."

Robert Maust
Harrisonburg, Virginia

"In the 1950s, my magazine assignments yielded few reusable pictures, but when I began writing and illustrating books for children and about photography, and specialized in articles about photographic techniques, building a personal stock file became important. This London street is typical of pictures that have sold to various publications over the last decade. I shoot as often as possible as I travel, and also sell through several agencies. I always try to envision possible markets as I take pictures."

Lou Jacobs, Jr.
Cathedral City, California

"I frequently work with freelance writers on picture stories. The material can often be rewritten and reslanted for extra mileage. I've been freelancing full time since 1973. I wear two hats. My work has ranged from portraiture and service photography to editorial, illustrative, and decor photography. This picture is an example of decor photography. I have made a concerted effort to establish myself in this area. My archival black-and-white decor prints have been selling well lately."

Bill Ellzey
Telluride, Colorado

"I've made thousands of sales in the twenty years I've been freelancing. Today I'm the photojournalism professor at CBN University in Virginia Beach. After hours, while others find excitement watching TV football games, I find mine making moving, graphic images that sell and resell and in filling the request lists that keep coming in. The rewards, which are much more than financial, include a recent Photographer of the Year award."

Bob Combs
Virginia Beach, Virginia

"I have been a writer for twenty years and a photographer for ten. The two go well together—editors are always happy to see that I can also supply the illustrations. I am a people person, so people are my main subject in my photography. That is not to say that I don't take a beautiful flower or landscape probably more often than I should! Since becoming involved in stock photography, my stock file has grown. So has my market list. I have received assignments from magazines such as *Woman's World*, *Ideals*, *News & Views*, etc. This picture is one of my most published, also one of my favorites. Having my photo published in *Ideals* (more to come) was a lifelong dream—and one of the great rewards of my lifetime!"

Joanne Kash
Holly Hill, Florida

"A freelance photographer for thirty years, my most-sold picture is a family of four singing at an upright piano, Mother playing. Naturalness and spontaneity seem to be the requisites. Posed pictures are out. This picture has been a very good seller. Today, most of my work appears in magazines and textbooks."

Vivienne della Grotta
Carpinteria, California

"When I started as a special education teacher, it seemed second nature to use my camera in the classroom.

Today, my work is used regularly in a variety of publications across the U.S. And many photos get used more than once. For example, this picture of a guest physicist demonstrating static electricity to third graders served one month on the cover of *Elementary School Journal* and the next month to illustrate an article in *National PTA Magazine*."

Harvey Phillips
Colts Neck, New Jersey

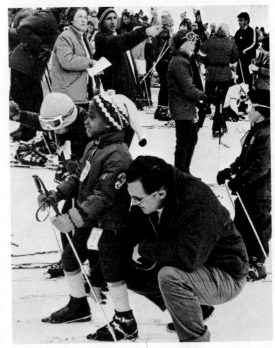

"Although I'm primarily a writer, I have also taken pictures for the past twenty years. My work as a part-time photo agent resulted in interviewing many well-known photographers for the book *Freelance Writing: Advice from the Pros*, published by Macmillan. Some of my subjects are the outdoors—skiing, mountaineering, and winter sports. I always advise students to learn how to use a camera. Photo illustrations make an article more salable."

Curtis W. Casewit
Denver, Colorado

3.
Finding
Your Corner
of
the Market

*No sales for your photos? Unemployment is a matter of self-assessment.
If you can photograph one subject well, you're needed somewhere by
some photobuyer.*
—H.T. White

First, Find Yourself

Who are you? Photographers who are successful in selling their pictures
have learned this marketing secret: *Know thyself*. That is, know your
photographic strengths and weaknesses before you begin marketing
your pictures.

You want to find your corner of the market. But first, you must find out
who *you* are, photographically. You can do that by completing the following simple exercise.

Photographically . . . Who Am I?

Save a Sunday afternoon to fill out this section—it will be invaluable in
terms of the wheel spinning you'll encounter if you jump into photo marketing without having the information in this chapter. If you are reading
this book a second time because your stock photography enterprise is
sputtering and coughing and you're wondering what went wrong, read
this chapter *carefully*. Many photographers fail to do so and then fail. As
the saying goes, "When all else fails, read the directions."

Take a piece of paper and make two columns like the ones in Figure 3-
1. Head the column on the left *Track A*, the column on the right *Track B*.
The columns can extend the length of the page or pages, if necessary.

Next, fill in the Track B column with one-line answers (in no special
order) to these questions:

1. What is the general subject matter of each of the periodicals you
subscribe to, or would like to subscribe to (or receive free)? (For example,
if you subscribe to *Today's Pilot* you would write: aviation.) Write something down for each magazine. Do you welcome catalogs in the mail?
What's the subject matter? Write it down.

Track A	Track B
scenics	gardening
flowers	electronics
fountains	grocer
insects	teacher
sunsets	scenics
historic sites	flowers
	fountains
	insects
	sunsets
	historic sites
	antique automobiles
	snowmobiling
	old barns
	old movies
	Minneapolis
	Wisconsin
	Mississippi River
	St. Croix River
	Interstate Park
	TV cameraman
	dentist

Figure 3-1. John's track list.

2. What is your occupation? (If you've had several, list each one.) Also include careers you'd like to pursue, or are studying for or working toward.

3. When you are on a photo-taking excursion, what subjects do you enjoy taking the most? (E.g., rustic buildings, football, celebrities, sunrises, roses, waterfalls, butterflies, fall foliage, children, puppies, Siamese cats, hawks, social statements, girls.) Use as many blanks as you wish. The order is unimportant.

4. List your hobbies and pastimes (other than photography).

5. If you were to examine all of your slides and contact sheets, would you find threads of continuity running through the images? (For example, you might discover that you often photograph horses, train stations, rock formations, physical fitness buffs, minority groups.)

6. What are your favorite armchair interests? For example, if a passing interest is solar energy, astronomy, or ancient warfare, write it down.

7. What is the name of the nearest city of more than 500,000 population?

8. What state do you live in?

9. List any nearby (within a half-day's drive) geographical features (ocean, mountains, rivers) and human-made interests (iron or coal mine, hot-air-balloon factory, dog-training school).

10. What specialized subject areas do you have ready access to? (For example, if your neighbor is a bridge builder or a ballerina, or a relative is a skydiver, or your friend is an oil rig man, list them.)

If the list in Track B includes any of the following, *draw a line through them*: landscapes, birds, scenics, insects, plants, wildflowers, major pro sports, silhouettes, experimental photography, artistic subjects (such as the "art" photography in photography magazines), abstracts (such as those seen in photo-art magazines and salons), popular travel spots, monuments, landmarks, historic sites, cute animal pictures. Transfer all of the subjects that you just drew a line through over to Track A.

You'll find your best picture *sales* possibilities in Track B. Track A is a high-risk marketing area for you. Most photographers have spent a great deal of their time photographing in the Track A area. Are you surprised to find that you have the most pictures in the weak marketing areas and few pictures in the strong marketing areas? Most photographers who want to market their pictures never learn their marketing strengths and weaknesses until they have failed at selling their photography. At that point, they believe they have failed at photography. There is a difference.

When you get off Track A and onto Track B, you'll stop wasting time, film, postage, and materials. You'll get published, you'll receive recognition for your photography, and you'll deposit checks. Let's examine the Track B and Track A of a hypothetical photographer, John, in Figure 3-1.

1. John subscribes to magazines dealing with gardening, electronics, and antique automobiles. Not only do these reflect John's interests, but the combined total for photographs purchased for magazines and books in these three areas can exceed $150,000 per month. Yet most of John's picture-taking energy and dollars have been put into Track A pictures, which have limited marketing potential.

2. John's occupation is grocer. The trade magazines in this area spend about $20,000 per month for photography. John could easily cover his expenses to the national conventions each year, plus add an extra vacation week at the convention site, with income generated by his camera.

John is a former teacher, and retains his interest in education. His experience gives him the insight and know-how to capture natural photographs of classroom situations. Such photos are big sellers to the education field, denominational press, and textbook industry. Let's make a conservative estimate of the dollars expended each month for education-oriented pictures: $500,000.

3. In his picture-taking excursions, John usually concentrates on scenics, flowers, fountains, insects, sunsets, and historic sites. These all have limited marketability for the independent freelancer without a track record with the big agencies and top magazines. However, John could place some of these Track A pictures in stock agencies for periodic supplementary sales. A stock agency that specializes in insects, for example, will be interested in seeing the quality of John's insect pictures. Some of John's other Track A pictures belong in different stock agencies. (Chapter 12 tells how to research which agencies are right for which pictures on your Track A list.)

4. John's favorite hobby is antique cars. He can easily pay for trips to meetings and conventions through judicious study of the market needs for photography in antique cars.

John also lists snowmobiling as a hobby. More than $50,000 a month is expended on photography in publications dealing with winter fun sports in season.

5. John finds that he photographs picturesque old barns every chance he gets. Market is limited (Track A). One day he may produce a book or exhibit of barn pictures, but it will be a labor of love.

6. His armchair interest is old movies. No marketing potential unless placed in a specialized photo agency.

7, 8. Nearest city: Minneapolis. Chapter 11 will explain how to capitalize on your travel pictures.

9. The Mississippi and St. Croix rivers are nearby, plus a state park; see Chapter 11.

10. John's neighbor is a TV cameraman. He could get specialized access to television operations and be an important source to editors who need location pictures dealing with the TV industry. John's brother is a dentist, so he has access to the field of dentistry. Publications in each of these areas spend easily a combined $15,000 per month for pictures.

Your PMS/A (Personal Photographic Marketing Strength/Areas)

Let's take a closer look at Tracks A and B:

Track A

These are the areas of formidable competition. Track A pictures are used in the marketplace all right, but it's a closed market. Photobuyers have tons of these photographs in inventory, or they locate them easily from their favorite top pros, or they contact a stock agency that has thousands upon thousands to select from. If you want to concentrate your efforts in the Track A area of photography, I suggest you stop reading right here, because you'll need to put every minute of your time into making a go of it. Only a handful of freelancers in this country—most of them full-time pros—are successful at making regular sales of Track A photographs, and the majority must still supplement their incomes with writing, consulting, speaking, or teaching.

If you're not planning to concentrate on Track A pictures, but you still want to take them, one solution is to put your Track A shots into a stock photo agency and then not worry about how often they sell for you. Every once in a while, you may get a nice surprise check. (Chapter 12 shows you how to determine which agencies are for you.) A second solution is to turn to producing decor photography (again, see Chapter 12). Keep in mind, though, that you can't expect either of these solutions to result in *regular* sales for you. Decor photography is a labor of love, and the big money maker at a stock agency is the director. Practically speaking, your forte and solid opportunity for immediate and consistent sales—in other words, your strong marketability areas—lie on Track B.

Track B

Take time to do a complete job of filling out Track B, and you'll find that you've sketched a picture of who you are photographically. This list is your PMS/A, your personal photographic marketing strength/areas. You have vital advantages in these areas. You offer a valuable resource to editors in these specialized subjects. You have access and an informed approach to pictures in these areas that many photographers do not have. Your competition in marketing Track B pictures is manageable. Throughout this book, I'll constantly refer to your PMS/A, your Track B list. You are already something of an expert in many of these Track B areas, and the subject matter appeals to you. Not all of your interests, of course, lend themselves 100 percent to photography. But you will be surprised how many do. For example, *chess* has spawned few periodicals that require pictures. But pictures of people playing chess have varied applications: *concentration, thinking, competition*—good illustration possibilities for textbooks or for educational, sociological, or human-interest magazines.

Photobuyers for the Track B markets will encourage you to submit pictures by purchasing more and more of your photo illustrations. Gradually you'll receive higher fees—and eventually assignments. Your efforts and sales in the nuts-and-bolts areas of Track B can also justify the time you still may wish to give to Track A photos, which actually *cost* you money to try to market.

Throughout this book when I refer to *you*, the photographer, I mean for you to adapt what I'm saying to *your* particular photographic strengths and approaches. Refer again to the photographic picture of yourself you've outlined on Track B. When I say *you*, I won't mean *me*, or any other reader of this book. Another photographer would fill out this chart differently. He would also be an important resource to an editor or editors, but rarely would the two of you be in competition for the attention of the same photobuyers. Your task will be to find your own mix of markets, based on the areas you like and know best, and then hit those markets with pictures they need.

This approach eliminates the drudgery associated with the admonition we often read in books and hear at lectures: "Study the markets!"

When I first began marketing my photographs, I also heard "Study the markets!" I've always associated the word *study* with tedium. I found it unnecessary to study the markets. The only studying I needed was to study *myself*—and then develop my personal photographic marketing strengths. If I listed the market in my PMS/A, I was already a mini-expert on the subject. If it wasn't in my PMS/A, I had no business either studying it or photographing it.

The Majors and the Minors

Do you know any successful photographers? *Success* eludes concrete definition. We all know that it is irrelevant to judge people's success by their net worth, or where they live, or the fame they have attained. When I refer to *success* in this book, interpret it not in terms of some stereotyped level of achievement, but in terms of the goals that are meaningful to *you*.

The major markets for your photo illustrations may not necessarily be the major markets for the stock photographer next door. Your neighbor's major markets may be your minor markets.

Will you have to change your lifestyle or your photography to apply the marketing principles in this book? Not at all. And breaking in won't put a dent in your pocketbook. Your major markets need not be in New York. They might be in your backyard.

The length of your Track B list will give you a good idea of the breadth of the market potential for your photography. Some stock photographers thrive in a very limited marketplace. Others find it necessary, because of the nature of their photographic interests, to seek out many markets. In my own case, I have six file drawers filled with correspondence with 830 publishing houses or photo-buying contacts developed over a period of twenty-five years. The files, like the publishing world, stay in a state of flux. Markets change focus, they fold, new markets appear, and personnel turnovers occur. (At the same time, many markets stay stable and dependable through the years.) I deal on a regular basis with about a third of the total number in my files. Yet I know of stock photographers who confine their photo-marketing contacts to only a couple dozen.

How to Use the Reference Guides and Directories

Once you know your photographic strengths, you'll find your corner of the market more easily. Several excellent market guides exist that will point you in the right direction. Keep in mind that directories, even telephone directories, because of publishing lead time, are up to one year older than the date on the cover. Use your directories to give you a general idea of potential markets for your photographic strengths. For specific names, titles, and updated addresses and phone numbers, keep your directories current yourself by making personnel changes whenever you learn them through your correspondence, phone calls, or newsletters.

Treat your directories like tools, not fragile glassware. Keep them handy, scribble in them, paste in them, add pages, or tear others out. Your directories are a critical resource for moving forward in your photo marketing. If you are computerized, begin to maintain a photobuyer file.

Table 3-1 tells you the names and addresses of published directories. Most of these you'll find at any large metropolitan library, and many of them are stocked by your local community or branch library.

Which directories are best for you? You'll find out by matching the subject categories in your Track B list with the market categories covered by the different directories. By far the most popular directory among newcomers to stock photography is *Photographer's Market,* an annual directory that lists over 2,500 markets. This directory not only tracks down personnel changes in the industry, but also lists the fees photobuyers are willing to pay for stock photos.

Using Your Local Interlibrary Loan Service

Some directories may be too expensive for you. They may also be too expensive for your community or branch library. Ask the librarian to borrow such a directory through the interlibrary loan service (or its equivalent in your area). If the book is not available at a regional library, the service will locate it at the state level. It generally takes two weeks to locate a book. Since the books you order will be reference manuals, your library will probably ask that you use them in the library. However, you can photocopy the pages you'll need, thanks to the *fair use* doctrine of the U.S. Copyright Act.

Chart Your Course . . . Build a Personalized Market List

Now that you have defined your photographic strengths and focused in on your accessible subject areas, you are ready to chart your market course.

Successful businesspersons in any endeavor aim to reduce the possibility of failure by reducing or eliminating no-sale situations. Why attempt to sell your pictures to a market where the no-sale risk is high? By using the procedure that follows, you will build a *no-risk* Market List and begin to see your credit line in national circulation.

Consult all of the directories available to you and build a list of potential markets for your material by combing through the categories that match your photographic strengths. This might take several evenings of effort, but the investment of time is worth it.

Here at PhotoSource International, we provide a computerized printout of names and addresses of contact persons or photobuyers in every imaginable area. Your homework will result in several similar lists (the number of lists depends on the length of your Track B column).

For example, the list below was taken from a single market directory, *Magazine Industry Market Place*. Although your areas of interest may not include things automotive, take time to read through the list to get a sense of the variety. The same variety of markets is waiting for you in your fields of special interest.

American Motorcyclist
Antique Automobile
Antique Motor News
Auto Merchandising News
Auto Racing Digest
Automobile International
Automobile Quarterly
Automotive Aftermath
   News
Automotive Age
Automotive Body Repair
   News
Automotive Design &
   Development
Automotive Fleet
Automotive Industries
Automotive Messenger
Automotive News
Brake & Front End
Car and Driver
Car Craft
Cars & Parts
Cars Magazine
Choppers/Big Bike
Commercial Car Journal
Consumer Guide
Custom Bike
Cycle Guide

Cycle News
Cycle World
Defense Transportation
   Journal
Diesel & Gas Turbine
   Progress
Dirt Bike
4x4's & Off Road Vehicles
Four Wheeler
Heavy Duty Trucking
Hemmings Motor
Hot Rod Magazine
Jobber Topics
Magic Circle
Mechanix Illustrated
Midwest Motorist
Modern Cycle
Montgomery Ward Auto
   Club News
Motocross Action
   Magazine
Motor
Off-Road
Old Cars
1001 Truck & Van Ideas
Owner Operator
Parking
Pickup, Van & 4WD

Popular Hot Rodding
   Magazine
Popular Mechanics
Popular Science
Q-Vo Magazine
Racing Pictorial
Rider
Road & Track
Snow Goer
Special Interest Autos
Stock Car Racing
   Magazine
Street Chopper
Street Machine
Street Rodder
Sun Magazine
Super Chevy
Super Service Station
Super Stock & Drag
   Illustrated
Today's Transportation
   International
Touring Bike
Traveler
Travelin' Vans, Mini
   Trucks & Pickups
Truckin'
Ward's Auto World

Advertising Photographers of America Directory 823 North La Brea Los Angeles CA 90038	**The Bowker Annual of Library and Book Trade/Information** R. R. Bowker 245 W. Seventeenth St. New York, NY 10011	**Educational Marketer Yellow Pages** Knowledge Industry Pub. 701 Westchest Ave. White Plains, NY 10604
American Book Trade Directory R. R. Bowker 245 W. Seventeenth St. New York, NY 10011	**Business Publication Rates and Data** Standard Rate and Data Service 3004 Glenview Rd.	**Education Directory: Colleges and Universities, 1986-86** (Stock Number 065-000-00268-0) Superintendent of Documents
American Hospital Association Directory 840 N. Lake Shore Dr. Chicago, IL 60611	Wilmette, IL 60091 **Canadian Almanac and Directory** Copp Clark Pitman Ltd.	U.S. Government Printing Office Washington, DC 20402
American Society of Journalists and Authors Membership Directory Directory of Professional Writers 1501 Broadway, Suite 1907 New York, NY 10036	495 Wellington St. West Toronto, Ontario M5V 1E9 Canada **Cassell's Directory of Publishing** Artillery House, Artillery Row	**Encyclopedia of Associations** Gale Research Co. Book Tower Detroit, MI 48226 **Gebbie Press All-In-One Directory** Box 1000 New Paltz, NY 12561
American Society of Picture Professionals Directory Box 5283 Grand Central Station New York, NY 10017	London SW1 1RT England **Consumer Magazine and Farm Publication Rates and Data** Standard Rate and Data Service	**Gift and Decorative Accessory Buyer's Directory** Geyer McAllister Publications 51 Madison Ave. New York, NY 10010
American Universities and Colleges Walter de Gruyter, Inc. 200 Saw Mill River Rd. Hawthorne, NY 10532	3004 Glenview Wilmette, IL 60091 **Contact Book for the Entertainment Industry** Celebrity Service International	**Guide to American Directories** B. Klein Publications P. O. Box 8503 Coral Springs, FL 33065
ASMP Stock Photo Handbook ASMP, 205 Lexington Ave. New York, NY 10016	Suite 300, 1780 Broadway New York, NY 10019 **Decor Sources Annual** Commerce Publishing Co.	**Harfax Directory of Industry Data Sources** Ballinger Publishing Co. 54 Church St., Box 281 Cambridge, MA 02138
Association For Educational Communications and Technology Directory 1126 Sixteenth St., NW Washington, DC 20036	408 Olive Ave. St. Louis, MO 63102 **Design Film Directory** Wefler & Associates 117 North Jefferson St.	**Information USA Directory** Penguin Books 40 West 23rd St. New York, NY 10010
Audiovisual Market Place R. R. Bowker 245 West Seventeenth St. New York, NY 10011	Chicago, IL 60606 **Directory of Free Stock Photography** InfoSource Publications	**Interior Design Buyer's Guide** Interior Design Publications 475 Park Ave South New York, NY 10016
IMS Directory of Publications Gale Research Book Tower Detroit, MI 48226	10 East 39th St. 6th Flr. New York, NY 10016 **Directory of Small Magazine Press Editors and Publishers** Dustbooks	**Internal Publications Directory** National Research Bureau 424 N. Third St. Burlington, IA 52601
Bacon's Publicity Checker Bacon's Publishing Company 332 S. Michigan Ave. Chicago, IL 60604	Box 100B Paradise, CA 95969	

Table 3-1. Directories.

The International Buyer's Guide of the Music-Tape Industry
Billboard Publications
1515 Broadway
New York, NY 10036

The Journal of the Society for Photographic Education Directory Exposure Magazine
P. O. Box 1651
FDR Post Office
New York, NY 10150

Literary Market Place
R. R. Bowker
245 W. Seventeenth St.
New York, NY 10011

Madison Avenue Handbook
Peter Glenn Publications
17 E. 48th St.
New York, NY 10017

Magazine Industry Market Place
R. R. Bowker
245 W. Seventeenth St.
New York, NY 10011

The Mail-Order Business Directory
Catalog Division
B. Klein Publications
Box 8503
Coral Springs, FL 33065

National Outdoor Guides Directory
Professional Guides Publishing
1904 Talpeco Rd., Suite A
Tallahassee, FL 32303

New York Publicity Outlets
Public Relations Plus, Inc.
Post Office Drawer 1197
New Milford, CT 06776

O'Dwyer's Directory of Corporate Communications
J. R. O'Dwyer Co.
271 Madison Ave.
New York, NY 10016

O'Dwyer's Directory of Public Relations Firms
J. R. O'Dwyer Co.
271 Madison Ave.
New York, NY 10016

Online Business Information Sources
Cuadra Associates
Suite 305
2001 Wilshire Blvd.
Santa Monica, CA 90403

Patterson's American Education
Box 199
Mount Prospect, IL 60056

Photographer's Market
1507 Dana Ave.
Cincinnati, OH 45207

Photographic Education Directory
Exposure Magazine
P. O. Box 1651
FDR Post Office
New York, NY 10150

Picture Sources V
Special Libraries Assn.
1700 18th St. NW
Washington, DC 20009

Reader's Digest Almanac and Yearbook
Pleasantville, NY 10570

Register of the Public Relations Society of America
845 Third Ave.
New York, NY 10022

Society of American Travel Writers Directory
1120 Connecticut Ave.
Washington, DC 20036

Standard Directory of Advertisers
National Register Publishing Co.
3004 Glenview
Wilmette, IL 60091

Standard Periodical Directory
Oxbridge Communications
Suite 301, 150 5th Ave.
New York, NY 10011

Stock Photo Source Book
The Photographic Arts Center
127 East 59th St.
New York, NY 10022

Talk Show Guest Directory
Broadcast Interview Service
Suite 930B, 2500 Wisconsin Ave.
Washington, DC 20007

Television Contacts
Larimi Communications, Ltd.
5 West 37th St.
New York, NY 10018

Traveler's Guide to Info
U. S. Dept. of Commerce
U.S. Travel Service
Visitor Services Div.
Washington, DC 20230

Travel Writer's Markets Directory
Winterbourne Press
P. O. Box 7548B
Berkeley, CA 94707

Ulrich's International Periodicals Directory
R. R. Bowker
245 W. Seventeenth St.
New York, NY 10011

Underwater Photography Directory
Sport Diver Publications
3299 K. St. Sixth Floor
Washington, DC 20007

Where and How to Sell Your Photographs
Amphoto
1515 Broadway
New York, NY 10036

Working Press of the Nation, Volume V, Internal Publications Directory
National Research Bureau
424 N. Third St.
Burlington, IA 52601

The World Almanac
Newspaper Enterprise Association
200 Park Ave.
New York, NY 10017

World Travel Directory
Ziff-Davis Publishing Co.
Room 1011, 1 Park Ave.
New York, NY 10016

Table 3-1. (cont.)

Writer's and Photographer's Guide to Newspaper Markets International Resources P. O. Box 1275 San Luis Obispo, CA 93406 A Writer's Guide to Chicago Area Publishers Writer's Guide Publications Gabriel House, Inc. Suite 7, 5045 W. Oakton Street Skokie, IL 60077	Writers Guide to San Francisco/Bay Area Publishers & Editors Zikawuna Books P. O. Box 703 Palo Alto, CA 94302 Writer's Market 1507 Dana Ave. Cincinnati, OH 45207	The Yearbook of American and Canadian Churches Abingdon Press 201 Eighth Ave. S. Nashville, TN 37202

Table 3-1. (cont.)

Setting Up Your List

Type the address of each market on a separate 3x5 file card, expandable personal directory, or computerized data base. On your lists you will want to include information about the photobuyers you deal with at each market—title, nickname, former position or title, fee range, plus a note or two about their photo-buying procedures, preferences, dislikes, and assignment possibilities. Leave room for code designations of your promotional mailings to them (see Chapter 10), and of course, space for changes of address, title, or personnel.

This system will allow you flexibility to delete, repair (e.g., make changes of address or spelling corrections), or add names easily.

You get the start for your personal Market List from the directories, but you can discover additional markets for your pictures at newsstands, doctors' offices, business counters, and reception rooms.

Your list is now tailored to your exact areas of interest. If you have several areas of interest, should you make several lists? My advice would be to keep one master list. Color-code the categories, or type them on different-colored file cards. Then, when you repair or replace a listing, you need do it only once. (For more on recordkeeping, see Chapter 13.)

The Specialization Strategy

Now that you have charted your course to sail straight for your corner of the market, you are bypassing the hordes of photographers on Track A to move along Track B, where you can manage the competition.

As you work with this system, you will discover that you can define your target markets even more specifically—and improve the marketability of your pictures 1,000 percent—through a strategy used by all photographers who are successful at marketing their pictures, the strategy of *specialization*.

We live in an age of specialization. Once we leave school, whether it be high school or medical school, we are destined to become a specialist in something. In today's world, with the immense breadth of knowledge, technology, and diversification, it's impossible for one person to be expert even in all aspects of a single chosen field. And in our culture, buyers of a person's services prefer dealing with someone who knows a lot about a specific area, rather than with someone who spreads himself too thin.

The same holds true for photobuyers. They know the discerning readers of their specialty magazines expect pictures that reflect a solid knowledge of the subject areas. Understandably, then, buyers seek out photographers who not only take excellent pictures, but who also exhibit familiarity with and understanding of the subject matter of their publications.

Technical knowledge alone is not sufficient to operate successfully in today's highly specialized milieu. Marketing has evolved beyond the "I buy a product because I like the product" stage. Marketing people have found that consumers often buy an image rather than a product. Their success at image-creating to sell cars, cigarettes, and beer attests to the power of images to move the buying public. Since most magazines (and, to a lesser extent, books) are extensions of the advertisers or supporting organizations, photo editors, directed by the publisher's editorial board, are constantly seeking out photographs and photographers who can capture the publication's image in pictures. The image projected in a yachting magazine will be subtly different than that of a tennis magazine. The image projected by a magazine called *Organic Fruit Growing* will be radically different from that of one called *Chemical Fertilizers Today*.

These nuances are important for you to be aware of. (In Chapter 9, I'll discuss these nuances further and show you an effective query letter for reaching editors.) Go over the list of markets you've compiled for yourself. You need to familiarize yourself with the publications (write for copies or find them at the library) to educate yourself on their individual themes. Often, the book or magazine publisher will supply you with photo guidelines. If you can't get a handle on the image of some of the markets, put them at the bottom of your list. Keep the areas you're more sure of at the top. You have now fine-tuned your list; you can be more selective in your choices. The top of your list has your target markets, the ones that best reflect who you are *photographically*, the ones that fall within your personal photo marketing strengths. Editors have specific photo needs, and the sooner you match your subjects and interest areas with buyers who need them, the sooner you'll receive checks.

You'll also be building a reputation among the photobuyers who need your specialized photography. Photobuyers pass the word.

Keeping On Top with Newsletters

Another way to discover additional markets for your list, or to keep abreast of current market trends, is to read the newsletters in the field.

You can usually find these in the library, or you can send for sample copies (include $1 and SASE), to gauge whether your particular photographic approach would be served by subscribing. For names and addresses of a dozen of the best in the field, see the Bibliography.

Track A: The Boulevard of Broken Dreams

Your Track A and Track B lists have probably proved revealing to you. They may have surprised you also. You've discovered that the kind of pictures you have spent a good deal of time producing, those on Track A, don't have much marketing potential. They sell, yes, but as we've discussed, they're not good marketable pictures—not at this stage of your career. You are in a game of chance with 50,000 other players. There's always a winner, but the odds aren't in your favor. There are 49,999 losers. That's why I call it *sweepstakes marketing*.

But don't consider this as a condemnation. Instead, consider it a challenge. If you follow the system outlined in this chapter, you can say goodbye to thinking that you have to depend on a stock photo agency to sell your work. You used to think that was the route to follow because a large stock agency can be in touch with buyers for your pictures on a national scale. But now you can move your own work more actively and consistently than a large stock agency. You have now tapped national, regional, and local markets who will buy your specialized photography, and they'll give you all the business you need, provided you continue to supply them with what they need.

For Sale or For Soul?

If you enjoy taking Track A pictures, continue to take them—but take them on Sunday along with your art pictures. Relegate those Sunday pictures to a photo agency for a sometime sale, or to your "famous" file. Then, like the poet or songwriter whose earlier work is unearthed, you too, when you become famous, can let the world discover your Track A pictures in exhibitions, anthologies, and art print sales. Remember, though, that selling your "poetry" is tough to do. Judson Jerome, the noted poet, critic and columnist for *Writer's Digest*, once estimated that about 500,000 poems are submitted annually but only 500 get published earning a total of $10,000. This "guess-timate" by Jerome would mean that a poet stands one chance in a thousand of earning about twenty dollars, and if that poet sent out twenty poems per year (too many, Jerome says, for quality), he would sell one poem for twenty dollars every fifty years. Until you become famous and your Track A pictures are in demand, direct your energies toward producing marketable pictures.

There's a Target Market for every photographer. Take the time to fill out the lists on the next few pages. They are designed to fine-tune your photo marketing. What follows is a tested timesaving system for finding an exclusive **Market List** tailored to your personal photographic marketing strengths areas.

1. Using the columns below, break down your photo-marketing potential into two areas—Track A and Track B, according to the instructions on pages 49-54.

(Weak Marketing Potential) *TRACK A*	*(Strong Marketing Potential)* *TRACK B*
	BOATING
	CARPENTRY/CONSTRUCTION
	BAY
	WILD LIFE
	HORSES
	FARMING
	FAMILY
	OCEAN
	EDUCATION

Before turning the page, draw a big
X over your Track A list.

Figure 3-2. *How to find your PMS/A.*

2. Which entries on your Track B list don't appeal to you photographically? In other words, you wouldn't enjoy photographing in this area.

List here:

_____

_____

_____

_____

_____

_____

_____

_____

_____

_____

Eliminate that list from your PMS/A. Write in your *new* PMS/A here:

_____

_____

_____

_____

_____

_____

_____

_____

_____

_____

_____

_____

Figure 3-2. (cont.)

3. Be realistic. Which areas on your PMS/A list would it be impractical for you to photograph? For example, if you listed as an *access* a relative in Alaska who is a shrimp fisherman, it might be difficult to photograph this area (unless you are reading this in Alaska).

Another consideration: Would concentration on any of the markets you listed require a heavy investment in new photographic equipment that you would prefer not to make at this time?

List here:

_____

_____

_____

_____

_____

_____

_____

_____

Eliminate the preceding list from your PMS/A. Write in your new PMS/A here:

_____

_____

_____

_____

_____

_____

_____

_____

_____

_____

Figure 3-2. (cont.)

4. Which areas of your PMS/A don't lend themselves widely to publishing? Few areas don't, but one or two of them might be on your list.

For example, there may be a very limited audience for pictures of antique clock repair. Or there may be too few picture possibilities for an armchair interest in unidentified flying objects.

List here:

_____

_____

_____

_____

_____

_____

_____

_____

Rewrite your list below, leaving out the subjects that are unlikely to apply widely to publishing. You have now further refined your PMS/A.

_____

_____

_____

_____

_____

_____

_____

_____

_____

_____

Figure 3-2. (cont.)

5. Decision! It's time to narrow down your PMS/A to *four* major areas. If you aim your marketing strategy at a minimum of four strength areas, you'll be able to develop them to their fullest potential.

Here are seven factors that will aid you in your decision. (Make an educated guess on some of them, since you probably don't have access to current circulation and payment figures in all of these fields.)

High	Medium	Low	
☐	☐	☐	• Your knowledge or expertise in this field.
☐	☐	☐	• Your personal interest in this field.
☐	☐	☐	• Your existing supply of pictures.
☐	☐	☐	• The payment range for pictures in this field.
☐	☐	☐	• The competition factor—is it high, medium, or low?
☐	☐	☐	• Your access to the field or information about it.
☐	☐	☐	• The audience (number of readers).

Using any other criteria you can think of, narrow down your PMS/A to four. Then decide which one of the four offers the best marketing potential for *you*. Then list the second best, and so on. Note your four strongest areas below.

My PMS/A

No. 1: _____

No. 2: _____

No. 3: _____

No. 4: _____

Figure 3-2. (cont.)

1. Now that you have found your top personal photographic marketing strength/areas (PMS/A), you are ready to find the *markets* that are looking for pictures in your PMS/A. Your library, depending on its size, can provide you with many of the directories and reference guides listed in Table 3-1. Your Market List is your gold mine; you will want to refine it in the same manner as your PMS/A. In the two columns below, list magazines and publishing houses that are potential markets for your PMS/A No. 1. Do your research thoroughly.

My initial market list for PMS/A No. 1:

_____   _____

_____   _____

_____   _____

_____   _____

_____   _____

_____   _____

_____   _____

_____   _____

_____   _____

_____   _____

_____   _____

_____   _____

_____   _____

Figure 3-3. Narrowing down your market list.

2. To tailor your list, ask these questions of each potential market on your list (you're going to do some shuffling):

A. What is the supply/demand factor? (Remember that *supply* in this case means the photobuyer's supply, not your supply.)

High supply, no demand = move to lower third of list.

High supply, high demand = move to upper half of list.

No supply, high demand = move to top of list.

No supply, no demand = move to lower third of list.

B. What is the competition factor?

No competition = move to top of list.

Moderate competition = move to upper half of list.

Fierce competition = move to lower third of list.

C. Miscellaneous considerations.

The magazine or house demands model releases = move to lower half of list.

The magazine or house has no track record (has been in business less than three years) = move to lower half of list.

Foreign market = move to lower half of list.

Slow or no payment reported = move to lower half or remove entirely.

Poor reliability factor reported (e.g., photobuyers reported as uncooperative, disrespectful, poor administrators, or inefficient in handling photographers' pictures) = move to lower half or remove entirely.

D. What is the publisher's purchasing power?

Rather than trying to determine a single magazine's circulation, research the entire publishing house's purchasing power. Most publishers concentrate on a specialized subject or theme. Often, if your pictures don't score with one editor, they are circulated among other editors within the house. (Some publishing houses have as many as twenty to thirty editors.) The best way to determine the buying power of a publishing house is to tally the number of periodicals and/or books published annually. If that figure is not available, you can get an idea of the house's purchasing power by looking at their circulation figures, number of pictures

Figure 3-3. (cont.)

purchased per year, or number of editors employed. Use Table 3-3, to rate your markets in order of purchasing priority.

Guide to Publisher's Buying Power

(Note: In this chart, *Publishing house* means book or magazine publisher.)

	Place at top of list	*Place in upper half of list*	*Place in lower half of list*
Number of editors at publishing house.	20 to 50	6 to 19	1 to 5
Number of periodicals at publishing house.	15 to 35	4 to 14	1 to 3
Number of books or magazines published per year by this publisher.	50 to 100	11 to 49	1 to 10
Number of photos purchased annually by publishing house.	400 to 3,000	49 to 399	1 to 50
Circulation figure (for single-magazine publishers).*	250,000 to 500,000	75,000 to 250,000	20,000 to 75,000

*Note: Magazines above 500,000 circulation are a closed market to most part-time stock photographers. Large-circulation magazines acquire their photos from (1) their staff, (2) stock photo agencies, or (3) long-time established local (or sometimes national) service photographers. Once your stock photo file grows to 20,000 and more salable images, you'll be eligible to deal regularly with top newsstand magazines.

Figure 3-3. (cont.); **Table 3-3.** Publisher's buying power guide.

3. What is the probability factor?

In the final analysis, you will determine your probability of scoring with a given magazine. Pictures in magazines can be broken down into two categories: advertising and editorial. As a stock photographer, your main concern is the *editorial market.*

These pictures are supplied by staff photographers, assignment freelancers, service photographers, stock photo agencies, and stock photographers such as yourself on the magazine's available-photographers list.

Using the magazines on your **Market List,** analyze their use of both advertising and editorial photographs. The amount of advertising in the magazine will give an indication of the magazine's picture budget. While you're at it, analyze the use of Track A pictures; this should convince you of the futility of trying to market Track A pictures yourself. (See Chapter 12 for methods to sell these.)

Rate the magazines:

30 to 150 editorial pictures = place on top of list.

10 to 29 editorial pictures = place on top half of list.

1 to 9 editorial pictures = place on bottom half of list.

_____   _____

_____   _____

_____   _____

_____   _____

_____   _____

_____   _____

Figure 3-3. (cont.)

_____   _____

_____   _____

_____   _____

_____   _____

_____   _____

_____   _____

_____   _____

_____   _____

4. You have shuffled and refined your Market List for PMS/A No. 1, and your strongest markets have come out on top. Go through the same process for your three other Market Lists.

   Transfer your four Market Lists to 3×5 file cards, a computer file, or a three-ring (expanding file) notebook (see Chapter 13). Make additions, deletions, and address changes to your Market List as soon as they occur.

   Some Market Lists are long because of the general nature of the subject. Others are short.

   Work closely with the top half of your list. But, because publishers' budgets change, continue to keep in contact with the lower half of your list as well.

   If in the future you acquire new knowledge or interest in another field, consider replacing one of your lists with a list for this new field.

Figure 3-3. (cont.)

4.
Getting
Started

"Many will come, but few are chosen." Will you be one of the chosen? Since 1981, when I published the first edition of this book, many photographers have benefited by it, and write to tell me they are now well-established in the stock photography field. What's their secret? Why have they been chosen?

Seize the Day

Throughout this book, I emphasize the importance of analyzing your personal photographic marketing strength/areas and then determining which markets need your kind of pictures. These invaluable assessments alone are an insurance policy against failure when you get started in your photo-marketing operation. Taking the time to pinpoint your PMS/A and research a sound Market List is fundamental to the success of your operation. If you skip this process or give it only short shrift, your photo-marketing prospects will be shaky.

Should you *start today*? My answer is yes, if you start by mapping out your PMS/A and Market List—*then* set aside four weekends to physically set up your operation.

That's right—in just four weekends, you can put yourself in business. We'll explore how to move step-by-step through those weekends in the "Four-Weekend Action Plan," but first let's take a look at a dozen roadblocks that may be standing in the way of getting started.

I've listed in Table 4-1 the twelve most common reasons people give as to why they haven't plunged into their photo-marketing operations. To the right are references to where each point is discussed and either solved or dissolved as a problem. If you've found any of the reasons mentioned in Table 4-1 to be roadblocks along your own route, now's the time to break through them and launch *your starting strategy*.

Breaking through the Roadblocks.	
"A dozen reasons why I can't!"	WHERE YOU'LL FIND THE REASONS WHY YOU CAN
Roadblock 1 "I don't have the time."	Chapters 4 and 13
Roadblock 2 "I have no experience."	Chapter 14
Roadblock 3 "There's too much competition."	Chapters 1, 2, 3, 6, and 14
Roadblock 4 "I only have one camera."	Appendix B
Roadblock 5 "I don't have a darkroom."	Appendix D
Roadblock 6 "Editors don't know me."	Chapters 7, 9, and 10
Roadblock 7 "It's too expensive."	Chapters 9, 14, and 16
Roadblock 8 "I live in a small town."	Introduction and Chapter 1
Roadblock 9 "I can't give it *full* time."	Chapter 14
Roadblock 10 "I don't know how much my pictures are worth."	Chapter 8
Roadblock 11 "I don't know *who* to sell to."	Chapters 1, 3, 7, and 12
Roadblock 12 "I don't know *what* pictures to sell."	Chapters 2 and 12

Table 4-1. "A dozen reasons why I can't!"

The Four-Weekend Action Plan

Most people have an aversion to starting things. Did you ever *not* start preparing a recipe because you weren't sure if you had all the ingredients? Did you ever *not* start work on a project because you weren't sure you would be able to find one of the necessary tools when you were halfway through it? Or you weren't sure *what* you'd need? Most of us procrastinate.

Well, you're lucky. You don't have to wait any longer to fire up your photo-marketing enterprise. Why not? Because the Four-Weekend Action Plan contains all the ingredients, all the tools, all the know-how you need to propel yourself into the field of photo marketing.

Your resolve will require some understanding on the part of your family and friends. Announce to your family that you are going to take the next four weekends to establish yourself in the business of marketing your photographs.

Now here's a paradox: As soon as you make your announcement, your loved ones will find every imaginable reason to distract you for the next four weekends. ("Johnny has a choir concert." "We're scheduled to play cards at the Howards.' " "Barbra Streisand is at Orchestra Hall.") After all, they like you so much, they don't want to see you invest yourself in something that they believe might not work out, and secondly they don't want to see you engrossed in something they are not part of. At this point, you are most vulnerable to being talked out of your Four-Weekend Action Plan. Visualize your goals and hold firm. If you can, turn your loved ones' reservations into an advantage by recruiting their help in some of the routine tasks needed to set up your office and recordkeeping systems. Remember, though, that *you* are running the show.

Your blueprint is in Table 4-2.

Don't fall into the trap of overpreparing: "One for the money, two for the show, three to get ready, four to get ready, five to get ready, etc. . . ." You are about to begin a long and adventurous journey. You must begin by taking that first step.

The photo-marketing enterprise you are about to embark on is going to take endurance. You are going to experience setbacks. You will no doubt encounter some trying times of reassessment. If your desire is strong, none of this will faze you. Welcome to a magnificent obsession with this profession!

WEEKEND ONE: Set Up Shop.

Take action. Announce your plan to family, relatives, colleagues, and friends. Enlist their help, but fly solo if they attempt to dissuade you from your plan.

Clear out a room, or partition off part of one, and set up a desk, chair, lamp, typewriter or word processor, and filing cabinet. (Consult the Yellow Pages for used-furniture bargains.)
Tack a sign above your desk, "_____Stock Photography."

Order your supplies:
> Magnifying glass (loupe)
> Personalized stationery
> Mailing envelopes
> Plastic sleeves
> Labels
> Slide view files
> Rubber stamps
> Business checks
> Simplified bookkeeping system
> Recordkeeping system
> Subscriptions to business periodicals

WEEKEND TWO: Zero in on Your PMS/A.

Determine your areas of strong marketing potential and the areas of poor marketing potential. Photo marketing is a *business*. Success comes when you eliminate the barriers and pitfalls that prevent you from succeeding (failure avoidance). Discover your personal photo-marketing strengths (who you are photographically).

Whether you have 500 or 5,000:
Catalog your slides (transparencies).
Catalog your black-and-whites.

Reread "First, Find Yourself" at the beginning of Chapter 3. Fine-tune your PMS/A (Figure 3-2).

Reread Chapter 2, "What Pictures Sell and Resell?"

Table 4-2. The Four-Weekend Action Plan to launch your photo-marketing enterprise is on the following two pages.

WEEKEND THREE: Capture Your Corner of the Market.

Why compete with an army of photographers in the general arena when you possess channels of knowledge and access to select areas that specific photobuyers are already looking for? Spend the weekend in your local library and compile *your own* Market List, a list of markets tailored to *your* photographic strengths. Request photo guidelines from each of your markets.

Reread all of Chapter 3, "Finding Your Corner of the Market." Fine-tune your Market List (Figure 3-3).

WEEKEND FOUR: Roll the Presses!

All of your supplies are in. Set up a simple recordkeeping system (nothing elaborate) to note what you send out, to whom, and what sells. Validate your Market List. Confirm spellings. Make address corrections. Verify current contacts' names. Mail out your first shipments.

Read Chapter 14, "Working Smart."

Read Chapter 16, "Your Stock Photo Business: A Mini Tax Shelter."

From here on out, make it a *habit* to work in your new home office on a routine daily basis, for one hour or ten hours, whatever fits your work style, lifestyle, and income projections.

Read your business and marketing periodicals, and expand your knowledge a little each day. Learn what others are doing; attend specialized workshops and seminars. Listen to business and marketing cassette tapes in your downtime (driving to and from work, in the darkroom, etc.). Incorporate elements of such information as they apply to you.

You are now on your way. Depending on the size of your stock file, you'll have many published pictures (and deposited checks) to your credit, by the time you're ready to celebrate your first anniversary.

5.
Producing
a
Marketable
Product

Some Basic Questions Answered

Color or black-and-white: Which should I shoot? Whether you shoot in black-and-white, color, or both, will be determined by your PMS/A (personal photographic marketing strength/areas) and your Market List. Many markets in the publishing industry lean heavily toward black-and-white. However, some periodicals deal exclusively in color. Make this test: Select a magazine from your Market List to which you plan to send your photo illustrations. Tear out any ads and put them aside. What's left are the editorial photo illustrations. What percent of them are black-and-white? Color? Checking each of your markets or prospective markets in this manner will give you a realistic appraisal of the black-and-white-versus-color needs of publishers you deal with.

Many photographers prefer to shoot exclusively in color. (Service photography market areas—ad agencies, graphic design studios, corporations, commercial assignments, and stock photo agencies—often require a heavy concentration on color.) In the near future, perhaps technology will provide a less costly way for publishers of books and magazines to employ color. Right now, in fact, trends in the magazine and book industry indicate a move toward more color. This may be because each new year brings the birth of new specialized magazines and book publishers, which increases the total amount of color (and black-and-white) used each year. The textbook industry, however, shows a marked increase in the use of color over black-and-white in the last two decades.

Is it cheaper to shoot in black-and-white or color transparencies? At first glance, black-and-white would appear to be less expensive. But if you take into consideration your developing/printing time and costs, plus the cost of maintaining a black-and-white darkroom (see Appendix D), color is actually less expensive.

Again, remember, photo editors buy pictures because they *need* them, not because they like them. If you enjoy shooting color, shoot color; but if your markets require black-and-white, shoot black-and-white, too.

What Film Should I Use?

Black-and-White

For indoor shots, the faster films are best, of course. Tri-X has proved popular with many photographers. I personally shoot it at EI 800; other photographers shoot it as high as EI 3200. Equivalents are Kodak's T-Max and Ilford HP5 (400 ASA).

If you're shooting outdoors, you might want to investigate a slower film, Kodak's Plus-X pan film, or its equivalent in other brands, such as the Ilford FP4 (125 ASA). When outdoors, I often shoot Plus-X at EI 320. I also shoot Tri-X in *outdoor* situations, and I find the results very satisfying. Generally speaking, no outdoor situation is too difficult for the faster Kodak Tri-X or T-Max film, even when you're shooting it at EI 800 with a shutter speed of 1,000.

Unless you enjoy and can afford working with several cameras, it's handy to explore the versatility of a single film. It's convenient to work with one film—no problems arise when you need to dash from inside a schoolroom to an outside playground in midroll, for example. You can develop a fine-tuned familiarity with the qualities of "your" film and what you can produce with it.

Color

First, plan on marketing color transparencies, not prints (see page 85). Both fast and slow color film will be valuable to you. For outdoor work, I use Kodachrome 25 film (daylight) ISO 25 and Kodak Ektachrome 100 film (daylight) ISO 100. Other equivalents are Fujichrome 100 (ASA 100) and the popular Kodachrome 200 film. The lower the ASA (or ISO), the better photobuyers like the results; the lower ISO speeds produce a tighter-grained transparency, which means the editor can blow it up larger and still get good definition. (Frequently, a photobuyer will use only a portion of a picture and enlarge it for the format.) Kodachrome 25 film, for example, is reported to have a resolution of 100 lines per millimeter, and Kodachrome 64, a resolution of 100 lines per millimeter. The Fuji films, by the way, have earned a solid position among assignment and stock photographers.

Color films for indoor use include Kodachrome 40 film 5070 (Type A) and Ektachrome 160 film (tungsten). These films are appropriate to use when you're inside under artificial light. If you're inside but able to shoot with available light from windows and doors, outdoor color film such as Ektachrome 200 and 400 films (daylight) work just as well as indoor film. Again, when you can manage it, it's handy to be able to use just one film both for outside and inside.

We've talked about the preferred size for black-and-white prints (8x10)—for color, it's not so cut and dried. Both 35mm and 2¼ are welcomed by photobuyers. In some cases, especially if you are a service photographer, 4x5 and even 8x10 will be useful and often required. For volume sales, such as inside editorial use, you'll find 35mm to be a consistent seller.

For covers, chapter heads, or advertisements, your best bet is the 2¼ format. Using 2¼, you will obtain the most consistent marketing of color photo illustrations, mainly because when editors confront two transparencies of equally fine caliber, one a 35mm and the other a 120, they usually choose the *larger* picture.

Why? Big is beautiful to the art director, and also to the business manager who is often called in when decisions about big expenses are involved. If a photobuyer is going to spend $750 for the use of a color transparency plus the cost for color separations, it seems logical to get the most for the money.

Later in this chapter, we will discuss the marketing advantages of duplicating and enlarging your best 35mm pictures to the larger 4x5 format.

Black-and-White: What Makes a Marketable Print?

We are gazing at a black-and-white photograph at a salon. Texture and detail in the shadows of the photograph come through superbly. The dark areas are black and rich; highlights sparkle with crisp whites. Between these poles flows a broad range of values that give the print an almost three-dimensional quality. We are looking at the classic *good print*.

In photo illustration, not every print needs to have this full range of tonal gradation in order to be marketable. Your pictures have to be technically good to sell, but they don't have to be technically perfect. Buyers of photo illustrations are primarily concerned with content, *communication*. A photo illustration taken in the fog, for instance, can have no highlights, yet still be effective. Or a picture of students in animated discussion around a seminar table, which exhibits only middle tones, will nevertheless make a successful photo illustration.

To add to the ambiguity, the same print can be treated different ways and achieve equal success as a photo illustration in each version. I once showed three variations of one print to a group of seven photo editors. One version was contrasty, one dark and moody, one a classic good print. The editors could not agree on which was the "best" print. The "rightness" of each printing approach depended on how the print would be used.

Print quality, then, is relative. David Vestal, photographer, lecturer, and critic, adds this:

> Most good prints are craftsmanlike. They tend to give maximum information and show all the tones that the photographer chooses to show, clearly, richly, and in an appropriate degree of contrast (dictated by feeling).
>
> Most good enlargements are in focus all over the paper, and are visually balanced, without unwanted inconsistencies. In poor prints, some areas usually "stick out" inappropriately, or fail to be clear, or both; usually because the photographer has not paid enough attention to his picture, or hasn't done the necessary work.
>
> In any mode, a good print is one where the photographer has seen accurately what the picture needs and has successfully used his craft to provide it. The technique can be simple, as with Edward Weston, or complicated, as with Jerry Uelsmann or Gene Smith. Either way, a good print normally reflects thorough craftsmanship, from shooting through fixing and washing.

How Extensive Should Tonal Gradation Be?

No experts will commit themselves to a firm definition of a good print. But even taking into consideration the leeway involved, good prints do consistently exhibit the photographer's concern for tonal gradation. You will create a good print if you are able to extract the appropriate range of gradation values inherent in your negative and select and match these with the mood and atmosphere you wish to convey in your photo illustration.

In order to consciously eliminate some tones from a print to create the desired feeling in your picture, you must be aware of the range of gradation available to you in that print. To say some prints come off well with portions of their full gradation missing does not invite you to settle for substandard or hurried printing results. Photobuyers will recognize poor quality immediately. Only by taking time to become familiar with the precise potential offered in the tonal range of any particular print is it possible to develop creative control over tonal results. Educate yourself on different degrees of tonal completeness for technical excellence, yet remember that in photo illustration you can depart from textbook definitions of good print quality if the content of the picture says what you want it to say.

Black-and-White: What Size Should I Print and What Paper Should I Use?

The standard black-and-white print size in the publishing industry is 8x10. This size fits conventional file drawers and is easy to handle. Here are some paper pointers, whether you do your own printing or farm it out and want to know what instructions to give the lab. Photobuyers nowadays rarely ask for glossy prints, primarily because semigloss gives them a closer idea of how the photograph will look when reproduced in their publication. Editors formerly asked for prints with high shine ("Gimme a glossy!") because in the old days printers required a glossy surface for best reproduction. This is not the case today.

Semigloss paper, such as Kodak's J-surface paper, is a good choice because it has a solid, professional look, and it takes spotting easily (see Appendix C). You can also get a semigloss finish by using glossy paper (e.g., Kodak's F-surface paper) and air-drying the prints in blotters rather than ferrotype-drying them. Because of their convenient air-drying feature, resin-coated (RC) papers are especially suitable for the stock photographer who has neither the space nor the time for mass-producing pictures. Another timesaver in developing is the stabilization process, which bypasses the conventional wet darkroom procedures. Since photobuyers are rarely interested in archival quality in your pictures, a stabilizer can be a convenient tool.

Should I Rely on Color-to-Black-and-White Conversion?

If you're strictly a color photographer, you'll find you have to deal with the fact that, despite the profusion of color used in the publishing industry, black-and-white is still popular.

"How about conversion?" you may ask. Many publishers refuse to incur the cost of converting color to black-and-white (usually about $10 to $15 a picture). "If we do decide to convert to black-and-white," says one photobuyer, "we'll charge off the conversion costs to the photographer." Other photobuyers don't like to convert to black-and-white because it isn't reliable. "You never know what you're going to get. Black-and-white conversions are usually lacking in technical quality." The time factor is also important. Editors, working against a deadline, don't like to be at the mercy of a lab. The editor will choose the next best picture, in black-and-white.

One answer is to shoot both color and black-and-white on the scene, with two cameras. Another is to use Eastman 5247 film, a negative 35mm movie camera film from which both slides and black-and-white prints can be made; however, it has limitations, which I'll discuss later. Another answer is to convert color to black-and-white yourself. The results aren't guaranteed, but if your original picture exhibits reasonable definition, the results are often acceptable.

Here are three processes:

1. Make an 8x10 negative (b&w) of your slide and then make 8x10 (b&w) contact prints.
2. Make a large-format internegative, then enlarge it to come up with the final print. This process can be markedly speeded up by the use of

Polaroid positive/negative film. The Polaroid film holder (Model 405 or 545) is placed on the enlarger baseboard, and the slide is projected directly onto the film. Exposure tests, of course, are necessary. The 405 holder uses type 665 pack film and gives a 3¼x4¼-inch negative; the 545 holder uses type 55 film and gives a 4x5-inch negative.

   3. A third, even easier, method involves the use of Kodak Direct Positive Paper. The paper is exposed to the slide in an enlarger like regular printing paper. Special processing produces a positive image in just one step—that is, no internegative. Print quality depends on both the quality of your original color transparency and your processing talents.

How Do I Make Sure My Color Will Sell?

What if your PMS/A points toward color and some of the buyers on your Market List require color? Can you make sure it's *your color* that hits often enough to make it economically viable for you? The answer is yes, you can put yourself strides ahead of the competition, *if* you put together a well-planned marketing strategy for your color pictures (transparencies).

   More than black-and-white, color requires extra technology, equipment, and know-how to produce the right marketable picture. Three-fourths of all the technical questions I receive as director of PhotoSource International pertain to *color* and how to avoid excessive expense in producing and marketing color photography. One of the first ways you can save is to ask yourself on your next photographic outing, before every shot: "Is this marketable?" With each frame you expose, ask yourself, "Will this one be on a photobuyer's desk next week for consideration, and will it have a good chance because I've researched my photobuyers and their specific needs?" If you find yourself shoulder to shoulder with dozens of other photographers on the bridge at Ellis Island, waiting for the right light at sundown on the Statue of Liberty, you can be reasonably sure you will get an excellent picture. You can also be reasonably sure the marketing potential of it will be zero. A dozen photographers waited on that bridge yesterday, and a dozen more will be there tomorrow.
   Get in the habit of asking yourself, "Is it *marketable?*"

The Most Commonly Asked Questions about Color

In figuring your color marketing strategy you'll need the answers to the following questions:

   What color film is most popular among photobuyers? When talking about film, technical quality looms as a more important consideration with color than with black-and-white. Photobuyers draw up their technical requirements for color on the basis of recommendations set by their printers; printers are at the mercy of their particular printing equipment.

If the equipment is sophisticated, they can sometimes excuse minor imperfections in a picture. If the equipment is mediocre, printers (and thus photobuyers) depend heavily on a technically fine picture from you.

Basically, an outdoor picture should be taken on a low-ISO-rated film such as Agfachrome CT-18 or Kodachrome 25 film. An indoor shot is acceptable when shot on the higher-rated ISO films such as Fujichrome 100, Ektachrome 200 (daylight), Ektachrome 400 (daylight), and Ektachrome 160 (tungsten) film. There are exceptions to all rules, of course. Having said that, I'll say the photobuyers seem to prefer K-25 (Kodachrome) and Fujichrome for outdoor and Ektachrome 100 film for indoor shots. These three films are very reliable and predictable.

And why the low ISO Fuji and Kodachromes? As I mentioned earlier, an editor may wish to use only a part of your picture or use all of it for a cover or a poster that would require magnification. If a higher ISO film is used, grain clumping might preclude using the picture. To get around the grain-clumping problem, a 5x7 internegative could be made, but often photobuyers don't want to go to the extra time and expense. Preparing color photography for publication already requires longer production time than black-and-white.

Should I indicate which film I used? Some stock photographers indicate on their slide mounts the film and film speed that were used. Although this might be helpful in your learning process, it could be detrimental to sales if your color, for example, is in the higher *ASAs*. Erase the information, or place your name and address label over it if it's in ink.

Should I shoot vertical or horizontal format? Editors continually lament that they do not have enough vertical shots to augment their layouts. "Printed matter is usually a vertical format," one editor told me. "Yet photographers persist in sending me horizontal pictures. I could use many more verticals than what I get."

One photographer friend told me that when she was starting out she pasted a label on her camera that read, "Is it a vertical?"

Do editors accept color prints? I've touched on this elsewhere, but let's examine this question in more detail.

Very few photobuyers, possibly 10 percent or less, accept color prints. Usually it's the *low*-paying markets that will accept color prints. When they do, they expect a *quality* 8x10 rather than the smaller "drugstore" prints. Incidentally, do not send your color negatives. Keep them home, safe, and on file.

The industry as a whole would certainly fare better if color prints, rather than color transparencies, could be accepted across the board. However, the industry has invested millions in color-positive (transparency) processing and printing machinery, and they are not ready to make the switch. Until they are, photographers are faced with the reality that the industry is geared for transparencies, not color prints.

I can liken the situation to taking $50 in foreign currency to a department store and trying to make a purchase. Yes, the manager will believe the money is worth something, but it's too much hassle to convert the currency to his needs.

So for now, although color negatives are more logical and convenient, and have a greater exposure latitude than transparencies, you're stuck with shooting transparencies. You must put up with the hazard of constant handling of your originals (your slides) by yourself and by photobuyers.

How can I get around the color print barrier? If you have a lifelong history of working only with color negatives, however, and are not willing to work with transparencies, read on. Some stock photographers have attempted to circumvent the color neg-versus-transparency situation via these four methods:

1. Make your shots in color negative and enlarge to 8x10 color prints. Send the prints, or color photocopies of the prints, to several potential buyers on your Market List. Put a label or rubber stamp on the back explaining that a color *transparency* is available on request. If a photobuyer does request the transparency, send a rush order to your custom processing lab and have the lab make a 4x5 reproduction-quality transparency which you—or the lab, depending on the deadline—can forward to the photobuyer.

Incidentally, this type of duplicate (dupe) is actually an improved version of your original. The 4x5 transparency will prove to be of great advantage to you. The large 4x5 size is impressive and sells more readily than the smaller 120 or 35mm. Even if your picture doesn't make the photobuyer's final cut, your 4x5 transparency has especially good potential for scoring with other photobuyers. You know it's a marketable picture because one photobuyer has already considered using it.

Make full use of this marketing maxim: If one photobuyer wants a picture, other photobuyers will want it *too*. Have duplicate or triplicate copies of your transparency made while it's at the lab. In multiples, the single cost is much less. Aggressively market your copies.

2. Make your photographs in color negative, select the most marketable, and have reproduction-quality transparencies made from the selected negs. This approach could be costly unless you are confident in your ability to choose marketable pictures.

Kodacolor VR 200 film, Fujicolor Super HR, and Kodak VR film provide high resolution and fine grain. Also, Fujicolor Super HR 400 and Kodacolor Vericolor III Professional 400 film provide excellent-quality images for indoor situations. Eastman Kodak will convert negs into display transparencies slides for about a dollar each, but the reproduction quality cannot be recommended in most cases. A custom lab will charge between $10 and $25 per transparency.

3. Eastman 5247 film is designed for use in the movie industry. It is a negative film that lends itself to 35mm camera use. Some photo illustrators may find it their film of choice. (See page 90 for more details on it.)

4. One other means: Do it yourself. Kodak provides two printing processes for making transparency enlargements from color negatives. They're called Vericolor print film for enlargements, and Vericolor slide film. However, making your own transparencies requires darkroom precision, patience, and time. The end product must be acceptable for reproduction.

I don't want the above four suggestions to give you the impression that the color-neg system is the answer. In most cases it is not, for this reason: Photobuyers want a picture *now*. Any extra steps, such as waiting for a transparency to be made, will often make the difference between a sale and no sale.

An excellent book that will guide you in producing excellent black-and-whites and color transparencies for reproduction is Norman Sanders's *Photographing for Publication* (R.R. Bowker Company). His book answers *all* questions you'll have, ranging from the type of photo paper to use to whether or not you should submit dupes.

Should you make duplicates of your slides? Newcomers to the field of photo marketing have a well-founded hesitation to send their original transparencies to some unknown entity. A seemingly popular answer is to make duplicates (dupes) of your originals. Before I launch into the pros and cons, here is the most convenient way to make dupes: *Make them during the original shooting of your subject matter.*

Since you know what pictures will sell to your Market List, you aren't gambling away film dollars by making several extra exposures of an especially marketable scene or situation.

Of course, depending on the scene or situation, your "originals" won't be exactly the same. Some you might even want to discard. Those that remain will share equally strong marketing potential. With several "originals," you'll have no worries about losing, misplacing, or damaging the original.

But what if you have only *one* original? I wish that I could say an inexpensive, quick, and high-quality method of duplication is available to you. There is none—not for reproduction purposes.

Let me explain: The photobuyer is midway between you and the printer (the pressman, platemaker, etcher, etc.), who demands the best-quality image in order to satisfy the publishers', advertisers', and subscribers' tastes, not to mention his own. The printer has a bag of tricks that can perform some limited miracles, but in the end, there is no substitute for a good original image.

This then rules out everything you've heard about making your own dupes or having them made professionally by a filmstrip company at fifty cents apiece. These products are duplicates, yes, but usually not dupes a quality printer can accept for reproduction.

But all is not lost. Reproduction dupes can be made, and the cost is usually comparable to a dinner at a first-class restaurant.

Here's how the pros make their dupes. Select an original that has enjoyed wide sales or has such sales potential. Contact a reputable color lab and have your original made into a 4x5-inch transparency. In many cases, your original can actually be improved by adjusting the color balance in the dupe. Slides that are too dark, but with adequate shadow and highlight detail, may be lightened either for a more pleasing effect or to bring their density into line with other slides in your presentation.

Overexposed slides may be darkened. Composition can be corrected or emphasis can be given to just a portion of the slide by cropping and copying a certain area. Color rendition can be changed by means of filters either for corrective or creative deviation from the normal. A sandwich can also be made at this time. This is the process used when you want to place two slides together, such as a seagull and a setting sun, and print them as one. If you want to have a sandwich made, tape your two originals together in the composition you choose. The lab will shoot them as a single slide.

The price quoted above is for a reproduction-quality dupe. At about half this fee, you can get a lesser-quality display-grade dupe.

Incidentally, many stock photo agencies (see Chapter 12) will make 4x5-inch reproduction-quality dupes of your 35mm. The reason? The improvement in color balance, plus the added size, improve sales. These agencies often have sales reps here and abroad who carry these dupes with them in their display cases. They sell the dupes directly from the case as originals, which they now are.

One quality color lab is *Creative Color,* 4911 W. Grace Street, Tampa, FL 33607, owned by Burton McNeely. In addition to producing reproduction-quality 4x5 transparencies from your 120 or 35mm originals, his firm also offers a full-line lab service. A lab that has often been recommended to our subscribers by photographer/writer Carl Purcell is Compcorps, Attn.: David Doody, Duplicate Services Division, 711 4th Street, NW, Washington, DC 20001. Ask for their 70mm film duping service. Others are:

Dale Color	Meisel Photochrome Corporation	Pro Color, Film Division
Box 3000	Box 666666, Suite 708	909 Hennepin Ave. S.
Bloomington, IL 61702	Dallas, TX 75266	Minneapolis, MN 55403
K & K Color Lab	Northwest Color Lab	
8302 S.E. Thirteenth Ave.	10245 Ninety-Fifth St.	
Portland, OR 97202	Edmonton, Alberta, Canada T5H 2B3	

A few stock photo agencies and a few publishers will invite you to send 35mm dupes to be held on file as display. When they require the original, they contact you for it. Such display dupes are inexpensive, usually under a dollar. The following filmstrip companies produce quality display dupes:

Atkinson/Stedco
7610 Melrose Ave.
Los Angeles, CA 90046

Color Film Corporation
West Coast Lab: 3212 Nebraska Ave.
Santa Monica, CA 90404

Color Film Corporation of America
East Coast Lab: 777 Washington Blvd.
Stamford, CT 06901

World in Color
Box 392
660 Cedar St.
Elmira, NY 14902-0392

A final option, of course, is to make dupes on your own—not only duplicates but restorations of existing slides, color changes, sandwiches, and experimental pictures. Type 5071 Ektachrome slide-duplicating film is the usual choice, along with a duplicator such as the Bowens Illumitran Model 3-C, which includes a special contrast control unit. The final results usually fall into Track A—pictures that are interesting but difficult to market.

Unusual duplication techniques will come and go, but the duplication technique of choice will probably remain: Make on-the-spot duplicates by shooting extra pictures as backups.

Can you submit display prints of your transparencies? Yes. The Cibachrome method of making prints directly from slides has become a popular way to show photobuyers your photography without having to send your original slides. The usual procedure is to enlarge six vertical or six horizontal 35mm slides to $2\frac{3}{4}$x$3\frac{1}{4}$-inch on an 8x10-inch sheet of Type A Cibachrome print material. Include your name and other details on the back of each sheet.

Robert A. Walsh at the Stock Photo Darkroom (158 Wyoming Avenue, Audubon, NJ 08106) and Ray Young, PhotoGenesis, 4418 Cabrillo Street, Suite 201, San Francisco, CA 94121, provide Cibachrome service.

A second way to reproduce your color transparencies for display purposes is the *positive-stat* method. No internegatives are required since the system is a direct reversal, positive process. Stats are made in standard sizes of 5x7, 8x10 and 11x14 inches. For stat services, consult the Yellow Pages under "Graphic Art Services" or "Graphic Designers."

A third method, mentioned earlier, is to make color photocopies of your slides. Twenty 35mm or twelve 120-size can fit on a standard $8\frac{1}{2}$x11-inch sheet. The image quality is passable. Instant-print shops, banks, and libraries often feature this service. Consult the Yellow Pages for Xerox Centers in your area.

A final method, and probably the costliest, is to gang-print a group of ninety-one slides (or black-and-whites) onto a 4x6-inch microfiche card. If the editor has access to a microfiche projector he can order slides from your card. Sid Bugelholl, 13854 Kinbrook Street, Sylmar, CA 91342, produces microfiches for photographers.

The advantages of submitting color display prints or dupes of your slides to a photobuyer are as follows:

1. You can circulate more copies of your slides to more photobuyers simultaneously.

2. Your originals remain safe in your file until a photobuyer makes an order.

3. You can try untested markets without fear of losing valuable originals.

4. You save on the extra postal costs of shipping original transparencies.

5. You can, in effect, establish a catalog of your pictures with certain buyers on your Market List.

6. The enlargements of your slides (the Cibachromes or stats) give the photobuyer a good idea of what your picture looks like when it's reproduced.

7. Your reliability factor (see Chapter 7) goes up a few notches because you look more professional.

Of course, all these fine advantages go flying out the window when the photobuyer says, "I can't hold up production. I thought we had the *original* here. We'll have to use this other picture instead, because we have it right here."

Is 5247 Film Useful for the Stock Photographer?

Eastman's 5247 is Kodak's standard movie film. It's an improved version of the earlier 5254 film, which didn't have the fine grain or wider latitude of the new film. Photographers have discovered that the 5247 film (it's a negative rather than a positive) can offer slides, color prints, and black-and-white prints—all from the same negatives.

Here are some advantages for the stock photographer:

1. The film can be shot indoors or outdoors at ASA 100. The corrections are made in the processing lab.

2. The film can be pushed to ASA 400 easily.

3. The color quality is comparable to Ektachrome. (As a movie film, it must be projected to movie-screen size.)

4. Several "originals" can be made and circulated simultaneously to photobuyers. The photographer never loses an original slide, unless the original negative is damaged.

5. You can use it to shoot black-and-white and color in the same shooting situation with only one camera. (No need to convert a color shot to black-and-white.) This film could prove to be very useful to the stock photographer who shoots mostly indoors and where a 100 to 400 ASA range is practical.

6. You can make color contact prints of your available slides for the photobuyer's file.

7. Processing labs for this film are plentiful, and the processing system is safe, since it's basically designed to service the 35mm film industry, which can't afford processing mishaps in valuable film sequences.

8. It's cheap. If you shoot regular color print film and do not cut the strip, the processor can print the entire roll to slide for about six dollars.

The disadvantages of 5247 film are few, but major:

1. Because it does not have the tightness of grain of the lower-rated ASA films, such as K-25, photobuyers will not accept its use in situations where K-25 could have been employed.

2. It is not standard. Photobuyers tend to be suspicious of any films that are not standard. So do photographers.

3. It is confining. For an outdoor stock photographer, the ASA is too high (100). For an indoor stock photographer, in classrooms, offices, or similar available light situations, the ASA is too low.

Following are labs that can process Eastman 5247 film:

Dale Laboratories
2960 Simms St.
Box 900
Hollywood, FL 33020

RGB Lab
816 N. Highland Ave. Dept. 18
P.O. Box 38903
Hollywood, CA 90038

Red Tag Photo
2214 Pico Blvd.
Santa Monica, CA 90405

American Passage
500 3rd Ave. West
Seattle, WA 98109

A recommended black-and-white printing lab for stock photography is: Photo Marketing Labs, Rt. 5, Box 42A, Menomonie, WI 54751.

Cut Your Photo Costs

If cash-flow problems cause your stock photography operation to bog down, it may be that you are over-spending in the wrong areas. An excellent book on this subject is *Cut Your Photo Costs*, by Robert McQuilkin (MCI Publishing, Box 162C-C, Winfield IL 60190).

6.
Taking and Making Photo Illustrations

Do You Take or Make Them?

Throughout this book, when I refer to *photo illustrations*, I am referring to the Track "B" stock photo—the *marketable* picture.

No book has been written on the subject of Track B stock photos, yet over the past half century a history of the photo illustration has been recorded in our magazines and books. The photo illustration as we know it today has evolved from a documentary snapshot to a subtle and sophisticated art form. This development can be traced in magazines that have existed for the past one hundred years, such as *National Geographic*. Following the progression in bound volumes at the library can be entertaining as well as informative.

As we learn in zoology class, ontogeny recapitulates phylogeny (that is, the stages in the development of the individual mirror those of the species). A photographer entering the field undergoes the same sort of progression. He begins by taking simplistic photographs, similar to the early photo illustrations, and gradually grasps new ideas and technical knowledge that enable him to produce better and more interesting pictures, until, if he survives, he eventually turns out fine photo illustrations. This evolution is a valuable learning experience for the photographer, but it *can* be accelerated. Here's how.

Many photographers are conditioned to *take* photographs—to reflect the world somewhat as a mirror does. A documentary photographer *takes* a picture. He records things the way they were.

But to limit photography to mirrorlike documentation is to circumscribe knowledge and understanding.

Photo illustration, on the other hand, opens up a vast new field of interpretive endeavor. The fact that photo illustrations are in large measure workaday pictures doesn't preclude innovative and creative treatment of them. Photo illustration allows a photographer to *make* photographs. The photo illustrator creates a situation as it could be, or as it should be. As we all know, painters rarely paint their landscapes true to nature. To limit their illustrations to exact duplications of nature would be to confine their creativity and their viewers' enjoyment. They rearrange the elements in their paintings to achieve a composition of wholeness and meaning that earlier did not exist. Jazz musicians improvise on the melody and rhythm of a familiar tune not because they wish to seem clever or self-consciously different, but because they wish to discover, for themselves and their listeners, new meaning in the music. Photographs, like other expressive media, can offer fresh insights and deep understanding. A photograph can become a telescope/microscope for the viewer to see into and beyond what is being photographed.

All of this, of course, does not apply to photojournalism or documentary photography. It would be dishonest to alter or shape a news photograph so as to misrepresent a scene or subject.

The line between photo illustration and photojournalism, however, can sometimes be thin. W. Eugene Smith, one of the all-time greats, was once criticized for moving the bed away from the wall for better camera angle in some of his photographs of a midwife for a *Life* magazine story.

Photo illustrators often confront ethical questions when it comes to such improvisation. For example, if you photograph a teenager whose blemishes are here today but gone tomorrow, do you leave them in the picture or retouch them out? Which is the truer interpretation? Are the blemishes inappropriate if you are illustrating the winners in a student government activity or a science fair? Should they remain if you are illustrating nutritional deficiencies, or youth gangs? Or should the blemishes remain no matter what the context?

The answers are ultimately left to you, the photo illustrator. It might appear to photography purists that allowing free rein to interpretive photography could lead to a lack of respect for the truth. However, before the arrival of the photograph and the photographer, pictorial illustrations came in the form of etchings, cartoons, drawings, and paintings. We accepted the artist's interpretations and managed to survive.

In photo illustration work, then, you are frequently and legitimately *making* a picture, not *taking* it. For example, you see something happen, you feel it was significant, and you would like to photograph it. You have two alternatives:

1. You can hope it happens again in your lifetime, or
2. While you are still on the scene, you can attempt to re-create it, "improving" on it (stripping it of distracting elements) as you do so with your $P = B + P + S + I$ principle.

In photo illustration, you can also create scenes that never did happen, but *could* happen. On an assignment to photograph a child's visit to a toy factory, for example, I realized my little model wasn't at all intrigued by the assembly-line production. The bits and pieces didn't look like toys yet; the pounding and banging of the machinery were hurting his ears; the paint smell was disagreeable. Yet I needed to illustrate a small boy's excitement at seeing toys being manufactured. In desperation, I wadded a piece of bubble gum (when working with kids, always have a supply of goodies handy) and stuck it on one of the toy trucks as it moved toward the next assembly stage. I stood on a ladder above the moving belt and asked my model to point out the bubble gum as it came into view. He did so with enthusiasm, and I snapped a picture of a delighted youngster pointing at a toy truck on an assembly line. In illustrations, it is true, you may bring elements together that never happened. You are, in effect, contriving. But you can keep your illustrations authentic by selecting situations that *could* happen, and then reenacting them in a way that appears unposed.

Danger Ahead: Trite Pictures

There's a trap waiting for the photographer who is new to photo illustration. Although I continually remind you in this book that workaday pictures are the most marketable, workaday subject matter can easily fall into the trite category—if you let it. Corny pictures are easy to produce. Beware of the temptation to take pictures that are trite, old hat, cute, clichéd.

"There's nothing new . . . !" you're probably saying.

Stop. Think about the pictures in your portfolio, print notebook, or recent slide show. If you were to eliminate (1) the dramatic silhouettes, (2) the sunset scenes, (3) the postcard scenes of mountains and clouds, (4) the portraits of the old men, (5) the father lovingly holding his daughter, (6) experimental abstract shots—how many pictures would you have left?

I don't want to imply that the above subjects are always trite. We have all seen these subjects treated with compassion, depth, and a sense of beauty. Many of them can qualify as standard excellent pictures. However, the more photographs we see of these familiar subjects, the less charity we have available for them in our appreciation bank.

The tendency to take trite pictures is almost a disease among photographers—even veterans. Because we see trite pictures every day in local, regional, and national publications, we become conditioned to the status quo. Photographers find an easy way to take a school portrait, or a commercial or architectural shot, or a standard stock photograph and gradually lock themselves into an effortless routine that stifles creativity.

Photography, especially photo illustration, has become a vibrant communication vehicle in our daily lives. The public expects not only to be entertained but to be informed by photos. It doesn't take well to stock photographs that, like old news or old jokes, are mere repeats. It wants new insights, angles, and interpretations of everyday subjects.

An Example

Let's say a publisher has assigned you to produce a photo essay on "The Circus." Take a scratch pad and jot down ten picture situations that come to mind. Don't read further until you've jotted down at least ten. . . .

That was easy, wasn't it?

Well, if it was, I'll bet you've listed ten trite picture ideas. Producing un-*trite* pictures takes a lot of thought.

Before you rush out and snap away five rolls of 35mm film on a subject that every man, woman, and child is familiar with, take at least a half hour to sketch out some picture possibilities. This brief exercise will save you hours of location and darkroom time spent on pictures that would probably be rejected by a publisher. It will also eliminate those blinders we often inadvertently wear when we arrive at a picture-taking locale and become immersed in the scope and immediacy of the situation. Objectivity is easier to retain if you have a preplanned sketch of what you want to photograph before you get there. By the same token, don't go overboard and lock yourself into a plan that has no room for spontaneity and innovation sparked by on-the-scene elements. Try to always be ready for new picture possibilities.

Let's take our circus example. These shots are not new to us: the clown in his dressing room; the elephant's trunk appearing through the window of the circus moving van; the tightrope walker silhouetted by spotlight against the tent's ceiling; the roustabouts taking a well-earned coffee break; the trainer at work with his chimpanzees; the cleanup crew the day after. We've all seen these pictures over and over again. Maybe the documentary photographer can be satisfied with such pictures, but not the photo illustrator or the photobuyer who strives to provide fresh insights, even on such familiar subjects as the circus.

What *do* we want to see in your essay on the circus? The answer will take thought, timing, and preparation on your part. Imagination, luck, and persistence will be important, too. You've got to zig when other photographers are zagging. You've got to anticipate. But most important, you've got to show us the circus as we never imagined it could be. (Caution: Please don't interpret this as a license to go out and shoot obscure, experimental, weird-angle pictures in an effort to be different. That would be equally trite.)

What nontrite pictures, then, will you shoot at the circus? For starters, let's see an extreme close-up of one of those curvaceous acrobats doing pushups in her dressing room. How about a mother with infant in arms happily holding a cotton candy cone up to a clown? Or an overweight father lifting his three-year-old up to touch the bar of the trapeze? How about a backstage shot of a roustabout pumping air into the tire of the goofymobile while the chimpanzee driver waits nearby? As a photo illustrator, you must remember that readers of publications are people and that people love to watch and learn about other people. You will record how people at the circus relate and react to the performers (with admiration?), to the animals (with fear or pity?), to the atmosphere generated by the circus (with awe?), to each other (with friendship?). When possible, you will include symbols of the circus in your pictures—a trapeze, a cage, a tent—but these will serve only as incidental elements to establish the circus atmosphere.

In most cases, you will want to apply the principle of *making* a picture rather than *taking* one. You can reenact or improve picture possibilities by asking the cooperation of spectators or performers. To a clown: "Would you mind taking a bite of that cotton candy again?" To a teenager: "Could I ask you to do that again—over here by the zebras?"

Photography is visual, and you can escape the plague of triteness by constantly *visualizing* picture-taking possibilities. Most successful photographers use this secret, so why not try it out yourself? In free moments, even days before you actually perform your assignment (circus, annual report, political convention, etc.), visualize the thousands of picture-taking possibilities that will probably come up. Eliminate the trite, the corny, and the cute. Concentrate on innovative possibilities that are practical and realistic. (This process will save you on-the-scene time, too.) If you visualize, you'll arrive at your assignment well prepared. Most important, you will have worked all of the tempting-trite pictures out of your system, and you'll be able to concentrate on a fresh approach to your subject matter.

A refreshing photo insight into the circus is the essay by Susan Felter, pages 58-65 of the January '86 issue of *American Photographer*. Your librarian can locate it for you.

Are trite pictures salable? They are. So are trite paintings, songs, and handicrafts. There are also books devoted to making trite photographs, and directories and catalogs devoted to displaying trite stock photos. But not this one. If after reading this admonition against trite pictures, you find some culprits in your stock photo file, send them off to a stock photo agency (see Chapter 12). Professionals are familiar with stock agencies' need to provide *standard trites* to their clientele. One photographer friend says, "I market my best pictures myself, and I dump my clichés on my agency, which can use all I can send."

How Do I Manage the Models?

Marketable photo illustrations are very often pictures of people doing things. How well the people in your picture perform can determine the success of your illustrations. The service photographer often has the convenience of working with professional models. In photo illustration, most of your models will be regular folks rather than professionals, and it's up to you to make them feel comfortable and cooperative.

You will encounter many of your models spontaneously in the course of your routine shooting. For the most part, children, teenagers, and adults will willingly cooperate with you for the fun or novelty of being photographed or being involved in the action. People are often intrigued that their picture might be published.

Before you begin photographing your on-the-spot models, let them know who you are and why you want to photograph them. And take the time to make them feel at ease.

Often their first question will be, "What's this photograph going to be used for?" Give your models a direct answer: "For a book. If this photo is selected for publication, you'll appear in a school textbook." Or, "For a magazine [name]."

Or, "For my photograph files. I'm a stock photographer and have a library of my pictures, which I sell to magazines and books." Give some examples of where the picture might be used.

Control the Conversation

If it seems appropriate, explain the mood you are trying to capture in your pictures. Control the conversation throughout the whole picture-taking session to trigger naturally the kind of expressions you're aiming for. Don't let the conversation slip into a subject that is contrary to the mood you are trying to create. For example, if your picture calls for a happy, gay mood, steer the conversation away from war, taxes, the storm or fire that took so many lives last week, or the twenty-car pileup on the freeway this morning. However, if your picture calls for somberness, guide the conversation in that direction.

Relax Your Models

Sometimes, to elicit the right kind of expressions from a nonprofessional model, you'll need to go a few steps further and become an actor—occasionally to the point of giving an award-winning performance as a clown, demagogue, or saint.

After a while, you'll find in working with people for your pictures that you develop a technique of gentle persuasion. You become adept at moving the conversation along the lines you want it to go.

Be as selective as the situation allows in your choice of models. Don't choose the model because he or she is a neighbor, relative, or friend. You'll make your task easier if you choose a model beforehand whose natural style or demeanor comes close to the expression you're aiming for—a serious thinker for sadness or weary expressions, a clear-eyed, optimistic individual for happy shots, and so on.

Here are some tips on how this works in practice:

Happiness. Don't ask for a smile. Instead, maneuver the conversation to some magic questions that always get smiles from—
SENIORS: "Do you have any grandchildren?"
ADULTS: "How's your golf [bowling, tennis] game?" Or, "Been on a vacation lately?"
TEENAGERS: Teenagers won't usually allow themselves to be categorized. I've found it best to learn the teenager's interests first (sports, music, movies, etc.), and then ask questions in those areas. Don't attempt to speak in their vernacular. They'll only become more suspicious of you.
PRE-TEENS: "Who's your boy- [or girl-] friend?"
SMALL CHILDREN: "What's your dog's [cat's/horse's] name?"
BABIES: If you make strange noises, you'll usually be rewarded with a smile (from everyone!).

Sorrow. Some people look sad naturally (Abraham Lincoln, for example). You can induce a sad-looking expression by asking a model to look tired. Another method is to catch him between expressions. The resulting expression is often pensive and sad-looking.

Intimacy. Shoot from a three-quarter view with a long lens. This will bring two people closer. Ask your models to look at each other's eyebrows. Unless they are pros, models who do not know each other will feel self-conscious, and your resulting pictures will look stilted. For your intimate pictures, choose models who know each other.

Illustration 6-1.

Overcoming shyness. Use a long lens when your model is shy about being photographed. The young Indian girl in Illustration 6-1 refused out of custom (on the Northern Cheyenne reservation in Lame Deer, Montana) to be photographed alone. I asked her brother to appear in the pic-

Illustration 6-2.

ture with her. The telephoto lens captured her alone on all of the vertical shots. The long lens also brought the teepee (symbol—see Chapter 2) closer. "Don't take my picture!" shy people will often say. To accomplish your mission, try taking a picture of what they are doing, as in Illustration 6-2.

Children are good models and can be diverted in ways that will enhance picture content. They tend to participate more fully than teenagers or adults. A good technique is to get your kid models involved in guessing games with you (the type of games we offer our children on long, boring car rides). Kids become animated when they like what they are doing.

Pictures of people sell. Photobuyers know that we're human, that nothing touches us more than a picture of someone feeling something we identify with—be it anger, humor, pensiveness, bewilderment, delight. Thus, when you aim your camera at your models with photo illustration in mind, you've got to adjust your thinking from the cosmetic approach usually employed when taking pictures of people. Your customer is not the portrait client or the bride or Aunt Harriet, but a photobuyer. And photobuyers are not interested in how pretty or handsome you have made your subject look, but in what emotion, what spontaneity, what insight into the human condition you have captured.

Should You Pay Your Models?

If you are shooting on speculation for inventory for your stock photo file, many models are satisfied with a copy of the published picture (tearsheet) if and when it is published. Other nonprofessional models are willing to cooperate just for fun or for the experience, especially if you are a beginner yourself. Still others are happy to have copies of the photographs. Give *them* your card, and have them write to you. If you do promise photographs, and they contact you for them, follow through.

Monetary payment would be in order for on-the-spot, nonprofessional models when you're shooting a commercial assignment as a service photographer. A good rule of thumb is to budget a minimum of 5 percent and a maximum of 10 percent of the fee you are receiving for the picture to pay your model(s). Seal your transaction by obtaining a signed model release.

Other Model Sources

A good source of models is your local community theater. Amateur actors always need portraits for their portfolios. You can trade them some portrait shots for their posing (in natural settings, of course) for your people-picture needs (e.g., people talking, interacting, or expressing fear, sadness, loneliness, joy, or another emotion).

Check also with local families and neighbors in need of family portraits. I often sketch out photo-illustration ideas (using my principle P = B + P + S + I—see Chapter 2) and have the members of the family act out the photo illustration situations. In return for their modeling services (about an hour's work), I supply them with a family portrait.

And What about Model Releases?

Are model releases required for all pictures you take, whether as a service photographer or as a photo illustrator? This question has several answers, depending on the situation.

If you anticipate that any of your pictures might be used for commercial purposes, build a model release file. Print up a 3x5 model release pad, then file the releases alphabetically in a 3x5 file-card box. The model release form shown in Figure 15-2 can be reduced easily to 3x5 size. Make one pad for adults and one pad for minors. An organization such as Associated Photographers International sells model release forms and similar photographer aids. Write them at 22231 Mulholland Highway, Suite 119, P.O. Box 4055, Woodland Hills, CA 91365.

Generally speaking, photo illustrations that are not used for advertising, endorsement, or similar commercial purposes do not need a model release. However, if the situation permits, obtain the release. Then, if any of your pictures are used for commercial purposes later on, you will have the release available and not miss a sale.

A general rule many stock photographers (and some service photographers) follow is to use photogenic neighbors, friends, and relatives as models. Then they can be fairly sure of finding their models to get a release if they need to in the future.

Occasionally I get a model release request for a picture I took a decade ago. I consult my model release file-card box and usually find that I received a blanket model release for an entire family when I originally took the picture. To obtain a blanket release, I had both parents fill out and sign the release and asked them to list their (minor) children. And what if I don't have a release? Because the model was usually a neighbor, friend, or relative, I can often track him down for the release.

In the early stages of my stock photography career, I obtained model releases on every occasion. I have since turned this completely around and almost never get one, because experience has shown me that this administrative disruption of the mood or atmosphere of my picture-taking session isn't necessary. Model releases are not required when a picture is used for educational or informational purposes. Since my personal Market List consists of magazine and book publishers, I rarely get a release request from an editor. However, since your PMS/A and Market List are different from mine, you will know how extensive you want your model release system to be. (See Chapter 15 for a full discussion of model releases.)

Dealing with Officials

The scene: An important high school football game, and you've arrived to get pictures of the kickoff for your stock file and an assignment. You'll leave as soon as you get the kickoff pictures, so you see no reason to pay admission. You enter by a side gate and are met by an attendant with an officious "Where do you think you're going?" expression.

You're not going to let this fellow steal your precious minutes, so you try to ignore him. You walk right past him. "Wait a minute!" he says, insulted that you have not recognized his importance. He has the right to detain you, and he does—long enough that you miss the kickoff shots.

Sound familiar? It will, unless you keep in mind this photo illustrator's motto: "Officials: Handle with Care."

As stock photographers, we frequently can't get our pictures without first having to get permission from someone. Security is getting tighter in many sectors, and it's understandable because past abuses—or the sheer numbers of people—have made it necessary to screen who takes pictures of what. You'll encounter officials in many forms: gatekeepers, receptionists, police, bureaucrats, teachers, secretaries, security guards. You'll even encounter unofficial officials: janitors, ticket takers, relatives of officials. But no matter who presents himself as an official barrier to your picture taking, handle the person with care, allowing for the amount of time you sense will satisfy his need to detain you.

One of the easiest official-eliminators is the "I need your help" routine. In the case of the football gate attendant, you say, "I need your help. I'd like to get a dramatic picture of the kickoff [look at your watch]—could you tell me the quickest way to the fifty-yard line?"

If an official wants to know something about you—why you're here, what the pictures will be used for—here's the answer: "I represent the John Doe Stock Photo Agency, and I'm John Doe. These pictures go into my files of over 5,000 stock photos. They're used in magazines, textbooks, calendars, anything that would be in the public interest—you name it! [Smile.]"

Try to cultivate officials who could have access to information relevant to your picture-taking assignment: ask questions such as "When will he be back?"; "How many players are on this team?"; "What time does the gate close?"

When you encounter an official who isn't cooperative, try offering a copy of the picture you're going to take. But don't take his name on a piece of paper; such papers either get lost or add to your office work. Instead, offer him your card and say, "Here's my address. Write me in about two weeks. The picture will be processed by then." (Experience predicts you have a one-in-a-thousand chance of hearing from him.)

Should you carry a press card? For large, important events, written permission from headquarters is your best introduction to on-site officials (headquarters usually issues its own press cards, stickers, passes). But for the 999 other events you'll attend, officials don't ask for a press card. If you're carrying two or more cameras around your neck (even if they're borrowed from a friend), that's official enough for them.

If you've found officials to be a constant thorn in your side, try the handle-with-care approach. However, there's an exception: if you stand to lose too much time by acquiescing to an official's demands ("Wait over there"; "Fill out this form"; "Stand in line"; "I'll put you on hold"; "I have to check with my boss first"), then take a different tack: try a *different* official. In the case of the football gate attendant, if he is uncooperative, walk away and find another gate. In the case of an uncooperative receptionist, wait until she goes on coffee break or to lunch. The replacement might be more agreeable (or you might think of a better approach).

In cases in which no officials appear, don't go out of your way to find someone to ask permission from. That someone may have no authority (a waiter in a restaurant, an attendant at a conference); he'll only pass the buck, detain you, and cause delays. Rather than take no pictures (because you didn't have permission), jump in and start clickin'. An official will usually come forward. Before he gives you *his* routine, give him your "I need your help" routine.

You owe it to yourself and the rest of us in the field to carry out your assignments in a professional way and in a manner that will earn the respect of the public.

Officials can sometimes delay, or even prevent, you from getting your picture. When all else fails, remember this: "It's sometimes easier to apologize than get permission."

Special Effects

Some photo illustrations can be converted into new illustrations through the use of posterization, special effects, and line conversion.

Photo editors welcome special-effect photography, provided that the pictures follow basic photo illustration criteria and conform to the magazine's or book's needs.

Special-effects aids are often advertised in photography magazines. Mine came from Edmund Scientific Co. (101 E. Gloucester Pike, Barrington, NJ 08007).

Special effects are often described in photography magazines. For example:

Petersen's PhotoGraphic, September 1977, page 12, "Mirror Images."
Popular Photography, May 1978, page 124, "Color by Laser."
Petersen's PhotoGraphic, October 1977, page 12, "Double Vision."
Popular Photography, October 1979, page 120, "Black Light for Halloween Magic."
Popular Photography, October 1979, page 112, "Through the Mylar Looking Glass."
Modern Photography, October 1983, page 10, "Out of Focus Images."
Darkroom Techniques, Jan/Feb 1983, page 53, "Soft Focus."
Popular Photography, March 1986, page 36, "Reflections."
American Photographer, June 1986, page 62, "Shots in the Dark."

Illustration 6-3. *A portrait can be converted to line art by using a special-effects screen.*

Illustration 6-4. *For special effect, the highlights were dropped out and the dark grays became solid black to create a high-contrast print.*

Illustration 6-5. *A photocopying machine will often produce interesting effects.*

Illustration 6-6. *Special-effects aids are often advertised in photography magazines. In this case, I placed an 8x10 special-effect "bullseye" negative and glass over the print paper.*

In addition, the following magazines and book, devoted to the dark-room, often include articles on special effects:

Darkroom Photography
9901 Agoura Rd.
Agoura, CA 91301

Darkroom Techniques
Preston Publications
7800 Merrimac Ave.
Box 48312A
Niles, IL 60648

The Basic Darkroom Book
by Tom Grimm
New American Library
1633 Broadway
New York, NY 10019

The Dramatic-Lighting Formula

As a photo illustrator gearing your pictures to the good marketable shots we've been describing, you may from time to time wish to treat a subject with unusual emphasis. The following comes in handy when you want to employ dramatic lighting with a subject, and it will enable you to produce top professional results every time. I call it the *Dramatic-Lighting Formula*. To check out the formula yourself, take a *spot meter* to Illustrations 6-7, 6-8, and 6-9. Measure these three areas in each one:

1. The main light falling on the face (M)
2. The shadow side of the face (S)
3. The background (B)

You achieve the most dramatic effect when the shadow side of the face is 2¾ stops lower than the lighted side of the face and the background is ¾ of a stop lower than the lighted side of the face. You see that in the actual photographs these gradations of light show marked contrast. On the scene, however, at the time you take the picture, there is not a corresponding marked contrast visible to the naked eye. What appears to the eye as very slight gradations of contrast will be definite contrasts in your print. With the aid of a spot meter, you can train yourself to perceive real-life light differences that are very subtle but that produce high-contrast results in your photographs. To achieve gradations in the face of your subject, use more or less fill light. To get the proper background ratio, move your background closer or farther away from your subject, or use a darker or lighter background area.

Here, then, is the formula:

$$P = M + S + B \text{ when } S = M - 2\tfrac{3}{4}$$
$$B = M - \tfrac{3}{4}$$

$$P = \text{Portrait}$$
$$M = \text{Main light area of face}$$
$$S = \text{Shadow side of face}$$
$$B = \text{Background}$$

Illustration 6-7. *The formula is most effective when you position your model so that the eye in the shadow side will pick up a glimmer of light. If it does, the light falling on the high areas on the shadow side, such as the cheek, will give your photograph a dramatic dimension.*

Illustration 6-8. *The dramatic lighting formula can be used easily in a "window-light" situation. In this case a window blind behind my model served as a plain background.*

Illustration 6-9. *The dramatic lighting formula is effective for portraits. The lighting may not always be flattering to your model, but it will be impressive to photobuyers, who are always interested in stock photography that catches readers' attention.*

Measure the light ratios in portraits you've taken in which you were aiming for a highly dramatic effect. Chances are you'll find that the light ratio of M to B and S is much higher than in the above formula, resulting in an overdose of contrast, a loss of detail, and an actual weakening of dramatic effect. Once again, you don't need to create lighting that gives high-contrast effects to the naked eye in order to get the kind of dramatic lighting you see in these illustrations. Quite subtle light gradations will give you dramatic contrast on your print, without losing the detail that gives life and breath to your picture.

Some Notes on the Taking and Making of Photo Illustrations in This Book

As I said earlier in this chapter, the photo illustrator not only records things as they are, he also often creates situations that could be or should be. You not only will be developing an eye for seeing potential illustrations in your viewfinder, you will also often be taking an active hand in the *making* of good marketable pictures.

The pictures I've chosen to head the chapters in this book are examples of stock photos with high resale value. Each of them has been published many times by many publishers; each follows the $P = B + P + S + I$ principle. The following are some insights into their taking and making.

Introduction. Photobuyers look for *naturalness* in your pictures. Because I used available (window) light and the dramatic lighting formula, the children felt at home, and not self-conscious. Studio lights or flash usually result in a posed look with nonprofessional models.

Chapter 1. Stock photographs are more successful when they *suggest* rather than *explain* a mood. In this case, I used a telephoto lens and backlighting for effect. I shot ten to one and selected the most successful picture.

Chapter 2. How do you illustrate the isolation of a nursing home? A hundred ways. The somberness of the silhouette in this picture makes a statement. So does the woman's interest in reaching the outside world through her newspaper. Notice the use of the $P = B + P + S + I$ formula.

Chapter 3. Choose your models carefully for their ability to project certain expressions or feelings.

Chapter 4. To show involvement with the lake, I wanted to make a ripple of water, but the pebbles the little boy was tossing didn't make much of a visual impact. I had a friend stand off to the left and out of the picture and throw large boulders at the designated spot in my composition. I asked the little boy to try to throw his pebbles at the ripple of water.

Chapter 5. Showing a relationship between elements in a picture is important. This picture might not be a successful portrait, but it is a successful photo illustration.

Chapter 6. Stock photographs with interesting graphic designs are always welcome with photobuyers. See page 28 for a further discussion of this picture.

Chapter 7. The right moment, and only that moment, is crucial for the stock photographer. At a ceremony at a Montana reservation, I stood behind these Indian mothers and snapped the picture just as the flag came into my vertical composition.

Chapter 8. Good ideas make good stock photographs. One day, I saw this happen but didn't have my camera along. I made a note in my idea file, and a year later, when I found the right situation, I made the picture.

Chapter 9. When a blizzard hit western Minnesota one year, we were staying overnight at a friend's farm. When my friend's wife said, "There'll be no mail delivery today!" I said, "Let's pretend there is." I used the "shoot ten-to-one" rule and this picture best told the story.

Chapter 10. Stock photography "portraits" are not always flattering, or glamorous. Photobuyers look first for an *illustrative* quality in your pictures. A special-effects technique was used in this picture to give it an engraved look.

Chapter 11. Interesting faces, especially close up, lend themselves well to stock photography. I took this picture with my 130mm lens on a crowded steet in Istanbul. I printed it on number 5 paper to give it extreme contrast.

Chapter 12. What attracted your eye first in this picture? Probably the highlight on the ocean. A successful stock photo leaves an element of discovery for the viewer—in this case, the bird.

Chapter 13. In Turkey, it is the custom not to allow dogs inside a home. But that isn't necessarily a measure of a boy's affection for his dog and vice versa. I wanted to show this in my photo story and coaxed the dog to the door stoop with some meat while the boy caught his attention.

Chapter 14. Joy, surprise, delight—these are a few of the messages photobuyers are continually seeking for their layouts. Notice how people express emotions (other than through facial expressions), and try capturing them with your camera.

Chapter 15. In Green Bay, Wisconsin, on a frosty February morning, I stopped my car to take a picture of the smoke. The smoke appears more ominous than it really is. I used a red filter. After taking pictures of the grain mill, I drove off and saw a sign that juxtaposed its message with the background. Just what the two together mean, I'm not sure, but this picture has sold often.

Chapter 16. In the principle $P = B + P + S + I$, sometimes the background can also serve as the symbol. The flag lent itself to a photo story on youth activists. I found the best lighting in the room first, moved the chair to it, and then hung the flag.

Chapter 17. The light rays in this picture were inspired when I saw the dust particles in the air after a pickup truck drove by our farm one mid-morning. The next day, at approximately the same time, I had my camera ready and I asked a neighbor to drive up and down our road; before the dust settled, I asked two friends to walk down the road.

Photo illustrations are successful when they capture a mood that lends itself to magazine-article or book themes and topics. This picture has served many books and articles.

7.
The Fine Art of Dealing with Photobuyers

Getting to Know Them

Thousands of photobuyers exist in market areas ranging from the commercial, such as advertising and public relations firms, to the editorial (books, magazines, publishing houses). In this book, when I refer to *photobuyers*, I will be referring almost exclusively to those (mainly editorial) who deal with the stock photographer and not those photobuyers (mainly commercial) who deal with the service photographer.

Art director, picture editor, designer, photo acquisition director, photo editor—are just a few of the titles bestowed on photobuyers at publishing houses and magazines. Photobuyers usually work out of an office, are usually between twenty-five and forty-five years old, and approve between $1,000 and $10,000 a month in photo purchases; probably half are female, and all are busy people. You'll find that photobuyers are interested in *photographs*, not *photography*.

Photobuyers tend to mellow with age. Younger photobuyers, new to the job, sometimes exercise their newfound decision-making power by exhibiting impatience or intolerance. Handle with care.

Veteran photobuyers have usually survived the rigors of the publishing world with enough aplomb to be able to take the time to admire a photograph now and then. They've also honed their viewing skills to the point where they can speedily select *the* picture out of a large pile as if by magic. Which brings to mind: Always send a picture buyer more pictures than you believe to be adequate, provided the pictures are appropriate. You'll often be surprised at the pictures the editor chooses. Don't edit your selection (except to delete off-target pictures). Let the editor do the editing.

A visit to an editor's office will bring home to you my adage about picture editors buying pictures that they *need*, not that they *like*. The walls of an editor's office are plastered with lovely Track A pictures: prints clipped from calendars or signed originals from friends. Track B pictures, the kind the editor authorizes a check to you for, are rarely on the wall. What editors *need* and what they *like* are different. *Marketing* is understanding that difference.

The Reliability Factor

One paradox in the story of creativity in the commercial world is that those who succeed are not necessarily the most talented. In all creative fields—theater, music, art, dance—talented people abound. But the world of commerce is a machine, and a machine operates well only if all parts are moving smoothly together.

The people who sign the checks will readily admit that **talent** does not head the list when it comes to selecting a new person for a part, an assignment, or a position. History has taught them that "the show must go on," that reliable people make commercial productions a reality. Since talent is plentiful, they can be selective.

Thus, an unwritten law in the world of commercial creativity is the **reliability factor.** How well would you stack up if a photobuyer were to ask, "Are you available when I want to contact you? Are you honest? Prompt? Fair? Dependable? Neat? Accurate? Courteous? Experienced? Talented?"

I placed *talented* at the bottom of the list because that's where most photobuyers will place it. They *assume* you are talented. Their basic question is: "Can you *deliver* the goods—and when I need them?"

Because you are talented in photography, you purchased this book. You knew you could easily compete with the pictures you've seen published. But talent will not be your key to success in marketing pictures. You will succeed in direct proportion to the attention you pay to developing and nurturing your reliability factor.

There are exceptions to everything, of course. Even with a low reliability factor, some creative people succeed. (Witness the temperamental screen idol or the eccentric painter.) But usually they are coasting on previously established fame, or they exhibit a unique ability. As a newcomer to the field of photo marketing, your greatest asset will be your ability to establish a solid reliability factor with the markets you begin to deal with.

The Photobuyer Connection

You will connect with photobuyers in person, by phone, and in writing, relying primarily on the latter. As a stock photographer who conducts business via the mailbox, it's important to express yourself well in your communications with photobuyers.

From my overview of photographer/photobuyer relations at Photo-Source International, I have noted that if a breakdown occurs, it's usually because the photographer didn't express himself clearly, whether in writing, in person, or by phone.

Many photobuyers reached their picture-editor post after serving in an editorial capacity—or continue to do both. They're often journalism or English majors initially attracted to editing and writing because of their communication skills. They have an advantage over the photographer, who frequently enters the field through the nonverbal avenues of art, design, or photographic technique.

In your dealings with photobuyers, if you experience a misunderstanding or mix-up in regard to purchase, payment, assignment, or whatever, here's how to handle it:

1. Give the photobuyer the benefit of the doubt. Despite the harangues we hear from some of our fellow photographers, rarely will you encounter an intentional hustle on the part of a photobuyer. If you are in a dispute with a photobuyer and you are positive the fault is his, rest assured it was probably an honest mistake. We're all allowed some of those.

2. Be firm, but not offensive. Consider the buyer's self-esteem, too.

3. If you are emotionally upset over a transaction between yourself and a photobuyer, wait a day (twenty-four hours) before you react.

Remember this: The photobuyer is probably dealing with you because he considers your work valuable, even essential. Don't let a harsh word or irresponsible statement slip out and get in the way of future opportunities to publish your work.

The newcomer to the field of photo marketing is often amazed and sometimes insulted by the casual approach many photobuyers take in their handling of photographers and the photographer's work. To a photographer, a photograph can be like a child, an extension of the soul, a piece of poetry or music. Photobuyers don't have the same reverence for your work that you do; they can't. You may consider your photograph a work of art; to them it's another piece of work to process. This is not to say they don't admire talent or good photography. They do—most of them. But to survive in their field, they have learned to separate their emotional appreciation from their career demands.

If you take the same approach with your stock photography—that is, separate and compartmentalize your photography into marketable pictures that will feed your family and not-so-marketable pictures that feed your soul—you will be able to suffer the jolts and inconveniences of photobuyers without feeling they are callous or insensitive. They usually aren't. They're just doing a job, and usually doing it well.

Should You Visit a Photobuyer?

If you tailor your marketing plan correctly, your specialized markets will be scattered throughout the nation. Unlike the service photographer who can work effectively with agencies within the confines of a single city, the stock photographer deals with far-flung buyers—mostly through the mail (see Chapter 9).

I myself have dealt with some photobuyers for a decade and have never met them. My reliability factor continues to score high with them. A personal visit would serve only to satisfy our mutual curiosity. Yet while personal visits are not always necessary, they can be a real plus.

Personal visits always help seal a relationship. If my itinerary and schedule permit, I drop in on photobuyers when I can to say a personal hello. People do respond more actively to a face than to a letterhead. If you are trying to develop a new market, a personal visit to a key buyer could be your turning point. Or a personal visit might help solidify your relationship with a market you've already been dealing with successfully. But you will not necessarily find photobuyers eager to set up an appointment with you, especially if they don't know you. Talent is plentiful. Besides, they have a deadline coming up tomorrow. If they need a photographer, they'll consult their photographer file. They know that personal visits take time and aren't often immediately fruitful. Their needs are too specific for a general, introductory visit to solve.

Don't make an appointment unless (1) you have sold a picture to the photobuyer in the past; or (2) you have something of value to give the editor, such as information or photos targeted to what you have learned is a current need for him. Photobuyers are understaffed and underpaid. They'll have little reason to welcome an "I'm me and I have photos" visit from you. You'll end up creating a reaction opposite to what you're after and get put on that buyer's blacklist. If you can make your visit worthwhile to the photobuyer, however, you'll be greeted warmly and your time will be well spent.

Realistically, a visit to a photobuyer can be extremely costly for you. In effect you are making a sales call, and in the corporate world a salesman's call costs just about the price of the suit he is wearing. As of this writing, the average cost of a sales visit is $192. If you live close to some markets, those visits need not cost that much. But for your far-flung markets, of course, the cost could be much more.

By working smart, you can cut such costs by diverting funds that might be spent for personal visits toward contacting buyers by mail. Since photobuyers buy pictures not because they like them but because they need them, your tailored selection of twenty-five to a hundred prints mailed to a buyer will serve the same purpose as a personal visit with your portfolio. Also, your selection will receive more attention from the photobuyer. Remember that as a stock photographer, your separate photobuyers will not require you to be versatile; therefore, a portfolio that demonstrates your wide range of photographic abilities will not be necessary.

Should You Write?

By far the most effective way to contact and deal with photobuyers is by mail. Chapter 9 shows you how to write the standard cover letter (Figure 9-1) and how to graduate to the "magic" query letter (Figure 9-2) that captures a photobuyer's interest every time. You'll also learn that looking like a pro is a key to the success of any correspondence you have with a photobuyer.

Letter writing is probably the least expensive method of contacting photobuyers. The corporate world tells us, nevertheless, that letter writing is not cheap: each business letter costs about the price of breakfast at a restaurant. As of this writing, the cost is $5.75. The stock photographer's letter can be much less expensive, as I'll show in Chapter 9. Because you have narrowed your list to a select group of markets, you'll find you'll need only about a dozen basic letters.

By using the mails to contact photobuyers, you'll also have the opportunity to include self-promotional literature that will serve as an effective reminder to your clients that you exist and can produce what they need.

Your letter, with its unique self-promotion piece, photo example or two, and cordial hello, can provide a pleasant interlude for the photobuyer with a succinctness that a personal visit cannot match. A few such letters over the period of a year will create and sustain a good working rapport between you and the photobuyer.

Is dealing through the mails effective? Take a look at Sears, L.L. Bean, and thousands of other mail-order houses. Granted, we call 90 percent of the solicitations that arrive in the mail junk mail. But the other 10 percent—a sale on Fuji film at a camera supply house, an antique camera catalog—hits our interest areas, captures our attention, and makes us want to buy.

Editorial photobuyers purchase nearly 100 percent of their pictures through the mail. They expect mailed solicitations. Part of your mail-marketing operation will be to establish a regular, daily letter-writing routine. Depending on the size of your Market List, you will want to write one or more letters a day to buyers on your list. Your letter should remind them of your continuing knowledge and interest (expertise!) in their readership area, update them on your trip plans or assignments pertinent to their subject needs, and include a photocopy of a recently published picture of yours. If your Market List is lengthy, a few months will pass before you come around again full circle to the first name on it. When you do, redesign your letter and your enclosures, and begin again.

This might seem like an endless routine to you, like the continual re-painting of the Brooklyn Bridge, but this system will reward you over and over. If you have built an effective Market List, your mail program will be effective.

Should You Telephone?

The telephone has evolved from a luxury to an important marketing tool—a tool that must be used skillfully to be effective. The key to successful phoning is understanding the principle of *give and take*. Most photographers, when they call, make the mistake of *taking* only. They take advantage of the photobuyer's courtesy by asking endless questions that could be answered through basic library research. (See the reference and directory list in Table 3-1 and the Bibliography.) They also take the photobuyer's valuable time. They come away with answers to their own questions and leave the photobuyer with nothing.

Multiply such a call by ten times a day, five days a week, and you'll understand why a photobuyer is not interested in talking to photographers. Persistence is a virtue. But it has a reverse effect for stock photographers who persist in phoning editors indiscriminately.

Here's the secret. Before you make your call, study the buyer's needs backwards and forward, then make up a *give list*. Decide what you will give the photobuyer.

How do his needs match your PMS/A, your personal photographic marketing strength/areas? You won't be wasting his time when you can say:

—"I'm a bass fisherman, and I have some excellent pictures of Florida, which I understand you'll be covering in your magazine next August." (Newsletters in the field such as Larami's *CONTACTS*, *Travelwriter Marketletter*, *and PARTY LINE* [see the Bibliography], will carry this kind of advance information.)

—"I regularly vacation in Maine, and I'd be available for assignment when you need to update your files of New England pictures."

—"I notice you have a continuing need for classroom pictures. My neighbor is a teacher. With a few guidelines from you, I could get the kind of pictures you want."

Once you establish rapport with some photobuyers by showing that you can offer *them* something, they won't mind giving *you* the information that you'd like. They'll also welcome your calls in the future because they'll know your calls will save them time. Because you have narrowed your photographic interests to your Track B strong areas, you can approach any of the photobuyers on your list with confidence.

Telephoning can be inexpensive when you prepare beforehand by doing your marketing homework to zero in on the editor's needs. Often you can limit your conversation to five minutes. The editor will appreciate this; so will your bank balance.

Because you will be dealing with photobuyers who are in time zones different from your own, phone them before 8:00 a.m. or after 5:00 p.m. your time, when possible, for savings.

Not every photographer has mastered the art of telephoning. Some are afflicted with *phonephobia*. Practice your telephone techniques with a friend or a tape recorder. Professional telephone marketing people tell us to write out our proposed message (script it), then refine it with rehearsals. Make your first call to a photobuyer for whom you have a strong give list. The conversation will go easily if *you* are doing all the giving.

As you become more adept at telephoning, contact more photobuyers on your list. Your *give list* might not be equally strong for each buyer, but as long as you figure out something to offer, what you pick up in your conversation might lead to picture ideas or subject matter that you can turn into a strong *give* the next time you call that same buyer. As you progress in your telephone-marketing program, make a record of your calls on 3x5 file cards, a Rolodex, or a notebook, and measure their efficacy. Eliminate from your telephone list those photobuyers who aren't productive for you. As you become more experienced in telephoning, you'll learn how to pick up leads in your conversations that will direct you to future picture-selling opportunities. You'll find it easier and easier to *give* to your photobuyers as you become more and more familiar with their exact needs.

Get on the Available-Photographers List

Your Track B list probably features several strong areas of special interest ranging from gardening to sailing. You have contacted a number of potential photobuyers in each of these areas, all of whom would like to know more about you because your photographic interests match *their* needs. They each maintain an *available-photographers list* in the office. If your reliability factor looks high, you could be on several dozen photobuyers' lists. Here's how you get on a list.

Make a *categories form letter* similar to the one in Figure 7-1, and send it off to photobuyers in your target market areas. Don't give in to the tendency to print only a few categories that match your Track B chart. List them all, but *check off only the ones that apply to your PMS/A* and the editor's needs. Photo editors will gravitate to their own immediate spheres of interest, and when they find those specific areas checked off, they'll take notice of you. Since you checked few of the other areas, they'll know you aren't dissipating your photographic talents over territory that is of little concern to them, and concomitantly that you must have *a lot* of material in the areas you concentrate on, i.e., what they specialize in. This is one of the reasons I suggest you curb your picture-tak-

YOUR LETTERHEAD

Dear Photo Editor:

Kindly include my name and work on your photographers list. I have checked off several areas below in which I feel I could be of photographic service to you.

FORMAT AVAILABLE:
☐ 8 × 10 black-and-white
☐ 35mm color
☐ 2-¼ color
☐ 4 × 5 color
☐ Other: _____

Reproduction fee for one-time North American rights:
B&W's: _____
Color: _____

Holding fee past 2 weeks:
☐ I charge none
☐ My fee is: Color _____
                    B&W _____

SOCIAL
☐ Health
☐ Welfare
☐ Drug abuse
☐ Alcoholism
☐ Sex education
☐ Rights movements
☐ Role reversals
☐ Juvenile delinquency
☐ Other _____

PEOPLE
☐ Preschool
☐ Elementary
☐ Junior high
☐ Senior high
☐ College
☐ Adult
☐ Families
☐ Senior citizens
☐ Multiracial groups
☐ Blacks
☐ Native Americans
☐ Chicanos
☐ Orientals
☐ Middle Easterners
☐ European-American
☐ Other ethnic groups ____
_____
☐ Customs
☐ Holidays
☐ _____

SPORTS
☐ Basketball
☐ Football
☐ Baseball
☐ Track
☐ Other: _____
_____
_____

NATURE
☐ Animals
☐ Scenic
☐ Seasons
☐ _____
_____
_____

RELIGIOUS
☐ Congregational worship
☐ Communion, Baptism,
    Bar Mitzvah
☐ Adult education
☐ Church school,
    age levels: _____
☐ Family worship
☐ Religious holidays
☐ _____

INDUSTRIAL/TECHNICAL
☐ Food
☐ Agriculture
☐ Industry
☐ Government
☐ Labor
☐ Manufacturing
☐ Mining
☐ Transportation
☐ Communications
☐ Fisheries
☐ Tourism
☐ Entertainment
☐ Medical
☐ _____

EDUCATION
☐ Adult education
☐ Primary
☐ Elementary
☐ High school
☐ College
☐ Vocational
☐ Other: _____
_____
_____

OTHER
☐ City life
☐ Rural life
☐ Environment/ecology
☐ Occupations
☐ _____

TRAVEL
I have current pictures (within the last three years) of the following COUNTRIES:

I have current pictures (within the last three years) of the following STATES:

[Your Name]

Figure 7-1. A sample marketing categories form letter.

ing in Track A areas and accelerate your Track B areas (Chapter 3). This form letter is another way of saying to photobuyers, "I'm the person for the job. . . ." The photobuyer will respond, "This photographer speaks my language."

The categories letter is appealing to photobuyers because it doesn't call for any action on their part. They can just have it filed for future needs. And it is concise and to the point.

Photobuyers will do one of four things when they receive your letter:

1. Throw it away.
2. File it to have on hand for reference.
3. Phone you because of an immediate need.
4. Put you on their available-photographers list.

Note: Resist the urge to appear versatile by checking off several categories. Photobuyers prefer dealing with specialists in *their* area. If you do check off plenty of squares, they'll say, "No one is that good!"—and choose the photographers who appear to have a large stock file in *their* area of interest.

The available-photographers list in the photobuyer's office can take many forms—3x5 file cards, a three-ring notebook, separate files, or a computer file. Photobuyers will add notes to your file, such as what they perceive to be your strong areas within their categories of interest. They may also add notes concerning conversations with you, assignments, or a running list of your pictures they have used to date.

Once you are on the photobuyer's available-photographers list, you will periodically be sent a *needs sheet*, which delineates the current photo needs of that publishing house, ad agency, or magazine. You'll send your pictures in for consideration whenever you receive a needs sheet. Since the needs sheet describes the exact photos needed, you'll find yourself saving postage and making points by not sending inappropriate pictures for consideration. The photobuyer will welcome your pictures because they are tailored to the publication's needs.

Since the publishing industry is forever in a state of change, mail your categories form letter to each entry on your Market List once a year. Why? Because some things might change: (1) your priorities; (2) the photobuyer's priorities; (3) your address; (4) your stationery; (5) the photobuyer's address; (6) the photobuyer.

Whether or not any changes have occurred, this letter is a good reminder to the photobuyer. New competition appears on the scene every day. Your letter will keep you and your work in the forefront of the photobuyer's mind.

Selling the Same Picture Over and Over Again

Multiple submission is the phrase often used when photographers submit the same photographs to different publishers at the same time. Unethical? Not at all. The reason? Your Track B pictures will be submitted to specialized markets targeted to different segments of the reading (viewing) public. There is no cross-readership conflict, especially if your markets are regional or local. In other words, the readers of magazine X never read magazine Y or Z. Feed those statistics into the 10,000 photo-buying markets that exist, and you can see why a photobuyer editor is not too concerned if your photo has already appeared, or will appear, in magazine X.

Sell & Re-Sell Your Photos

What's the appeal of multiple submissions to photobuyers? Savings. Most editors don't have the budget to demand more than one-time rights. They know they can get a picture much cheaper if they rent the picture from a photographer on a one-time basis.

And the multiple-sales system is healthy for you, the stock photographer. It will encourage you to research more picture-taking possibilities as well as to produce more photographs.

Multiple submission, of course, does not always apply to exclusive national publications, such as *People* or *Ladies' Home Journal* who would prefer that you sell them first rights to your picture. Nor does it apply to commercial accounts where you have signed a work-for-hire agreement in which you transfer *all* your picture rights to your client. (This is a procedure I do not recommend to the stock photographer—more about this subject in Chapter 15.)

But you'll find you can use the multiple-submission system with 95 percent of the photobuyers you deal with. The exceptions will be large-circulation newsstand magazines, and most calendar and greeting card companies, ad agencies, PR agencies (service photographer areas), and other commercial firms that require, because of their nature, an exclusive right to, or sometimes ownership of, your photograph. (But unless a photobuyer offers you a fee you can't refuse, don't sell anything but one-time rights.) The picture on the cover of this book and on page 139 has earned me nearly $3,000. If I had sold all rights originally for $500, I would be out nearly $2,500! But I didn't, and the cash register keeps ringing. I'll also be able to pass the rights to the photo on to my heirs.

Photocopying Your Photographs

A great boon to stock photographers has been the practice on the part of photobuyers of photocopying certain pictures (black-and-white or transparencies) when you send them in for consideration.

The advantages to you are many:

1. Although photobuyers may not be able to immediately use a picture you have submitted, they might anticipate its future use. A photocopy in their file will serve as your calling card. When the need arises for your picture, the photobuyer contacts you for the original.
2. Some buyers might hold photocopies of twenty to thirty of your photos in their central art libraries (see next section). Often as many as ten to forty other photo editors at the publishing house can have the opportunity to view the pictures.
3. Since your *original* is returned to you, it can be sent elsewhere. Conceivably, photocopies of the same picture can be working for you in a couple dozen central art libraries at the same time.
4. You incur no costs.

And the disadvantages? Unauthorized use of your photocopies for rough layouts might occur. But that's a small price to pay for the marketing potential your pictures enjoy while on file.

Copyright infringement? There is none. The photobuyers are using your picture for the purpose of research (Sections 113(c) and 107 of the Copyright Act). They are required neither to ask your permission nor to compensate you for its use.

A potential disadvantage might occur in the future when the digitizing of black-and-white and color transparencies is refined to the point where it would be difficult to tell the difference between your original picture and the resulting copy. But that's in the future, and then again such a technological advancement just might turn out to be a *plus* for the stock photographer, much as the introduction of the recording industry made residual sales a boon to songwriters and musicians.

Color copiers now exist (at libraries, banks, and instant-print shops) that will make reasonable *color* copies of your slides (twenty 35mm to a sheet). These, or Cibachrome copies, serve as excellent samples to leave on file with photobuyers. (For information on file prints, see Chapter 5.) For your own purposes, photocopy your slides in color at a Xerox Center and cross-reference the results in a three-ring notebook as a handy office reference guide to your available color photos. You can also make documentary copies of your color slides by placing them on a light table and snapping a shot of them when you send a shipment off. File the resulting slide in the photobuyer's file for future reference.

Finally, photocopying has come into its own as an art. Recent exhibitions have featured visuals produced by the photocopying duplication process. Stock photographers have also produced interesting copies of their own photographs and then rephotographed them for illustrative impact.

To increase sales, whenever you contact photobuyers—by letter, phone, or in person—encourage them to photocopy your pictures.

The Central Art File

Publishing houses usually start from a modest venture, which then expands, sometimes over several generations. The main theme of the publisher usually remains the same. For example, automotive publishers expand with things automotive, and so on.

As you research your market possibilities, geared to your photographic strengths, you'll plug into some large publishing houses with twenty to fifty or more editors for as many periodicals and/or book specialties. In marketing your pictures to such houses, you of course save yourself time and expense. You need send only one shipment of one set of prints or slides, rather than thirty sets to thirty separate photobuyers.

Large houses have large photography budgets—$20,000 to $40,000 per *month* is not uncommon for a large publishing house. If you have done your research well, part of that budget can be yours, because you can supply pictures that fill their needs.

In most magazine or book publishing houses, you'll find a *central art library* (sometimes called the *photo library* or the *photo file*). Incoming pictures are logged by a librarian and then distributed to the appropriate photo editors (or art editors or designers) for viewing. If your picture(s) is selected, the art librarian puts a purchase order into motion, and within a month, you receive a check.

Color is returned to you, but once your black-and-white is used, it is tagged and placed in the central library's filing system, usually by subject, age bracket, or activity. Some libraries will make photocopies and cross-reference them in other related files for possible future use.

"But isn't a used picture less salable?" you might ask. On the contrary. The fact that your picture sold once puts a stamp of approval on it. The next photobuyer who comes along and sees your picture in the file, its previous use noted, will be *more* likely to use it since it has received prior approval from a colleague.

You'll receive, generally, 75 percent of your original fee when your picture is used again. If the repeat sale is for other than inside editorial use, you should receive a higher fee (see Tables 8-2 and 8-3).

About once a year, the art librarian will conduct a spring cleaning of the central art file and return outdated photos to photographers.

The Permanent-File System

Large publishing houses, especially the denominational houses that employ fifty or more editors, are always in need of up-to-date photographs that reflect society. Their need is so great (they produce several dozen periodicals and as many book titles each year) that editors keep a permanent file of black-and-white photographs in their art libraries. These photographs are chosen because of their broad appeal to the particular readership reached by that publishing house. The editors welcome additions to this file to keep on hand for immediate use when needed.

Photobuyers are fond of saying, "Send me pictures that I can always find a place for in my layouts." Of course, it would take a mind reader to score every time, but if you have been successful in selling to a certain market several times, in all probability you have a keen understanding of the photographic needs of that publishing house. Ask all your contacts if they have a permanent file. If they do, submit your pictures for consideration. They can be included in the file, and each time a picture is used, you will receive a check. Most photobuyers prefer original slides, and you may not wish to place your originals with a central art librarian. However, the system works well for black-and-white's, and for some textbook publishers, who will accept display dupes as file copies.

Can you depend on publishing houses to be conscientious in their dealings in this kind of arrangement? The risk factor of a mix-up in use and payments is low when you consider an honest mistake every now and then compared with all those checks you would not have received if you had never placed your pictures with the permanent file. Your greatest risk will be investing in multiple prints of your black-and-whites and then relying on your judgment as to which publishing houses would be likely to use them most frequently.

From time to time, you'll want to update your supply on file by sending in a fresh batch of photos. From time to time, too, the art librarian will return pictures to you to make room for more recent submissions.

The Pirates

Some newcomers to photo marketing bring with them misconceptions about the ethics of photobuyers. From my conversations and correspondence with beginners, I'm always amazed at how many have visions of picture-buyer pirates lurking in their office coves, ready to seize some unsuspecting photographer's pictures and sell them on the black market.

Such infringers might exist in the field of service photography, where stakes for a single picture are known to reach impressive heights (such cases are reported in trade journals such as *Photo District News*), but in twenty-six years I have never run across a deliberate case of piracy in the editorial field. An occasional inexperienced photobuyer may make an error of omission or commission. Photographers have been known to do likewise. The lesson here is to be cautious when working with new publications that don't have a substantial track record or publishing houses that have a history of hiring greenhorns. I suggest that you deal with publishers who have been in business a minimum of three years.

All in all, you'll find photobuyers of stock photography reliable and interested in you as a person and as a photographer. If you operate with the same attributes, you'll find dealing with photobuyers an easy task.

8.
Pricing
Your
Pictures

Master Your
Marketing System
First

As I cautioned earlier, it is foolhardy to jump right into trying to sell your photo illustrations before you understand how to market them. *Selling* is what happens naturally, after you do your *marketing* homework. In Chapter 2, I explained the difference between a good picture and a good *marketable* picture, and why (unless you break into that small elite of top professionals) it is almost impossible to sell with regularity to the big-money markets.

Rather than rely on luck, i.e., selling your pictures in scattershot fashion, use the system in Chapter 3 to tap dozens of markets that will *consistently rent* your pictures from you on a one-time-use basis. Some of these markets have monthly photography budgets of $10,000 to $30,000. Yet they are markets that the pros rarely have the time to discover or to research.

Chapters 2 and 3 show you how to set yourself apart from the hordes of stock photographers trying to sell the standard excellent picture (Track A) to photobuyers who already have hundreds or even thousands of such pictures in inventory or on tap. Chapter 3 explains how to analyze your personal photographic marketing strength/areas (PMS/A), and in so doing, immediately become a valuable resource to specific photobuyers.

Be sure, then, to get Chapters 2 and 3 under your belt before moving to this chapter on pricing. In other words, set up your *marketing* strategy first—before you attempt to sell. It will save you time and money spent on postage and packaging that bring only "nice work, but . . ." letters from photobuyers, if they respond at all.

Trusting you've done your marketing homework, then, on to pricing your pictures. Figuring prices need not be a mystery. The system I outline will aid you in keeping your prices professional and acceptable to photobuyers.

It's important to remember that you will be dealing with photobuyers as a photo illustrator (stock photographer), not as a service photographer. Therefore, you can enter this field in high gear, provided your pictures are good and your reliability factor is high (i.e., you present yourself and your pictures in a professional way and on time).

Sell and Re-sell

There is a myth I will ask you to unlearn at this point: " 'Selling a picture' means selling it once—you can't sell it again."

This myth is perpetuated because it can be true in the field of service photography. It doesn't apply to photo illustration (stock photography).

You can sell your pictures over and over again, because in selling a photo illustration, a stock photograph, you are selling *one-time use* of the picture, not the picture itself. Naturally, you must exercise common good judgment, and not simultaneously submit a picture to three sailing magazines that could have cross-readership. But you *can* submit the same picture to a sailing magazine, an elementary school textbook publisher, and a denominational publishing house simultaneously. Photobuyers rent a photo for one-time use, whether for cover or inside editorial use, to obtain quality pictures at fees lower than they would have to pay to purchase the picture outright. They do not attempt to exercise any controls over where else you might market the same picture—it is understood that you observe the ethics of the business in not sending the same pictures at the same time to competing publications.

Photobuyers recognize that the risk of the same picture appearing simultaneously in another publication is minimal. It rarely happens. In the nearly three decades I have been submitting pictures on a multiple basis, only one photo editor has been hesitant, and that was back in 1963 when the field was young and editors weren't always familiar with the benefits of renting pictures.

The Price Range

Should you set a fee for your pictures and stick with it? If you are a service photographer, perhaps, yes. But if you are selling stock photographs, you'll learn that the different photobuyers on your Market List have different budgets. If you have three hundred potential markets on your list, you are going to find a wide range of fees paid for your photos.

A low-circulation magazine will not have the budget of one with a high circulation. A high-circulation publication sponsored by a non-profit organization might not have the budget of a low-circulation magazine sponsored by an oil company. Another consideration is advertising. Some trade magazines are heavily supported by advertising; other magazines with the same circulation figures have little or no advertising and are supported by subscriptions. You'll find the latter category on the lower end of the payment range. You, of course, have the option to choose what markets and what price ranges you want to deal with.

Base Camp: Inside Editorial Use

As a newcomer to the stock photography field, you deal basically with photo editors, designers, and art buyers at publishing houses. Your pictures are usually bought (rented) to illustrate the editorial content of periodicals or books. You'll find that 90 percent of your pictures go to *inside editorial use* in magazines, periodicals, encyclopedias, textbooks, and trade books. Payment for this type of use spreads across the six basic fee ranges shown in Table 8-1.

These six categories reflect the circulations and budgets of the existing market areas, from local newspapers to major magazines and book publishers. If a picture is to be used for a purpose other than inside editorial (for example, as a cover, chapter head, or informational brochure), you should charge a higher fee, and you can use the above standards to figure what that higher fee should be. (We'll cover how to do this shortly, under the heading "Using the Pricing System: What to Charge.")

To apply to publishers and publishing companies
for one-time inside editorial use (as of 1988)

Range No.	Black-and-White	Color
1	$100 to $250	$300 to $500
2	$ 50 to $100	$150 to $300
3	$ 35 to $ 50	$125 to $150
4	$ 25 to $ 35	$100 to $125
5	$ 20 to $ 25	$ 75 to $100
6	$ 15 to $ 20	$ 50 to $ 75

Table 8-1. Pricing Guide One.

Which Range for You?

The lower-ranging fees on the chart represent those you will receive from, say, your local newspaper, a nonprofit organization, or a small church magazine. The higher range looks more enticing. I would like to comment on both. I mentioned earlier that you can start your photo marketing in high gear—at the top, so to speak. However, if you are a newcomer to the field of photo marketing, you will find the lower-paying markets a good testing ground. The smaller markets are more likely to tolerate errors as you refine your professionalism. And they offer other pluses: Many of these lower-paying markets are based on special-interest themes that might reflect your own views. Their editors often have small budgets, but big hearts. They are willing to give helpful advice and to provide you with copies of your published photographs for your files.

Depending on your Track B list and your Market List, you'll probably be dealing primarily with editors in fee ranges 5 to 2.

And why won't you deal with Range 1? Although I've covered this question in Chapter 3, it bears repeating. Range 1 is a closed market. Photobuyers who can pay $100 to $250 (and more) for a black-and-white photograph also enjoy the convenience of having a number of top-flight stock photographers at their disposal, as well as access to the major stock photo agencies. Getting excellent pictures is no problem for them. Neither is the question of cost. The modus operandi of Range 1 markets is to deal with pros they've bought from before and who have established a track record with them. You don't necessarily have to live within the shadow of the World Trade Towers to be included in the stable of photographers of a photobuyer who pays in Range 1, but you do have to have high visibility and a known reliability factor. For example, if you are listed in *Magazine Industry Market Place, The Black Book,* or *Stock Photo Assignment Sourcebook* (see the Bibliography), etc., as a photographer, or if you subscribe to *Photobulletin* or *Photomarket* (see the Bibliography) you no doubt already have high visibility. This chapter may not apply to you.

If this sounds like a chicken-or-egg situation, it is. It takes an immense investment of time and concentration on the single-minded goal of breaking into Range 1 to create a chance for yourself in this closed market. It can be done, but as I've mentioned before, it requires a freewheeling lifestyle, frenetic work habits, and a willingness to be always on call. Some thrive on it. If your inclinations aren't in this direction, the struggle to break into Range 1 will deprive you of valuable progress you could be making in establishing your own gold mine of markets in the 5-to-2 ranges.

This may sound as if I'm attempting to protect the established stock photo professionals. I'm not. They protect themselves by working at their careers ten to fifteen hours a day. Range 1 photobuyers realize this, and when they award a large commission, they turn to the established stock photographers or stock photo agencies who have proven performance records.

Some books say, in effect, "You, too, can start today successfully writing and selling screenplays, television scripts, and songs." I'm aware that some books on marketing photographs similarly imply that it's possible to step right in and sell your photographs to the Range 1 markets. To that I say it's also possible to win a game of chance with 50,000 players. This book and the pricing system it sets forth show you how to avoid such a sweepstakes marketing approach—an approach that, from my experience, is nothing short of misleading. Every now and then, you do hear about someone new to the field who sold a single picture for $750. My own research shows that most such cases result in small actual return, once out-of-pocket marketing costs, downtime expense, and mental investment are considered. Also, the one-picture sale frequently has little bearing on establishing possibilities for repeat sales. You can expect a larger return, for a smaller investment of time, in selling one of your pictures ten times for $75.

The established pros in the field have a distinct advantage over you in approaching Range 1 markets: their names. (Remember, photobuyers aren't bowled over by a portfolio of excellent pictures. Excellent pictures and talent are everywhere.) But you have an advantage in approaching Range 2-to-5 markets: you can sell pictures of your own choice on your own timetable without changing your lifestyle.

Using the Pricing System: What to Charge

As I indicated earlier, the fee for a particular photograph will vary according to who is using it. This presents the problem, "How do I determine which range to charge a particular market?"

There are three standard answers: (1) Guess; (2) ask; (3) research it. All three are viable alternatives.

Guessing—educated guessing, that is—will become an important tool for you as you progress. You'll be able to judge a magazine by its cover. Once you know what comparable periodicals and books are paying, you'll find it easier to be on target with your pricing. Figure on using guessing later in the game, after you've racked up some experience.

Asking would be easy if the information were readily given by buyers, but photobuyers are sometimes hesitant to reveal such information to unknowns. Most photobuyers, however, provide *photographer's guidelines*. Write to each photobuyer on your Market List, using professional-looking stationery, and request a photo guideline sheet. (Be sure to include SASE.) The guidelines (of their picture needs) often include price information. If you approach a photobuyer by phone or in person, phrase your question this way: "What is your payment range for black-and-white and for color?" Since photobuyers always work within a given range, you are saying two things to photobuyers: (1) you know something about pricing if you ask for a *range* rather than a set fee; and (2) you allow editors to save face and not have to commit themselves (which means you won't be coming back later with, "But you said such and such. . . ."). Editors will usually cooperate when your question is worded in this manner. However, before you embark on your quest for price-range information, review Chapter 7, on dealing with photobuyers by phone, by mail, and in person.

Researching your answer might be easiest for you. The first direction to turn would be to the marketing directories and reference guides listed on pages 57, 58, and 59. Remember that fees quoted in a national directory are probably going to be conservative, that is, they will be the lower figure (the minimum) on the pricing guide in Table 8-1.

As an example, let's say in your research you find that the published fee for a black-and-white print for *Golf Today* magazine is $35. You can assume that this magazine will pay in Range 3 ($35 to $50 for a black-and-white, $125 to $150 for a color transparency, inside one-time use).

Many market directories will also give circulation figures, which are invaluable in determining the price ranges of publications that are similar. For example, if *Golf Today* pays in Range 3 and their circulation is 800,000, we can assume that another magazine, *Teen Golf Digest,* with a circulation of 400,000 and with similar advertising accounts, might pay in Range 4. If *National Golf Review* has a circulation of 1,000,000 and stronger advertising support than *Golf Today,* we can figure that they probably pay in Range 2 ($50 to $100 per black-and-white or $150 to $300 per color, inside, one-time editorial use). These examples can give you a base from which to start.

Payment for Other Uses

Again, the fee ranges in Table 8-1 apply to *inside editorial use.* As I mentioned, if your photograph is used by the publisher for a different purpose, you should receive a higher fee.

Publications, of course, will be local, regional, or national in scope. You should be compensated accordingly. National use carries the most generous compensation, of course, but keep in mind that sometimes a national magazine will be limited to a highly specialized audience and thus yield a lower pay rate. For example, a skydiving magazine would be limited in its impact, even though it might have national circulation. So would a national magazine directed to Baptists or Methodists.

Table 8-2 provides a system for arriving at a fair price to charge for other-than-inside use of your photos, no matter what level publishing market you're dealing with. Take the price you normally receive for one picture from that market, then multiply it by the factor that represents the purpose for which the photo will be used.

To arrive at a "ball park" fee for use of your picture when it is used for a purpose other than inside editorial use, multiply these factors times the figures in Table 8-1.

**Advertising

National	7.144
Regional	3.155
Limited	2.867
Local	1.621

Annual Reports	1.429

Audiovisual packages

National	1.621
Limited	1.429
Cover	2.859
Advertising	3.155

Brochures

Inside

Limited	1.429
National	2.867

Cover

Limited	1.621
National	2.859

Calendar

Exclusive (limited three-year rights)	2.143
One-time	1.429
World rights	50% additional
Advertising	3.155

Coffee table books (for inside editorial use, see Table 8-1)

Chapter head	1.621
Cover	2.859
Advertising	3.155

Contests (Payment based on contest rules. Allow only limited rights to your winning entry, never all rights.)

**Curriculum

Chapter head	1.429
Cover	1.621
Advertising	2.143
Montage	negotiable

Decor photography

Sold by an agency

Framed prints	(find out what royalties the competition is paying)
Limited editions	Negotiate

Sold by yourself

Framed prints	(sell to a distributor in volume at one-third his retail fee)
Limited editions	Negotiate, but expect a wide range depending on client, use, and your "name."

**Encyclopedias

Chapter head	1.621
Cover	2.143
Advertising	3.155

Table 8-2. Pricing Guide Two.

Filmstrips

Educational	1.429
Industry	1.621
Cover	2.859
Advertising	3.155

Gift wrap   2.859

Greeting cards

Exclusive (limited three-year rights)	2.143
One-time	1.429
World rights	50% additional
Advertising	3.155

**Hardcover books

(See also: Paperbacks, Coffee table books, Textbooks, Encyclopedias)

Jacket or cover

National	2.859
Limited	1.621

Chapter head	1.429
World rights	50% additional
Advertising	3.155

**House Magazines

Cover

Limited	1.429
National	2.143

*Magazines

Cover

Limited	1.429
Regional	1.621
National	5.716

Motion pictures

Nonprofit	1.255
Experimental	1.429
Test	1.621
Limited	1.429
Regional	1.621
National	2.143

*Newspapers, news, news services

Cover

Limited	1.429
Regional	1.621
National	2.143

Spectacular exceptions (disasters, etc.): Consult your directories (or the library) to determine competing national news agencies or periodicals and then put the picture up for bids on a limited-rights basis. An agent might be your best bet.

*Nonprofit organization

Regional	1.429
National	2.143
Poster	3.155

Paperback books—editorial (see also Hardcover books)

Cover

National	2.859
Limited	1.621

World rights	50% additional

Place mats

Exclusive (limited three-year rights)	2.143
One-time	1.429
World rights	50% additional
Advertising	3.155

Table 8-2. (cont.)

Playing cards		Puzzles	
Exclusive (limited three-year rights)	2.143	Exclusive (limited three-year rights)	2.143
One-time	1.429	One-time	1.429
World rights	50% additional	World rights	50% additional
Advertising	3.155	Advertising	3.155

Postcards		Record covers	
Exclusive (limited three-year rights)	2.143	Limited	1.621
One-time (national)	1.621	National	
One-time (regional)	1.429	Front	2.143
One-time (local)	1.077	Back	1.621
Advertising	2.188	Wraparound	4.211
World rights	50% additional	Advertising	3.155
		Promotion	1.429

Posters		*Textbooks (see also Hardcover books)	
Exclusive (limited three-year rights)	2.143	Chapter head	1.429
One-time	1.429	Cover	2.143
World rights	50% additional	Advertising	3.155
Advertising	3.155		

Product packages		*Trade publications	
		Cover	
Limited	1.621	Limited	1.429
National	5.716	Regional	1.621
		National	3.155

Public relations		Video	
		Commercial	
Limited	1.429	Nonprofit	1.621
Local	1.429	Limited	2.444
Regional	1.621	National	6.152
National	3.155		
		Video disc	
		Educational	1.429
		Industry	1.621
		Advertising	3.155

*For inside editorial use, see Table 8-1.

**A general rule for photographs used in a publisher's advertising campaign: charge 5 percent of the space rate the publisher is paying. Space rate information is available by phoning the newspaper, magazine, etc.

Note: If your photo is digitized and used as part of a digital photo, use this formula: Ascertain the advertising page-rate of the periodical. Depending on image-use, size, and what percent of your photo was used, charge accordingly.

Table 8-2. (cont.)

For example, if a photobuyer in Range 3 (see Table 8-1) who normally pays $50 for a black-and-white would like to use one of your photographs for local public-relations use, multiply $50 by the factor 1.429 to come up with a round figure of $75 ($71.450). To figure the fee for the same black-and-white photograph to the same market for use in a *national* advertisement, multiply $50 by the factor 7.144 and you get $350 ($357.200).

For the sake of completeness, Table 8-2 includes uses such as advertising, calendars, record covers, postcards, and video discs; these are all commercial areas that publishers sometimes delve into. (Table 8-2 applies to projects by publishers or publishing companies, not to commercial uses by ad agencies, calendar companies, and the like.) Most often, however, you will use Table 8-2 to figure fees for book or magazine covers, catalog promotions of a periodical or book, chapter heads, informational brochures, and similar editorially connected uses.

Pricing your photographs for covers or other special uses is easy if you follow the pricing guidelines in Table 8-2. The key is to determine the photobuyer's basic budget range. Once you have that, all other prices will fall into line when you use this factor system. Considerations such as inflation or a drop or raise in the photobuyer's fee structure will not be a problem. You simply adjust the price-range number accordingly.

One final word regarding the use of Table 8-2: When you take the appropriate factor, whether you multiply it by the lower or higher figure of a fee range or pick a figure in the middle depends solely on your own experience and/or judgment with regard to that particular market or photobuyer. If your reliability factor has been high with the client and you're confident of the quality of your pictures, aggressively market them. Aim for the highest fee practical (see "Negotiating Your Fee" in Chapter 11) that still keeps the door open for future assignments from the same people.

In the end, the buck stops with you. You will have to be the final judge in setting the price. As you gain experience, you will come to know each magazine or publishing house; you will know their photobuyers and the temper and tone of your relationships with them. All of these factors will help you to fine-tune your pricing.

Within the Price Range, Should You Charge the High End or the Low End?

There's an adage in the business world, "You can always come down in your fee, but you can't go up." For the service photographer this is usually true. As a stock photographer, it will also be true when you seek assignments. You will want to negotiate for the highest fee (see Chapter 11).

As a newcomer to the field of stock photography, however, initially you will want to charge the lower figure of the price range. Why? Because you are an unknown to the photobuyer. He has little to gain if you charge the maximum fee within the range. He already has a roster of high-priced but familiar photographers with a known reliability factor who would require less time to deal with. But if your pictures are on target and your fee is at the lower end of the range, he can justify the time taken out from his busy day to instruct you in the submission procedures, holding requirements, payment policies, etc., unique to his publishing house. Once you have made two or three sales to the photobuyer, test the waters by raising your fee on your next statement. Since you already know the photobuyer's price range, you know you won't exceed his maximum.

Think in terms of long-range goals. You have done your marketing homework. You know that your PMS/A is matched with your personalized Market List. By progressing patiently up the pay-range scale, you'll gain experience and eventually become a top-notch contributor to each of the outlets on your Market List. Most successful pros in any field will tell you this is the way it's done. After all, actors start at the community theater level; baseball players start in the minor leagues.

Second Use of Your Pictures

As a stock photographer, you price your pictures on a one-time-use basis. In effect, you are renting your pictures to the photobuyer. What happens if the photobuyer wants to rent your picture a second time? Should he use it free, or at a discount, or at the same fee?

Many publishing houses have set policies on photo re-use. But you can set policies also. For a starting point, you can use the guide in Table 8-3.

Here is an exception to these re-use guidelines: If a publishing house has retained your picture in its central art library and re-uses it in a new format, you should expect 75 percent and not 100 percent. The 25 per-

	Percent of original fee
For use in same format as original use (e.g., in a revision, new printing)	75%
For use in an anthology	75%
For use in a new format (a new or different project)	100%
For use as a cover, in advertising, public relations, filmstrip, etc.	See Pricing Guide Two.

Table 8-3. Pricing guide for photo re-use.

cent in such a case is understood as a privilege fee for holding your pictures in the library; it goes toward the library's operating costs and services.

State Your Fee

Always state your fee when you submit pictures to a photobuyer (assuming you've done your homework and can quote a fee you know is within the photobuyer's range). This practice will increase your chances for sales. Why? Photobuyers tell me that one of the main deterrents to purchasing a picture from a submission is that the photographer failed to state a fee in the cover letter.

When I first began submitting photographs, I fell into the hesitancy trap. I hesitated to put down a fee. I believed that the photobuyer would want my picture so much that he would phone me or write and ask for the fee, or better still, tell me what he would pay.

It didn't work out that way. Yes, the photobuyer wanted my picture. But he would have to go through the busywork of getting in touch with me (and what if I were out of town?), perhaps negotiate with me, and endure time-consuming back-and-forth communication for someone he wasn't even familiar with. And he had a deadline to meet. So to avoid those problems, he would use a second-best picture that was available and had a price on it. (Have you ever wondered why some pictures are published that are not as good as yours? This is one reason.)

The fee you are charging is the most important element in your cover letter (except for spelling the photobuyer's name correctly). If you can't come up with a price you know is within the buyer's range, make an educated guess based on your research. Even a guess too high or too low can result in a sale that you might not have made if you had quoted no fee at all. When all else fails, use a rubber stamp that says "for publication at your usual rates." By telling you this, however, I hope I haven't given you license not to do your homework.

Pricing the Service Photo

Although this book is written for the stock photographer, from time to time every stock photographer finds himself involved in a service-photography assignment. Briefly, here are some tips for gauging a fair price for your now-and-then stints as a service photographer.

Three excellent guidebooks exist for the person who sells photography in the following assignment areas: advertising illustration; architectural; general commercial (studio and/or location); photojournalism, photo reporting; public relations; publicity.

These are the price guides:

ASMP—*Guide to Professional Business
Practices in Photography*
205 Lexington Ave.
New York, NY 10016

ASMP—*Stock Photography Handbook*
(same address as above)

Blue Book of Photography Prices
by Thomas I. Perrett
Photography Research Institute
Carson Endowment
21237 S. Moneta Ave.
Carson, CA 90745

ASMP—Guide to Professional Business Practices in Photography is a compilation of rate surveys made among the highest-paid photographers in the country. If some of the markets on your Market List are over a quarter-million in circulation, this book could be worth the investment (around $25). The ASMP (American Society of Magazine Photographers) is an organization of more than three thousand media photographers. (I was a member in the 1960s but dropped my membership when I changed my focus from service photography to photo illustration.)

Service photography, because of the complexities and the high fees often involved, requires extra attention to precision when you negotiate a picture sale or an assignment. The ASMP book will inform you about book-publishing contracts, settlement of disputes, trade definitions, photographer-agency relationships, copyright, stock photo sales, and insurance. It also contains forms (which you can adapt to your own needs) for assignment confirmations, delivery memos, and model releases. Remember, though, that the mission of the ASMP book is to guide the photographer who operates in a city of at least one million population, or who deals with publications of 250,000 circulation or higher. If you employ the ASMP guidelines or forms outside of those parameters, you and your clients might find the experience less than optimum. Keep in mind that it is the photobuyer who approves the assignment, initials the proposal, or forwards a statement for reimbursement.

So use the ASMP book wisely. It was conceived and produced for top pros in the big leagues of Madison Avenue and parts West. A book is always the extended shadow of its author; in this case, the book was written by a committee. Unless you have lucked into a top-paying, Range 1 assignment, modify the ASMP guidelines accordingly. (Incidentally, the ASMP underscores that fees mentioned in the guide are only guidelines by stating in their introduction, "ASMP DOES NOT SET RATES.")

The ASMP is a group of hardworking photographers who devote their energy and time to setting and maintaining high standards for the industry. As a group they are in a position to exert pressure for the betterment of working policies for service photographers. If you lean toward service photography and would like more information about the ASMP, write to them at 205 Lexington Avenue, New York, NY 10016.

As a service photographer, you probably know that a Hilton hotel room or a Hertz rental car costs about 25 percent less in smaller cities. The same reduced rates hold for photography assignments and stock sales in smaller cities. The *Blue Book of Photography Prices* has been produced by Thomas Perrett since 1972. Although the *Blue Book* is more costly than the ASMP book, it may be of greater value to you if you are a service photographer and working with accounts in smaller cities.

The *Blue Book* is actually a three-ring notebook, and it's revised every month to reflect inflation and changes in the industry. Because the book was originally compiled from questionnaires sent to photographers throughout the country (as was the ASMP *Stock Photography Handbook*), you can be reasonably sure that the suggested prices for architectural, public relations, fashion, and advertising photography are realistic. The *Blue Book* can save you research time as well as dollars by telling you what photographers across the nation actually receive for their service photography.

If you don't wish to invest in either of these pricing guides, you can determine the going rate in your area by a somewhat roundabout route. It's sometimes difficult to get the information from other photographers or the photobuyers themselves. (Unlike photo illustrators who work in their own market and subject areas, and therefore don't compete with other photographers for the same dollar, service photographers very often compete with each other for specific assignments and are not eager to give information to newcomers.) Do ask other photographers and photobuyers, but do it long-distance—go to a large library and get hold of the Yellow Pages of several cities around the country that are of comparable size to your own. Pick out several photographers and photobuyers and phone them (before 8:00 a.m. and after 5:00 p.m. your time, when possible, to take advantage of lower rates) to find out what they consider fair fees. Be sure to establish early in the conversation that you are calling long-distance. The time and money spent in such research will save you hundreds of dollars in either underpricing or accounts lost (assignments missed) because of overpricing.

The Lowest Fee Possible: Nothing

I can't close this chapter without a word about zero-price marketing.

Some publishing houses have no budget for photography. They have budgets for carpenters, secretaries, printers, and the IRS, but they don't budget for you, the stock photographer.

If you discover some of these nonpaying markets on your Market List, chalk it up to the research and refinement inherent in hammering out a strong Market List, and delete these markets or let them sink to the bottom.

You may wish to let one or two no-pay markets stay in at the bottom because you feel they'll serve as a showcase for your photography. As a newcomer, you want to build your published-pictures file as quickly as possible. Your credit line beside your pictures will establish your credibility and lead to other sales. Aside from the free-advertising benefit you reap from such publications, you can request copies (tearsheets) of your published picture(s) as payment. The usual method is to request three copies after publication. If you're interested in several dozen copies, contact the photobuyer a month before publication and ask the publishing house to give you or sell you *overrun* pages. (They'll let the press run a little longer for your order, generally for a dime a page.) Request a number of these copies, and use them as stuffers in your mailings to other prospective photobuyers. (See Chapter 10.) There's also a chance that some no-pay markets may be ground-floor businesses with promise— i.e., markets that eventually will grow to healthy budgets for photography, and that will remember and appreciate you when they do, *if* you keep reminding them of your existence. (It's always up to you to keep the communications alive.)

Once you have attained whatever benefits you sought in allowing your pictures to be published free, begin working up toward the top of your Market List, where pricing is healthy and lucrative.

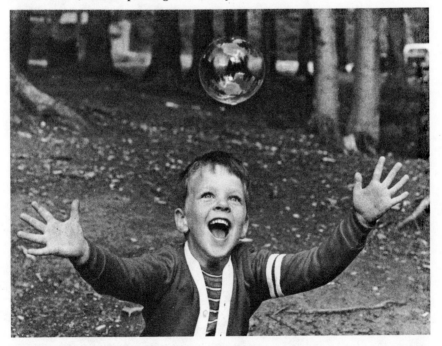

Joy! to the reader, and also to the photographer—me! Because this picture taught me how to market my pictures. It was taken twenty years ago, sold right away, and has been selling over and over again ever since. Sales from this one picture have paid for all of my camera and darkroom equipment. Editors use it for articles on children's games, summer recreation, health, playtime activities, camping—not to mention articles in textbooks on happiness, sorrow, depression, and exuberance. To date, it has earned nearly $3,000. The cash register keeps ringing.

9.
Managing
Your
Mail-Marketing
Operation

Our Postal Service—A Bargain for the Photo Illustrator

As a stock photographer, you can market your pictures almost entirely by mail. Photobuyers like working this way. It saves them time and it's efficient. For you, marketing by mail is less expensive than costly personal visits. The risk? Minimal. Here at PhotoSource International I've been engaged in a long campaign to debunk the myth of photos missing in the mail.

We've all heard horror stories about the U.S. Postal Service, but I've found the vast majority of those "lost picture" stories to be untrue. For example, at my seminars I ask people to describe their experiences with photographs *lost* in the mail. When the facts are laid out, I've yet to discover one case that could be documented. When photos fail to arrive at their destination or return home, it most frequently is the photographer's fault: typical reasons are incorrect address, incorrect editor, no editor, no ZIP code, no return address, no identification on prints or slides, poor packaging. We sometimes get a call from a photobuyer who asks, "Can you locate the address of Harrison Jones for us? We want to send him a check, but all we have is a slide with his name on it. No address. No phone."

Stock photo agencies and film processors must know something about the U.S. mail. They have shipped pictures across the nation and the globe for years. Magazines use the postal service successfully, as do Sears, Spiegel and Calumet.

Not that it isn't easy to have a photograph damaged or lost in the mail. Simply ship it out in a flimsy envelope and don't identify it as yours. The odds are you'll never see the picture again.

If there is a risk, it is in *not* sending your pictures through the mail. Pictures gathering dust in your files are hazardous to your financial health.

Preparing Your Stock Photos for Market

The first impression a photobuyer has of you comes from the way you package and present your material. Photobuyers assume that the care you've given to your packaging reflects the care you take in your picture taking and your attentiveness to their needs. They believe they are paying you top dollar for your product. They expect you to deliver a top product. If you want first-class treatment from a photobuyer, give *him/her* first-class treatment.

Sending Black-and-Whites

If your black-and-whites are dog-eared, in need of trimming and spotting, they may miss the final cut. Often excellent pictures never reach final layout boards because they make such a poor first impression that nobody looks beyond it. As the saying goes, "You never get a second chance at a first impression." Your stock photos make the rounds of many buyers, so check your prints regularly to trim any edge splits or dog-ears. Before submitting black-and-white 8x10s, retouch any flecks. For tips on how to spot your black-and-whites, see Appendix C.

Use plastic sleeves to protect your black-and-whites. These sleeves present a fresh, professional, and cared-for appearance, and they hold your prints in a convenient bundle for the editor. They come in 8½"x11" (or larger) size and are available from the plastic distribution houses listed in the Yellow Pages of metropolitan phone books. One sleeve can hold up to fifteen single-weight or ten double-weight black-and-white prints.

Print Multiple Copies

Successful stock photographers develop a solid Market List and then supply on-target pictures to photobuyers on that list. To save darkroom time, print several copies of each black-and-white at one session, and distribute them simultaneously to appropriate buyers on your list, or keep them on hand as backups in your files. Use a similar technique for color by shooting several originals of your subject when on the scene. (See Color, Chapter 5.)

Should you send contact sheets as part of your mail marketing system? Only rarely will a buyer want to see contact sheets. If you were on assignment, for example, it's conceivable the editor would want to see other selection possibilities. He would ask you to pre-edit them, and you would circle with a grease pencil alternative shots. Otherwise, don't display your less-than-perfect pictures by sending contact sheets.

Should you send negatives? If an editor wants your negs, it's probably to make better prints than those you have submitted. Rather than run the risk of damage to your negatives, volunteer to reprint the pictures or to have a custom lab print them. Avoid sending negatives to photobuyers.

Sending Transparencies

To best protect your transparencies, send them in vinyl sleeves. Don't send glass mounts. Photobuyers don't work with them; they're cumbersome, and they do break. Use slides that have been mounted in plastic or cardboard, or else unmounted. For mounted slides, use the popular vinyl pages that have twelve 2¼-inch or twenty 35mm-size pockets on one page. For unmounted transparencies, the vinyl pages are also useful. Four 4x5s, two 5x7s, or one 8x10 can fit in one page. If you have only a few transparencies to submit, cut the page in half or quarters. Send your selection in a smaller envelope. Single acetate sleeves are another option for protecting mounted or unmounted transparencies. They're available at photo supply houses. In the past, there has been some concern as to whether the polyvinylchloride (PVC) in vinyl sleeves can damage a slide. Use this rule: Ship your slides in thick vinyl (or nonvinyl) sleeves, but store your slides in archival plastic pages. A thin plastic page should not be used to ship your slides because the slides fall out too easily.

When you submit transparencies, you might wish to keep not only a numerical record of your submission but a visual record as well. Here are two ways:

1. Make a color photocopy (at a library, Xerox® Center, bank, or print shop).
2. Make a 35mm (black-and-white or color) shot of your slides on your light box. Keep the results on file until your slides are returned.

How can you caption unmounted transparencies? Fit your information on an adhesive label and place this at the bottom of the protective sleeve or vinyl page pocket where it won't cover the image. If you decide you would like to mount your transparencies at a later date, you can order mounts from Kalt Corporation, 2036 Broadway St., Santa Monica, CA 90406.

Inexpensive protective vinyl (or similar plastic) transparency-holder pages are available from the following:

PHOTAK
P.O. Box 2104
Neenah, WI 54956

Bardes "Clearlast"
5245 W. Clinton Ave.
Milwaukee, WI 53223

Light Impressions
439 Monroe Ave.
Box 940A, Loop Station
Rochester, NY 14603

Kleer Vu Plastics
Kleer Vu Dr. #7
Brownsville, TN 38012

Phototix
Princeton Retail Systems
4 Village Cir.
Westfield, NJ 07090

Plastican
10 Park Place, Butler Court
Butler, NJ 07405

20th Century Plastics
3628 Crenshaw Blvd.
Box 15715A
Los Angeles, CA 90016

Unicolor Photo Systems
7200 W. Huron River Dr.
Dexter, MI 48130

These companies also produce single-slide vinyl protectors. Insert the protected slide in the pocket. When a buyer extracts it from the full-page sheet, you'll be doubly protected.

Identify Your Prints and Transparencies

Identify each of your black-and-white prints with a rubber stamp on the back that includes the © copyright notice and your name, address, and telephone number. (Print neatly and lightly on black-and-whites so the impression doesn't come through.) Include also your picture identification number (see Chapter 13).

RC papers do not take the standard rubber-stamp ink. Circumvent this problem by first placing a blank label on the back of your print, then rubber-stamping the label. Or use spirit-base ink and pen the identification information by hand. The ink has a tendency to dry up, but keeping it in a Ziploc bag solves this. An excellent source for rubber stamps and inks is Jackson Marking Products Company, Brownsville Road, Mt. Vernon, IL 62864. 1(800)851-4954. Their fast-dry stamp pad is called the Mark II.

Do not include a date code in your identification system. Editors will recognize the date, and your picture will be dated before its time. If slides have a date printed on the side, cover it with a label imprinted with your identification details. If for some reason you need a date, put it in Roman numerals, or use an alphabetical code—for example, A = 1, B = 2, C = 3, etc. The fifth month could be E, and the year '87 would be HG (E/HG).

Captions

Because your pictures will be used as illustrations, not as documentation or news pictures, captions will seldom be necessary. Besides, in most cases the editor is looking for a picture to fit a theme or use he has in mind; he may already have written the caption.

Captions are sometimes necessary for travel pictures, wildlife, horticulture, and related themes, or picture sequences. When you need to include captions, type them all on one page, and key them by number to each photograph or slide. Keep a carbon or photocopy for yourself. As a general rule, make your captions brief, and include who, what, where, when, why. The editor will tailor the information to the publication's style.

Before packing up your photographs to send off to a prospective buyer, give them this checklist test:

Selection—Do your photographs fall within the specialized interest area of the photobuyer?

Style—Do your photographs follow the illustrative style the buyer is partial to?

Quantity—Are you sending enough? Generally, you should submit a minimum of two dozen, a maximum of one hundred. There are exceptions to this, such as the single, truly spectacular shot that you might rush to an editor because of its timeliness or for another reason.

Quality—Can your photographs compete in aesthetic and technical quality with stock photos the buyer has previously used?

Appearance—Are your prints and transparencies neat and professionally presented? If your photos don't conform to the suggestions I've given, then hold off submitting. Eagerness is a virtue, but as in any contest, you must match it with preparedness.

Packaging: The Key to Looking Like a Pro

Once you have your photos prepared, present them in a professional package. One editor told me that she receives about 20 pounds of mail every morning. She separates it into two piles: one that she will tackle immediately and a second that she will look at if and when time permits. I asked her how she determined which pile things belonged in, and she answered, "By the way they're packaged."

Your package will be competing with all those other pounds of freelance material when it arrives. The secret of marketing your pictures is to match your PMS/A with the correct Market List. But if the editor never sees your pictures (because of faulty packaging), they won't get their chance.

Use a packaging system that is trim, sturdy, and stands out. I recommend large white mailers made of stiff cardboard. They give an excellent appearance and have a slotted end-flap that makes them easy and fast to open and close. Buyers can use the same mailer to return unused photographs. (Since you can't be sure the buyer will automatically reuse your envelope [or mailing carton as it's called in the industry], have a rubber stamp or label made that reads: "Open Carefully for Reuse," or "Mailer Re-usable," and put it on the flap of the envelope.) The mailers can be recycled several times, since they are made of heavy material and hold up well. Place your new address label over the existing label, and white self-apply labels (available at stationery stores and through computer sales catalogs) over previous stamps and markings. (I've tracked down six manufacturers of white mailers: Calumet Carton, 16920 S. State Street, South Holland, IL 60473; Curtis 1000, 1000 Sun Valley Drive, Rosewell, GA 30076; MAIL SAFE, Chicago Packaging, Station 12, 1350 South Canal, Chicago IL 60607; PACK•A•LOPE, International Envelope Company, Number 11 Crozerville Road, Box 2150A, Dept. 52, Aston, PA 19014; and Columbian Safeway Mailer, WESTVACO, Envelope Division, Springfield, MA 01101; Freestyle Sales Company, Dept. B, 5120 Sunset Blvd., Los Angeles, CA 90027.)

This type of mailer also saves you from having to pack your photographs between two pieces of cardboard, wrap rubber bands around same, and then stuff the result into a manila envelope. When editors have to unwrap this type of submission twenty times a day, you can understand why they welcome a submission in a cardboard envelope, where pictures tucked in a plastic sleeve slide in and out easily. Manila-colored envelopes also have the disadvantage that postal workers tend to identify the manila color as fourth-class. Also, photobuyers might think of your photos as fourth class and worse, you may think they are. Go first class, and mail in a white envelope. It will help your package receive the tender care it deserves both coming and going.

Another alternative, especially when you are mailing out large shipments of pictures (50 to 250) is to use the mailing cartons used for 16mm movie films, available at film carton supply houses. Since these cartons are circular or oval in shape, place styrofoam inside and cut a hole $8\frac{1}{4}$x$10\frac{1}{2}$ inches in the center for your prints. Your pictures will be well protected.

As long as we're considering the book-by-its-cover judgment, invest in some personalized, self-apply address labels. Your reliability factor will gain points if your logo on the labels is distinctive. Also have return labels printed with your name and address, which you'll include on the inside of your package with a SASE for the editor.

How to Send Your Submissions

Unless you ship via the "express" services or subscribe to the UPS service (for a monthly fee, UPS comes to your home or office every day for pickup), you will no doubt be sending your package via the U.S. mail. I have found the mail and UPS equally acceptable. Assuming you will use the U.S. Postal Service, you will find that *priority mail* treats your packages with respect and moves them quickly to their destinations, for the least cost. (Straight fourth-class mail is less costly, but receives rougher handling.) Priority mail is placed in the first-class bin.

If you prefer to ensure that a package receives extra care, send it fourth-class, *special handling*. It will cost more than priority mail, but your material will be handled with care. Fourth-class mail, however, does not arrive as quickly as priority mail.

Whether you use priority mail or fourth-class special handling, you might want to consider insuring your package. (The best bargain is the $15 to $50 coverage for less than a dollar. Postal insurance rates change, so give your local post office a call for current rates.) Keep in mind that in the event of damage or loss, the U.S. Postal Service considers your pictures worth only the cost of replacement film. Your main reasons for getting insurance will be the extra care it guarantees your package and the receipt the delivery person collects from the recipient. The post office will have documentation that your package arrived if you need to trace it. (For less than a dollar more, you can also have a return receipt sent directly to you.) This document can come in handy if the photobuyer ever says, "I didn't receive your shipment."

Shipping your photos by registered mail is good insurance, too, of course, but expensive. The lower cost of sending material via fourth-class/special handling or priority mail for regular shipments usually outweighs the speed advantages of registered mail or Express Mail. I'm aware that many photography books recommend sending your shipment via registered mail. I'm also aware that the authors of those books are not engaged in stock photography as their principal source of income. Registered mail is expensive.

Insuring or registering your photos for $15 or $1,500 will not ensure that you will receive that amount if they are lost or damaged. Only if you have receipts, showing how much you have been paid for your pictures previously, will you have a case. Otherwise you'll receive only the replacement cost—about fifty cents for each slide or print. The best insurance is *prevention*. Use the packaging techniques I've described here and you will have little or no grief.

Be sure to include some kind of return postage in your package. Buyers not only expect it, they demand it. Some refuse to send photographs back if return postage is not included. Purchase a small postal scale at a stationery store, and you can easily figure your postage costs at home.

There are three acceptable ways to include return postage (SASE) described as follows:*

1. If you use a manila envelope packaging system, affix the stamps to a manila envelope with your return address, fold, and include in your package.

2. Place loose stamps in the amount of the return postage in a small (transparent) coin envelope, available at hobby stores. Tape (don't staple) this envelope to your cover letter. This method has the advantage that often the photobuyer will return the stamps to you—unused. You can interpret this as a sign that the photobuyer is encouraging you to submit your pictures again in the future.

3. Write a check on your business checking account for the amount of return postage. Make it out to the publishing house, agency, etc. Your reliability factor will zoom upward, and nine times out of ten, you'll receive the check back, uncashed. Besides, the bookkeeping department at the photobuyer's probably has no accounting system for such checks. Another advantage: Say by rare chance the client happens to lose or damage a print and reports to you they have no record of receiving the pic-

*Foreign subscribers: Contact your local Postal Service and purchase International Reply Coupons and include them as equivalent return postage.

tures; if they cashed the check, you would have proof that they received your submission.

Writing the Cover Letter

Always include a cover letter in your package. But remember that photobuyers are faced with the task of sifting through hundreds of photo submissions weekly. They don't appreciate lengthy letters that ask questions or detail F-stops, shutter speeds, or other superfluous technicalities. Such data is valid for salon photography, or the art photo magazines, but not in stock photography.

If you do feel compelled to ask a specific question (and sometimes it's necessary), write your question out on a separate sheet of paper and enclose SASE for easy reply.

The shorter your cover letter the better. Your personal history as a photographer, or where and when you captured the enclosed scenes, are of little interest to the photobuyer. All you really need in the cover letter is confirmation of the number of photos enclosed, your fee, and the rights you are selling. Let your pictures speak for themselves.

Your cover letter should be addressed to a specific person, whose name you'll find by consulting your Market List or by calling the reception desk of the publishing firm or agency. A typical cover letter might read like the one in Figure 9-1.

This cover letter may not win any literary awards, but it's the kind photobuyers welcome. It tells them everything they want to know about your submission.

Photobuyers like to deal with photographers with a high reliability factor—photographers who can supply them with a steady stream of quality pictures in the photobuyers' specialized interest areas. They don't want to go through the time-consuming process of developing a working relationship with photographers who can supply only a picture or two every now and then. The right cover letter will signal to the photobuyer that you are not a once-in-a-while supplier.

First-Class Stationery

To give a professional impression, have your cover letter typeset. If this isn't practical, type it on a carbon-ribbon typewriter and then have it printed at one of the fast-print services, on 24- or 28-pound business stationery. Include your letterhead and logo for a first-class appearance. Leave the four blanks in your letter to fill in by hand for each submission (see Figure 9-1).

The strategy here is that photobuyers will not be offended by receiving a form letter but rather will welcome it as the sign of a knowledgeable working stock photographer. The message the letter telegraphs is that someone who's gone to the expense of a printed form letter on quality

YOUR LETTERHEAD

Dear _____:

Enclosed please find [number] [slides, 8x10 B&W prints] for your consideration. They are available at $_____ (color) and $_____ (B&W)*, for one-time publishing rights, inside editorial use. Additional rights are available. Please include credit line and copyright notice as indicated.

You are welcome to photocopy the enclosed picture(s) for your files for future reference. My name, address, and print no. are on the reverse side of each picture.

I'd appreciate it if you would bring the enclosed pictures to the attention of others at your [publishing house or company office] who may be interested in reviewing them.

You are welcome to hold this selection for two weeks (no holding fee). I have enclosed postage for their return.

Thank you for your attention.

Sincerely,

[Your name]

Figure 9-1. Sample cover letter to send with submissions to photobuyers.

*It's essential that you state a fee. (See Tables 8-1 and 8-2.)

stationery has more than a few photographs to market. If the pictures you submit are on target and you include an easy-to-read, concise form cover letter, you are on your way to establishing yourself as an important resource for the photobuyer.

If you have learned of a specific need a photobuyer has (through a mailed photographer's memo, announcement in a photo magazine, or listing in a market service such as *Photoletter*, *Photomarket*, *Photobulletin*, *or Photonet*), what kind of letter should you send? Again, your letter should be brief. Include many of the details listed in Figure 9-1. However, also include the number or chapter of the book, brochure, or article, for which the photos have been requested. Photobuyers often work on a dozen projects at a time. Knowing which project your pictures are targeted for helps!

Use a form letter if I've convinced you; otherwise, send a neatly typed letter.

Deadlines: A Necessary Evil

Because photography is only one cog in the diverse wheel of a publishing project, photos are necessarily regarded by layout people, production managers, printers, and promotion managers not as individual aesthetic works, but as elements of production value within the whole scope of the publishing venture. Book and magazine editors often have a tendency to treat photography as something that should support the text rather than the other way around. Hence, they load photo editors with impossible deadlines. If your photographs are due on such and such a date, the photo editor is not kidding. Being on time can earn you valuable points with a photobuyer.

Develop the winning habit of meeting deadlines *in advance*. It will increase both your reliability factor and the number of checks you deposit each month.

Unsolicited Submissions

The word in the street is that photobuyers look upon unsolicited submissions with disdain. This is partly true. If you were an editor of an aviation magazine and I sent you, unsolicited, a couple dozen of my best-quality horse pictures, you'd be righteously perturbed. However, if I sent a group of pictures, unsolicited, that were tailored to your needs, and showed a knowledge of aviation plus some talent with the camera, you'd be delighted, especially if I sent you an SASE for those you couldn't use.

"Most freelancers send me views of birds against the sun or close-ups of flowers, and maybe a kid with a model sailboat. Don't they ever look at our magazine?" an editor of a sailing magazine asked me.

You can understand why some editors have a tendency to lump freelancers and unsolicited pictures into the category of *undesirable*.

If you've done the proper marketing research, photobuyers will welcome your unsolicited submission. On the other hand, if you haven't figured out the thrust of the magazine or the needs of the publishing house, don't waste your time or postage and earn their ire by submitting random photos to them. You won't last long as a stock photographer, no matter how good your pictures are. Ask yourself before you send off a shipment, "Am I risking a *no-sale* on this one?" Choose a market whose needs you've pinpointed—one that you're sure of scoring with.

The Magic Query Letter

If you have advanced to a stage in your photo-marketing operation in which you are prepared to contact multiple markets on your list, here is an introductory query letter system that will prove helpful. This system is designed to hit the right buyer with the right photograph every time.

When postage was cheap (pre-1975) and photo paper was cheap (pre-1970), photographers used a shotgun method of contacting prospective markets. That is, they sent samples of their photographs almost indiscriminately to any photobuyer on any mailing list. Today's economics encourages, instead, the rifle method of reaching buyers, that is, narrowing down your prospective photobuyer list to a select Market List.

When you are ready to select targets for your query letter, concentrate on the fields of your particular interest, for example: education, medicine, sailing, gardening, botany, automotive, camping. Within your personal interest fields, you'll find specialized magazines, specialized publishing houses, specialized readers, specialized advertisers.

The age of the general audience magazine disappeared with the weekly *LIFE, Look,* and *Saturday Evening Post.* Their place was filled by the special-interest magazines, which contain subject matter ranging from hang-gliding to geoscience to executive health. The diversification continues. Gardeners have their interests featured in magazines covering houseplants, ornamentals, backyard farming, organic gardening, flowers, etc. Boat enthusiasts all have their own special magazines ranging from sailboats to submarines. Horse lovers have their own private reading magazines on the Arabian, on the quarter horse, and so on. Why venture into fields that have little or no interest to you when you are already a mini-expert in at least a half-dozen fields that could provide you with more than enough markets to choose from?

The key to the magic query method is an initial query *letter* to each prospective editor. What you say in this letter will move the editor to invite you to submit your photographs. (For simplicity I'll use the pronoun *him* throughout, with the reader's understanding that the editor can be him or her!)

The query letter, to be effective, must be brief and simple—yet spur the editor to reply immediately and request your submission for consideration. Here's how to plan your letter, individualized to each market.

You must immediately hit the buyer where his heart is: in your first sentence you must include a magic phrase that will grab his attention and rivet him to your letter.

It will take some research on your part, but once you've worked out that magic phrase, not only will your letter be read, but it will also be hearkened to and acted upon.

The majority of publications today are designed for specialized audiences. Imagine the structure of a special-interest magazine as a pyramid. At the base of the pyramid are the thousands of readers and viewers who are fans of this special area of interest. Next up on the pyramid are the people with an economic interest in this specialized area: the advertisers. Further up are the creative and production people who put the magazine together—the writers, designers, layout artists, printers, photographers, etc. At the top of the pyramid is the publishing management. The pinnacle of our pyramid contains the concept, the idea or theme upon which the magazine is based.

Now here's the key to that magic phrase. Outside appearances would have you believe that the essence of, say, a magazine called *Super Model Railroading* would be model railroads. It is not.

You're only one-eighth right. (And this is where most suppliers—writers, graphic designers, photographers—lose the trail when they initially contact a prospective editor.) Here's the essence of *Super Model Railroading*: to allow adults the *license* to buy and play with expensive toys.

In the first sentence of your query letter to the editor of this magazine, you would use a magic phrase like this: "I specialize in photographs of people enjoying their hobbies."

Let's take another example. A magazine called *Today's Professional RN* appears to have professional nursing as its theme. Yes, that's the magazine's *stated* theme. But what is its unstated theme—the subject that touches the heart of its readers, and therefore the publication's management? The essence of *Today's Professional RN*: to remind nurses that they deserve the respect and esteem accorded to other community health-care professionals such as physicians, psychologists, dentists, etc.

In the first sentence of your query letter, you would use a magic phrase like this: "I specialize in health-care photography and have in my stock file a large selection of pictures showing nurses playing a key role in our health-care system." The editors of specialized magazines are always looking out for their readers, advertisers, bosses. If the first sentence in your query letter indicates you can help in that mission, the editor will say to himself, "Now here's a person who speaks my language!"

Your job as a query-letter writer becomes one of separating illusion from reality in the publishing world. As you can see, it will take some

YOUR LETTERHEAD

Dear _____,

I am a photographer who specializes in* _____
_____ [Note: It's on these lines that you enter _____
_____ your magic phrase or sentence.] _____
_____

May I be of assistance to you? I'd like to send you a selection of my photographs for your consideration. They are available at $ ** for one-time rights, inside editorial use.

I have enclosed an SASE for your convenience. I'd look forward to working with you.

Thank you for your attention.

Yours sincerely,

[Your name]

Figure 9-2. The magic query letter.

*Or—you could say, ". . . I am a photographer who has a file of pictures that . . ."
**Insert your fee (see Chapter 5).

study on your part. But the study becomes pleasurable if you direct your research to magazines you already enjoy reading. Make a game of distinguishing between a magazine's stated theme and its real theme. You'll be surprised how easily you learn this technique, especially in the magazines on your Market List.

And what is the reaction of an editor who receives a query letter that shows no preparation on the part of the photographer? He feels insulted. He runs a tight ship. He has deadlines. He tosses the letter into the wastebasket. He's not about to show any consideration to a photographer who has not shown him the courtesy of studying his magazine.

But if you've done your job in your first sentence, and your first paragraph shows you are interested in both the magazine and the photo editor, you will have his attention. He will be alerted to your inventory of pictures, but beyond that, a few more ideas will be occurring to him:

1. If you are an informed photographer (in his field) you are a mini-expert and therefore a valuable resource to him, and you could be available for assignments.

2. Although you've said you have certain photographs which you believe to be adaptable to his needs, you might just have many more photographs that are adaptable to his needs. For example, perhaps his publishing firm is starting up a sister publication and is on the lookout for additional pictures in an allied area of interest.

The second paragraph of your query letter should confirm the attitude expressed in your first paragraph, namely that you are aware of his photo needs.

And how do you become aware of those needs? By studying the magazines you find in libraries, dentists' offices, friends' homes, business reception rooms, etc. Photo-marketing directories such as *Photographer's Market* and those listed in Table 3-1 describe thousands of magazines and list them by special-interest areas.

Before you send your query letter to an editor, request his photographers' guidelines. Most magazines provide a sheet of helpful hints to photographers, and if you contact the photobuyer on deluxe, professional stationery, complete with your logo, he'll send a sample issue of their publication as well.

You are now ready to write the magic query letter. Type it on a handsome letterhead with a clean ribbon. Figure 9-2 shows you a sample of how your query letter should sound.

You'll notice in the magic query letter that there is an abundance of *I*'s. This may seem contrary to your writing style (or training), but those *I*'s are there for a purpose: to give the editor the impression that this new recruit is dynamic, aggressive, and self-centered. (Note: Welcome to the

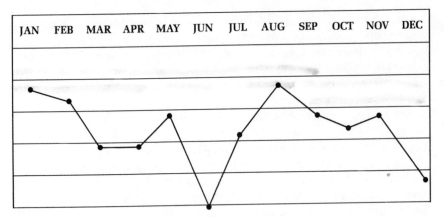

Table 9-1. Seasonal trends in photobuying.

world of business! If being dynamic, aggressive, and self-centered turns you off, you've got to reexamine and adjust your thinking. Timidity, modesty, and humility are nice attributes, but not if you want the world to see your pictures.)

In this letter, there is a good balance with the word *you.* (Most schools of persuasive writing teach that *you* is the most beautiful word in the language.) Your job as a letter writer is not really to *inform* an editor, but to move him to action, to make him *want* to see and buy your pictures. The magic query letter will put you leaps ahead of your competition because editors will *act.*

Should You Deal with Foreign Markets?

Once you are settled in to dealing with domestic markets for your stock photography, you might want to investigate the hundreds of foreign markets, some of which might be target markets for you. The easiest way to break in is to work with an established foreign stock photo house. An excellent "how-to" manual is *The Foreign Syndication Handbook* by Vicki Comiskey (Haberman Press, Bank Station Plaza, P.O. Box 71B, Merrick, NY 11566). A newsletter on the subject (in English) is *Markets Abroad,* Michael Sedge, publisher, Strawberry Media, 2460 Lexington Drive, Suite C, Owosso, MI 48867.

What Are the Heavy Purchasing Months?

Recently I sent out a questionnaire to one hundred photobuyers, asking them which months of the year are their busiest in terms of picture buying. Table 9-1 indicates that the thirty-five photobuyers who responded share one of two prime purchasing periods: midwinter and midsummer. My more than two decades of experience as a stock photographer marketing by mail confirms that these are heavy purchasing periods for a good proportion of the publishing industry.

Why midsummer and midwinter? At first glance, one might suspect editorial reasons: In midsummer, photo editors are buying for the holiday-oriented projects; in midwinter, they are buying for the beginning of the next school year.

But editorial considerations don't appear to be the case. My guesstimate would be budgetary reasons. Publishers are working on either a fiscal (July 31) or a calendar (December 31) year, which means cash flow is down in July or December, and up again in August or January.

How does this information help you as a stock photographer? Moralewise, it might help you to know why those checks aren't coming in during the months of July and December. It can also help you to market more accurately. Your marketing strategy calls for periodic mailings of photo illustrations for consideration. Note in Table 9-1 that you can increase your chances of scoring if you aim at the midwinter and midsummer months.

But before you decide that you have photo marketing down to a formula, don't forget that Table 9-1 represents a sampling of only thirty-five publishing houses. Also, some of the photobuyers, such as Rodale Press and Highlights for Children, reported that "All months are equally busy." And what about the peak in the graph in May and the dip in June? I have no concrete explanation, save editors have been known to clear their desks before departing for summer vacation! The last two weeks of December are especially dead in the publishing industry.

If your Market List leans toward textbooks, you'll want to consider this: Many textbook companies work with two different printing dates during any given year—June, for the regular September delivery date on textbooks, and December (usually the month of kickoff sales meetings) when all new special books and textbooks are presented to the sales staff for the coming year's sales efforts. You can figure that picture selections for books and textbooks are made anywhere from two to four months before the printing date. This average, of course, is relative and subject to variations (both yours and the photobuyer's), so be sure to consider Table 9-1 only as an indication of what happens much of the time in much of the market—to be balanced against your own PMS/A, your Market List, your experience, and your schedule.

If nothing else, Table 9-1 might help to explain that slow payments or slow sales do not necessarily reflect a stock photographer's ability to photograph, or a photobuyer's ability to pay. To everything there is a season.

Don't forget: When preparing seasonal pictures, check with your individual markets as to their lead time (usually about six months). In other words, be prepared to send springtime pictures in September. Photobuyers usually work that far in advance.

How Long Do Photobuyers Hold Your Pictures?

"The photobuyer is holding my pictures an unreasonably long time, don't you think?" a photographer recently asked me. He had sent his pictures six weeks previously.

"Not so," I said. "Especially if the photobuyer makes a purchase."

The buyer subsequently bought the pictures in question. Everyone was happy.

How long should a photobuyer hold your pictures? Two weeks to two months is a safe answer. Magazine editors, for example, will hold your pictures about two weeks, sometimes four. However, if you've requested in your cover letter that the editor circulate your submission to others at the publishing house who might be interested in reviewing them, and the publishing house is a large one, you may not see your pictures again for six weeks.

If you've directed your pictures to a book or textbook publisher, they could remain at the house for as long as eight weeks, since book production schedules often require more complex dovetailing and coordinating than magazine schedules. Ad agencies and PR firms are less likely to hold your picture for an unreasonable length of time. The reason? They are usually working on a tight deadline. Their decision must be quick.

You will not notice how "unreasonably" long photobuyers are holding your pictures if you make several duplicates of your black-and-whites and offer them to your Market List simultaneously. If you have made reproduction dupes of your transparencies, offer them simultaneously to several noncompeting markets.

Here are a few variables that can result in photobuyers' holding your pictures for a while:

1. The deadline for the project (textbook, brochure, article, etc.) has been extended, giving the buyer more time to make a decision on your pictures.

2. The buyer likes your pictures and has set your package aside for further consideration.

3. The buyer likes your picture but wants to do a little more shopping, in case he can find something even more on target.

4. The photobuyer has forwarded your pictures to the author (of the textbook, book, etc.) for consideration. The author is holding up the decision.

5. The buyer's priorities have changed and your picture is now in the #2 (or #6) priority stack.

6. The photobuyer is a downright sloppy housekeeper and your pictures won't surface until spring housecleaning time. (Fortunately, there are very few photobuyers in this category.)

If a photobuyer keeps your pictures longer than four weeks (and you are certain the selection date has passed), drop him a courteous note.

You can expect a form-letter reply (letting you know of the disposition of your pictures). Textbook editors hold pictures longer, as mentioned earlier. Usually if a picture lingers at a textbook publisher's, you'll be notified within three months that it is being held for final consideration.

Most editors, however (textbook editors included), when looking over photography (especially general submissions), attempt to review pictures the very same day they arrive, and if none of the pictures is to be considered for publication, the editor will have them shipped back the following day. This makes good sense both for insurance purposes and for office organization. If one or more of your pictures is being considered for publication, the photo editor might hold your complete package until a decision is made.

Again, the best answer to the "unreasonable" length of time a photobuyer may hold your pictures is to make several duplicates. Get many, many black-and-white prints and transparencies out working for you, and you'll be so preoccupied with sending them out and reaping the rewards that you won't have time to track down tardy photobuyers.

What insurance coverage does a publishing house have that would cover your pictures being held in case of fire or similar calamity? Generally speaking, publishing houses have a blanket insurance policy on your photographs. This blanket policy also includes their office equipment, light fixtures, and other tools of the trade. Your pictures are treated as pieces of paper or acetate, and the insurance covers only the cost of material replacement.

Nevertheless, publishing houses do not like to keep your pictures any longer than they have to, because as long as your pictures are in their possession, they are responsible. Between your place and theirs, the U.S. Postal Service or UPS has that responsibility—if you happen to insure your package. (Note: UPS insures all your packages, free, to a maximum of $100, but again, will reimburse for loss only to the amount of film or print replacement.)

Using Postcards to Relieve the Agony

If not knowing the disposition of your photos is frustrating to you, take a tip from stock photographers who include a return postcard with their submissions. The self-stamped card is addressed to the photographer and says in effect that the photo shipment was received by so and so on such and such date.

Another effective contact with a photobuyer would be to affix your letterhead on a memo with the message shown in Figure 9-3. The accompanying postcard reads as shown in Figure 9-4.

A Holding Fee—Should You Charge One?

As mentioned before, some editors must of necessity hold your pictures for several months. This in effect takes your picture out of circulation. If it's a timely picture, such as a photograph of performers who will be in

TO:

FROM:

PROJECT:

On _____

I sent _____ [transparencies] [B&W's]

to your office for consideration. Kindly let me know their disposition

on the enclosed return-reply postcard.

Thank you for your interest in my work.

Yours sincerely,

[Your name]

Figure 9-3. Memo to inquire about pictures being held too long.

We have received your (transparencies) (B&W's)

☐ Your pictures were returned to you on _____.

☐ We are still holding your pictures for final selection. You should
hear from us by _____.

☐ _____ of your pictures have been selected. You will receive payment on _____.

☐ Enclosed are _____ of your pictures. We are still holding _____
pictures for final consideration.

Remarks:

_____
Name   Title

_____
Firm

Figure 9-4. Postcard form for editors' reply about late pictures.

town in two weeks, or a photograph taken at the fair that ends this week, you could lose sales on it. By the time it's returned to you, it could be outdated and lose its effectiveness. To compensate for this potential loss, the holding fee was born. (Happily, most of your photo illustrations are universal and timeless if you've applied the marketable-picture principles of this book.) Some photographers have been known to charge a holding fee for pictures held beyond two weeks. The holding fee ranges anywhere from $1 to $5 per week for black-and-whites to $5 to $10 per week for color.

To make a potentially lengthy discussion short: Don't charge a holding fee unless you are a service photographer dependent on quick turnover of your images, or you are an established stock photographer working exclusively with price range 1 (see Table 8-1).

As a newcomer to the field, you'll find, of course, exceptions to my dictum. And you'll have to be the judge when the situation arises. Generally speaking, editors will frown on an unreasonable holding fee and on you, especially if you are a first-time contributor to their firm.

As I mentioned, the secret to overcoming the possibility of losing sales on your timely pictures: *Make duplicates*, and have several of them out working for you simultaneously. (For information on quality color reproduction duplicates, see Chapter 5.)

Sales Tax—Do I Need to Charge It?

Not every state charges sales tax, but if you live in a state that does, contact your state Department of Internal Revenue for details. If you make a sale within your state, you need to charge a sales tax. If the sale is to an address outside your state, no sales tax is required. Generally speaking, most stock photographers deal long distance and sell outside their own state. Since you are "re-selling" a product (photographic paper or transparencies), you are probably eligible to receive a "Seller's Permit" which exempts you from having to pay a sales tax when you buy your supplies such as paper and film.

In California the question of "one-time" use of photographs came up and the State Board of Equalization addressed it with this ruling: "Photographers who license their photographs for publication should be aware that merely because the photographer owns the rights to the photographs and retains the negative does not mean that a sale has not taken place. The transfer of possession and use of a photograph for a consideration (license fee) is a sale and is subject to state sales tax. There is only one exemption to the above which is for newspaper use—but not for magazines, or any other commercial use—even if for 'one-time use only.' "

You'll need to check what your state's policy is.

When Can You Expect Payment?

Most photobuyers on your Market List will pay on *acceptance* rather than on *publication*. If they don't, drop them to the bottom of your Market List. After all, your PMS/A matches only certain markets, but you bring to those markets an exclusive know-how that other photographers do not possess. You are an important resource to editors. Be proud of your talents. If some editors don't reward you with payment on acceptance, replace them.

Photobuyers usually send a check to you within two to four weeks after they've made their decision to purchase. However, each publishing house works differently. Some will pay more quickly, others take longer in their purchase-order and bookkeeping procedures. However, if a publishing house has a $30,000-a-month budget and is slow in paying, I'm sure you won't be too irate if the several checks a month addressed to you customarily arrive a little late. Many publishing houses across the nation have $30,000-a-month photo budgets or close to it, and they're seeking your pictures right now. If a publishing house is late with its payment, spend your energy sending them more pictures rather than composing letters of complaint. (If you've built your Market List correctly, you'll find few deadbeats in it.)

How Safe Are Your Pictures in the Hands of an Editor?

Contrary to popular opinion, photobuyers do not have machines that split and crack 8x10s, scratch and crinkle transparencies, and sprinkle coffee over both. Your submission will receive professional handling if you are careful to submit only to the professional. If you aren't sure whether a publishing company is new to the field, check a previous edition of *Photographer's Market* or similar directory. If the house was listed three years ago, that's a factor in its favor.

Here at PhotoSource International I receive occasional complaints from photographers about a photo editor's handling of their pictures. Invariably, mishandling of pictures can be traced to employees of a company new to the publishing business. It's rare that a publishing house with a track record will mishandle your submissions. The reliability factor works both ways. If you find that a publishing house projects a low reliability factor, avoid it.

Don't spend sleepless nights fretting about your pictures. Instead, imagine your stock photography operation as a long tube. You put a submission in one end, and keep putting submissions in, moving down the tube. Instead of waiting by the mailbox, put in more time in the darkroom, or snap more slides for your stock photo file. Keep the submissions moving down the tube. One day, you'll hear a sound at the other end—the check arriving!

Lost, Stolen, or Strayed?

Stock photos don't offer much temptation to a thief. In order to be useful, they have to be published rather than hoarded. A stolen photo that's subsequently published increases the thief's chances of being discovered. You'll rarely hear of a stolen stock photo.

Lost pictures more accurately describes a possibility. However, as I mentioned earlier, when a picture is lost, whether in the mail or at a photobuyer's office, the record reveals that it is most often the fault of the photographer.

Here are some common reasons:

1. No identification on the pictures, or identification that is blurred or unclear.
2. Return mailing information missing, incomplete, or unclear.
3. Erroneous address on the shipment to begin with.
4. Failure to include return postage (SASE) when appropriate.

I have talked with many photobuyers who say they have packets of photographs, and single photographs, gathering dust in their offices because the photographers did not include an address on the pictures. Once pictures become separated from the original envelope, the buyer has no way of knowing where to return them. Many orphan black-and-white photographs hang temporarily on photo editors' walls, they're that good!

I myself have lost one shipment in my twenty-five years of photo illustration. I should say temporarily lost, because after five years, the editor's replacement discovered my ten photographs in the back of a filing cabinet. My mistake: sending a shipment to a novice editor.

Loss of your black-and-whites or transparencies is best avoided through prevention. Don't send pictures to photobuyers or publishing houses that have no track record. Prevention is cheap. And it's a good habit to get into in photo marketing.

Your Recourse for Lost Pictures

This is not to say that an honest error can't be committed by a photobuyer. Let's say that some of your pictures are lost and the photobuyer appears to be at fault. Your best policy is good old-fashioned courtesy. Otherwise, a good working relationship between you and the photobuyer can break down, sometimes irreparably. Don't be quick to point an accusing finger and lose a promising client. Consider the following:

1. Have you double-checked to see if the person you originally sent your picture to is the same person you are dealing with now?
2. Have you waited ample time (four weeks for a magazine, eight

weeks for a book publisher) before becoming concerned?

3. Have you asked if your picture is being considered for the final cut?

4. Have you checked with the postal authorities on initial delivery?

If you definitely establish that your picture arrived and is now lost, three options are open to you, depending on who lost your picture, the photobuyer or you.

When I speak of a lost picture, I am referring now to one or more transparencies, or a group of black-and-whites. Photobuyers generally do not expect to engage in negotiations over a single black-and-white that they know can be reprinted at much less cost than the cumulative exchanges of correspondence over it between photographer and photobuyer. If a single black-and-white disappears, my suggestion is to accept the loss and tally it in the to-be-expected-downtime column.

Transparencies are another story. A transparency is an original. Photobuyers are are prepared to talk seriously about even a single transparency—if it has been established that they did receive the picture. One excellent way (mentioned earlier) to keep tabs on delivery of your shipments is to insure each package for $50. The post office will provide you with documentation that someone signed for the package.

Another protection is a liability stipulation, which you include in your shipment, to the effect that if the buyer loses or otherwise damages your transparency, his company is liable to you for $1,500.

Does this latter course seem excessive? Many photobuyers think so, and you get on their blacklist if you try it. There's an old story about Joe Namath demanding a special jersey number, a special footlocker, and white football shoes. The coach just laughed at him. Joe was thirteen at the time. Even Ernest Hemingway in the early stages of his career had to settle for less than optimum contract agreements. So did Van Cliburn, Burt Reynolds, and Barbra Streisand.

When you're an unseasoned freelancer, you takes what you gits. Initially, exposure and credit lines are your prime rewards. Only when you have proved to an art director or photobuyer that you can deliver the goods, and that he or she needs you, can you call the shots. Until you've proved yourself valuable to a photobuyer or publishing house, you're not in a position to talk liability stipulations.

In this age of malpractice suits, some publishers have become gun-shy because a small but significant number of photographers have aimed at ensnaring companies by pressing suit for loss of transparencies (rarely are black-and-whites involved). Consequently, publishers shy away from dealing with new and untried stock photographers, or they take precautionary measures with them such as having the photographer sign a waiver that in effect releases the publishing house from any or all liability.

That's why it's important to discern who's doing the talking when you hear ol' pros advise that "you ought to require photobuyers to sign liability agreements." When the pro advises you to get a liability release from the publisher, he just might be using one of the tricks of the trade (any trade) to eliminate competition. They know that photobuyers will steer clear of you if you summarily present them with a liability requirement. Or it might be an ego trip for the pro to suggest that you get the release. Only the known and the best can make demands, as Joe Namath eventually learned.

The service photographer and the stock photographer may have different attitudes toward this liability problem. As a stock photographer, your interest in photography as an expressive medium differs a lot from that of the photographer who concentrates on photography as a graphic element in advertising, fashion, or public relations. The service photographers' rights to sell their services and to protect their business with holding fees, liability terms and conditions, and so on, should be honored. But their business is not stock business, and their markets are not stock markets, when it comes to dealing with photo illustrations. Yes, of course, if you're dealing with a buyer in Range 1 (see Table 8-1), you'll probably arrive at some mutually reasonable liability agreement before too long. If you deal with buyers in Range 6 the subject may never come up.

How Much Compensation Should You Expect?

The compensation you should expect from a photobuyer for a lost picture is relative to several factors: (1) the value of the picture to you and to the photobuyer; (2) the anticipated life of the picture itself; and (3) which price range (1 to 6) the photobuyer is in. I have talked with photographers who have received compensation ranging from $100 to $1,500 for an original transparency. A good rule of thumb is to charge three times the fee you were originally asking. If the lost transparency is a dupe, only the cost of replacement would be in order. One final consideration: There's some politics involved here. Each photobuyer can be a continuing source of income for you. How you handle these negotiations will influence how much of that income continues to come your way.

In the September 1987 *Photoletter*, photographer Joe Viesti told readers he solved the problem this way:

It's not going to happen to you very often in your photomarketing career, but when it does, it's devastating: One of your favorite photobuyers calls and says, "We've looked everywhere and have to admit we've lost your photo."

What are your alternatives? As you probably know, they range from a court case to just forgetting it. It's a case of politics, isn't it? You ask yourself, "Do I really want to take this photobuyer to court?" In the end, what with attorney's fees and your own time spent on the case, you might break even and be left with a lost account.

Here's what worked for me in one of these situations. I sat down with the art director and said, "Look, rather than me sending you a bill for $4,500 (three transparencies were lost), and your boss refusing to pay it, let's do this. Just guarantee to me this value ($4,500 for three pictures) through your use of stock photos from me and/or assignments to me plus expenses over a reasonable period of one year." The art director was relieved.

Next month I got an assignment to fly to South America. And I'm still getting assignments from the same photobuyer. Sometimes it pays to turn a lemon into lemonade.

If you are still not convinced that a liberal policy toward a photobuyer's liability is sound, consider this: *Two* other entities *also* handle your transparencies, the film processor and the delivery service (U.S. Postal Service, UPS, Federal Express, etc.). None of these organizations will accept liability for your transparencies (or prints) beyond the actual cost of replacement film and paper, unless *gross* negligence can be proven. You've seen this in small print, but as a reminder, see Figure 9-5.

(These notices are all from reputable film-processing companies.)

Neither the U.S. Postal Service, UPS, nor Federal Express will award you more than the *replacement cost* of the film or prints. If you've insured your package for the intrinsic value of your pictures, in the event of damage or loss, the carriers will want to see a receipt establishing that value. If you don't have one, they will pay you only what it would cost you to print the pictures again or have a duplicate made. The insurance would not cover sending you back to France to retake the pictures.

If you were a service photographer and the loss was substantial, and gross negligence by the carrier was involved, you might want to consider taking the carrier to court.

Such harsh terms should encourage you to *prevent* loss of your film or pictures by packaging them well.

If you have arrived at a point in your own stock photo career where you'd like to test the reaction of your photobuyers to a Terms and Conditions Agreement form, write for a current copy of *Business Practices in Photography* ($29.50) to the American Society of Magazine Photographers (ASMP), 205 Lexington Avenue, New York, NY 10016. It includes the following sample forms (which you can photocopy or modify): Assignment Invoice, Stock Photo Submission Sheet, Stock Pictures Invoice, Model Release, and Terms of Submission and Leasing (which lists the compensation for damage or loss of a transparency at $1,500). Write to me here at PhotoSource International for a free copy of a "transmittal form" we provide our subscribers (please send SASE). For readers who

LIABILITY: Submitting any film, print, slide, or negative to this firm for processing, printing, or other handling constitutes an AGREEMENT by you that any damage or loss by our company or subsidiary, even though by our negligence or other fault, will only entitle you to replacement with a like amount of unexposed film and processing. Except for such replacement, the acceptance by us of the film, print, slide, or negative is without other warranty or liability.

Customer's film is developed by_____
_____ without warranty or liability of any kind, except to furnish the customer with replacement film at least equivalent in number of exposures to negatives lost or damaged in processing.

NOTE: Responsibility for damage or loss is limited to cost of film before exposure.

Figure 9-5. Liability notices.

would like to know more about assuring their rights when a transparency or shipment of black-and-whites is lost or damaged, here are four references:

Law and the Writer (see page 99)
Kirk Polking and Leonard S. Meranus, editors
Writer's Digest Books
1507 Dana Avenue
Cincinnati, OH 45207

Stock Photography Handbook
ASMP
205 Lexington Ave.
New York, NY 10016

Photography: What's the Law? (see page 94)
Robert Cavallo and Stuart Kahan
Crown Publishers, Inc.
One Park Ave.
New York, NY 10016

Selling Your Photography
Arie Kopelman & Tad Crawford
AMPHOTO BOOKS
1515 Broadway
New York, NY 10036

Remember, the key to successful marketing of your pictures lies in effective communication with the people who approve payment of your pictures—the photobuyers.

A Twenty-Four-Point Checklist to Success

Sending out a submission to a photobuyer? Run your package through this quality control:

Packaging

1. ☐ Clean, white, durable outside envelope.
   ☐ Correct amount of postage.
2. ☐ Professional-looking label, with your return address and logo printed on it.
   ☐ Address that is legible and correct.
3. ☐ SASE enclosed.
4. ☐ Photos that are all identified: picture number, plus your name and address.
5. ☐ Copyright notice.
6. ☐ No date on your slides or 8 × 10s (unless you use a code).
7. ☐ Captions when appropriate.
8. ☐ Transparencies: in vinyl pages.
9. ☐ Cover letter (printed form letter) that is brief and on clean, deluxe stationery.

Cohesiveness

10. ☐ Solicited submission: Pictures are on-target as per request of photobuyer.
11. ☐ Unsolicited submission: Pictures follow style and subject of photobuyer's publication. They fit the buyer's graphic and photographic needs.
12. ☐ Pictures are consistent in style.
13. ☐ Pictures are consistent in quality.

Quality

Color

14. ☐ Color balance is appropriate for subject and is suitable for reproduction.
15. ☐ Chromes are used for outdoor 35mm.
16. ☐ Dupes are reproduction quality (with proper filtering) or else identified as display dupes.
17. ☐ Each slide has been checked with a magnifying glass or a loupe for sharpness. No fuzzy shots!

Black-and-White

18. ☐ Good gradation: stark whites; deep, rich blacks; appropriate gradations of grays.
19. ☐ Spotted.
20. ☐ Trimmed: Edges are crisp and straight; no tears or dog ears.

Both Color and Black-and-White

21. ☐ In focus, sharp, good resolution (no camera shake).
22. ☐ Current (not outdated).
23. ☐ Appropriate emphasis and natural (unposed) scenes.
24. ☐ $P = B + P + S + I$. Pictures evoke a mood.

Can your subjects look straight at the camera without diminishing the effectiveness of your photo illustration? Yes—but not always.

10.
If You
Don't Sell
Yourself,
Who Will?

Promoting
Your Photography:
How to Blow
Your Own
Horn

The greatest hurdle in the area of self-promotion, it seems, is not *how* to advertise oneself (many clever and creative methods are open to you), but the reticence most of us have when it comes to self-advertising. We're uncomfortable talking about ourselves in glowing terms, afraid of seeming pushy or immodest.

Many a talent has gone undiscovered because he or she failed to act on the salient reality: if we're going to be discovered, it's our job to orchestrate it. The number of talented photographers in this country alone must run in the hundreds of thousands. Picture the Bronx telephone directory, and then imagine that all those names are modest, talented photographers and your name is among them. It would seem preposterous to think that the world of its own accord is going to come along and pick you out from all those other fine talents, wouldn't it? Sometimes it's actually immodest to be modest.

Society has ingrained in us the idea that unless we exhibit an acceptable degree of self-effacement, we won't be thought well of. ("He's so conceited!" "She's stuck on herself!" "What an ego!")

But the viewing public deserves to see and enjoy your pictures. You deserve to have your talent rewarded with what allows us to survive in today's world: money. You must overcome the conditioning our culture lays on us and accept the fact that if your stock photographs are going to be seen and enjoyed, you are going to have to blow your own horn.

With good judgment, you can accomplish this and come off looking not like an overbearing egomaniac but like a talented businessperson who knows how to keep his product in the marketplace.

Talent Can Take You Just So Far

Here are four tips that should help you maintain your resolve to promote yourself—and to keep on promoting:

1. Many stock photographers, once they have achieved a name in their local area, lull themselves into supposing that the *world* is aware of their work. Not so. Think big. Don't just toot that horn, *blow* it.

2. If you want your photo illustrations to continue selling, you have to continue selling yourself. Horn blowing is an ongoing task. Don't be satisfied that photobuyers, or potential clients, are going to remember you next week because of your success with them last week or month. Today's successes will become history tomorrow.

3. Once you begin to promote yourself, you will be pleasantly surprised to find that the people you thought would be highly critical of your promotional efforts will actually be the first to compliment you.

4. Because part of your motivation as a photographer is to share your insights, your vision of the world with others, you will find that the rewards of promoting yourself (and therefore your stock photography) will far outweigh the personal discomfort you sometimes feel when writing and distributing press releases about yourself or when enclosing in business correspondence tearsheets of your triumphs. Without such promotion, you leave yourself at the mercy of chance. Sure, a few photographers are going to make it by sheer luck alone. Someone always wins the Irish Sweepstakes or the $200,000 jackpot at Atlantic City. But the majority of photographers who become successful have managed it by means of effective self-promotion.

Look Like a Pro Even if You Don't Feel Like One Yet

This applies to everything from your stationery to your flyers. The adage at work in this business is *Appearance communicates quality of performance*.

Your new contacts in the photo-marketing field, since they rarely meet you in person at first, will rely heavily on the appearance you project via your communication materials. Your photography speaks for itself. Your promotional material speaks for you. It tells photobuyers how serious you are about your work—whether you're a good bet to be producing the same fine photography next month, or next year, at an address they can reach you at (your *reliability factor*). Photobuyers assume that your performance and dependability will match the quality of your presentation.

As publisher of the *Photobulletin*, I have the opportunity to see numerous creative methods of self-promotion. I've included some examples in the following sections. They will give you an idea of the possibilities open to you: producing brochures of photo samplings, making catalogs, enhancing your stationery with examples of your work, designing a distinctive logo. Limitations on space preclude my showing many more fine examples.

Your Personal Trademark

Your photography itself becomes your trademark once you get established. But before you reach that point, a trademark may very well be an important element contributing to your success. A distinctive logo or design can help your correspondence start looking familiar to buyers—and your name to start being remembered.

When you design your symbol, or logo, be aware of a common error: the temptation to use the obvious—a camera, a tripod, a piece of 35mm film, etc. You may, of course, want to choose from things photographic, but try for a combination or adaptation that's all your own. Make it simple and easy to remember. Recruit that graphics student or that friend who's good at designing, drawing, or critiquing your work, to help in the decision, based on the pointers mentioned above. Flip through the Yellow Pages or a business directory to see how others have tackled the question of logo. Don't be too cute in your design—the novelty will soon wear off, or even be offensive to clients. Don't be obscure, either. I consider the design of a stock photographer's stationery so important that I prepared a kit for our newsletter subscribers that aids them in selecting a letterhead and logo for their stationery. To obtain a kit, send $2.50 to cover cost, postage and handling to me at: PhotoSource International, Pine Lake Farm, Osceola, WI 54020. Mark your request: "Stationery Kit."

If your photographs are highly specialized in one area, be specific with your trademark. If you are a nature photographer, you can choose a design that reflects your photography—a silhouette of a fern or a close-up of a toad. Children's photographer? Choose a classic shot of yours that lends itself to a simplified sketch or drawing. As your photo-marketing enterprise grows, you'll be building equity, exposure, mileage in your trademark. Decide your specialty early and produce a trademark that will cause editors to say, "Aha—he's a transportation photographer," or "She's a tennis photographer." However, don't worry if you don't have a strong specialty yet. You can work gradually toward becoming strong in one or two defined areas on your personal marketing strength/areas (PMS/A) list, and then alter your trademark from a more general design to one tied into your specialty.

Your personal trademark doesn't necessarily have to include a design (logo) or photograph. It can also consist of the name you give to your stock photo business, with or without an identifying design. The name can be your own name or a product of your imagination. Choosing your trademark is like naming a child. The result is here to stay, so do it carefully.

It's not necessary to formally register your trademark (thirty dollars, at this writing), but if you wish to explore the process to ensure that no one will copy your design, you can write: Trademarks, Superintendent of Documents, U.S. Government Printing Office, Washington, DC 20402, and enclose one dollar (price subject to increase). You can also register your *mark of trade* with your local state officials.

Your Letterhead

Your letterhead is often your first contact with a photobuyer. Put special care into designing it. For your lettering, try the distinctive press-on letters available at the printer's. If you have a general mood running through your pictures, match it with a typeface that has the same feel to it. And consider incorporating a carefully chosen sample of your photographs themselves in the design. Barter with a graphics student to conjure up some ideas for you to choose from. Outside help is usually more objective. As I've mentioned throughout this book, "You don't get a second chance at a first impression." You are working long distance with your buyers. The first impression they have of you is the piece of paper with which you contact them. When you initially write for photo guidelines, contact the photobuyer on *deluxe* stationery. If it's costing a dime a sheet, you're on the right track. At a quick-print shop, get only 100 printed at a time. It's costly, but if you change your address or your mind, an investment in 5,000 sheets isn't lost.

Envelopes

Make your envelope a calling card. How to decide which logo or photograph you should use on your outside envelope? Use one that (1) commands attention and (2) reminds photobuyers and the public of your specialties. If your specialty is agriculture and an extensive portion of your Market List includes publications in the area of farming, a strong agriculture photograph or logo will serve well. Keep in mind the purpose of your envelope promotion. You want your name to become synonymous with agriculture photography. When photobuyers in the farm-publications industry ask themselves, "Who has good agriculture pictures?" you want your name to come up.

And what if you have two or three specialties? Print two or three different envelopes targeted to the different segments of your Market List.

Business Cards

A distinctive business card will keep your name circulating. They're inexpensive, and any printer can produce them. But don't fall into the trap of acquiring a couple thousand business cards that are cheap-looking and indistinguishable from your competition. Make your next business card something people will remember: a photograph (see Figure 10-1). Consult the Yellow Pages for printers. A good source for photographic business cards is Camera Art, Suite 82, Box 100, Lewiston, MN 55052.

Build a Mailing List

The core of your operation is your Market List—the list of your photo-buyers—past, present, and future. Your promotional mailing list should start with your publication Market List. Now begin to extend it to camera columnists, local galleries, photography schools, camera clubs, camera stores, radio and TV stations, and newspapers that will receive the press releases you'll periodically circulate.

The question naturally arises: Should these names and addresses be on several different lists or one major list? Generally speaking, it's better to maintain one master list. If your list is on file cards or Rolodex cards, you can code by color or symbol those that are markets, those that are columnists, etc. Having one list will help you avoid duplication in mailings and time-consuming tracking when an address changes.

Compare the problem if you had a friend's name on your current Christmas card list, a business firm list, a potential client list, and a general mailing list. Any change in address would have to be made (or possibly missed) on each of the four lists.

Keep your list faithfully up-to-date. Print "address correction requested" on all of your envelopes. The cost from the Postal Service for the correction is currently twenty-five cents, but it's worth it. Whenever you make a mailing, code the mailing on your master list with a color, symbol, or date so that you'll have a means to measure how many mailing pieces certain markets or columnists, etc., are receiving. If your list is on computer, design your program to anticipate categories that may be useful in the future, such as number of sales per individual market and type of sales (book, curriculum, magazine, etc.). Clean your list often (i.e., weed out addresses that have changed or are no longer useful).

Mailers—They Pay for Themselves

Probably the most cost-effective means of self-promotion is the use of mailers (also called flyers, inserts, or stuffers). These promotional pieces are similar to brochures (described later in this chapter) and serve the same purpose, but they are less elaborate (thus less costly), and you can make them yourself if you wish. They consist of a grouping of examples of your pictures, in whatever size you wish to make them.

In my own business, I use mailers as my principal form of advertising. I send them out regularly every three to six months to the photobuyers on my Market List.

Figure 10-1. Photographers' business cards.

My most effective mailers consist of eight current black-and-white prints reduced together to 3x9. Each group conveniently fits in a No. 10 (business-size) envelope.

Rather than print the mailers myself, I send them out to a studio in Minneapolis that handles volume printing accounts. They shoot my eight pictures on an 8x10 neg and mass-produce the results.

I order 250 and mail out 100 to a portion of my Market List. They usually cost from fifty to seventy-five cents apiece, but they invariably pay for themselves, because a good percentage of the photobuyers either see a picture on the mailer that they want to order or they're triggered into requesting other photos from me.

The remaining 150 mailers remain at my desk to stuff into my regular business correspondence with potential as well as current photobuyers. You can add other inserts to bring attention to your photography: press releases, tearsheets of news about you, change-of-address notices, announcements, and press kits.

Other types of mailers are 3x5 or Rolodex-size cards (2¼x4, in various colors) with promotional reminders on them. Rolodex cards are available through Printcrafters, Inc., P.O. Box 5157, Hamden CT 06518 (203/387-2253). A punch-out Rolodex card is available through Ticket Shack, 12896 Highway 55, Minneapolis MN 55441 (612/559-3846). Promotional postcards are available from Pate Poste, Ad Cards, 43 Charles St., No. 5A, Boston, MA 02114. Color "stamps" are available from Double Image, P.O. Box 3970, Berkeley, CA 94703, and from Photolabels, 333 Kimberly Drive, Station 12, Carol Stream, IL 60188.

Brochures

Design and produce a professional-looking four-page brochure—that is, one large (8½x9½) sheet folded once. It will be a showcase for you, and it will pull in sales and assignments. Use as guides the brochures or pamphlets found in airline or travel offices. Such a brochure usually pays for itself whether you invest $100 or $1,000. My advice, if you have the cash, courage, and marketable pictures available, is to bend your budget and produce a full-color brochure aimed at a specific market that has both the need for your PMS/A and a pay rate that will make it worthwhile. How many photographs should you include? Look at other brochures to see which appeal to you most. When you find one, adapt the design, using pictures you think will appeal to your Market List.

Handsome, four-color brochures can cost as much as ninety-five cents each. A good place to find a wide selection of samples of these exquisite brochures is in the wastebasket of your local post office. Does this tell you something? Make sure your brochure reaches the right target.

How many brochures should you print and where? Take your mock-up to several four-color printers for quotes on one thousand, three thousand, and five thousand copies. The quantity depends on the size of your market. I've always found that it's better to print more than you think you'll need. It's cheaper per unit; besides, you'll discover new uses for your brochures once you have them.

Such brochures need very little copy. Put your photographs into the space. About the only words you'll need are your name, address, and phone number.

Postcards

Four-color postcards that show off a single example of your photography serve to remind buyers who you are and what you can produce. Here are some suppliers:

Gerson Printing
6301 Biscayne Blvd. #206M
Station 74
Miami, FL 33138

MWM Dexter
P.O. Box 261
107 Washington
Aurora, MO 65605

Spruiell Company
444 West Mockingbird Lane
Dallas, TX 75247

Catalogs

Have a catalog printed displaying a selection of your stock photos based on your PMS/A. Assign numbers to each picture. Three-hole punch the left side of each page. Send it to current and prospective editors (see Figure 10-2).

The cost for this 8½x11 black-and-white, eight-page catalog is currently "$700 for 3,000 copies," says Robert Maust, a stock photographer, of Harrisonburg, Virginia. "That amount was paid off in sales I made directly related to the catalog in only a few months."

Here's how to put together such a catalog: Place sixteen verticals or fifteen horizontals on one page. Using 8x10s, make a huge paste-up of each half of the page. The printer shoots it in halftone, reduces it, shoots the other half, tapes the upper and lower halves together, and prints.

Another type of catalog useful in promoting current pictures to prospective photobuyers is one displaying a group of actual prints (8x10s). Punch holes down the left side of the prints, and bind them in a plastic binder that covers front and back. I assemble seventy-five double-weight pictures of a particular category and include an invoice form.

Editors order from the invoice form, which is coded to the catalog pictures. When the print edges of the catalog become worn, I send the catalog back to the bindery and they trim the book a few millimeters.

I also assemble smaller catalogs of pictures from recent trips. I print three or four pictures to a page and include a picture identification number for each.

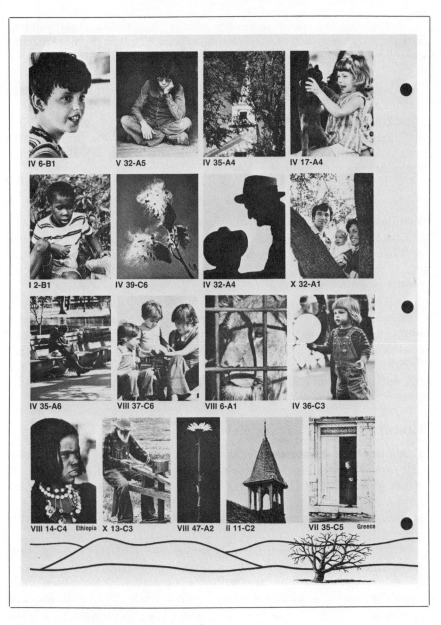

Figure 10-2. A photographer's catalog.

Photographers have asked me if printing (lithographing) their catalogs would be just as effective. In my own experience, there are three reasons why a "print-your-own" catalog is more advantageous:

1. You have complete flexibility as to how many editions you wish to produce.
2. You have complete control over the quality of the pictures.
3. Printers require a minimum run whose cost might be prohibitive to you. Also, with printing (by litho) you are at the mercy of the printer's technical capabilities and experience.

The Phone

Telephone marketing is an effective way to sell yourself. Each phone call is actually a self-promotional opportunity. Be sure to prepare for it with a give list. If you call a prospective photobuyer with nothing to give, your intended promotion may end up as demotion. (For more on dealing with photobuyers by phone, see Chapter 7.)

Your local telephone company will have promotional aids available to you, ranging from WATS-line information (wide-area telecommunication system) to literature on how to overcome "phonephobia." Practice your promotional calls on a tape recorder. If your voice sounds too high, too low, or unenthusiastic, keep trying until you get it right. Then practice with a few trial calls. You'll know by the response if the phone is for you.

Credit Lines and Tearsheets—Part of the Sale

Credit lines and tearsheets of your published stock photos are significant self-promotional tools for you. How do you get them? Request them when you are notified that your picture has been purchased. Even better, in your original cover letter to an editor, you can include a courteous statement that the terms of sale include use of your credit line and provision of a tearsheet upon publication.

Major markets ordinarily print credit lines as a matter of course; they expect you to purchase the publication and get your own tearsheets, however. Textbook editors also will expect you to make your own photocopies of your published pictures. Photo editors of regional, local, or specialized limited-circulation publications, however, work with smaller budgets, and will usually supplement the dollars with a credit-line guarantee and will forward tearsheets to you. Some of your markets will have the provision of tearsheets built into their standard operating procedure. They automatically send them to all contributors of a given issue to confirm for their own records that the photographer (or writer) has been correctly credited and paid. (To help ensure a correct credit line for your photographs, use the identification system described in Chapter 13.)

You can use tearsheets for self-promotion in a variety of ways. Make photocopies of them to tuck into your business correspondence, to show prospective clients how other publishers are using your stock photographs, and to remind past photobuyers of your existence. Dave Strickler of Newville, Pennsylvania, regularly includes such samplings in his correspondence with editors and art directors. Inexpensive and immediate, such promotions often pay for themselves through orders for the actual stock photos pictured in the photocopy. You can also use groups of tearsheets (originals or photocopies) to send to a prospective photobuyer to illustrate the depth you have available on a given subject.

When you gather a good number of tearsheets, file and cross-reference them to use as tools to locate subject matter you've previously photographed.

Credit lines, besides the good advertising they provide for you, can be instruments for additional sales. Art directors and photo editors are always on the lookout for promising new stock photographers. When your credit line appears (next to your photo illustration or in the credits section of a publication), it's available for all to see and make note of. If you're doing your self-promotion job correctly, your credit line will be popping up often, and photobuyers will become familiar with your name.

In some cases, photobuyers will want to reuse a published photo that catches their eye, and they will seek out the photographer to make arrangements. Without a credit line, this would be a complex detective task the buyer doesn't have time for.

What if a photobuyer doesn't give you a credit line? Beyond an approach of courteous insistence, your hands are tied. The use of credit lines, in the majority of cases, is left up to the editor or art director of the publishing project. You're fightin' city hall when you vent righteous indignation at the lack of a credit line. But have faith. As in city hall, administration changes occur in the publishing world, and the next art director you deal with at a particular publishing house may have the "right" attitude toward including credit lines. An examination of magazine and book layouts over the last decade will show that the trend is decidedly moving toward the use of credits. Meanwhile, it is up to you to politely but firmly continue to press for the use of your credit line next to your published photograph.

Show Yourself Off

Your promotional tools are working for you to make sales of your pictures. Now you want to begin getting some promotional exposure for you as a photographer.

Trade Shows

Publishing trade shows, book fairs, and magazine workshops always attract publishers and photobuyers. Invest in trade shows with either an exhibit booth or a ticket to the event to personally meet publishers and photobuyers, who represent potential markets and/or new members for your promotional mailing list.

To learn which trade shows would be most productive for you, ask buyers on your Market List which ones they personally attend. Since these people are your target markets, you can be sure the events they deem worthwhile will pay off for you in opportunities to become aware of new, similar market areas.

Carry your business cards and several packets of your stock photographs with you, each packet representing a separate area of your PMS/A. I went to my first trade fair with a general portfolio of pictures. Photobuyers weren't interested in seeing my pretty pictures. The next year, I built three packets, each with twenty-five 8x10 black-and-whites and two vinyl pages of color (forty 35mm), enclosed in a plastic folder. Each aimed at a specific market: education, gardening, teens. I talked only with photobuyers in each of those three specific interest areas and showed only the photographs they were interested in seeing. My visit more than paid for itself in the subsequent sale of pictures.

Speaking Engagements

Here's a simple way to promote yourself, and it doesn't cost you anything. If you communicate effectively with your camera, you may have the potential to communicate effectively as a speaker. Take to the platform!

In the trusty Yellow Pages, you'll find a listing of community and photographic organizations, clubs, and associations. Most have a regular need for interesting program speakers. Let the program chairpersons of several groups know that you are available. In most cases, they'll be happy to book you.

How do you get started? What should you talk about? As a stock photographer, you have a wealth of subject material available to you—and since 90 percent of your listeners fancy themselves photographers, too, you'll have a receptive audience.

Build your talk around a how-to subject, for example, "How to Take Pictures of Your Family," "How to Take Indoor Natural-Light Pictures," "How to Make a Photo Illustration." You are welcome to use any of the ideas in this book.

For some ideas on titles for your speech or speeches (there's nothing wrong with having one basic speech for quite a while), order Kodak's free catalog entitled "Your Programs from Kodak." These are basically movie and slide programs, but their titles alone are enough to stir your imagination for your own speech. (Write to: Audio-Visual Library Distribution, Eastman Kodak, Rochester, NY 14650.) Give your speech title this test: "Am I speaking about something that applies directly to my audience?"

Your listeners don't want a lecture. If they did, they'd register at the local adult education center. Tailor your speech to be entertaining. Include anecdotes, personal experiences of your own or of photographer-friends, humor. Use audiovisual aids such as charts, slides, or blackboards. You'll get audience response (feedback), and this will aid you in refining your speech. Eventually, program chairpersons will seek you out.

Payment? At first, charge nothing, except perhaps a fee to cover your out-of-pocket expenses such as baby-sitting, gas, and the meal (if part of the meeting). At this stage, the speaking experience and exposure are more valuable to you. As you progress, start charging by the hour—for example, $25 per hour. Increase the fee as demand for your services increases. As your track record grows, so will your fee.

And how does all this relate to self-promotion? You'll discover some surprising spinoffs from your public appearances. Local publishers will hear of your talents. Assignments will be directed your way. You'll learn of places, people, and happenings that you'll want to photograph. Photobuyers will contact you. Your name as a stock photographer will be catapulted ahead of equally talented but less visible photographers.

Another spinoff: If you find that you enjoy speaking, the field is wide open to you. Eventually, you may want to promote your own seminars.

For good advice and direction on speaking engagements, there's a newsletter that could be helpful to your speaking career: *Sharing Ideas*, Dotty Walters, Royal CBS Publishing, 600 W. Foothill Boulevard, Glendora, CA 91740. If you branch out into seminars, a valuable book for reference is *Photography Seminars* by Robert McQuilkin (Lightbooks).

Radio and TV Interviews

Make yourself available to community radio talk-show hosts. They are usually interested in interviewing people engaged in out-of-the-ordinary pursuits, and you qualify. Photography is an ever-popular subject, as listeners are always eager to learn how they can improve their picture taking. Add some local or farther-afield radio-show hosts to your promotional mailing list. Some radio hosts will phone across the nation for an on-the-air phone interview if they believe that their listeners would be interested in what you have to say.

A good source to locate radio stations and the addresses of hosts of talk shows is *Contacts*, Larimi Communication Associates, 5 West 37th Street, New York, NY 10018. The same organization can give you the names and addresses of TV show hosts. Television interviews are possible if you can present your story in a five to nine-minute segment. Since photography can easily hold viewer attention, your chances are better than average for making a TV appearance, particularly in a nearby city. For a fee, you can get yourself listed in a "Talk Show Guest Directory" called the *Directory of Experts, Authorities, & Spokespersons* (Broadcast Interview Source, 2500 Wisconsin Ave. NW, Washington, DC 20007 (202)333-4904).

Contact the producer of a local talk show (by letter, phone, in person—or all three). You could offer to serve as the resident critic for photography submitted by viewers. Build your format around a how-to theme. Tailor your critiques so that the average snapshooter will understand and be able to improve the family's scrapbook photographs.

All this, again, is in the interest of exposure and self-promotion.

Press Releases

If you've been making speeches, giving talks, making appearances at vo-tech graphics or design classes, or giving interviews on radio or TV, someone's going to be mentioning you in your community news media. But whether you've been engaged in these activities or not, you can write your *own* press releases: they are an excellent form of promotion for your stock photo business. Newspapers and magazines are willing to accept news about you and your photography; so are the specialized newsletters and trade magazines that reach photobuyers and publishers. You must contact *them* and send them your press release. You'll find that about one-third of the media channels you contact will print your release.

When you consider that the average advertising rate is $50 per inch, when your press release is used, you receive a sizable amount of advertising space—free. What's more, your release is read as editorial, human-interest material, rather than advertising.

When can you send a news release about your photography or yourself? Depending on whether the item would be of interest on a local, regional, or national level and whether your target is a trade publication or a general-interest one, your press release can center on a recent trip; your photo exhibit at the local library; an award you received; your move to a farm, garret, former carriage barn; your donation of photo illustrations to a nonprofit publication or auction; your publication of a photo in a national magazine or book; or a recent speech or interview.

Press releases follow a basic format: double-spaced on a half page or a full page. Write your release as if the editor (or radio commentator) were writing it. Remember: It is not an ad. This is not the place to speak in glowing terms about yourself or your photography. A good handbook on this subject is *Public Relations Basics for Community Organizations* by Sol H. Marshall (Creative Book Company, Box 2244, Hollywood, CA 90028). See also *The Successful Promoter*, by Ted Schwarz (Contemporary Books, 180 N. Michigan Avenue, Chicago, IL 60601). A newsletter that broadcasts the current press needs of authors, columnists, and editors is: *Partyline*, PR Aids, 330 West 34th St., New York, NY 10001.

You don't need to include a cover letter, but do enclose a black-and-white photograph (5x7 is acceptable) when appropriate and practical. (Don't expect its return.)

Your best teachers for learning your way around press releases are news items you discover in the press. If you find yourself saying "That could be me!" rewrite the item to reflect your own information and send it to similar media channels.

Occasionally you will learn that a trade magazine in one of your fields of interest will be devoting an issue or an article to a certain subject. If you or your stock photographs can comment on that subject matter, volunteer to contribute (for free) to the issue. The resulting exposure of your name and your stock photos, in both the publication itself and the subsequent press release you write about it, will more than compensate for your effort and expense.

Once a press release is used, capitalize on the published article by making copies and sending the news item along in all your business correspondence and/or in a mailing to your market and promotional list.

Promotional News Features

Local, regional, or trade publications often welcome articles or short features (250 to 500 words) on somebody who's doing something interesting—you. You don't have to wait until a magazine or newspaper contacts you. Write your own material.

Photographer Bill Owens of Livermore, California, gets more mileage out of free advertising by turning a news feature about himself into a productive promotion mailer.

Advertising

Straight advertising is of course a direct method of self-promotion, but here you'll have to experiment—and it's usually expensive. Ordinarily, ads will not be the most cost-effective route for you as a stock photographer, unless you have strong depth in an unusual specialty with a known targeted market.

The following publications can be useful advertising vehicles—depending on what you're planting—as some photobuyers cull photo contacts from them. (Most of the ads are run by stock photo agencies and a few stock photographers who have extensive coverage of specific, select subjects.)

American Society of Picture
  Professionals Newsletter
Box 5283 Grand Central Station
New York, NY 10017

The ASMP Book
American Society of Magazine Photographers
205 Lexington Ave.
New York, NY 10016

The Creative Directory of the Sun Belt
Ampersand, Inc.
1103 South Shepard Dr.
Houston, TX 77019

Publishers Weekly
R.R. Bowker Company
1180 Avenue of the Americas
New York, NY 10036

Editors Guide to Freelance Photographers
Publishers Network, Inc.
828 Charcot Ave.
San Jose, CA 95131

Chicago Talent Sourcebook
212 West Superior
Chicago, IL 60610

Photo District News
Suite 6, 6th Flr.
49 E. 21st St.
New York, NY 10010

Madison Avenue Handbook
Peter Glenn Publications
17 E. 48th St.
New York, NY 10017

Magazine Industry Market Place
R.R. Bowker Company
1180 Avenue of the Americas
New York, NY 10036

Folio
125 Elm St., Box 697
New Canaan, CT 06840

Stock Workbook
940 North Highland Ave.
Los Angeles, CA 90038

Adweek Creative Services Directory
820 Second Ave.
New York, NY 10017
(212)661-8080

The American Photographer
American References Publishing
919 N. Michigan Ave. Dept. PSI
Chicago, IL 60617
(312)951-6200

Although you may not wish to invest in a costly display ad in any of the above, you could test for response with a classified ad. A typical example, which appeared in *Folio* magazine listed under "Photography, Stock," reads like this: "Emphasis on the Southwest. 150,000 images. Color and black-and-white. Write for free catalog [name, address, and phone]."

In deciding where to place an ad, one helpful route is to ask the photobuyers on your Market List which trade publications they read. You can assume that other publishers with similar editorial thrust read the same publications, and there is where you'll want your ad experiments to start. Following are some of the questions you should ask yourself when you're thinking of buying an ad: Who are the readers of the magazine? Do they buy photography? Will my ad get effective placement in the magazine? What do I expect to achieve from this ad?

Whenever you advertise, key your ad with a code number (for example, add *Dept. 12* to your street address). You'll be able to tally the replies to check how well an ad pulls for you.

To measure the response rate to your ad, divide the number of queries you receive by the circulation of the magazine. Expect a response of between 0.1 and 1 percent. Compare the response from each ad with those from the rest of the ads in your advertising program to weed out ads that are ineffective or reaching the wrong audience.

Another type of advertising tool, which you can use year-round, is a handy calendar of a size you can include in correspondence.

Or you can engineer this kind of arrangement: When I was starting out in business, I cooperated with a Midwest printing firm in a wall-calendar project. In return for the use of twelve of my photos, they paid me with a prominent credit line and 500 calendars, which I distributed as promotional pieces. The optimum ad is one in which a manufacturer or supplier or photography magazine highlights (promotes) you and your photography. Nikon, for example, featured different photographers and their work in a series of full-color, full-page ads that appeared in national photography magazines. In my own case, features and photographs of me have appeared in *Time*, *Money* magazine, *Changing Times*, *USA Today*, many newspaper photo columns, computer magazines, and most of the photography magazines. Was this luck? No. I applied the principles outlined in this chapter.

Again, you don't *wait* for things like this to land in your lap. You do something interesting and then let the industry and the media know about it. You keep alert for openings, and *you go for them.*

Reassess Your Promotional Effectiveness

Periodically monitor the effectiveness of your promotional efforts. Chart the percentage of your releases that are used; document the response to them and any ads you place by including a code; match numbers of mailings to specific markets with numbers of sales; analyze feedback from your photobuyers. Continue to test new ideas. Drop those that show no promise, and produce more of those that have been effective.

Postscript

The central message of this chapter has been to blow your own horn. Let people know who you are; get your name known, your work seen. The more exposure you give yourself, the more sales you'll make.

"What about portfolios, exhibits, or contests?" you may ask. They seem to be good sales tools and exposure opportunities. For the stock photographer, however, these elements, thought of almost synonymously with photography, either don't help at all or do very little to increase sales. Let's examine them.

Portfolios

A portfolio is an excellent tool for a *service* photographer because of the types of markets the service photographer works for. A portfolio exhibits the breadth of a photographer's talent and experience to a potential client who may wish to contract for his *services*. Legwork and personal visits are part of establishing credibility when one is selling *oneself*.

On the other hand, for the *stock* photographer—the photo illustrator—a portfolio and personal visits are not necessary. You work primarily by mail, and your kind of photobuyers are not interested in looking at portfolios—they want to see pictures geared to their current layout needs. Your pictures, if they're on target, sell themselves.

A stock photobuyer isn't interested in your versatility. In fact, he wishes you weren't so versatile. He'd prefer you concentrate more thoroughly on one subject—his favorite, the subject of his magazine or books. It stands to reason that a stock photographer who mails apple-orchard pictures in response to a photo request from the editor of an agriculture magazine is going to make a lot more points with that editor than a stock photographer who takes up time showing him a portfolio of underwater, aerial, and architectural photography.

The stock photographer's portfolio, in effect, is each sampling of pictures he sends to a photobuyer for consideration. But the pictures must be on the subject of domestic animals if you're sending them to the editor of a veterinary magazine, on the outdoors if you're sending to a camping magazine.

Exhibitions

Exhibitions are monumental time-consumers and have limited influence on sales, but they don't hurt, and they're good PR, especially when you attain national prominence. Your exhibit area can range from your local library, bank, restaurant, insurance office, or church to a city gallery or art museum. For the latter, a theme exhibit, rather than a general across-the-board show, will get more response from a gallery director. An exhibit built around a specific theme affords the viewing public insight into aspects of society with which they have little familiarity, or into some weltanschauung of your own, which they may find entertaining or informative. Once you have pinpointed your PMS/A, your thematic material should build rapidly. Later on, these same photo illustrations can lend themselves to books—another advantage for you as you build your career with marketing precision.

Exhibits can run from thirty to fifty mounted prints, ranging in size from 8x10 to 16x20 or larger. Usually an exhibit shows for two to four weeks. Capitalize on the exhibit through news releases and posters, plus radio, TV, and speaking appearances.

Salons

Salons, usually sponsored by local and national photography organizations such as camera clubs, offer you little promotional value. Salons are a cross between exhibits and contests. They are extremely—I would say unrealistically—formalized. Salons, in fact, perpetuate many of the myths that photo illustrators must unlearn in order to understand what is a marketable picture and what is not. Salon photographs are usually the standard excellent pictures, exquisite clichés. In fact, unless an entry conforms to this pattern, including the utmost technical perfection, the judges usually look on the entry with disdain. Salons remind me of outdated laws that no one ever questions. In a day when photo illustrations are meaningful tools of communication among strata of society that are drifting further and further apart, salons are an anachronism.

Contests

Contests are somewhat different from salons in that they can offer national publicity plus cash awards to the winners. Contest sponsors tend to judge pictures on their photo-illustrative merit rather than outmoded classical-composition rules that limit a photographer's creativity and expressiveness. If you win a prestigious photo contest, let the photobuyers on your Market List know about it through a press release or photocopy of the news announcement. However, enter photo contests with caution. Read the rules carefully. Many times it's the sponsor of the contest who is the *real* winner. Rule Number 6 or Number 7 will sometimes state, "All photos that receive cash awards become the property of the sponsor, including original negatives and transparencies, and picture rights." The film or camera manufacturer who sponsors such a contest requires the photographer to give up *all* rights to the picture. In other words, you transfer your copyright over to the sponsor—who can then use your picture whatever way he wishes, ad infinitum.

Keep in mind that if your picture is good enough to win a national contest, it's good enough to earn you several thousand dollars in the marketplace in its lifetime. (You can even pass the rights to a picture on to your heirs, by the way.)

Here at PhotoSource International, we have been engaged in a ten-year war with the nationally known firms that sponsor such photo contests. To date, about half of them have rescinded their ownership policy regarding the winning pictures.

If you come across any contests that require you to give up the rights to your photo, I suggest you remind the sponsors that you, the stock photographer, own your own creation. Write them postcards that say, "If my picture is good enough to win a national contest, it is good enough to earn me many dollars over its lifetime. I choose not to relinquish its copyright." Remind the contest sponsor of the Copyright Act, with this line: "Copyright privileges remain with the photographer as per Section 203(a)(3) of the Copyright Act of 1976, Public Law 94-533 (90 Stat. 2541) Title 17 USA Copyrights."

Decor Photography

Producing artful Track A prints for use in commercial buildings or residences can result in excellent showcases for your talents. As you'll read in Chapter 12, *decor photography* (or *photo decor*, or *decor art* as it's sometimes called) will take special administrative (as well as photographic) talent on your part. One approach is to become associated with an existing decor photography business that has already solved the administrative problems. Place your Track A pictures with them, much as you would with a stock agency, and receive a percentage. Beware of new outfits, though—they often tie up your pictures for lengthy periods while they learn the ropes themselves.

Greeting Cards, Calendars, and Posters

Greeting card, calendar, and poster companies offer you other showcase opportunities but have drawbacks of their own (see Appendix A).

From time to time you may decide it's worth your while to barter a supply of cards, calendars, or posters in return for certain rights. Depending on where you stand on the ladder, such an arrangement may be of self-promotional value to you.

Some Final Self-Promotion Suggestions

1. Have several current photographs of yourself on file for promotional use. Often, stock photographers have to make a quick Polaroid of themselves to meet a deadline. Have a press kit handy that includes a couple of black-and-white prints of you plus a biography of you and your accomplishments.

2. Don't do it all yourself. *Get help.* Promotion is always more effective if you can get someone else to write it for you, or at least read it and suggest corrections.

3. You can't measure promotion such as news releases, interviews, and exhibitions as effectively as you can direct advertising. If your business grows, you can assume that your promotional efforts are on the right track and are having an effect.

4. Be helpful. If a writer requests information or an interviewer wants answers, cooperate. *Any* kind of publicity is good. As Huey Long once said, "Say what you want about me, just spell my name correctly."

5. Share the news with others. If an article about you appears in a magazine or newspaper, share it with the photobuyers on your Market List. They'll be interested not so much in you, but in the confirmation that they chose rightly in adding you to their available-photographers list.

6. Here today—gone tomorrow. Promotion—like fitness—is short-lived. Your smashing success today will be past history tomorrow. Photobuyers forget. Oh, do they forget! Keep reminders flowing their way every three to four months.

7. Your promotional tools—your stationery, brochure, catalog, labels, business card, and envelopes—can speak as eloquently as your photographs.

8. Don't expect overnight results. Expect to move mountains, yes, but only stone by stone. Promotion works slowly. But it works.

"Include minorities when possible" is a request you'll often get from publishers of books and magazines. Such pictures will be highly marketable. The young people in this picture were playing a game of touch football and were discussing their next play. By moving in close, the football is eliminated and it appears they are in discussion.

Is grain objectionable in a photo illustration? Photo editors are more artist than engineer. If the picture fits their need, they tend to excuse what a photography purist might call technical imperfection such as the grain in this picture.

11.
Assignments

An Extra Dimension for the Stock Photographer

Buzz Soard of Denver was making a family vacation trip to New Zealand, and he decided to query editors on his Market List before he left. The result was a four-page article on New Zealand's flora and fauna for *Adventure Travel*.

Gene Spencer of Virginia queried his Market List before he left for the Northwest and learned that one photobuyer needed a picture of the Olympia brewery in Washington. "I did several other assignments, too," Gene said, "but that one picture nearly paid for all my gas!"

Assignments can be fun, lucrative, and fascinating, and you can generate them yourself, as well as experience those happy times when the phone rings unexpectedly. One of the biggest rewards, even for those workaday situations ("We need a shot of the National Balloon Race winners") is the satisfaction, and yes, glow, that come from the professional recognition of your competence implicit in any assignment.

As a stock photographer, you can nail plenty of assignments—many of them by mail. Once you have sold several pictures to a photobuyer, you become a valuable resource for that buyer. The situation can arise where the buyer needs a particular picture in a particular part of the country. He consults his index of available photographers (in much the same way as you consult your Market List) and finds that you live near the area. He contacts you and offers you the assignment.

It also works the other way. You are planning a trip, and you inform several of the photobuyers on your Market List of your itinerary, as Buzz and Gene did. One might respond with a two-day assignment, another might tell you that he needs one picture dependent on the weather ("I need clouds in the sky"), and a third might imply that he needs three different pictures if you'd like to take them on speculation. Assignments come in all varieties and will be limited only by the focus of the markets on your personal Market List.

Are assignments in your future? It all depends on your own personal interest in being mobile in your photo-marketing operation. Some stock photographers thrive on travel; others like to work from their homes. If you opt for assignments, you'll find it rewarding to apply the principles in this chapter.

Negotiating Your Fee

How much should you charge when you get an assignment?

I could give a quick answer to this question by referring you to ASMP's guide, *Professional Business Practices in Photography* (American Society of Magazine Photographers, 205 Lexington Avenue, New York, NY 10016); but this guide doesn't have all the answers since it reflects top-dollar fees commanded from top-drawer markets by top pros—and pertains primarily to the world of service photography, where fees range from $600 per day for corporate photography to $4,500 per day for national ads.

As in any business, until you have an impressive track record and your name is known, it's unrealistic to expect top dollar. But perhaps the most basic point to keep in mind is this: Many of the markets you deal with as a stock photographer are publishing markets that consistently pay you respectable fees for your photos, but they can't match New York day rates. Your fees will depend entirely on your own mix of markets. Some of the photobuyers on your Market List may indeed have healthy budgets for photography assignments, but feel them out—don't price yourself beyond what they can bear.

Essentially you are left on your own to judge the particular market and your track record with it, and to negotiate accordingly. Effective negotiations will make the difference between making or missing an assignment.

Now that I've delivered a caution to not overprice yourself, I want to emphasize on the other hand not to *undervalue* your services. Many creative people tend to put too low a price tag on their talents. A good formula to follow is to take whatever you decide to quote to the photobuyer as your day rate—and quote half again as much. You will be surprised how many will accept your higher fee.

In other words, say you have a chance at a plum assignment from an oil company's regional trade magazine. Taking into consideration that you have already sold two pictures to this magazine and this is your first assignment opportunity, you arrive at a $600-a-day rate for such a market. Instead, quote $900. You're probably worth it—and the photobuyer probably agrees—but you won't know until you start negotiating. In a situation like this, think big. With assignment work, while you have to walk a fine line and not charge beyond the range for the particular market, if you quote too low a figure you lose not only the photobuyer's dollars, but also his esteem.

Also, in a situation like this (with the higher-paying trade magazines), you probably will be invited to the photobuyer's office rather than having to negotiate by phone or mail. Being there in person is an advantage in this case, because you can watch the photobuyer's expression and body language when you quote your fee. He'll let you know if you're on target or not.

If your figure is high for his budget, you'll get some resistance. However, remember that he invited *you* to the office; thus, you know he thinks that:

1. You are an established photographer.
2. You bring specialized knowledge and talent to the assignment.
3. You have access to a certain profession and/or geographical area in relation to the assignment.

He who Speaks First . . .

Keep in mind that there are a dozen other photographers he *could have* invited to his office. It may seem like a disadvantage to have all that competition, but it's actually a plus in this case. By inviting you, he has established in his own mind that he has chosen the *right* person. If you quote a low fee, it might lower his estimation of you.

Remember, the photobuyer must report to his superiors. A high fee tends to justify his choice of photographer.

How you state your fee should go like this:

When the photobuyer inquires as to your rate, state your prepared answer confidently, and then—remain quiet. Don't say another word. This is a well-established principle of negotiating. The person who speaks next is at a disadvantage in the bargaining process.

Let the buyer do the talking. When he speaks, it'll probably be to commit himself to your fee or to indicate his budget. He'll probably indirectly answer some questions that are important to you:

1. How badly is the picture needed?
2. What is the competition charging?
3. How easily can he get the picture from some other source?

If you discern that the photobuyer is genuinely resistant to your fee, determine the basis for his resistance, and you will be able to figure the direction you should take in the negotiations.

Here are some guidelines:

1. He'll probably come back to you quoting a lower figure (you've tossed the ball to him—now he's tossing it back . . .). Don't immediately accept it. Why? He is probably feeling you out with a figure lower than what he actually could pay. He'll make some concessions if you press him.

2. Don't concede anything if you can help it, or at least don't be the first to concede ("OK, I'll complete the assignment in two days instead of three . . ."). If you concede first, the picture buyer has the upper hand.

3. If you have to concede something (the buyer tells you he can't cover the cost of developing your film, for example), then ask him for a concession, too ("I must have double mileage for this trip. There are a lot of dirt roads out there in West Texas!").

4. If you must match concessions with the picture buyer, remind him that these concessions are valid only if you and he are able to reach a final overall agreement on a contract or a fee for the assignment.

5. Decide beforehand what you want: a minimum and a maximum. (Make sure these figures are realistic.) Keep score as you negotiate.

6. If you come out smelling like roses, don't feel guilty about it. Remember: You don't always win in such negotiations. Enjoy the glow while it lasts. Next time you may not come out so well.

7. What if the photobuyer says, "This is the fee we can pay—you can take it or leave it!"? You can either say "thanks but no thanks" or explore with him the possibility of retracing your steps to either narrow or broaden the scope of the assignment. Offer more or fewer pictures, discuss travel expenses, change the length of the assignment. These are areas where you can concede wisely. Don't agree, however, to give up your negatives or to grant the buyer ownership (all rights) to your pictures. Even in these areas, though, it isn't a case of "never"—you may get in situations where the fee for all rights is sky high, or where you are eager to get that particular assignment at all costs. (See the discussion of work-for-hire in Chapter 15.)

Negotiating can be challenging—even fun. Practice makes perfect. Try out variations of your routine with your spouse or a friend playing the part of photobuyer. If you will be doing your negotiating by phone, then do your practicing on extension phones or in a couple of phone booths. You'll find that just running through your script is a tremendous catalyst to new thoughts, new ways to phrase your points.

In the long run, a photobuyer will appreciate your efforts to get the best fee for your pictures. Even if you come away with $600 a day instead of your $900, remember that's the fee you originally were willing to settle for.

Expenses

The quote you make for your day rate to a photobuyer does not include your expenses. These are over and above the day rate you receive, and they depend on a number of variables.

When negotiations reach the point where you address expenses, your reliability factor will be strengthened if you hand the photobuyer a copy of your Expenses form.

Have typeset and printed a personalized business form that lists expenses involved on assignment work. When I first started out, I had my own form printed on 4½x9½ paper in three different colors—white, blue, and pink—then collated and gum-sealed into a pad. I use carbon paper above the blue and pink, and I send the first two copies to my client and keep the third for my records. The pad paid for itself on my first assignment.

In a corner of the pad, in small print, is this message: "This sale or assignment is in accord with the code of practices as set forth by ASMP."

Although you may not be an ASMP member, or even if your client cannot afford ASMP rates, your expenses are a fixed cost, and you should expect reimbursement accordingly.

Your expense form should read as the one in Figure 11-1.

An equally effective approach, if you are computerized, is to present to the photobuyer a (dot-matrix) printout that includes not only your expense estimates but other points you agreed upon during the negotiation.

Extra Mileage from Assignments

Your assignments will take you to locations you might not ordinarily visit. Carry along an extra camera (or two—one for black-and-white and one for color), and shoot some stock photos for other photobuyers on your Market List. These are called *sister shots.*

This will not be as easy as it sounds. Full concentration on your assignment is essential to producing quality results, which is also the way you maintain a strong reliability factor with your client. Anything less than 100 percent attention to your assignment will give you mediocre, or at least ordinary, results. When you shoot "side" pictures while on assignment, then, plan to shoot them on your time and at your expense.

Many assignments call for only specific pictures. This situation allows you to add the sister shots to your stock file. Some stock photographers arrive early on the scene or stay later on an assignment. As long as the client has paid the transportation expense, you can capitalize on the (sometimes exotic) locale and shoot for your stock file. Some photographers shoot to add to their collection of pictures on special themes. Simon Nathan of New York, for example, snaps pictures of clothes hanging

---

YOUR LETTERHEAD
EXPENSES

From: Your Name

TO:
DATE:
SUBJECT:

TRAVEL
Taxi...$_____
Auto (_____¢ per mile) ....$_____
*Plane, train, bus ....$_____
*Car rental ....$_____
Tips..$_____
*Meals _____ *Lodging _____ ....$_____
PHOTOGRAPHIC
Processing
*Color: _____ Rolls @ $ _____ ....$_____
*B&W: _____ Rolls @ $ _____ ....$_____
*Rental of special equipment......................$_____
Other:

$_____

PROPS ....$_____
(Construction of or rentals)
MODEL FEES....................................$_____
(Hiring or nonprofessional releases)
LOCATION CHARGES ....$_____
MAILING, UPS CHARGES, TRUCKING ....$_____
INCIDENTALS
Long-distance phone calls ....$_____
Messenger, porter, assistant, guard...............$_____
Liability insurance ....$_____

SPECIAL SERVICES
Casting...$_____
Hair and makeup ....$_____
Home economist ....$_____
Costumes, clothing................................$_____
Location search ....$_____
OTHER...$_____
TOTAL EXPENSES: $_____

*Receipts attached   This sale or assignment is in accord with the
                                      code of practices as set forth by ASMP.

Figure 11-1. A sample expense form.

on clotheslines all over the world. "One day I'll have an exhibit—or publish them in book form," says Simon.

Do you own the pictures you take on assignment? It depends on what type of contract, if any, you have signed, or what rights agreement you and your client have arranged (see Chapter 15).

The Stringer

Another assignment channel is open to the photographer who is on tap for picture-taking services for a trade magazine, news service, newsstand magazine, or industry account. The photographer in this situation is usually called a stringer. You are, in effect, a part-time freelancer who sometimes works on a retainer basis—that is, for a regular monthly fee. In most cases, however, you work on a per-assignment basis. You get paid only when you produce.

Being a stringer falls primarily into the area of service photography, but stringer opportunities are also there for the stock photographer. By working out a flexible contract with a trade publication, you can arrange, for example, to supply them on a regular basis with single pictures relating to their subject theme.

For example, if one of your PMS/A areas is breed dogs and you travel often to dog shows, you would be a valuable resource to editors of various dog magazines, which have audiences ranging from breed associations to veterinarians. (We're talking about good working shots of dogs in action or breed portraits—remember, if you emphasize cute-puppy pictures, that's crossing over into Track A, pictures that you'll want to place in a photo agency; see Chapter 12.) If you travel often, you could tie in your mobility with other photobuyers on your Market List (recreational pictures for outdoor magazines, horse shows for horse magazines, equipment in use for heavy-equipment magazines).

Your contract need not be any more formal than a letter of agreement stating that you will supply them with X pictures a month (week, or year) for X dollars. The fee will not be monumental, but if you have several contracts, the sum will more than cover your expenses to those dog shows.

Competing magazines, of course, would not appreciate your supplying the same photographs simultaneously across the market. So by researching the specific needs of the photobuyers on your Market List, you can guard against inappropriate multiple submissions, yet set up an operation to receive checks with regularity.

Self-Assignments—Where Do You Start?

If assignments aren't coming your way yet, give them to yourself. Such self-assignments will reward you with new insights into lighting, working with models, using the $P = B + P + S + I$ principle (see Chapter 2), and using varied lens lengths for effect, as well as pulling elements together to make a cohesive and interesting feature.

You can start right away, and at the same time give yourself a course on producing the picture story, if you're not afraid to copy. Through the ages, creative people have learned from each other by imitating each other. As the Bible says, "There's nothing new under the sun!" A simple, effective technique based on this principle is *the switch*. Here's how it works:

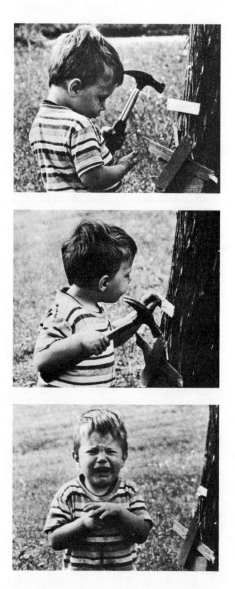

THE PHOTO ESSAY. *Want to make your picture stories come alive? Learn from the pros. A moviemaker in Africa taught me this trick, which you can apply to your photo stories. "Every story has a beginning, middle, and end," he said. "Whenever I get spectacular footage, say, of a successful rescue in a river, or one of my African crew fending off an attack by an animal, I consider that the climax footage. I then go back and film footage that will lead up to my climax footage. This subsequent footage I then use as my beginning and middle shots." In the case of the little boy at left, I shot the third picture on Saturday, and on Sunday I shot the first two.*

Let's say you're reading one of the magazines on your Market List and you come across a one-page, three-photo picture story about a young Eastern boy who is spending his summer in the West, earning money for college by working as a wrangler at a horse ranch in Wyoming. The copy block contains about 300 words. The pictures are a close-up of the young man and two middle-view shots, one a vertical, the other a horizontal.

You will use this story as a blueprint. It shows you what the requirements are for a similar picture story (not the same story, but one that's similar). In your case, you know of a young Dutch girl down the block who is in the United States for a year as a high school exchange student. In order to improve her English and to earn spending money, she is working as a babysitter for your neighbors.

The city-boy-turned-cowboy story pictured the boy with a ten-gallon hat. You will picture the Dutch girl in a native Dutch hat. The blueprint story showed the boy helping in the early morning roundup of the horses. You will show the Dutch girl with neighborhood children explaining how wooden shoes are made. The blueprint story showed the boy at breakfast with companions, downing heaps of flapjacks. You will picture the Dutch girl cheering with friends at a high school football game.

The original article is also a blueprint for the writing. You will tailor your writing to match the content and style of your blueprint. Insert quotes and anecdotes in much the same proportion as your model. If your writing skills are weak, find a friend who writes well and team together. Or simply amass the details (who, what, where, when, how), and submit them to the editor with your pictures. The editor will find his own writer.

Where to market your picture story? Start with the local metropolitan Sunday paper. They're always interested in seeing this slice-of-life kind of story. Also send it off to noncompeting magazines on your Market List that accept brief photo stories.

Expand certain aspects of your story to fit other markets. The wooden shoe, emphasized correctly, would appeal to trade magazines in the shoe industry. Periodicals in the educational field would like to see emphasis on the Dutch girl's learning experience in this country.

Submit at least a half-dozen pictures to give the editor a choice for his layout. Again, tailor your story line to your original blueprint, and you will earn not only the price of this book, but possibly the price you paid for the camera that took the pictures.

The key is to locate your blueprint example in the magazines on your Market List. This way you know you're on target with subject matter and treatment that are coordinated with your PMS/A.

Such self-assignments may not prove immediately marketable as picture packages, but certain of the photographs may turn out to be individually marketable stock photos.

Speculation

On self-assignments, you're working on speculation. Is this a "no-no" in stock photography? Not if you've used some savvy and done some homework to identify your PMS/A and become familiar with the kind of pictures needed by those on your individual Market List.

This way, if your stock photo picture doesn't sell the first time around, it's a valuable addition to your files and stands a good chance of earning its keep over the long haul.

You can also take pictures on speculation in response to a specific photo request by an editor, and this, too, is not a no-no. In fact, it is especially helpful to the newcomer to the field. When you speculate by following the guidelines of a photobuyer, you are, in effect, receiving free instruction in what makes a good, marketable stock photo. The editor's specifics will tell you what to include and what not to include. Subscribers to our *Photoletter* will often use a current photo-need listing as a guide, take the picture, and submit it to the photobuyer, if the deadline is within reason.

There are times, however, when you shouldn't speculate: a timely picture will quickly lose its marketability. A highly specific picture will probably not be marketable to many targets. Going after a picture that entails a good deal of expense (in time, travel, special arrangements) is questionable. (The President's visit to Ohio might attract so much freelance and staff-photographer competition that it wouldn't be cost-effective for you to get involved.) Finally, a picture that is outside your PMS/A might reflect your lack of expertise, and that would limit its marketability.

Take a Free Vacation

One type of self-assignment you can give yourself with assurance, over and over again, is the travel assignment—but with a switch: If you're planning a vacation or a business trip, plan to profit on your trip through your photography. (Because your travel can be a business expense when it involves getting pictures to add to your stock photo files, your travel expenses can be a tax write-off—another way your trip pays for itself. Chapter 16 gives more details on the tax benefits of making a business out of your photography expertise.) However, rather than aiming your camera at standard tourist attractions (Track A pictures, with limited marketability), concentrate on pictures where the supply is short and demand is great.

Another free vacation is one that is offered to established stock photographers and writers by public relations firms representing shiplines, ski resorts, hotel chains, spas, and so on. Invitations are issued regularly in the *Photobulletin* and *Travel Writer Market Letter* by firms that will provide lodging, meals, and often airfare to writers and photographers who have firm assignments relating to areas of the world they represent.

Who buys travel pictures? Travel editors, of course, but they are so deluged with travel pictures (exquisite clichés) from freelancers, government agencies, stock photo agencies, PR people, and authors of travel
stories, that this market takes time to break into. At first, you represent
more work for the travel editor as someone new that he has to deal with,
communicate with, explain his picture needs to—all of which he wants
to avoid, since he already has established picture sources that supply his
needs. Instead of aiming at travel editors at first, direct your marketing
efforts toward the publicity offices of airline, bus, train, ship, and hotel
organizations; city, state, and national tourist offices; PR agencies; filmstrip companies; ad agencies (who represent the country or state); plus
encyclopedia and other reference-book publishers who are continually
updating their publications. Also, it's helpful in some cases to contact
photo agencies. (See Figures 11-2, 11-3, and 12-1.)

Standard travel pictures are difficult to market because of the competition. Do not submit spectacular (in your estimation) pictures of standard tourist sites. The publicity officer or editor has already rejected
hundreds of them. You can, however, include pictures of new travel attractions, or changes in existing attractions.

What does the travel photobuyer really need? Current pictures in
their locales of these areas of interest: agriculture, mining, transportation, cuisine, contemporary architecture, celebrities, communications,
recreation, education, industry, labor, sports, and special events.

Your travel pictures, then, are not really travel pictures at all—but pictures of factories, airports, new sports facilities, freeways, festivals,
open-pit mines, housing, people, and skylines.

To know what to take and where to find the subject matter, write to the
Department of Economic Development and/or Department of Tourism
(or Consulate/Embassy, if foreign) of the area you will be visiting. They
will supply you with several pounds of literature—all of which needs
updating. Travel agencies can supply similar literature. Consult the encyclopedias at your library, as well as other reference books, maps, filmstrips, and pamphlets that feature your area of interest. All of this material will serve as a blueprint for the kind of pictures that photobuyers need.
Make photocopies of pertinent leads, pictures, and details (these will aid
you in your query letter).

The agencies you will be working with are actually promotion agencies. They want to put their client's best foot forward. In these changing
times, the profile of a city, tourist attraction, national park, or monument
changes rapidly. Updated quality pictures are always of interest to trav-
el-picture buyers. (Note: Remind the photobuyer that your picture is an
update.)

Stock agencies (see Chapter 12) are interested in seeing specific quality travel pictures. If they like your selection, they'll probably ask to see
more from other areas of the country or the world that you could take or

may have in your files. If your pictures are large-format (120-size, 4x5, 8x10), you'll probably have a better chance of scoring at an agency than if they are 35mm. However, some agencies will enlarge your 35mm to 4x5 for you. Other stock agencies deal strictly in 35mm.

But scoring depends on factors other than size. One of the most important is *content*. If they are pictures of a relatively untraveled area of the world or of places currently in the news, they will probably interest an agency more than if they were taken in, say, New York or Paris.

Here's another buyer for your kind of travel pictures: book publishers. New books on the area you just photographed will be coming out shortly. Why not have your pictures appear in them? The departments and offices mentioned above are often aware of books in progress. They will steer you in the right direction (since their job is PR) if you mention in your letter to them that you would welcome information on forthcoming publications about their area. Photo agencies, too, are aware of new books in progress because photo researchers are knocking on their doors, looking for a picture from such and such a place. While you're checking at the photo agencies, tell them you have fresh, updated pictures of the place(s) you've visited. Frequently, photo agencies miss a sale because their locale pictures are outdated.

PR (public relations) agencies will be interested in placing your photos if your pictures match their client's area of interest. Let's say, for example, you just returned from a trip to Venezuela, where you got forty marketable pictures of birds. Using the SATW directory (see page 58), find out which PR agency(s) represents Venezuela. For example, XYZ Agency will have an in-house writer prepare an article on "Birds of Venezuela." Using your photos, the agency will sell the article to a nature magazine. You will receive payment for your photos, as well as national recognition.

What about postcards? Postcard companies (see Appendix A) are rarely good markets for your travel pictures. They pay low fees, your picture is bucking hundreds or thousands of others for selection, and the companies usually want all rights. The competition is stiff in the postcard/gift area and the fees are generally low. Unless you have a special reason for marketing in these areas, avoid them.

Making the Contact

When possible, contact picture buyers *before* you go on your trip rather than after you return. Photobuyers, editors, and agencies can inform you of their current needs and suggest side trips to collect pictures (on speculation or assignment) to supplement or update their files. Independent photographers do sometimes shoot first and ask questions later (the *shotgun method*). But most veterans inquire first, with a letter like the one shown in Figure 11-2, and then shoot (the *rifle method*). Here are some letter-writing guidelines:

YOUR LETTERHEAD

Dear _____:

On August 15 through August 20, 19____, I will be traveling in the state of Minnesota. My itinerary will include Duluth, the Iron Range, Charles Lindbergh's home, a visit to Control Data in Minneapolis, and stopping points in between.

May I help you update your files with pictures from these areas? I shoot B&W and color, in both 35mm and 2¼-inch format.

If you have specialized photo needs along this itinerary, I would be interested in learning about them. Perhaps we could work out an assignment that is mutually beneficial. I would submit my pictures to you, of course, on a satisfaction-guaranteed basis.

My pictures, including the several thousand I have in stock, are available on a one-time basis for publication at your usual rates.

Thank you for your attention, and I look forward to hearing from you.

Yours sincerely,

John Doe

Figure 11-2. *A typical assignment query letter.*

1. This is a form letter you will send out to a number of promotion directors or editors, so type an original on your professional letterhead, which includes your address and phone, and then photocopy or instant-print it. Leave a blank in the salutation to fill in the name, with space above for each different address. (You can write to "Editor," "Photo Editor," or "Art Director," but if you can find out the name of the individual, this, of course, is preferred.) The form-letter format is an asset in this case because it tells the picture buyer two reliability factors about you: that you deal with many photobuyers who are interested in your pictures—and he gets the impression that if he acts quickly, he can be first to review them; and that you do business in *volume*, so you must be competent and familiar with the marketing process—someone he could develop as a consistent source of pictures. Photobuyers usually aren't interested in dealing with one-shot photographers.

2. In your first paragraph, let the photobuyer know *when* you're going, for *how long*, what your *itinerary* is (only the routes that will relate to his area of interest), and how you'll be traveling (car, plane, train, bus).

3. Never ask if he'd like to *see* your pictures of *standard* tourist attractions—national monuments, parks, etc. (You should know that he already has these covered.) Instead, ask if he would like his files of these pictures *updated*. Your recognizing his need to constantly update his files puts you in a professional light.

4. Explain whether you will shoot in black-and-white, color, or both. And tell him the size of your camera(s).

5. Suggest that if he has some upcoming photo needs, you can save him time and expense by shooting them for him—if it's not too much out of the way for you. Assure him that you are not locking him into any definite contractual arrangement. (It's easy to say no to those.) Let him know your pictures will be taken with no obligation or precommitment on his part. Mention in the next paragraph your stock file of several thousand. The editor will interpret this to mean there will be no loss to you if he does not accept your pictures—that you are an established stock photographer with a high reliability factor and plenty of available markets. Let him know you are renting these pictures, not selling them. Try to find out the going rate for his publication or publishing house before you contact him, but if you can't, tell him your pictures are available for publication at his usual rates.

Figure 11-2 is a typical assignment query letter—you'll notice it's brief. No photo editor wants a history of you or your photography. If your photos fit his needs, he'll buy. If they don't, he won't.

Let's say you didn't contact anyone before your trip, though, and you've just returned from Poland with many fine pictures. What do you do now? Contact all promotion bureaus, offices, and agencies that represent Poland. These will include government agencies as well as private Polish and American agencies such as airlines, ship lines, and hotel chains. Your list might also include American ad and PR agencies that handle these accounts. Design a form letter that informs these agencies of your pictures of Poland. Do not send actual pictures or a Poland portfolio until an agency expresses interest to you. Visit the agency in person, if possible, with a portfolio of pictures tailored specifically to the agency's interest. Use the tips in Chapter 7 on how to contact photobuyers by phone, by mail, and in person. It's on these visits that you might receive referrals for your pictures ("No, we can't use them—but I know Joe Jones is preparing a book on Northern Poland").

Here's how you would develop your after-the-trip query letter (see Figure 11-3 for a sample):

1. See Number 1 of the instructions for writing a letter of inquiry.

2. In your first paragraph, let the editor or director know who you are, where you're from (your letterhead will help), and when you were in his state or area. If your pictures are fresh updates, he is going to be interested. Mention specific areas that you have photographed.

3. Ask if you may send a selection of color and/or black-and-whites for his consideration. (Don't send photos with this first letter.) If you know what he pays, mention this fee in your letter. This will save both of you an extra exchange of negotiating correspondence. If you don't know his fee range, apply some of the pricing tactics outlined in Chapter 8.

4. Being an unknown photographer puts you at a disadvantage. Editors sometimes ignore introductory letters such as this. They prefer to stay with their own cadre of familiar and reliable photographers—rather than go through the extra work of establishing contact with a new photographer. It's a good idea, therefore, to insert a line in your letter to this effect: "Requesting review of these pictures does not obligate you to any purchase."

5. Ask outright which pictures (of those you've listed) the photobuyer would like to review.

6. The copywriters of the world tell us that the section of your letter that gets read first (if your letter gets read at all) is the *postscript*. You can attract the editor's attention by listing some of the places you have previously (or recently) photographed in his city, state, country, etc. Since these names will be familiar to him, this will help personalize your letter to him.

If the director or editor does ask to see your pictures, you should enclose a cover letter when you submit them for consideration. Again, a form letter is useful both to you (for your own records) and the editor. Your pictures, of course, will sell themselves, but as consumers, we all know that we are not likely to buy a new product (in this case, you are the new product) if service and support are not available. In other words, if the editor suspects you are a fly-by-night, that you have no reliability fac-

YOUR LETTERHEAD

Dear _____:

My name is_____ , and
I recently updated my stock photo files of several thousand transparencies and B&W prints when I traveled through [state/country] in
[month]. My files now include substantial coverage of these points of
interest:*

_____

_____

_____

I would be happy to send you a selection of B&W prints and
transparencies for your consideration. They are available at
$_____ on a one-time rights basis. Request to review these pic-
tures does not obligate you to any purchase.

Which pictures would you like to receive for consideration?

Yours sincerely,

[Your name]

*P.S. I also have strong coverage in my stock file of these areas:

_____

_____

_____

Figure 11-3. Sample shotgun (after-the-trip) query letter.

tor, that your business address or telephone might change next week, he is not likely to give your submission much attention. Photobuyers recognize the professional touch in submissions accompanied by a form cover letter. Again, it must be brief. Editors are faced with the task of sifting through hundreds of photo submissions weekly. They don't appreciate lengthy letters that ask questions or relate irrelevant details about the enclosed submission. If you do feel compelled to ask a specific question (and sometimes it *is* necessary), write it out on a separate sheet of paper and enclose an SASE for easy reply.

If your form letter is neatly typed (never handwrite queries to editors), the editor will greatly appreciate your professionalism. Better yet, have it printed by one of the fast-print services (ask for 70-pound stationery stock), leaving blanks to fill in specific details for each different situation. The editor will then recognize you as not a one-shot photographer, but as someone with a good supply of pictures and, therefore, as an important resource for handling future stock photo needs and assignments. (The thinking here is that no one would go to the expense of a printed form letter if he had only a few photographs to market.)

A typical form letter to accompany your submissions could be the standard cover letter in Chapter 9 (Figure 9-1). (If your submission is solicited, you can lead the letter off with the line: "Thank you for your request to see my coverage of _____.") Be sure to mention in this letter that "captions are included."

Ordinarily, stock photos (unless they are meant for technical or scientific use) do not require identifying captions. But travel and location pictures generally do. In your captions, identify the location and the action/situation in the picture. For a sample, see the illustrations of Poland in the following sections.

One final suggestion for *free travel*. If your forte is glamorous pictures of resort areas, Caribbean hotel owners are willing to barter with you. Send a sampling of your work to the sales manager of a Caribbean hotel with the explanation that you will provide brochure-quality pictures (twenty to forty) of his hotel environs, complete with models and model releases, in return for a one-week stay for you and your models. Provided your sample pictures are good and your male/female friends who accompany you have an All-American look, you will be hosted in the Caribbean next February for a week. In some cases, airfare can also be arranged.

To reiterate, your prime travel markets will be reference books, PR agencies, Bureaus of Tourism, publicity offices of airline, bus, train, and ship companies, hotel organizations, and other offices whose mission is to promote travel and economic development in the state or country they represent. These offices actively seek new and updated views of their areas of interest. Your secondary markets can be stock photo agencies, travel-oriented magazines, calendar and greeting card companies. The addresses of hundreds of such markets are easily available in reference guides such as *Photographer's Market*, 1507 Dana Ave., Cincinnati, OH 45207; and *Magazine Industry Marketplace* (MIMP), R.R. Bowker, Inc., 1180 Avenue of the Americas, New York, NY 10036. These reference guides are available at most libraries. A newsletter with markets for travel writers and photographers is Bob Milne's *Travelwriter Marketletter*, Rm 1723A, The Plaza Hotel, New York, NY 10019. Another is Nadine Orabona's *Photo Traveler*, P.O. Box 3768, Costa Mesa, CA 92628. An annual seminar for travel (tourism) photography is Lisl Dennis's Travel Photography Workshop, held at Santa Fe around Labor Day (one week), Box 2847, Santa Fe, NM 87501. The widely read syndicated column by Carl Purcell in 172 newspapers, called "Travel," is a good resource. *How to Get the Best Travel Photographs*, by Frederik Bodin is available through Focal Press, Suite 17, 5 Wiley St., Gloucester, MA 01930.

A Sampling of "Hot Sellers"

Each of your prime travel markets (e.g., mining, transportation, education) will present varied opportunities for stock photos. The following pictures of Poland are a good indication of the style and type of pictures sought by encyclopedias, textbook publishers, airlines, ship and rail lines, heavy-equipment trade magazines, agricultural periodicals, and Bureaus of Tourism. Instead of aiming your camera at tourist attractions, produce pictures such as these for repeat sales.

*Photos courtesy of
Polish Embassy.*

12.
Stock Photo Agencies and Decor Photography

Outlets for Track A

Stock photo agencies can offer opportunities or headaches. This chapter will help you avoid the "stock agency blues" and capitalize on the dollars available to the photographer with the right kind of stock photographs at the right agency.

If you choose wisely, you can approach agencies as an investment—one that should pay off in time.

You will gain most by selling your prime Track B pictures yourself, to your hot Market List. Let agencies handle your Track A pictures—those standard excellent photos that are so difficult to market on your own, because of excessive competition and the fact that the buyers who look for those types of shots are the ones who usually turn to agencies or their own list of favorite pros, not to a lesser-known freelancer.

I myself have pictures at three agencies: in New York, Chicago, and Colorado. My first contact with a stock photo agency was in 1958, when I had just returned from a trip through Africa. In New York, a friend introduced me to Anita Beer (who later merged her stock photography agency with Photo Researchers, Inc., New York City). In those days, agencies were not plentiful, and they attempted to be all things to all people. Emphasis was on black-and-white. Today, the emphasis has moved to color, computerization, and specialization. Although some large, prestigious agencies still hold out as general agencies, new ones have seen what happened in the magazine industry to general magazines and have taken the hint to specialize.

Most of the better-known stock photo agencies (sometimes called *picture-rental libraries*) are located in New York. The Manhattan telephone directory lists sixty-five of them. The photobuyers who use stock agencies range from book and magazine publishers to ad agencies and PR firms. These photobuyers have one thing in common: they can pay the high fee stock agencies demand.

Prepare to Share Your Profit

Stock agencies do demand high fees. They can afford to, because they offer the photobuyer something he can't get anywhere else—a huge selection at his fingertips. It's this fact, so attractive to photobuyers, that is your disadvantage. If your picture of a windmill or frog or seagull is being considered for purchase among dozens and dozens of others in the same agency—never mind competing agencies—your chance of scoring is minimal.

Even against this reality, however, the chances of that kind of Track A picture selling are greater at an agency than if you tried to market it yourself. Does big money await you when you go with an agency? It depends on how well you choose your agencies and how often you supply them with your targeted photos. Agencies will tally their sales for you on a monthly, quarterly, or half-year basis and send you a check. And although this check is for only 40 to 50 percent (sometimes 60 percent) of the agency's sales (the agency receives the remainder), it's always welcome. (From $40 to $150 is the present range of your share of an average transparency sale.) Most photographers, whether they are service or stock photographers, count on agency sales only as a supplement to the rest of their photography business.

A good rule of thumb, according to stock-photographer Ellis Herwig, is that you can expect one dollar annually for every photo you have in an agency. If you have 500 photos with the agency, you can expect annual revenues of $500; if you have 5,000, you can expect $5,000, and so on.

Newcomers to photo marketing (and some not so new) sometimes think they can relax once their pictures are with an agency—they believe that now they can concentrate on the fun of shooting and printing and check cashing, and let the agency handle the administrative hassles of marketing.

Agencies: A Plus with Limitations

It just doesn't work that way. In fact, it's a bit like gambling. You can increase your chances of making regular sales through agencies if, as at the baccarat table, you study the game.

Agencies offer the pluses of good prices and lots of contacts, but they have limitations that affect the sales of your pictures. One is that monumental competition faced by any one picture. Another is that no agency is going to market your pictures as aggressively as you do. The agency has something to gain from selling, yes, but it spreads its efforts over many photographers.

Another limitation, which you can turn to a plus once you're aware of it, is that different agencies become known among photobuyers as good suppliers in some categories of pictures but not others. Like art galleries, agencies tend to be strong in certain types of pictures. Sometimes, however, an agency will accept photos in categories outside its known specialties. If you place your pictures in the *wrong* agency, they'll not move (sell) for you.

When a photobuyer at a magazine or book publishing house needs a picture, he assigns the job of obtaining that picture to a photo researcher, a person (often a freelancer) who is adept at finding pictures quickly, for a fee. The researcher makes a beeline for an agency that he knows is strong in the category on the needs sheet.

If a book publisher, for example, is preparing a coffee-table book on songbirds, the researcher will know which agency to visit, and it might not be an agency you or I have ever heard of. And it might not even be in New York.

Photo researchers know that agencies, like magazine and book publishers, have moved toward specialization. By going to an agency that he knows is strong in songbirds, the researcher knows he'll have not a handful of pictures to choose from, but several hundred. Often the picture requirements will demand more than simply "a blackbird"—they'll specify the background: the type (Brewer's or red-winged), the time of the year (courtship? nesting? plumage changes?), the action involved (in flight, perching, or a certain close-up position)—and the wide selection will be particularly necessary.

Researchers feel that they're doing their client justice in choosing an agency they know will have a wide selection. If your pictures of birds or alligators are in a different agency, they may never be seen.

The first order of business in regard to agencies, then, is to research the field and pick the right ones for your mix of categories. You can have your picture in several agencies at once, chosen on the basis of geographical distribution (an agency in Denver, one in Chicago, one in New York), and on the basis of picture-category specialization (scenics at one, African wildlife at another, horses at another).

How to Find the Right Agency

If your photography is good, just about *any* agency will accept it, whether or not they're looked to by photobuyers as strong in your particular categories. That's where the danger lies. How, then, can you find the right agency or agencies for you?

It takes time, but here's one approach. Part of your task on the second weekend of your Get Started Action Plan (see Chapter 4) is to separate your pictures into Track A categories on the one hand and your PMS/A on the other. Take both your Track A and PMS/A lists and narrow them down to the areas where you have the largest number of pictures.

Let's invent an example. Let's say that in Track A (the standard excellents) you isolate three areas in which you are very strong: squirrels, covered bridges, and underwater pictures. In your Track B PMS/A you isolate five strong areas: skiing, gardening, camping, aviation, and agriculture. Taking your Track A pictures first, rather than placing all three Track A categories with one general agency, do some research and find which agencies in the country are strongest in each of your three categories.

You might find that your covered-bridge pictures land in a prestigious general agency in New York that happens to have a strong covered-bridge library. You will supply that agency with a continuing fresh stock of covered bridges, and they will move your pictures aggressively. Your underwater pictures might land in a small agency in Colorado that is noted for its underwater collection. Again, your pictures should move, since photo researchers will know to look to this agency for underwater shots.

Your covered-bridge pictures fall into Track A; you would probably have difficulty marketing them on your own. But how about your Track B pictures, like your camping or agriculture shots? Should you ever place them in an agency, too—or will you be competing against yourself, since you will be aggressively marketing your Track B pictures to your own Market List?

Your answer will depend on your Track B pictures themselves, their particular categories, and your Market List. If your own marketing efforts are fruitful, you will do best to continue to market your B categories yourself. If certain of your Track B pictures move slowly for you, you might find it advantageous to put them in an agency. (If you do, place your slower-moving Track B categories in different agencies with the same forethought you gave to your Track A categories.)

Researching the Agencies

Tracking down the strengths of individual agencies will take some research on your part. The magazines and books that are already using pictures similar to yours will be your best aid. As an example, let's take your Track A squirrel pictures.

Being a squirrel photographer, you naturally gravitate to pictures of squirrels. If you see one in a newspaper, encyclopedia, or textbook, it attracts your eye. Make a note of the credit line (if there is one) on each squirrel photograph. It will be credited with a photographer's or agency's name in about a third of the cases. (Picture credits are sometimes grouped together in the back or front of a magazine or book.) If after six months of this kind of research the same stock photo agency name keeps popping up, your detective work is paying off. (Sometimes, depending on your Track A category, two or three agency names will appear. This is a plus—it means you can be choosy about whom you eventually contact, basing your decision on how long each agency has been in business, their location, whether they have a WATS line, etc.) Locate the photo agency's address in a directory such as *Photographer's Market*.

You can also check agencies out by contacting the Picture Agency Council of America (PACA). Send $2 plus SASE for a list showing their membership's specialties. (This list will prove helpful in locating agencies and the categories of pictures they carry, but you'll learn more about where photobuyers go for what through your own research.) The address is 32 East 31st Street, Comstock Suite, New York, NY 10016.

How to Contact a Stock Photo Agency

Agencies, like photobuyers, expect a high reliability factor from you. If you are certain you have discovered an agency that is strong in one or more of your categories, contact the agency with a forceful letter.

Your first paragraph should make the agency director aware that you have been doing some professional research, and that you aren't a fly-by-night who just happened to stumble onto his agency's address.

Let the agency know the size and format of the collection you are offering, and whether it's black-and-white or color (a surprising number of agencies require black-and-white in addition to color). If you place special emphasis on a certain category, or you live in or photograph in a unique environment, state this also.

Impress upon the agency that your group of pictures is not static, that you continually add fresh images. (Some photographers hope to dump an outdated collection on an agency.)

Tell the director you are considering placing this particular collection in a stock house. Give the impression that you are shopping, *not* that you are expecting or wishing to place your pictures with him.

A typical letter that you can tailor to your own style is shown in Figure 12-1.

If your research is accurate and your letter professional in tone and appearance, the photo agency will welcome your contribution to their library. More important, your pictures will be at an agency known for a specialty—that happens to be *your* specialty.

In some cases, you can make a personal visit to an agency instead of writing a letter. A few agencies in the large cities designate one day of the week when photographers can come in to display their photos for consideration.

One photographer I know walked into a New York agency with ten notebooks of vinyl pages (about four thousand slides). The director said, "I can't look at that many slides. Weed them down to one book and come back tomorrow." The photographer went back to his hotel room and spent until 3:00 a.m. narrowing down the selection to one book rep-

---

YOUR LETTERHEAD

Dear _____,

I have noticed your placement of [category] pictures with many national accounts and want to compliment you on your success.

My collection of [same category] photographs is [600] strong [400 color, 35mm, and 200 B&W] and I am adding fresh images [weekly; monthly; regularly]. I am presently seeking a photo agency that will aggressively market my [category] pictures.

May I send you a sampling for your consideration? How many?

Yours sincerely,

[Your name]

Figure 12-1. *Sample contact category letter to a stock photo agency.*

resenting his best. He returned the next day, and the director said, "This is nice stuff. Do you have any more of these 'people having fun in winter sports'? We get a lot of calls for outdoor recreation."

The photographer went back to his hotel, went through the selection process again, and rushed back to the director with a book of outdoor-recreation pictures. The photographer has since sold outdoor-recreation scenes through the agency and continues to update his file there. Learn from this example. Categorize your pictures before you step into an agency. The director will want to see the best you have—on the subjects that interest him.

Once an agency says "OK, we'll carry your pictures," how many should you leave for their files? If it is a highly specialized agency, a minimum of forty black-and-white prints or slides (two vinyl sheets) is acceptable. A general agency would expect ten to fifteen of your vinyl pages and/or two hundred to three hundred black-and-whites. They would expect you to update this selection with twenty to forty new photos at a time, every six months to a year.

The agency will specify how your pictures should be identified and captioned. For example, on slides, most agencies want their agency name at the top, the caption information at the bottom. Your identification code, name, address, and telephone number should appear on the sides. They'll want to know which pictures have a model release (MR) or a model release possible (MRP).

The agency will send you their standard contract form in which they'll stipulate, among other things, that they will take 50 percent (sometimes 40 percent, sometimes 60 percent) of the revenue from picture sales. Expect them to require you to keep your pictures on file with them for a minimum of five years. (If after a period of time you want your pictures returned, an agency may take up to three years to get them back to you.)

The PhotoDataBank and Compu/Pix/Rental

Nothing is more important to a photobuyer than to have the picture he needs in hand, in front of him, ready to go.

As the demand for photography in publishing grows, the need outraces the supply, and immediate access becomes increasingly difficult for a photobuyer.

That's why a market letter like my *Photobulletin* has been successful. Editors with highly specialized needs cannot always find their pictures readily, since stock photo agencies hold in inventory only pictures with the potential to sell over and over. Where does a photobuyer go for that picture of Albuquerque after a winter snowfall taken within the last two years? Or a picture of a carbonized piece of grain, or a scene of the plains in Iowa as the Mormons might have seen them in their trek across the country in 1847?

The *Photobulletin* broadcasts such needs to our subscribers, and invariably some photographer can supply the picture. We also offer a free stock photo service to our subscribers and buyers, called the PhotoDataBank. Our subscribers list up to one hundred subject areas (e.g., snails, windmills, Memphis) on 3x5 file cards with their name and address. When an editor wants to locate pictures of collies, for example, we make a photocopy of all the 3x5 cards that designate collies and send them to the editor so he can contact the photographers directly.

An organization in California called Compu/Pix/Rental (C/P/R) has a computerized list of over two thousand picture categories and the photographers who have them. A photographer submits a sampling of pictures (which are returned), and if the photographer is accepted, he pays a fee to enter a category (with cross-references) on the C/P/R computer. If an editor needs a picture of an eagle, the computer in microseconds flashes on the screen the names, addresses, and phone numbers of photographers who can supply eagle pictures. The photographer deals directly with the photobuyer, and if a sale is made, pays 10 percent to C/P/R. C/P/R is currently not accepting new photographers, but if you would like to contact them, their address is 22231 Mulholland Highway, Suite 119-20, P.O. Box 4055A, Woodland Hills, CA 91365.

The Timely Stock Agencies

A few picture agencies deal in current photojournalism and sell for the service photographer who supplies fresh, news-oriented pictures. The agencies, again, are based in New York, and they send individuals or teams to trouble spots or disaster areas, much as a local or regional TV camera crew covers news of immediate interest. Most of these agencies, with channels or sometimes headquarters in Europe, sell single photographs and provide feature assignments around the globe for their top-ranking photographers. If you happen to photograph a subject, situation, or celebrity that you think has timely national impact, phone one of the following agencies and feel them out:

Gamma-Liaison, 150 E. Fifty-eighth St., 15th Fl., New York, NY 10022 (212) 888-7272.
Black Star, 450 Park Ave. S., New York, NY 10016 (212) 679-3288.
Sygma Photo News, 225 W. Fifty-seventh St., New York, NY 10155 (212) 765-1820.
Contact Press Images, 415 Madison, 23rd Fl., New York, NY 10017 (212) 750-1042.

Payment for your picture or picture story is based on several factors: (1) exclusivity (Has the rest of the world seen it yet?); (2) impact (Would a viewer find your picture(s) of interest?); (3) your name (If your name is Rick Smolan, add 200% to the bill.); (4) timeliness (Is it of immediate interest?). The following agencies will accept the kind of pictures and picture stories mentioned above, but will also accept nondeadline, human-interest pictures and stories:

Associated Press (AP), 50 Rockefeller Plaza, New York, NY 10020 (212) 262-4000.
United Press International (UPI), 220 E. Forty-second St., New York, NY 10017 (212) 682-0400.

Possible Problems in Dealing with Stock Agencies

In dealing with a stock photo agency, remember: You are the creator, you are in control, and you own your picture.

Contracts

Read any stock agency contract *carefully*. Most photo-agency contracts ask you to sign with them exclusively. Some stipulate that if you market any picture on your own, 50 percent of those revenues become theirs. Some agencies ask that you shoot stock pictures on a regular basis and send the results to them. If you fail to do so, they assess a maintenance charge to your account.

Contracts should be treated as agreements to be modified by both parties. Draw a line through any section in the contract that you disapprove of, and initial it. If your pictures aren't returned to you shortly thereafter, you'll know that the agency values the opportunity to market your pictures more than having agreement from you on the point or points you deleted from the contract. (Be prepared for possible negotiation and sharing of concessions with the agency.)

Conflicts

Some photo agencies may express wariness of a possible sale conflict— say, two competing greeting card companies buying the same picture—if the agency, plus you, plus one or two other agencies in the country are marketing your pictures. Explain to the agency that you have placed your pictures *by category* with agencies who are strong in these differing categories—and have not placed the same picture (or a duplicate) in competing agencies, and you don't intend to.

Could a problem still arise on a major account where significant dollars are involved? In such a case, the art director would thoroughly research the pictures with you for releases, history of the picture, previous uses of it, etc., before it is used, and any inadvertent duplication or possible sale conflict would come to the fore at that time.

In any case, if you have signed up on a nonexclusive arrangement with a stock agency, you put the burden of follow-up on the history of sales of a particular picture with the stock agency that handles your photos, not on yourself.

Delays

You'll be more likely to run across a problem in this area: By far the highest percentage of complaints that come into my PhotoSource office are about the slowness of stock agencies to move pictures. ("I know they could sell my stuff, but they don't try. They don't actively keep my pictures moving for sales. They're selling other photographers' work, but not mine!")

I've followed up on every complaint and have found that in all cases the grief could have been avoided. The problem usually lies in the *eagerness* of both parties.

The eagerness of stock photo agencies to supplement their stock of pictures by accepting categories of photos outside their known strength areas can be likened to the well-run garage that keeps its well-paid mechanics busy. They accept any job, any make vehicle, foreign or domestic. They pride themselves on their versatility. The fact is, no one is *that* versatile. Someone usually loses: the customer. With a little research, the auto owner could have found the *right* garage for his car and his pocketbook.

By the same token, the eagerness of photographers to have their photos accepted into a prestigious stock photo agency for the name, rather than on the basis of research showing the agency as strong in their specific categories, gives rise to the complaints, "They don't aggressively move my material!"

If your pictures of Alaskan wildlife, for example, were placed in the ABC Agency—a well-known, prestigious agency—a photo researcher seeking wildlife pictures would bypass that agency if it were not known for a strong wildlife selection, and instead head for the little-known XYZ Agency, strong on wildlife. Do your research, and choose your agencies with care.

There are other complaints and problems. I often hear them in this form: "Are they honest? I'm not receiving checks for all the pictures of mine the agency is selling."

If it is any consolation, I have never heard of a documented case in which it turned out that a major stock photo agency purposely attempted to carry out the above. I know it happens, but I believe it rarely happens on purpose. Stock agencies trade on their own reliability factor, just as you do.

As a free agent stock photographer, you place yourself at the mercy of the basic honesty of all the contacts you make in the world of business. That's one of the disadvantages of being a freelancer, and probably a good reason that there aren't too many of us. Before you place your pictures with a stock photo agency, find out as much as you can about the agency and then take a leap of faith.

Do You Need a Personal Rep?

What stock photo agencies do for photographers on a collective basis, representatives do on an individualized basis. A rep earns a living by se-curing the best price for your single pictures and the best fee for your photographing services. There's an old saying in the business, "You'll know if you qualify for a rep because the rep will come to you—just when your photography has finally arrived and you don't need him any-more."

Can a rep be of benefit to you? Yes, especially by freeing you from the confinements of administering your sales. You'll have more time to take pictures. But reps can be expensive. Depending on the services they pro-vide to you, they take from 20 percent to 50 percent of the fee. Most reps are in New York, where so many commercial photobuyers are.

Unless you live in a city of over a million population and your name is well established in the industry, you and a rep would not find each other mutually beneficial. For further information on reps, contact the Society of Photographers' and Artists' Representatives (SPAR), 1123 Broadway, Room 914A, New York, NY 10010 (212)924-6023.

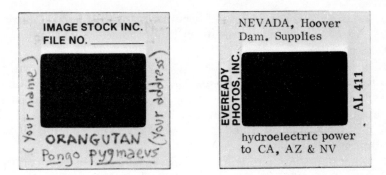

Figure 12-2. Ways to identify transparencies left at stock photo agencies.

Start Your Own Mini-Agency

If a large stock agency or a rep is not for you, but you want the photo-agency system for marketing your pictures (i.e., you want someone other than yourself to handle the selling), and you want a more aggressive approach to the sale of your photographs than you get with a regular agency, then establish a mini-stock-photo agency of your own to handle your pictures. You can do this either on an individual basis, or else get together with one or more other photographers to form a co-op agency. Both forms of mini-agencies have advantages.

The Individual Agency

Find a person (friend, neighbor, spouse, relative) who has spare time, an aptitude for elementary business procedures, and a desire to make some money. An interest in photography is helpful, but not necessary. More important, the person should have the temperament for recordkeeping and the ability to work solo.

Your job will be to supply the finished pictures. (You absorb all costs for film and processing.) Your cohort's job will be to search out markets, send out the photos, keep the records, and process the mail. From the gross sales each month, subtract the expenses off the top and split the net fifty-fifty. (There won't be many expenses: postage, phone, mailing envelopes, stationery, invoices, and miscellaneous office supplies such as rubber bands and paper clips.)

Before you start up your mini-agency, decide on a name and design a letterhead and invoice form. Open a business checking account. Work up a letter of agreement with your colleague that in effect will say:

1. You will split the proceeds fifty-fifty after business expenses, and all pictures, transparencies, and the *name* of the agency will revert to

you, the photographer, in case of termination of your business arrangement. Also, the back of your prints will show your personal copyright— not the agency's.

2. Bookkeeping records will be kept by your colleague, who will pay you from the business checkbook. Major purchases will be mutually agreed upon and the cost divided between the two of you. (Should you incorporate at this point? Probably not, but it depends on many variables that only you can answer. See the list of business information books in the Bibliography.)

3. Other photographers' work may also be collected by your colleague to market. Reason? IRS rules state that if other photographers' work is also represented, then your colleague is not an employee of yours (which requires employment records), but rather an independent contractor, which requires no government paperwork on your part. Your colleague fills out his own tax forms.

Personalized photography business forms are available from the New England Business Service, 500 N. Main St., Groton, MA 01471. They may have photography forms adaptable to your mini-stock agency. Their toll-free number is 800-225-9550.

The success of your mini-agency will depend on the efficiency of your retrieval system—designed for the convenience of both the office help and the walk-ins (i.e., photo researchers looking for pictures). Pictures should be categorized and filed with attention to physical ease of retrieval. (Chapter 13 will give you help on this.)

A trend for the future of one-person agencies or mini-agencies might be digital pictures, but until costs become practical, the good ole-fashioned microfiche, the convenient information storage method used by libraries, banks, and some publishing houses, will suffice. In this method, documents are photographed and then reduced to a miniature size and placed on film for easy recall.

Bud Kimball of Steilacoom, Washington, has made a unique use of the microfiche. He specializes in scenics and panoramic views of the West. He isolates categories, such as his collection of Mount Saint Helens views (see Illustration 12-1), and puts eighty-two shots on a 4x6 microfiche card. The first two frames are used for identification. He sells the microfiches to photo libraries, who hold them on file, and if they want a print (black-and-white or color) they order it from Bud. "Customers have a choice of many views," says Bud, "just like at a stock photo agency."

The equipment to make microfiches is not cheap: $18,000 is the cost of apparatus to shoot the microfiche. Bud has his processed by Sid Bugelholl (908 Richmond Road, Edmund, OK 73034).

For business reasons, as a mini-stock agency, you may want to explore joining the following three organizations. (Membership can add credibility on your business stationery, and all three provide newsletters with information from the picture-buying point of view that can be valuable to your operation.)

Illustration 12-1. *A full-size copy of Bud Kimball's microfiche. Eighty-two views are on one fiche. Two of the squares are used for identification information. Kimball sells his fiches to libraries and other information sources that rely on such research materials.*

Illustration 12-2. *An enlargement of one of the views of Mount St. Helens from the microfiche.*

SPAR (see p. 222)
PACA (see p. 217)
American Society of Picture Professionals, Inc., 5283 Grand Central Station, New York, NY 10017

Once your one-person agency is set up and rolling, if you've chosen a good, aggressive colleague, you'll find you'll be able to concentrate more on picture-taking and less on administration.

The Co-op Agency

Some photographers prefer to band together and form a cooperative agency, an establishment in which nonphotographer members handle the administration and photographers handle the picture taking. They share office-sitting chores, and they are compensated on a total-hours-contributed basis.

I have watched the demise of many such agencies—and the failure can always be traced to a concept problem: they attempted to be a general agency servicing local accounts. This seems logical enough, but a local account figures if it's going to pay national prices, it ought to get its pictures from a national source—and it does. Using convenient express services, such as UPS or Federal Express, it bypasses the local agency.

The *solution* for a small regional agency is to specialize. For example, a small agency in Nebraska might specialize in submarines, an agency in Vermont might specialize in things Mexican, and an agency in Florida might specialize in pro-football celebrities. In today's world, where distance has been annihilated by telecommunications, Express Mail, and computers, there's little reason for a Montana agency to specialize in the obvious: cowboys. It's more important to be a mini-expert on one subject. You'll then gather the pictures from all over the country, and the world, if need be. Here is a list of popular request categories, any one of which could be the specialty of a co-op mini-agency: celebrities, movie stills, historical, natural history, fine art, industrial, agricultural, food, sports, glamour, scientific, geographic, and still lifes.

The local accounts might continue to ignore you—but not when they need your specialty. You'll find them standing in line with the rest of your national accounts.

How many pictures should you have on file to start your mini-agency? At least 5,000 if you specialize and 20,000 if you are a *general* agency. How do you find qualified stock photographers? A few will come out of the woodwork locally, but the majority you will find through directories (see Table 3-1) such as *Literary Market Place, Stock Photo Assignment and Source Book,* ASPP, APA, and ASMP membership directories.

Decor Photography:
Another Outlet for Your Standards

As a stock photographer, you will find that many of your Track A pictures lend themselves to a photo-marketing cousin of stock agencies: decor photography (or *photo decor,* or *decor art,* or *wall decor,* as it's sometimes called)—photographs that decorate the walls of homes, public places, and commercial buildings. In contrast to your work in stock photography, you will be selling color *prints,* not slides.

Following are the two basic ways to sell photography for decoration: (1) *single sales* (yourself as the sales person), and (2) *multiple sales* (an agent as the salesperson). In either case, you, or the person you appoint to select your prints for marketing, should have a feel for the art tastes of the everyday consumer. You are headed for disaster if you choose to market prints that appeal only to your sophisticated friends. You'll ring up good decor sales if you can match the kind of photos found on greeting card racks.

I suggest that you, as a beginner, offer your photo decor *on consignment.* Your sales outlets will expect to sell your decor at twice the fee you charge.

Single Sales

Art shows, craft shows, and photo exhibits of all kinds are typical outlets for single sales of your decor photography. Aggressively contact home designers, architects, remodelers, and interior decorators. They are in constant need of fresh decorating ideas. Your pictures can add a "local" touch. Gift shops and boutiques can be regular outlets.

Art fairs provide an opening into the decor photography market. Offer your pictures at a modest fee. (Most visitors come to an art fair expecting to spend no more than a total of forty dollars. Let this be your guide.) You'll find you can make important contacts at art fairs that will lead to future sales. Pass out your business cards vigorously. There are two categories of decor photographers at major art fairs: Those that net $40 for the weekend, and those that net $4,000. The former, in work jeans, relax at their booth in beach chairs. The latter are equally excellent photographers who have studied the needs of consumers, present their work in a professional-looking booth, and are aggressive salespersons. For a listing of national and local art fairs and international photo contests and grants, write Gadney's Festival Publications, Dept. PL, Box 10180, Glendale, CA 91209.

Photo galleries offer important exposure and sales opportunities for your decor photography. Max Lent has produced *The Art Photography Directory* (24 Wellington, Rochester, NY 14611). The Photographic Resource Center produces aids for photographers, including *The Photographer's Guide to Getting & Having a Successful Exhibition* (127 East 59th St., New York, NY 10022 (212)838-8640). Visible Spectrum (808 Post, #1601B, San Francisco, CA 94109) produces catalogs of fine art photography.

The single-print-sales system that requires person-to-person contact can be time-consuming, cutting into your profits. However, if you enjoy the excitement and camaraderie of art fairs and public art exhibits, it can be rewarding. Probably the most lucrative market for single sales is architects and interior designers, who are in a position to sell your pictures for you.

Multiple Sales

If you want to spend your time shooting rather than selling, use the multiple-sales method. As with decor photography, your pictures must be a reflection of the common denominator, but even more so—because your aim is to sell your pictures in volume to masses of people. If Sears can do it, if Vincent Price can do it . . . why don't you try it?

Ken Townend of Burlington, Ontario, tried it, and he's doing it. In the last four years, he's averaged around ten thousand sales—about $70,000 clear profit. "It's just a Ma-and-Pa operation," Ken says. "I wouldn't want this business to grow any larger. It's very rewarding. I take the kind of pictures I prefer, and they are seen in thousands of homes yearly. I'm paid very well in the process."

He says the secret is to find a good agent. Where? In the Yellow Pages. "Sixty of them are listed in the Chicago telephone book alone! [Note: See Giftware Wholesalers and Manufacturers.] These are the fellows who also sell Dresden china to the department stores."

Ken was originally an advertising executive and now applies his marketing knowlege to his photography. He finds that sepia-toned pictures on RC paper sell the best. He has written a book revealing more of his secrets. It's called *How To Produce and Mass Market Your Creative Photography*. Write to: Photographic Publisher's Guild, 220 Main St., Suite 3A, Nevada City, CA 95959 (916)265-8819.

Another entrepreneur in the field of decor photography is William R. Eastman III. Rather than selling in great volume through an agent, he leans toward low-volume sales directly to stores and other outlets. Whereas Ken Townend's finished product sells for $15.95, William Eastman's sells for $95. The latter's forte is the *limited edition*, which enhances the value of a print once the entire edition (usually two hundred to five hundred) has been marketed and the original destroyed. This encourages patrons to buy for investment reasons. Eastman tells all in his excellent book, *How to Produce and Market Your Own Limited Edition Photographs*, also available from PPG (see address above).

What Makes a Marketable Decor Photograph?

One that makes your viewers *wish they were there*. Choose a view or subject you would enjoy looking at 365 days a year. If *you* don't like the view or subject, chances are your customers won't either. Keep in mind that most buyers of decor photography enjoy pictures of *pleasant subjects* because they find in such pictures an escape from the hassle and routine of everyday living. That's why for this market it's important to take your scenics without people in them. Your viewers would like to imagine *themselves* strolling through the meadow or along the beach. Figures that are recognizable as humans in your picture are an intrusion on their own quietude and privacy. In addition, people included in decor-photography pictures can date the pictures with their clothes, hairstyles, etc. Here are some excellent standards that sell over and over again for decor-photography purposes:

Nature close-ups*. Zooming in on the details of the natural world at the correct F-stop always produces a sure seller. They rarely become outdated: dandelion seeds, frost patterns, lichen designs, the eye of a peacock feather, the quills of a porcupine, a crystal-studded geode.

Decor-photography buyers tend to buy *easily recognizable subjects*. An antique windmill would consistently sell better than an antique wind generator (the kind with propeller blades). A still life of a daisy would sell better than a still life of potentilla. Keep your photography salable by keeping your subject matter simple. (Feature only one thing at a time, or one playing off another, rather than a group of things.)

---

*An excellent quarterly that brings wildlife and nature photographers up-to-date is *The Guilfoyle Report*. (See Bibliography.) Bill Thomas's "Nature Photojournalism" seminars come highly recommended; write to "A Touch of Success," R4, Deer Trails, Box 387, Nashville, IN 47448.

Animals. Both wild animals and pets are perennially popular. Choose handsome and healthy subjects. Keep the background simple so it will enhance, rather than overpower, your subject. An excellent book on the subject is *How to Shoot & Sell Animal Photos,* by Walter Chandoha (Writer's Digest Books).

Dramatic landscapes. Shoot landscapes in all seasons, especially with approaching storms, complete with lightning and rolling thunderclouds. The effects of ice storms are always popular, as are New England pathways in the fall, and rural snow scenes.

Len Nemeth of Northfield, Ohio, sells landscapes to hospitals. "They use them for the ceilings of intensive-care rooms," says Len. "I find that the scenics that work best are those that have a splash of *light* somewhere off in the distance. If a path or road in the scene leads to the horizon, it must lead to a light area rather than a dark area. This seems to have a positive psychological effect on patients who have little to do all day but to look at my scenic above them on the ceiling. The light area seems to represent hope."

Bill Ellzey of Telluride, Colorado, also sells decor photography for use in waiting rooms, hallways, and patients' rooms. "Local scenes offer more than decoration," Bill says. "Administrators know the cheering effect decor photography can have on both patients and their relatives, not to mention the staff." Bill also sells to insurance companies, professional offices, and government offices.

Nostalgia. This is a winner—if you can find the right rustic pioneer's cabin or antique front-porch swing; historical sites with patriotic significance such as Paul Revere's home or Francis Scott Key's Fort McHenry; still lifes containing memorabilia such as Civil War weapons or whaling ship artifacts. Again, choose the easily recognized subject.

Abstracts. Your pictures can range from bold urban shadow patterns to the delicate network of filaments in a spider's web. Abstracts lend themselves well to waiting rooms, attorneys' offices, and professional buildings, as well as homes.

Sports. Capitalize on the nation's avid interest in sports personalities and the games they play. Close-ups sell best. Scenes of sporting events such as football, soccer, tennis, and skating lend themselves to game rooms and family playrooms.

Portraits. Model releases are necessary. Close-ups sell best. Exotic, interesting, quizzical, yet pleasant (Mona Lisa) faces sell to legal suites and corporation offices.

Erotic. Eroticism finds a market in private clubs. Subject matter can range from newsstand pornography to esoteric nude studies.

Industrial. Sell your best industrial scenes to engineers' offices. It goes without saying that your pictures should be well composed, visually exciting but easy to look at, and of high technical quality. Sell to industry itself. Capture the strength of industry (a la Ayn Rand), its contributions to society: visually appealing abstract patterns, close-ups of computer chips, laborers in meaningful work, factories at sunset after a fresh rainfall. Deemphasize the negative aspects of industry.

Underwater. The quietude and exotic nature of underwater scenes is appealing to consumers. For an example of excellent decor photos, many of which include underwater scenes, send $10 to Creative Color, Station 17, 4911 W. Grace Street, Tampa, FL 33607, and ask for their catalog *Beautiful Photography.*

What to Charge

Prices depend on whether you sell in volume or individually. In either case, after markup, the buying public will pay about $45 for an 11x14 and $25 for an 8x10. Before you decide on your own price, see what the local department stores are getting for similar decor photography. Also, check out the fees in catalogs such as *Beautiful Photography,* mentioned above.

Limited editions are another question. You can demand a higher fee. And, of course, if you keep a couple prints for the grandchildren, they just might become heirs to a *very* valuable print. How do you limit the edition? As with other printmaking (silk screen, etching, lithography), you destroy the original after making 100 to 500 prints. In decor photography, you destroy the negative.

What to charge for limited editions? Keep in mind the professional artist who once said, "If you are going to price your watercolor at $15, you'll find a $15 buyer. If you price it at $75, you'll find a $75 buyer. And if you price it at $850—you'll find an $850 buyer. Just takes time." The going rate for a 16x20 color limited edition photograph is between $75 and $150.

Black-and-white or color? Surprisingly, black-and-white prints sell well as decor photography if they are sepia tones. But color probably has the edge over black-and-white. Shoot in transparencies rather than negatives—for three reasons:

1. You can project them effectively when you are demonstrating your subjects to a potential client.
2. Processing-lab technology can handle transparencies cheaper than negs and prints.
3. As a photo illustrator, you'll also want to market your color through regular publishing channels, and they require transparencies.

Size. If you sell your prints on a single-sales basis, you'll find that the larger 16x20 print (and higher fee) will result in more year-end profit than smaller (11x14 or 8x10) prints (and lower fee). On the other hand, if you go to *multiple sales* and smaller prints, and aim for the volume mar-

ket in high-traffic areas such as arts-and-crafts fairs or sh
you will be equally successful.

Production. The resin-coated papers make black-and-〉
tion on your own very easy. Color production is usuall〉
plished by a lab. Shop around. In New York, for example, an 11x14 costs
$24 and a 16x20 costs $45 to print. Quality is superb, and the delivery is
one-day. However, the decor photographer couldn't survive at those
rates.

Here's a processing firm which has taken an interest in serving the decor photographer: Dale Color, Inc., Bldg. G, Box 2460, Bloomington, IL
61701 (309)663-7325. They currently charge about one-quarter of New
York prices—but you have to order a minimum of three. Write them for
details, and they'll send you a free pamphlet called *Sell Prints for Profit*.

How to Make Your Decor Photography More Salable

Frames. Framing or matting your print definitely enhances its appearance and salability. Some prints can be improved by using textured or
silk-finish print surfaces. Dry mounting materials, glass, and hinge
mattes are available everywhere. Dale Color (mentioned above) offers
protective *shrink wrap* (a thin, close-fitting clear plastic covering). The
following company offers inexpensive imported frames (write for a catalog): Picture Frames by Caroline Kingcade, 1313 Atlantic St., North Kansas City, MO 64116 (417) 474-5230. And finally, try making frames on
your own. How-to series are often featured in photo and hobby-and-craft
magazines; consult your library's *Reader's Guide to Periodical Literature* for back issues. Or if all else fails, team up with a frame shop and
split the profits.

Promotion. This is the key to your selling success. If you've sold a series of prints to one bank in town, let the other banks know about your
decor photography. Work for ways and places to exhibit your pictures often. Sign your prints or mattes for added promotion and referrals. Offer
your services as a guest speaker or local TV talk-show guest. Produce
brochures, flyers, or catalogs of your work. (For more hints on self-promotion, see Chapter 10.)

Leasing. Start your own leasing gallery. Businesses know that leasing
anything can be charged against expenses. By leasing decor photos to
corporations, small businesses, or professionals, you'll get more mileage
out of your photos.

More information on decor photography. Kodak has produced *Photo
Decor* (available for $10.95 plus $3.25 postage and handling); write to
Eastman Kodak, Dept. PSI, 343 State Street, Rochester, NY 14650). Associated Photographers International (API) has produced four reports on
decor photography in its newsletter, *APIdea* (issues #57, #59, #92 and
#108); write to P.O. Box 4055A, Woodland Hills, CA 91365.

Decor photography and stock photo agencies both offer opportunities as outlets for your Track A pictures. The main message of this chapter has been to emphasize that success with these two secondary marketing channels takes research and time on your part. If you're willing to give what it takes, you can realize rewards.

I have a room all to myself; it is nature. It is a place beyond the jurisdiction of human governments.

—Henry David Thoreau
The Journals

13.
Keeping Records: Knowing Where Everything Is

The Lazy Person's Way to Extra Sales—Knowing What Is Selling

I'm lazy at heart. I like to put the lawn rake back when I'm done with it. Because I've learned it's a lot more work next time to search, and possibly not even find it, when I really need it.

This lazy kind of thinking got me into a very good habit after a while. By having (or finding) a place for everything here at the farm, I got into the habit of putting *everything* away.

I take the same approach to filing away slides, negs, and black-and-white prints. If something's worth having, I figure, it's worth knowing where it is when you need it.

I was happily spurred along in this principle when I inherited several hundred used file folders from a businessman who was retiring. By using a separate folder for each separate stock illustration, I could note right on the folder whenever a picture sold. I put a matching contact print on each folder, thus giving myself an immediate visual reminder of what's selling.

After a few years, my recordkeeping system was teaching me what pictures sold best, and therefore, which pictures I should take more of. By continually supplying my Market List's buyers with the kind of pictures they needed, I survived as a stock photographer.

File It! How to Avoid Excessive Recordkeeping

Here at our barn office, we bought a computer. We use it primarily for our newsletter records and mailing systems. I don't think it will ever replace the good old-fashioned filing system of slipping 8½x11 sheets in a filing cabinet or putting information on a cross-referenced 3x5 card. (See Chapter 17.)

One advantage of my noncomputerized file system is that it gives me a day off every year in April to do my spring cleaning. I thin out the files by eliminating from the front end of many files the material that dates furthest back and is no longer needed. I save only essential papers or correspondence and eliminate the rest of the file. I also eliminate categories that are outdated or no longer relevant, and thus free some folders for new use. For a list of the files I consider essential, see Figure 13-1.

I don't believe in excessive recordkeeping, and my spring-cleaning day helps keep things to manageable proportions.

Another method I use to minimize recordkeeping is to direct new projects to a minifile rather than into the central files. I find that miniprojects are usually completed in about a year. Researching for and purchasing our computer was a miniproject; so was remodeling our office in the barn. Others revolve around collecting material for future photo stories or photo essays.

Here's a simple technique for a minifile. The essential ingredients: two dozen file folders numbered 1 through 24; a temporary portable open file cabinet (like a box), usually made of pressed cardboard or metal and available at stationery stores; and two 8x10 cards—one numbered from 1 through 24 and the other from A through Z.

Each entry is given a numerical designation, filed numerically, and entered on the numbered card. The category is also entered by title and subject on the alphabetical card, with its numbered designation under the appropriate letter. The alphabetical listing also allows you to cross-reference the subject of the project or category. Since the file is small and portable you can carry it between home and office or store it in a regular file drawer. I often have as many as six or seven projects going at one time, with information building in twelve to fifteen others, and the mini-file system aids me in being a lazy shopkeeper. I never have to work at finding anything. When the project is completed, the file either earns a spot on my central files or is tossed away.

Knowing How to Put Your Finger on It:
Cataloging Your Black-and-Whites and Transparencies

Efficiency is essential if you market your pictures by mail. Establish a workable identification system—and stick to it. But which system should you use? I once asked Jane Kinne, Director at Comstock, Inc., what system proved best to locate pictures—a computer? an elaborate access point system? Her answer: No system replaces the device we all carry between our ears. "The nuances inherent in both the photo request and the image itself can't be captured by existing personal computers. I depend on our cataloging system to bring us to a certain point. From there on, I depend on the judgment of our researchers."

Before I go further, I should mention *Organizing Your Photographs* by Ernest H. Robl (Watson-Guptill). This book outlines in detail a system for filing photos along the lines a library employs in its card catalog system. The system utilizes punched 3x5 cards, the Anglo-American Cataloging Rules (AACR2) and the Library of Congress Subject Heading System. Since Robl is a photographer and also a librarian with a track record, he speaks with authority.

If you're a newcomer to stock photography, you may not want to invest your time into a cataloging system of such horsepower. On the other hand, if your aspirations have you heading toward a file, say, of 20,000 images and up, and your collection includes a plethora of pictures outside your PMS/A, then the Robl system can be the answer for you.

However, if you follow the marketing principles in this book and resist snapping pictures of every subject that comes into your viewfinder, limiting your picture taking to your PMS/A instead, you will find you are spending more time at picture taking than at picture filing.

Stock photo sales come from photos that you can access quickly. If finding a picture for a photobuyer takes a long time, the business of stock photography soon becomes discouraging to you.

Photobuyers want to see a selection of photos and then choose one. That's why your photos should be filed by PMS/A. You can quickly browse through your file on, say, aviation, when an editor requests jet engines. You'll also come across other jet engines that might not have been cross-referenced in your filing system.

Your filing system should meet the needs of your marketing system, not the other way around. With that in mind, I will describe a general example of a photographer whose file ranges from 100 to 3,000 marketable pictures, and who plans to follow the principles in this book and limit his weekday shooting to his PMS/A. What follows is a cataloging system that is flexible, simple, and photographer-tested.

Black-and-White

Here is the heart of your black-and-white cataloging system: negative sleeves, contact prints of each roll, PMS/A identification system, a 3x5-card cross-reference system (or computerized, if you wish, on today's available programs—see Chapter 17), and a contact-sheet file. Your system can begin inexpensively with these essentials. You can add on as your stock of pictures increases.

One of the best ways I've seen to identify your black-and-whites is the letter/number system. Here's how to set it up: For your identification on each print, use a letter of the alphabet to signify which category of your PMS/A the print is in. For example: A = Camping, B = Rural/Agriculture, C = Aviation, D = Family Living, E = Automotive, F = Construc-

Your files will grow, both in size and diversity, as your operation grows. Listed below in order of importance are a dozen basic files.

FILE:

— Transparencies

— Black-and-white prints

— Contact sheets

— Negatives (black-and-white) (color)

— Market list (file by publishing house rather than an individual file for each editor—some publishing houses have as many as thirty editors)

— Cross-reference list (your photos, both color and black-and-white, are cross-referenced on 3x5 file cards)

— General correspondence and business files

— Tearsheets (file by frequently-asked-for categories, according to your PMS)

— Story/article (file story ideas, finished stories, and those in progress)

— Accounts receivable/payable

— Reminders (file by month for future reference)

— Sample copies of market list magazines

Figure 13-1. What files will you need in your photo-marketing operation?

tion, G = Underwater Photography. Follow the letter with a number to signify the number of rolls you've taken in that category. Example: You are on your fifteenth roll of black-and-white underwater photography, and you are printing frame number 24. The number of your print would be G-15-24. (The number on the contact sheet would be G-15.) Table 13-1 will give you some more examples.

Of course, there are times you do not devote a complete roll of black-and-white film to one subject. In this case, you can cut the film and make two or more contact sheets (each with a different ID number), or you can let the subsequent subject matter remain on your underwater-photography roll and cross-reference it by 3x5 card. No big problem.

In any case, identify your negs. If you already have a large collection of black-and-whites taken over several years, you can still use this system. Arbitrarily assign a neg number to all your negatives.

I have seen some photographers use a month/year system to identify prints. However, this doesn't work out well for the stock photographer. For one thing, since the first number in this system should denote the number of rolls you have taken to date in that category, after a few years of taking many rolls of film, your left-hand number will get quite lengthy (somewhat like how unwieldy the number on your checks in your checkbook can get). For example, 3675-24. If you added a date in front of this, say, April '87, your number would read 4-87-3675-24. As a stock photographer, you might make a dozen prints of the same picture for multiple-

Letters	PMS/A Categories	No. of Rolls Taken	B&W Frame No.	Print No.
A	(Education)	708	12	A-708-12
B	(Rural/ Agriculture)	556	6	B-556-6
C	(Aviation)	28	36	C-28-36
D	(Family Living)	28	30	D-28-30
E	(Automotive)	138	6	E-138-6
F	(Construction)	250	15	F-250-15
G	(Underwater Photography)	15	24	G-15-24

Note: File your black-and-white negs alphabetically. File your black-and-white prints in manila folders numerically by first number, then alphabetically. Thus, G-15-24 goes before C-28-36, which is followed by D-28-30, then E-138-6, F-250-15, B-556-6, A-708-12.

Table 13-1. Sample print ID numbers for black-and-whites.

submission purposes. That's a lot of numbers to be writing on invoices and the backs of prints, not to mention negs and neg sleeves. If you need to know when a picture was taken, write it on the back (or front) of the contact sheet.

The biggest hazard with the date system is that you reveal the age of your pictures. Labeling a picture "4-82" will dampen its reception by a photobuyer. (Like day-old bread at the bakery, somehow it's not fresh.) Out of a selection of equally excellent pictures, a photobuyer tends to purchase the most recent. He is not fully up on equipment or style changes, and feels safest buying the most recent. If you are compelled to include a date, put it in Roman numerals or use the letter system explained on page 144.

For ease in writing your ID numbers on your negs and contact sheets, shoot blank the first two frames of your roll (numbers 1 and 2). Cut off frame number 1, and write your number and any other identification on frame number 2 in India ink. When it's dry, make a contact print. (Since black-and-white rolls are actually thirty-seven frames long, if you didn't snip off the first frame, you would have to snip off the thirty-seventh frame and have it float loose in your negative sleeve. The last picture on a roll is usually an important one.) Your shortened roll of developed film will fit exactly (cut into groups of six frames) in your neg sleeve. Store your negs in flat or fold-up (accordion-style) sleeves. I found that trying to save film by writing my ID number in tiny letters on some unused portion of the film was counterproductive. In the long run, it cost me more in time spent deciphering my numbers. Also, I found that by allowing myself a full frame for identification purposes, I had more room for identification of the subject matter—for example, "Gaines Farm, Aug '87," and so on.

Your ID number should also be written on the back of each print, with a china marker or very soft pencil and very light pressure. In a corner near the edge of the print (but not too near, to leave space for trimming the edges later), gently press your rubber stamp or label with © 19__, your name, address, and phone number. Do not enter the year on your copyright notice. If you are using RC paper, place a blank label on your print and then rubber stamp the label.

After you've made and coded a black-and-white print, you're ready to file it. Here's where your photocopy of your contact sheet comes in handy. Cut out the photocopy contact print of the picture you just printed, paste it under the file tab on a manila file folder, and mark the tab with the print number. This will readily identify the print inside the folder, plus serve as a visual guide when the folder becomes empty because the print is out making the rounds.

Note that the manila-file-folder system works better than storing pictures in, say, 8x10 Kodak boxes. Used manila folders are often available (cheap) from companies switching over to hanging file folders or computers. So are used dental and X-ray cabinets, for black-and-whites, negatives, or slides. Or if you want to go first class, order a prebuilt slide cabinet from Display Fixture Company (1579 Larkin Williams Road, Fenton, MO 63026); ask for the Multiplex Cabinet.

When you file your black-and-white stock photo file *folders*, file them not alphabetically, but in numerical order, using the first number in your identification code. For example, A-708-12 would be filed somewhere after our earlier example of G-15-24 (as in Table 13-1). Z-8-36 would be filed in front of A-708-12.

A word about printing: It's a good idea to print your black-and-whites on double-weight (or RC) paper: they last longer, and they just plain look and feel better to a photobuyer. Print four or five at a time. Store the extras in your manila file folders. When a picture is sold, indicate it on the file folder. This will be your best sales barometer. For example, if sales are brisk on a certain picture—and it is a timeless picture—this system will visually suggest to you that you ought to make ten or fifteen more prints of it when you're next in the darkroom.

Keep a running record of your submissions to your Market List. A simple *in/out* ledger is all you'll need.

Transparencies

Here's the best system for the newcomer to stock photography I've come across to date: Use the alphabet/number system. File your transparencies numerically in plastic three-ring sleeve pages and a three-ring hanging-style notebook. This type of three-ring binder—usually free when you buy a couple dozen vinyl (plastic) pages—hangs upside down in a letter-size filing cabinet. Since they hang free, the vinyl pages do not buckle and curl as they do when in an upright notebook. Figure out basic categories that reflect your picture-taking interests: camping, rural subjects, classroom, snow skiing, fishing. Decide on your categories when you evaluate your PMS/A, in the beginning, and prepare several three-ring books. When you expand your supply of pictures, your numbering system will grow along with you. (Three-ring hanging notebooks are available at stationery stores. See Chapter 9 for addresses of suppliers of plastic pages.) Tom Stack, who operates a stock agency out of Colorado Springs, prefers to use a *Pendaflex* holder, a plastic spine available at camera stores. The spine will hold as many as ten hanging vinyl sheets and can be flipped over a light table to locate a picture quickly. A similar product is the Snap-Hinge, available from Bardes Products, 5245 West Clinton, Dept. 8, Milwaukee, WI 53223.

Toss away all inferior slides. Hand-letter the code numbers (neatly!) on your slides on either vertical side, near the top. You can file in-camera duplicates (or reproduction-quality dupes) in sequential order by giving them subsequent numbers. To give a professional appearance, use a system such as Numbatabs, available from Saunders Photo/Graphic Inc., Box 111, Rochester, NY 14601. (These stick-on tabs sometimes cause problems in projectors, but stock photographers rarely allow their slides to be projected.) The slides should always remain in plastic sleeves. As a protection, if your budget can afford it, encase each of your slides in a single-slide protective sleeve before inserting it into your plastic page.

To be able to locate specific pictures, cross-reference your picture subjects on your 3x5 file-card system.

Rubber-stamp the right-hand or left-hand vertical side of your slide (as you look at it, right side up) with the copyright notice © 19__ (your name).* Include your address, and if possible, your phone number. The top and bottom of the slide should be left clear in case your slide ends up in a stock photo agency. They'll want that space for their identification system and description.

If your mounts have a date imprinted on them, place a label with your name and the copyright symbol over the top of this date. Self-apply labels, such as Avery #S828, are available in one-quarter-inch size: rubber-stamp a whole page of them at a time, with your name and address, etc. Printed labels are available from stationery houses mentioned elsewhere in the book.

As you begin to increase the number of slides in a particular category, you'll find you're developing a substantial portfolio of pictures on a single subject—for example, agriculture—so that when a photobuyer calls for farm scenes, you'll be able to quickly and efficiently sort out specific pictures to send off for consideration. Since all of your agriculture slides are filed collectively under one category, selecting pictures become less of a chore than if you had to search through your whole selection of slides.

A Cross-Referencing System for Retrieving Your Pictures

A photobuyer contacts you and wants a certain item—a lake in Utah or a picture of a bulldog, for example. Can you locate it readily? If not, it might mean a missed sale.

However, if you are able to consult a 3x5-card cross-referencing system that will pinpoint these subjects quickly for you, the sale could be yours.

---

*The Copyright Act (see Chapter 15) allows (in fact, encourages) you to personally affix the copyright notice to your pictures. Again, do not enter the last two digits of the year so as not to date your photo and diminish its sale potential. The art director or photo editor can enter the current year next to the published picture when (if) he puts your copyright notice and credit line in the layout for printing. I say *if* because this isn't put in automatically. You should always request the © and credit line in your cover letter to a photobuyer, both for your use of the tearsheets later for self-promotion and possible copyright registration, and for documentation of the picture as your property.

Letters	Film Type	Transparency No.
A	35mm (1-500)	A-493 (35mm) A-1008 (4x5)
B		B-623 B-624 (120) B-628
C		C-735 C-860 (120) C-1210 (4x5)
D	120 (501-1000)	D-493 E-488 (35mm)
E		
F	4x5 (1001-1500)	
G		

Note: File numerically, then alphabetically. Thus, E-488, A-493, B-623, B-624, B-628, C-735, C-860, A-1008, C-1210. You know immediately that the first two in the list are 35mm, the next five are 120's, and the last two are 4x5s.

Table 13-2. Code for filing transparencies.

Here's How to Do It

Black-and-white. After you develop each roll of film, make a contact sheet on 8½x11 paper. Always place your black-and-white number (as shown in Table 13-1) on the upper left of the sheet, so that when you're looking for a particular picture, you can flip through the upper-left corners of the contact sheets rapidly (a Graphics box usually holds forty to fifty contact sheets). Next, make a photocopy of your original contact sheet. File the original alphabetically then in numerical order in a contact-sheet carton.

On the back of the photocopy, jot down several subject titles that could be used to refer to the subject matter of the pictures on that contact sheet. Be liberal with your cross-referencing. For example, *aviation* could also be cross-referenced as *flying*. On the other hand, keep it simple, too. You should manage the files, not the other way around. A complicated filing system geometrically expands its complexity as your files grow.

When making subject references, keep in mind that photobuyers are usually seeking out prominent aspects—nothing obscure—in each of your images.

Set the photocopy in a special file or shelf. When you've amassed a few dozen photocopies of contact sheets in this way, set aside an evening to enter the lists of subjects and their ID roll numbers in your cross-reference 3x5-card system. (Keep the photocopy sheets; don't toss them away.)

I found that by paying our babysitter an extra fee per hour to tackle the cross-referencing chore, I could get the job done efficiently. By selecting the right babysitters, I found few errors or omissions. If your family situation doesn't include a babysitter, you'll find that time passes quickly on this tedious job if you plug in to your favorite VCR movie or stereo program.

Color. Cross-reference your color basically by the same system. The ID numbers on your transparencies will have a letter designating the category and only one number (e.g., 5 for the fifth horse picture in your files; 52 for the fifty-second). On your cross-reference 3x5 cards you'll recognize which are referring to color and which to black-and-white if you put a *c* (for color) beside the entry or use a colored pen to make the entry.

Since your color may consist of different formats (35mm, 120, 4x5), allow a space on each card between the lists of numbers referring to the different sizes of transparencies, and give each size a characteristic number. For example, under the category of *A* (we used *camping*), start your 35mms at number *1*; start numbering your 120s at number *5001*; and your 4x5s at *8001*. This will also give you a quick reference—if an editor refers to one of your transparencies over the phone by ID number, you'll know the size.

If your 35mm transparency collection in any one PMS/A category or size grows beyond 5,000, you can revert to the beginning and assign a small letter *a* to the next series of 5,000.

Again, use the hanging file folder system and vinyl pages to store your transparencies. File them in the notebook pages or *Pendaflex* spine by letter, and then within the pages by number.

Protecting Your Files

Humidity is the greatest enemy of your transparencies (and sometimes of your prints). For ten dollars you can buy a humidistat (from the hardware store) to locate near your storage area; it should read between 55 and 58. If the reading is lower, you'll need a humidifier; if it's higher, a dehumidifier. Moisture settles to the lower part of a room. Depending on the area of the country you live in, store your negatives and transparencies accordingly.

Damage from fire, smoke, or water can put you out of business. Locate your negs and transparencies near an exit with easy access. If your budget permits, invest in fireproof cabinets. If you live in a flood-prone area, store your film as high as possible. Excessive temperatures will also damage your transparencies and negatives. Store them where the range of temperature is between sixty and eighty degrees.

Everything Has Its Place

We've all seen cartoons picturing busy editors, their desks piled high with terribly important papers. The caption usually quotes the editor in some defense of his "filing" system.

Stock photographers can't afford the luxury of an editor's haphazard filing system. As your stock photo library grows, so will your need to be able to locate everything, from pictures to contact sheets, negs to notes.

Keep in control. If everything has its place, nothing should get lost. If you use an item, put it back when you're finished. The editor's desk got that way because he didn't follow these two principles:

1. Make a place for it.
2. Put it back when you're finished.

Is the editor lazy? To the contrary. It's a lot more work to shuffle through that heap on his desk to locate something.

Time lost can mean lost sales for the stock photographer. Take the lazy person's approach—know where everything is.

14.
Working
Smart

The
Success Habit:
Following Through

"There's no big secret about how to succeed as a stock photographer. You simply take good pictures. They'll sell themselves."

Wrong.

For every picture that sells by itself, there are about 100,000 waiting in files, unsold, because the photographer believed the above. Good pictures are only half of what you need. The other half is *working smart*.

Photo marketing is a business. And the principles that help business people to make a success of their efforts will also help you. Imagine your business as a locomotive. It rides on two rails. One rail is the quality of your photos, the other, your business know-how. One supports the other.

Knowledge is useless unless it is applied. That's the first thing novices learn when they venture into the business world. Photographers who succeed do so not because of their knowledge of photography or photo marketing, but because they apply what they know.

Sounds simple. But wisdom in business is not a one-time move, it's a continuing movement, a momentum, a follow-through, until it becomes habit. If you take the principles in this chapter and make them habits of your photo-marketing lifestyle and work style, you are on the road to success.

Setting Goals

Where is your ship headed? Are you on a fishing expedition, heading out in the bay and hoping to get a bite? Or do you have a definite destination, a well-researched spot where "they're bitin' "?

The SBA (Small Business Administration) tells us that most newcomers venture into a new business as if they were going fishing, with a lot of anticipation and enthusiasm and most of the emphasis on externals instead of on precisely where they want to go and how to get results.

Your chances of getting your stock photos published and your photographic talent recognized will be excellent if you form the winning habit of setting goals for yourself *before* each move you take in your business development.

Are you captain of your ship? If you're not, then you're letting others steer your ship for you. You have no way of knowing where you're going or how you will get there.

But if each day you plan to reach a point by the end of that day and a further point at the end of the week, and another by the end of the month, your ship will travel the most efficient way between where you are today and where you want to be. This is not to say that your ship can't stop at an undiscovered island or explore a new channel along the route. You may even want to change your short-term goals as you move steadily toward your long-term goal.

The reward in this way of operating is that you don't cut into your free time, or playtime, in the process of accomplishing your goal. You replace wasted time and lost motion with productive energy directed toward your destination.

Getting Organized

Have you ever tried to enter a sailing race without checking for torn sails, sizing up your competition, charting the course, figuring what currents and river traffic you'll have to buck, knowing when and where to tack, being prepared to adjust to the vagaries of the weather, sandbars, or reefs? An organized and efficiency-conscious person will be on the dock, enjoying wine and cheese, while the person who thinks he can enter the race without setting goals and making plans will still be out in the elements attempting to get to shore, paying the price for his lack of preparation.

"But I'm a creative person. I'm not organized," you might say. "I believe in the spontaneous approach."

People who visit me here at the farm are surprised to see how organized I am. They expect disorganized bliss. They find instead self-discipline and a smooth-running operation.

Some talented musicians, artists, writers, and photographers feel it's unfashionable, uncomfortable, even un-American to be organized. But creative people, the ones who accomplish with consistency, *are* organized. They can't afford not to be. Time is too important to them. Anyone who values his time and expects to accomplish anything of note *is* organized. A disorganized person will sometimes attain momentary fame and brandish his disorganization as a badge of distinction. But the ones who sustain and expand their success have learned to quietly get organized.

Lou Jacobs, Jr., photographer and author, once told me, "The only time I'm unorganized is when I'm on vacation." Like Lou, save your spontaneity for your Sunday shots and days off. As you build your photo-marketing business, set your goals, follow through, and be prepared when opportunity beckons. These are the secrets of creative success.

Time Your Goals

Set short-term and long-term goals. Make them realistic.

For a short-term goal, aim to be sending out a certain number of pictures by a certain month. Aim to cut your processing, film, and paper costs by a certain percentage within the same month (by shopping for the best price and streamlining your buying procedures—order by mail or phone rather than in person, and order in quantity).

For a long-term goal, aim within two years to be selling three times the number of pictures you are currently selling.

Goals need not be rigid and inflexible. They can be changed—upwards or downwards—depending on many variables. Write them down, though. Spoken goals don't have the same impact.

Write down a few dream goals, also. They're free.

I'd advise you not to share your written goals with anyone, save your spouse or cherished friend. Few people will share your enthusiasm. Friends, colleagues, and relatives are often experts at giving advice, though their experience and personal life situation may not justify it. Keep your goals to yourself, and share them by accomplishing them.

Is It Easy? A Survival Secret

Probably the most frequent question put to me is "How can I become successful at publishing my pictures?" The answer is simple, though it's not the answer most photographers expect. And that may be one reason the answer is so elusive to so many.

We might expect the answer to be "Be born with *talent*" or "Work hard!" Having talent and working hard can help, of course. But we all know photographers with a lot of talent who are going nowhere. We also know a lot of hard workers who are headed for the same place. To get to the point: If your desire to become a published photographer is so strong that your personal constitution will allow you to "put up with and do without," then success is just around the corner.

Whenever I follow up photographers who expressed dreams and aspirations of publishing their pictures, I find the ones who have met with success are the ones who have persisted and endured.

First of all, they have "put up with" the unglamorous chores inherent in this business. As they faced each day, they didn't avoid the tedious tasks. They had *true grit*. They knew that if they avoided an irksome job, it wouldn't go away, but would grow into a larger problem the next day, and by the end of the month, it would be an insurmountable barrier.

And what are these unpleasantries? As a stock photographer, you face them daily: retyping a poorly composed letter to a prospective photo-buyer; spotting a black-and-white print; making a phone call that will straighten out a disagreement; cross-referencing your pictures; filing your transparencies; packaging photos and licking stamps.

If you are new to the field of stock photography, you'll nevertheless recognize those drudgery jobs in a different form at your household. Every uncleaned paintbrush, or tool unreturned to its shelf, that unbalanced checkbook, and every unanswered letter in that pile of important letters—all are examples of things we don't like to do, things that pile up until it becomes a habit to *not* get them done. That habit then becomes our style, or *us*. Wishing away drudgery jobs never works. We cannot become a success at anything until we face the fact that a goal or a purpose must be worth *more* than the inconvenience of tackling the chores most people just don't like to do.

In my experience, I find that stock photographers who throw in the towel do so not for lack of talent, but because they are victims of their own failure to recognize this essential point: *Put up with the drudgery.*

The second dictum is: Do without the creature comforts. Hopefully, this will be necessary only in the initial stages of your career. How long you will do without depends on the goals you have set for yourself. Some goals are short-range and easily attainable. Other goals are long-range, worthwhile, and rewarding to the soul, but not immediately rewarding to the pocketbook.

In order to get established as a stock photographer, one must frequently do without the conveniences Madison Avenue continually reminds us we must possess: a VCR, a color TV, the latest model car, a new wardrobe. In order to meet film or postage costs or to purchase a new enlarger, we must often change lifestyle or supermarket habits to economize. We must do without.

If you begin today to economize, and tackle each drudgery chore as it comes along, you'll be surprised to find that you'll get into a habit of successfully meeting challenges. What was once an annoying task will become a joyous one for you, because you'll welcome and recognize it as another milepost on your journey to your goal as a successful stock photographer. If you persist and develop the inner constitution to "put up with and do without," you will begin your success where others failed.

"Victory belongs to the most persevering."—Napoleon

Think Small

In a few pages, I'll be asking you to think big, once you get your stock photo-marketing operation rolling. But Rome wasn't built in a day. Aim high in your photography aspirations, but initially aim low in your sales targets. Make your first mistakes where large audiences and your later market photobuyers won't see them.

I'm not proposing mediocrity, simply advising you not to fall into the "glory" trap: You'll run up against the wall built by experienced competitors, only to become discouraged and take that lucrative job offer at the local car wash. The result: You'll become another name in the Directory of Also-Rans. Work smart = think small in the early stages. Give yourself production and fee goals that are immediately reachable, and then move along in steps on your way to thinking big.

Don't Misdirect Your Work

Working smart includes not working—on projects or in directions that offer little promise. If you gauge in advance what to avoid, you can save yourself money and time. As a stock photographer breaking into the markets, assess beforehand the degree of difficulty you will face when approaching a particular magazine or publishing company. Is the market crowded? (For example, Ski magazine, in New York, stated in an edition of Photographer's Market: "Presently overstocked with photos.") Is it a closed market for you, such as Time, People, National Geographic? Or is it wide open? (Open markets include local magazine supplements for Sunday newspapers; denominational publishers, listed in Photographer's Market under Book Publishers, which publish dozens of magazines and periodicals; association and organization magazines like the Rotarian or Kiwanis magazine.)

What is the supply/demand ratio involved for each type of market? Some photographers do not learn the answer until they have uselessly spent a fortune trying to market pictures to a virtually closed market. Read the cues: "No use for this type of photography." "We're overstocked on those." "Bring more detail into your pictures if you want to sell to us." "We have a photographer who does those and don't need any more."

When you fill in your yearly assessment of your best markets, you'll know which ones to shut out. With each sale, you'll gravitate closer to your ideal markets.

The typically closed markets (see Appendix A) are the calendar, greeting card, poster, and placemat areas. The market is glutted with fine photographs and fine photographers, many of whom have worked for a particular company for decades. Why try to drive through a stone wall for occasional sales, when lucrative avenues await you? Magazine and book publishers with $10,000-, $20,000-, and $30,000-a-month budgets for photography await the stock photographer who has discovered his own PMS/A and has zeroed in on a specific Market List.

Your research and your own personal experience will determine which markets are closed to you. If the situation doesn't look promising in light of your current degree of expertise or depth in a certain photographic area, don't knock fruitlessly at a door that isn't ready to open to you yet. First put your energies and your dollars into tapping the lesser-known markets. You'll save money, gain experience, build your picture files, sell photos—and that's working smart.

Draw up a weekly report that tallies work activity scores, such as how many shipments were sent out, how many pictures were sold, and so on. Analyze these on a continuing basis to see if your sales are growing and what categories and which shipments have been most successful. Continue to revise your Market List priorities from these figures.

Your PMS/A—The Heart of Working Smart

At the heart of how smooth your business will run is a solid understanding of your personal marketing strength/areas (PMS/A), well coordinated with a sound Market List.

To photograph and attempt sales outside of your PMS/A or Market List is akin to being adrift out there on the bay on that fishing trip—yet many photographers are slow to switch over to the habit of concentrating on marketable stock photos.

Decide early in your stock photography career what portion of your photography is your hobby and what portion is business. Learn the difference between pictures that are marketable as stock photos and pictures that feed your soul but are monumentally difficult or even costly to market. Concentrating on producing marketable pictures can add up to sizable savings for you, as well as sizable earnings—and that's working smart.

Learn how to specialize. Don't be a photographic jack-of-all-trades. Instead of spreading yourself thin, get to know your strong areas even better. Provide your photobuyers with expertise that matches their readers' interest. You'll be in control of a well-managed stock photo business if you concentrate on your areas of personal marketing strength.

You Manage the Business/Not the Other Way Around

Being one step ahead of the competition, whether in a footrace or a pass pattern in football, makes all the difference between winning and losing. In business, it works the same way. If you get behind, you lose control, and get behinder and behinder. The business begins to manage you. You can be out front, even if it's by inches, if you adopt the winning habit of daily keeping your ship on course.

In stock photography, this applies especially to the routine you establish to get your shipments out to photobuyers. Establish a written plan (this will help to crystallize your thinking), and follow through.

If you are not a self-starter, here's a technique many people have used effectively: Hire a part-time assistant to come to your office certain days of the week to send out shipments of pictures. To keep your helper productive, you must always have new work ready to send out.

A Self-Evaluation Guide

How do you tell if you're making any progress? By measuring it. Too often, photographers and other creative people find one year running into the next without ever analyzing their efforts to see if they're really moving or just running in place. A well-received exhibit or a TV interview might create an illusion of success, but if the bottom line shows zero at the end of the year, it's time to assess your efforts.

Your measuring system doesn't have to be elaborate, but to be effective it should encompass at least a three-year span, so that you have a meaningful basis of comparison. (Quarterly or monthly assessments—based on your photo submissions in/out ledger—will be helpful until you reach the three-year mark.)

You will want to keep a running tally on four areas: pictures sent out; pictures bought; money received; and film, paper, and processing costs. Chart these monthly, as shown in Table 14-1, and at the end of three years, you will see your progress. (Pictures bought in one month may include many pictures actually sent out during previous months.)

How to Measure Your Sales Strengths

Here's how to chart your sales strength areas your first year. A spreadsheet program on your computer will tally these figures for you. Otherwise use a simple ledger sheet and a pencil.

Start any month of the year.

1. Assign a code number to each of your sales areas.
2. Make a sales slip (use carbon paper, photocopy, or mimeograph) that includes a blank space for:

Sales Slip
Date:
Amount:
Code Number:

3. Each time you receive a check for the sale of one of your pictures, record the above information. If one check is for two or three different sales areas (code numbers), make two or three sales slips.
4. File your sales slips in a drawer until the end of the month.

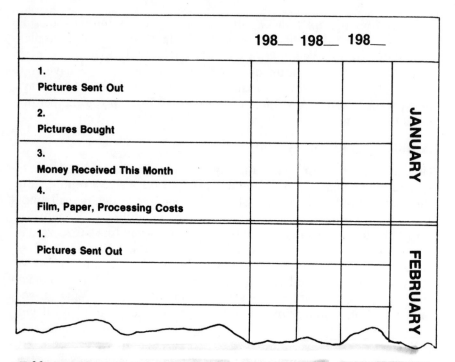

	198__	198__	198__	
1. **Pictures Sent Out**				JANUARY
2. **Pictures Bought**				
3. **Money Received This Month**				
4. **Film, Paper, Processing Costs**				
1. **Pictures Sent Out**				FEBRUARY

Table 14-1. Your success scorecard can be on a simple ledger sheet or a computerized spreadsheet.

5. At the end of the month, enter the information from the sales slips onto a chart (ledger) similar to the example in Table 14-2.

6. Make a total of the previous months and the current month for a year-to-date total.

Your sales totals are your best marketing teacher. Which code area(s) shows the highest income? By monitoring these statistics, you will be able to accurately document in which areas you should concentrate your sales efforts.

Pictures Just Aren't Selling?

Working smart includes reevaluating your working procedures now and again, too. Start with your packaging presentation. Here's a trick you can use to assure that you're maintaining top quality: Ask the person closest to you to be your quality-control engineer. Every so often, when you prepare a package for a photobuyer, don't let it out of the house until your spouse or special friend has given it the quality-control go-ahead. Let this person critique it, acting out the role of photobuyer. Painful as it might be, you'll form the habit of giving every detail of your presentation your best.

MONTH: _____		CODE NO.	TOTAL SALES PREVIOUS MONTH	TOTAL SALES THIS MONTH	TOTAL SALES YEAR TO DATE	TOTALS FOR 12 MONTHS BEGINNING: _____ ENDING:___
PRIMARY MARKETS	MAGAZINES					
		SPECIAL INTEREST	100			
		TRADE	101			
		BUSINESS	102			
		DENOMINATIONAL	103			
		ASSOCIATIONS, ORGANIZATIONS	104			
		LOCAL MAGAZINES	105			
		STATE & REGIONAL MAGAZINES	106			
		NEWS SERVICES	107			
		OTHER	108			
	BOOKS	TEXTBOOKS	200			
		CHURCH RELATED BOOKS	201			
		ENCYCLOPEDIA	202			
		CONSUMER TRADE	203			
		OTHER	204			
SECONDARY MARKETS	STOCK PHOTO AGENCIES	AGENCY A	300			
		AGENCY B	301			
		AGENCY C	302			
		AGENCY D	303			
		OTHER	304			
		MAJOR NEWSSTAND MAGAZINES	400			
	DECOR PHOTOGRAPHY	MARKET A	500			
		MARKET B	501			
		MARKET C	502			
		MARKET D	503			
		OTHER	504			
THIRD CHOICE MARKETS	PAPER PRODUCTS	CALENDARS	600			
		GREETING CARDS	601			
		POSTERS	602			
		POST CARDS	603			
		OTHER	604			
	COMMERCIAL ACCOUNTS	ADVERTISING AGENCIES	700			
		PUBLIC RELATIONS FIRMS	701			
		RECORD COMPANIES	702			
		AUDIO/VISUAL HOUSES	703			
		GRAPHIC DESIGN STUDIOS	704			
		OTHER	705			
	ART PHOTO SALES	MUSEUMS	800			
		PRIVATE INDIVIDUALS	801			
		OTHER	802			
	OTHER	GOVERNMENT AGENCIES	900			
		NEWSPAPERS	901			

Table 14-2. A ledger to assess your sales strengths.

The Five Reasons for Rejection

If you're not getting the sales you feel you ought to be getting, give the following points some serious thought. Often, success can be a process of elimination. By avoiding failure, you succeed. Get back to the basics, and turn your marketing sales spiraling upward.

There are five basic reasons for photographs being rejected. If you are guilty of any of them, you should reassess your marketing methods.

1. Poor presentation. Are you mailing in a crisp, white, cardboard envelope? Are you using a professional label or imprinted logo? Did you include SASE with your submission (if you are a new contributor to the publication)? Are your transparencies packaged in protective sleeves? Are they clearly identified? Have you checked for the current address and photobuyer's name? Is your cover letter a professional-looking printed form letter (which saves your time and the editor's) rather than a rambling handwritten letter?

It may seem unfair that the outside appearance of your package is so important. But photobuyers are busy people and have found through experience that amateurish packaging usually reflects the contents. Often they relegate a sloppy package to the *return* bin—without opening it. If you want first-class treatment from photobuyers, give them first-class treatment.

2. Off-target and unrelated submissions. Does the material you've submitted stick to the point of the buyer's request? Do your pictures hit the mark? Or has the buyer asked for pictures of waterfalls, and you've submitted pictures of brooks and streams just in case the buyer might want to see them?

Also, are your pictures *cohesive in style?* Do the pictures themselves have a consistent, professional-looking appearance? That is, do they all look like they came from the same photographer? A good way to test the cohesiveness of your pictures, and their professionalism, is to gather pictures from magazines and periodicals on your Market List, lay about twenty of them on the living room floor, and then place *your* pictures beside them (or if you deal in slides, project them on a screen with the tearsheets taped to a nearby wall). Do your pictures fit in? If so, you are on target. If not, retake the same pictures, incorporating into your new pictures what you have learned from this exercise.

3. Poor quality. Take a look at your pictures again. Assuming you are using a top-quality lens, is your color vibrant and appropriate for the mood and scene? Have you properly filtered your indoor shots where fluorescents are involved? If you've used flash or lights, have you avoided hot spots?

How sharp are your color and black-and-white? Published pictures must go through several generations before they reach the printed page. Your pictures must be appropriately in focus, with good film resolution (sharpness), with no grain (unless appropriate), and with no camera shake, as these faults will be magnified in your published picture.

Are your prints technically good? Have you achieved the best possible gradation in your black-and-white prints: a stark white (with some details), several gradations of grays, all the way down to a deep, rich black (also with some details)? If you've used burning/dodging techniques, they shouldn't be apparent to the photobuyer. Have you spotted your prints (see Appendix C), especially the 35mms?

Are your b&w pictures dog-eared, with rough edges, cracks, stains, folds, tears—or scratches?

All of the above are quick evidence to a photobuyer of poor craftsmanship and low reliability factor.

4. Outdated pictures. Outdated pictures can be another enemy to your sales. Photobuyers expect a fresh batch of new pictures from you on each shipment. Some pictures are long-lived, timeless: fifty years from now, your heirs could continue to benefit by their sales. The majority of pictures, however, are short-lived because they reflect the *now*. In a matter of years (usually between five and ten), you will want to extract these pictures from your files because they are dated by clothing and hair styles, equipment, machinery, furnishings, and so on.

Some stock photographers have attempted to circumvent this problem by eliminating anything from their pictures that would date them. This (generally speaking) means excluding people. However, the one most essential element in a successful photo illustration is people. Exclude them and sales diminish.

Putting your dated pictures out to pasture is not an enjoyable prospect. Be as objective as possible in your weeding-out process. If you find it difficult to eliminate pictures, ask a friend to look through a group and to try to guess what year the pictures were taken. Your friend's objective assessment will be very similar to a photobuyer's.

We all have a tendency to rationalize our pictures' usefulness and stretch their life span beyond marketing reality. It's no fun sending them to the incinerator. At the risk of sounding like dial-a-mortician, I'm asking you to be *realistic*. Photobuyers are. Outdated pictures will outdate your business operation, and will possibly eliminate you from the photobuyer's roster.

5. Poor composition. Assess the *composition* of your pictures. Do they adhere to the $P = B + P + S + I$ principle? (See Chapter 2.) Do you zero in on your subject matter with the appropriate emphasis for each situation? When you work with people in your pictures, do you orchestrate the scene so that the results are natural and unposed? In other words, are you producing marketable stock photos?

If this section on why pictures fail to get published is discouraging to you, it shouldn't be. Remember that the stock photographers who are successful at photo marketing are not those who occasionally produce a brilliant photograph, but those who periodically assess and evaluate their progress. If they find deficiencies, they take the next step: they do something about it.

Please be cautioned that some photographers take to extremes my suggestions for avoiding failure. These folks are *perfectionists.* "Do it right or not at all." "There's always enough time to do it over—but never enough time to do it right in the first place." These admonitions are certainly well-founded, and many successful stock photographers can trace their success to adherence to such good rules. The paradox is that many unsuccessful stock photographers can trace their failures to them, also. Why? The procrastinator, under the guise of perfectionism, accomplishes nothing for fear of not doing it flawlessly.

Procrastinators spin wheels reading and studying about cameras and equipment and how to take pictures. They keep telling themselves they don't know enough to start, that their pictures aren't good enough yet to send to an editor.

If you find yourself justifying procrastination, ask yourself to redefine *quality.* You can pride yourself on quality presentations without crippling yourself by equating quality with perfection.

A Potpourri of Additional Aids in Working Smart

Remember the Law of 125

When you get upset with a photobuyer, remember the Law of 125. Each person you deal with influences 125 other friends, neighbors, relatives, or business colleagues. It works this way: If you produce a good product for a person, that person will probably tell five people (5) who may each tell five people (25) who may tell five people (125).

$$1 \times 5 = 5 \times 5 = 25 \times 5 = 125.$$

If you turn away a prospective customer with an angry remark or letter or poor attitude, you may be turning away 125 prospects.

Let Magazine Articles Teach You

Photography magazines can help you learn the techniques of successful stock photographers. Ask your librarian to help you locate back issues. An excellent desk top reference is the *Photography Magazine Index* by Stu Beger, Paragon Publishing, Santa Rosa, CA. It's updated every four years.

Insurance

Are you insurance-poor? That is, are you putting a disproportionate amount of your dollars into insurance instead of film and photo supplies? Don't allow yourself to be talked into equipment insurance plans that will put you in a bind. Talk around with other photographers. If you hear of many instances of stolen equipment, then a solid equipment or business protection plan might be in order for you. Reexamine your policy from time to time. Some of your equipment may have depreciated to the point where it isn't cost-effective to continue to insure it. On the other side of the coin, the incidence of theft may have increased in your neighborhood. Protect yourself accordingly.

Here's an interesting fact: The *Milwaukee Journal* does not insure its cameras and equipment. They have found it not to be cost-effective.

Buying insurance is like gambling. You play the odds. However, some careful research on your part can establish how much insurance is enough for you. Shop around. If you're quoted disproportionately different rates, read the fine print and investigate the company through *Consumer Reports* or your local Better Business Bureau.

The best insurance is the daily habit of prevention. *That's* affordable.

1. Know the high-risk areas for thievery.
2. Don't tempt thieves with flashy camera bags or unlocked car doors.
3. Invest in a burglar-alarm system or a dog who likes to bark.
4. Inscribe your name on your equipment. Your local police department will help you on this.
5. Ask for references from the people you employ.
6. Keep receipts and serial numbers of all your equipment.

Toll-Free Numbers

The telephone is rapidly becoming an important resource for the stock photographer. The numbers listed here are toll-free, and the people on the other end of the line stand ready to serve you in some aspect of your photo operation. This is only a sampling of the toll-free numbers available to you. For a number not on this list, call the toll-free information operator at 800-555-1212 and ask if the company has a toll-free number. You'll save on your phone bill, and you'll get your answers from the experts, fast. The major photography magazines often list toll-free numbers in the ads for camera equipment and film processing. A toll-free directory is available from *Toll-Free Digest*, Box 800, Claverack, NY 12513. Companies will change their toll-free number. If this happens on any of the following numbers, just call 1-800-555-1212 and ask for the new number.

800-422-7220 **U.S. Postal Service.**

800-348-2220 **Fox Professional Color Labs** (processing).

800-238-5355 **Federal Express** (common carrier).

800-343-5000 **Polaroid** (film).

800-638-4480 **Ritz Camera** (cameras, equipment).

800-628-9265 **U.S. Envelope Co.** (inexpensive envelopes).

800-331-1212	**Avis Rent-a-Car.**
800-527-0700	**Budget Rent-a-Car.**
800-654-3131	**Hertz Rent-a-Car.**
800-433-7300	**American Airlines.**
800-327-8376	**Eastern Airlines.**
800-221-1111	**Pan American Airlines.**
800-221-2000	**TWA Airlines.**
800-555-5340	**Bausch & Lomb** (optics, lenses).
800-654-4488	**E. Leitz** (cameras).
800-645-6687	**Nikon Inc.** (cameras).
800-223-0125	**Olympus Corp.** (cameras).
800-257-8354	**RapidForms** (business forms).
800-451-8113	**RapidForms** (fast fax orders).
800-328-9555	**St. Paul Book and Stationery** (office supplies).
800-243-5250	**Grayarc** (business forms, labels).
800-225-9550	**NEBS** (business forms, labels, printed custom forms).
800-527-9530	**The Drawing Board** (business stationery, office supplies).
800-523-0163	**Fenton** (labels).
800-328-3034	**Fidelity Products Co.**
800-323-6230	**Moore** (business forms, labels, etc.).
800-421-4662	**20th Century Plastics** (plastic slide pages).
800-638-3033	**Stationery House** (office forms, stationery).
800-238-3957	**Tie Officemates** (plastic products).
800-421-1222	**Viking Office Products** (computer supplies).
800-523-0552	**Bell Atlantic Business Supplies** (office equipment).
800-328-2179	**The Bill-a-Pak Co.** (printed promotional items).
800-558-0220	**Miles Kimball Company** (office products).
800-237-8207	**CBI Corporation** (customized business forms).
800-431-1095	**Dexter** (colored post cards).

Federal Tax Information. Provides answers to your questions, plus assistance on your federal tax questions. Number varies by state.

Grants, Loans, Scholarships, Fellowships, and Aids

Assistance is available to photographers on local, regional, and national levels. The funds come from state and federal agencies as well as private corporations and foundations. The monies are awarded usually for specialized photographic projects. If your idea for a grant, fellowship, etc., is accepted, the grant can provide a boost for your supply of stock photos in one of your PMS/As.

To apply, photographers propose a photographic project, and if select-ed, receive a stipend ranging from $500 to $1,000 a month for a period of several months.

You can learn more about how to write proposals for and receive such funds through the following books:

The Art of Winning Foundation Grants
by Howard Hillman and Karin Abarbanel
Vanguard Press
424 Madison Ave.
New York, NY 10017

Gadney's Guide to Contests, Festivals, &
    Grants
Festival Publications
Box 10180
Glendale, CA 91209

Documentary Photography Grants
by Bill Owens
Working Press
Box 687
Livermore, CA 94550

Foundation Grants to Individuals
The Foundation Center
888 Seventh Ave.
New York, NY 10016

Getting a Grant
by Robert Lefferts
Prentice-Hall
Englewood Cliffs, NJ 07632

Grants and Aid to Individuals in the Arts
Washington International Arts Letter
Box 9005
Washington, DC 20003

Grants in Photography—How to Get
    Them
by Lida Moser
Amphoto Books
1515 Broadway
New York, NY 10036

Grants Register
St. Martin's Press
175 Fifth Ave.
New York, NY 10010

National Endowment for the Arts
1100 Pennsylvania Ave. NW
Washington, DC 20506

The ultimate in working smart, of course, is doing work that you don't consider work at all. If you've defined your PMS/A well and tailored your Market List to markets that offer you the best potential, you'll find that you'll automatically be working smart.

15.
Rights
and
Regulations

Copyright

Who owns your picture? You do! The Copyright Law speaks loud and clear.

Back in 1976, the U.S. Congress revised our ancient Copyright Law (the first major revision in sixty-nine years), and the revised edition has been in effect since January 1, 1978. The new law generally gives you, as the author of your photos, copyright for each picture from the moment you snap it. Ownership of the copyright enables you to limit the use of every photo in whatever way you specify, to resell various rights in the work, and to have your work protected by a court of law in case of infringement.

The easiest way to assert your claim is to affix a copyright notice— © 19_____/Your Name—to each photo. You can also formally register your picture with the Copyright Office for a fee (currently $10). You then receive a registration certificate, the prerequisite for taking an infringer (one who has used or reused your picture without authorization) to court. If you don't register your picture, it is still protected by copyright, as your property, and you still have legal claim to it. However, formal registration helps to cement your claim and if you register within three months of the first publication of your work, you have a better chance at receiving full financial recompense in the event of infringement.

Copyright Infringement

Let me say at the outset that I believe that the spirit of the Copyright Law is to encourage the free flow of information in our society, and that the law is a basic protection for that exchange. It was written to protect not just photographers, but the users of photographs as well: the photobuyers. Copyright infringement in stock photography is rare (as opposed to service photography, where infringement does happen). In twenty-five years as a stock photographer, I have personally experienced only one instance of possible infringement. And in that case an art director, new on the job, made an honest mistake.

If you wish to be super-safe, you can register your extra-special marketable pictures. When you do, you'll receive the benefit of the Copyright Office's documentation and recording, and you'll have copies of your work filed with the Library of Congress. But generally, in stock photography work, you won't find it necessary to register every picture. The © symbol affixed to the back of your picture (or the front if you wish), or next to your credit line in a layout, offers a warning to would-be infringers. The right to use the © is yours; it costs you nothing. The law recognizes that you own your picture once you have it on film. The 1978 law is, in effect, a photographer's law, rather than a publisher's law as it was prior to 1978.

Remember, a copyright protects only your picture, not the *idea* your picture expresses (Section 102[b]). If someone improves your idea with his picture, that's not copyright infringement; that's free enterprise. For example, if your photograph shows a tiny kitten hanging precariously by its tiny claws from a clothesline, it is generally not copyright infringement for another photographer to photograph his own kitten (or mouse or raccoon) in the same situation.

Group Registration

Another option—and to the photographer, quite an advantage—is that under the revision, you can "group-register" photographs that have been published in periodicals. Whether you're registering five pictures or fifty, whether they're from one magazine or newspaper or many, a single fee (currently ten dollars) is charged. The requirement for a group registration is that the pictures must be published within a twelve-month period in a periodical and that your copyright notice appear adjacent to your photo. You need to file one copy of the entire issue in which the photo appeared for each photo you are registering, and if your copyright notice is not included with your credit line, you cannot group-register your picture.

Omission of the adjacent notice does not, however, void your copyright. The picture will still be protected by the publisher's copyright notice, usually included in the masthead, which protects all editorial matter and photographs (except advertising) within the publication.*

Group registration is also possible for your unpublished photos; unpublished works may be re-registered after publication. Registering un-

---

*Service photographers, take note. Since noneditorial photographs (ads) are not protected by the blanket copyright, insist that your copyright (unless you worked "for hire") be included with your picture.

published works is usually unnecessary but can expedite getting into court in the event a work is infringed.

How to Contact the Copyright Office

For more details on specific points in this chapter, phone the Copyright Public Information Office (202)479-0700 between 8:00 A.M. and 4:00 P.M. (their time), or write: Register of Copyrights, Library of Congress, Washington, DC 20559. If you feel you need legal advice, contact an attorney. For a free copy of the Copyright Act of 1976, Public Law 94-553, write to the Register of Copyrights.

The Copyright Law is lengthy (twenty-two pages) and covers all aspects of creative endeavor, from book publishing to motion pictures. We'll be addressing here only the portions of the law that relate to stock photography.

Interpreting the Law

Writing and commenting on "the law"—any law—is like discussing philosophy or religion. A point of law might be stated one way, but it's open to different interpretations. Only time and court tests solidify the interpretation. Even then, there are exceptions to the rule. As each stock photographer's Market List and PMS/A are different, so is the photographer's need to interpret the Copyright Law. I have made every effort to ensure the accuracy of the information contained in this chapter, checking it with copyright officials and attorneys, but I cannot guarantee the absence of error or hold myself liable for the use or misuse of this information.

To sum up the points of law covered so far:

—You own your picture (unless you have signed a "work-for-hire" agreement, discussed later in this chapter).
—You can register your pictures for added protection.
—You can group-register your photos for a reasonable fee.

Be Wary of Dates

All of your pictures published prior to *January 1, 1978,* that appeared in copyrighted publications are copyrighted jointly by you and the publisher. The Copyright Office does not recognize you as the sole owner of the copyright on such a pre-1978 picture unless you can show proof that you leased the picture on a one-time basis or that the publisher reassigned all copyright privileges back to you. It is doubtful that this situation will cause you any problems, unless the picture concerned is one with great market potential (such as a person who recently catapulted to fame). Nevertheless, pre-1978 pictures are generally protected by copyright, and it may even be possible for you to assert your sole right to them at the time of renewal (more about this later).

Though your rights in pictures published before 1978 may be limited by the arrangements you originally made with the publisher, pictures taken before 1978 but not published until after 1978 will enjoy the benefits of the revised Copyright Law.

Now for the bad news. It is possible for you to lose the right to your pictures and for them to fall into public domain. Here's how it can happen: If your work is published without your copyright notice in an uncopyrighted publication (e.g., a literary magazine or a low-budget regional publication), and if you do nothing about correcting the error within a period of five years from the date your picture was published, then the Copyright Office will refuse to register your picture. It is then implied that your copyright has expired and that your picture belongs to "the people." It is in the public domain. Anyone can use it.

This, of course, is an extreme example—but how would you correct the situation? If it's an important picture, you should register it immediately with the Copyright Office. Send two copies of the original (8x10s of black and white, dupes of a transparency) along with your registration fee. Ask for form VA.

If you attempt to register a work that has been published without notice, you will have to show the Copyright Office that either: (a) the notice was omitted from only a relatively small number of copies distributed to the public, (b) a reasonable effort has been made to add notice to all copies distributed once the omission was discovered, or (c) the notice was omitted in violation of your express requirement, in writing, that your notice appear.

The easiest way to avoid this predicament is to stamp (or write) your notice on all photos sent out, along with a letter stating that if the photo is published, your notice must appear beside it. Notice consists of the word "copyright" or the abbreviation "copr." or a © symbol (leave the year blank) and your name (©19_____ your name).

The revised Copyright Law offers the machinery to protect your ownership of your pictures, but ultimately the burden of protecting your rights is on you. The rationale behind the public domain concept goes like this: A created work deserves to be enjoyed by the people. Credit and reward should go to the creator, but if the artist, by choice or circumstance, is not in a position to reap the potential benefits, then the public at large can lay claim to the creation. In that case anyone who sees potential in them that you may have missed can capitalize on your pictures.

The Copyright Office can offer you no protection if you have relinquished your rights through neglect, ignorance, or your own wishes.

I suggested in Chapter 13 that you leave the year blank when you order the rubber stamp for your copyright notice, so as not to "date" your pictures and lose potential sales. The Copyright Law is not clear as yet as to strict adherence to date requirements. The Copyright Office is interested in the date the picture is (was) published, not the date you took the picture or had it processed. Therefore, the layout person or art director can insert the date of publication in small print adjacent to your picture in the layout and satisfy this requirement.

However, some art directors don't include the © notice and date next to your picture. What, then, if there's an infringement question? If you have notified the art director that your notice must appear as a condition of publication, the work will be considered "unpublished" (because it was an unauthorized form of publication). Then the © notice with the year blank would be accepted by the Copyright Office, since you can register an unpublished photo that has no publication date. You also have the advantage of not dating your pictures when this occurs.

Laying Claim to Your Picture

The Copyright Law doesn't specify what else you should have on your picture for identification other than the notice. (Always copyright under your name, not the name of your business. Otherwise if you sell your business, with it would go the copyright to all your pictures.) For your own ID purposes, however, always include your address and phone number. I also advise ordering a stamp with the memo shown in Figure 15-1. (Use two stamps—the other for your address and phone.)

(Your slides will require an abbreviated form of the stamps shown in Figure 15-1 because of the border-size limitation, but be sure to include all the information on your accompanying invoice. Computer labeling programs like those mentioned in Chapter 17 can also be used to accomplish this.)

There are sound reasons for going to the trouble of a memo stamp:

1. *Licensed* implies that this picture is not work-for-hire.* (In work-for-hire, the copyright may not belong to you.) "Licensed" implies that you have not entered into any separate sales arrangement with your client, and that you want any transparency returned to you, and, when practical, you'd like any black-and-white print returned to you.

2. "One-time" assures that you are not assigning any rights other than rights to one-time use. If you wish, include this sentence in your invoice: "Additional rights available."

3. "Inside editorial use" simply lets the client know that if he decides to use your picture on a cover, he must pay extra. (See Table 8-2 for how

---

*If the purchase order or agreement—or even the check—you receive from your client requires you to sign anything that implies that you are offering more than one-time publishing rights, or states a work-for-hire arrangement, don't sign it. Cross out and initial that portion of the purchase agreement, stamp your rubber stamp on the margin, send it off with the picture (also stamped), and let them carry the ball from there.

Stamp 1   **Stamp 2**

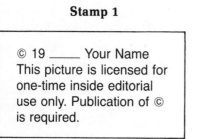

Figure 15-1. Stamps to protect your prints.

to increase your fee when a picture is used for a cover, advertising, etc.) This phrase will also protect you in the future if an art director happens to use your picture without authorization for commercial (trade) purposes or advertising. If a suit were to arise relating to trade and advertising use because of the people pictured in the photograph, you could show proof that the picture was leased for only editorial purposes (which usually require no model release).

4. Include © credit. Shows proof, in case of infringement, that you asked the publisher to name you as copyright owner.

Some Drawbacks of the New Law

INFRINGER (Section 501[a]): Someone who violates any of the exclusive rights of a copyright owner.

The revised law, although of benefit to the stock photographer, must be seen realistically as also of potential benefit to an infringer—a person who innocently (or knowingly) pirates your pictures. To illustrate how an infringer might have more muscle than you do when it comes down to the bottom line, consider this: The cost for registering a picture is in actuality about $24, if you consider the cost of the initial correspondence, the duping of your slide or printing of your 8x10 (deposit), postage and handling, clerical work at your end, and the $10 registration fee. If you were to discover an infringement, five more exchanges of letters or phone calls to your attorney and the infringer would amount to about $150. The attorney's pretrial consultation fee would be $45 to $125, and a day in court would cost you $350 to $1,500. And here's the curve ball: Section 504(c) (2) and Section 504(b) provide that when an infringer is not aware that he has reason to believe that his acts constitute an infringement, the court is allowed to reduce the minimum statutory damages to $100 (even if you had your picture registered!). As a result, you could lose money in the deal. If you won the case you might be lucky and the court might award you reasonable attorney's fees as part of the costs. But as we all are aware, sometimes it's nonproductive to sue.

Your greatest protection, then, is to place the copyright notice on *each* of your pictures. (Remember, the notice costs you nothing.) An "innocent infringer" would rarely pirate your picture if identification were on it, and most assuredly not if you had it stamped with a copyright notice. It carries clout. Like the average citizen who never removes the mattress label (Do Not Remove Under Penalty of Law), the infringer is likely to shy away from anything that looks like a federal offense.

In the rare instance where you might discover an infringer within three months after you have published an unregistered picture, if you choose to press charges, you can get your picture registered at the Copyright Office (special speedy handling will cost you [at this writing] an extra $200—by certified check!) and haul the infringer into any court having jurisdiction in a federal civil action. If it's past the three-month deadline, you can still register your picture, but damages you would receive if you won the case would be limited.

The process of registration is simple for authors who register an entire book for $10. For stock photographers, who produce thousands of pictures, the administration and expense of registering each photo might be likened to separately registering each paragraph in a novel or textbook. As stock photographers, then, we continue to be left to the mercy and basic honesty inherent in most people. God won't save us from "innocent infringers" but we can do a lot to eliminate their "innocent" status by putting notice on every photograph that leaves our hands.

A Remedy

If you discover someone or some business or organization has used your picture without your permission, send them a bill. How much? $300 to $500 would be normal. If they've got "deep pockets," charge them $1,500, an acceptable fee in the commercial photo community.

Under the new law (Section 113(c), 107, the "fair use" doctrine), libraries, schools, and noncommercial broadcasters (such as public television) can sometimes use your pictures without requesting your permission, provided their use is limited to educational and noncommercial activities and does not diminish the future marketing potential of your picture.

This latter ruling will need further interpretation because of the paradox involved when a picture receives wide exposure. Consider the broadcasting of pro football—leagues are still not sure whether broadcasting enhances or decreases gate sales. Hence the blackout provision. This provision of "fair use" by the nonprofit sector, which has yet to be fully tested in court, could prove to be a great disadvantage to the stock photographer. "Fair use" is, however, limited by many of the provisions detailed in Publication R-21, which describes some of the limitations on fair use. If your work has been used extensively, the use may not be "fair"—reading Publication R-21 may shed some light on this for you.

And remember, as one sage put it, "A new law is like a new baby; it's created, but that's only the beginning. Then we watch to see which way it will grow."

Q & A Forum on Copyright

In the following Q & A Forum, I'll give detailed answers to some significant questions as they apply to you, the stock photographer, first citing the source in the Copyright Law of 1978.

Can the © be placed on the back of
my picture, or must it appear on
the front?

Section 401(c)
and
House Report
ML-182

Your copyright notice can be rubber-stamped, printed on a label, or handwritten on the back or on the front of your prints. In the case of a transparency, it can be placed on the border (back or front). Be sure the © is enclosed in a circle, not just parentheses.

Who owns my picture?

Sections 201(a)
(b)(c) and
203(a)(3)

You do, from the moment you snap the shutter ("fix the image in a tangible form"). Before 1978, it was assumed the person who *used* your picture (publisher, ad agency, client, etc.) owned the copyright. The new law assumes *you* own all the rights to your pictures unless you have signed those rights away. Except in a case where you have entered into some kind of transfer-of-rights agreement with a client or publisher, such as a work-for-hire agreement, no one else can exercise any ownership rights to your picture. Even if you do sell "all" rights to your picture, in thirty-five years if you or your heirs take appropriate action, the copyright can be taken back.

How long do I own the copyright
on my photograph?

Sections 302(a)
and
304(a) and (b)

The 1978 Copyright Law says your picture "subsists from its creation" (when you snap the shutter), and you own copyright to it for as long as you live, plus fifty years. (The old law, by the way, allowed you only twenty-eight years to own your picture plus a renewal period of twenty-eight years (for a total of fifty-six years). That renewal has been extended to forty-seven years (for a total of seventy-five years)—if you register. If you don't register your copyright in a pre-1978 work, you can't renew it, and at the end of twenty-eight years it will fall into public domain. To register pictures that hold special importance for you, the current fee is $10. Ask for Form VA. If you wish to register nonphotographic work such as writing, ask the Copyright Office for Form TX.

How can my picture fall into the public domain?

Section 405, 406

Theoretically, if you were to publish your picture without a copyright notice, or if your name was misspelled on your notice, your picture could fall into the public domain. If you didn't register a claim to correct the error with the Copyright Office (i.e., register your picture) within *five* years after the picture was published without the notice, or with the error, then the picture's copyright could be invalidated. However, the law bends over backwards to maintain the copyright in works first published after 1978. Your supplying proof that the picture was published without notice in violation of your express requirement that your notice be published with it could preserve your copyright. But publication without notice before 1978 did mean your picture was in the public domain—that is, anyone could use it and not be required to pay you for it.

What is group-registration and how do I do it?

Section 408(c)(2)

This provision of the law says you can register any number of pictures from any twelve-month period for one price. Whether you're registering five pictures or fifty, and whether they're from one magazine or newspaper or many, the fee is currently only $10. (Group registration for your pictures appearing in books, however, is not possible. They must be registered separately.)

How to do it: For each photo you choose, obtain one copy of the entire periodical in which it appeared. Under the current rulings of the Copyright Office, it is mandatory that a bona fide copyright notice appear adjacent to your published picture for it to be group-registered*—another reason to encourage photobuyers to include your © and credit line next to your picture in their layouts.

To group-register, fill out Forms VA and GR/CP (available from the Copyright Office, Library of Congress, Washington DC 20559) and send them along with your $10 fee (in check or money order payable to the Register of Copyrights) and copies of the periodicals or newspapers in which your published pictures appeared.

For unpublished pictures: Submit several contact-size pictures on one 8x10 sheet or submit photocopies of unpublished transparencies or

---

*This requirement of the law [Section 408[c][2]) is especially disadvantageous to photographers, since few art directors wish to include © notices alongside photographs in their layouts.

black-and-white prints (not photocopies) of the pictures you wish to register. Since unpublished works must be in the form of a collection, call this collection of pictures "Collection of Photographs by [Your Name]." A handy way to group-register a collection of slides is to put twenty images in a plastic sleeve, photograph them in color on your light stand and then blow them up to 11" x 14". You can submit any number of multiple sets under one title and the cost is still $10 (at this writing.) Fill this title in at space #1 on Form VA. The law is undergoing interpretation in this area.

If I ask a publisher to include my © notice alongside my picture when he publishes it, but the © is omitted, does this invalidate my copyright protection?

Sections
401(a)(c)
405(a)(2)(3)
407(a)(2), and
408(a)

No. Your copyright protection exists if you can show proof that your picture was (1) rubber-stamped, printed, or handwritten with the copyright notice on the front or back before it was published, or (2) was accompanied by a letter insisting on the publication of your notice with the photo in the publication, or (3) published in a copyrighted publication. Since *all* of the pictures (except advertisements) in a publication are covered by the blanket copyright notice in the masthead, copyright protection for you is implied—but make sure that the publication's copyright notice is correct (you'd be amazed at how many publications print partial notices—or erroneous ones!).

Can I place the © notice on my slides and photographs and be protected in court even if I didn't register my picture with the Copyright Office?

Sections
401(a)(c),
405(a)(2)(3)
407(a)(2), and
408(a)

Yes. The © notice that you put on it is "official," and it is free. If a picture is not registered (with the Copyright Office), it does not mean it is not copyrighted. Like your automobile, if it is stolen, it is a lot easier to prove it's yours if your automobile were registered with the Department of Motor Vehicles, than if you could produce only your title to your automobile, but no registration. Your remedies through the courts are more extensive if your picture happens to be registered.

If I do not register my pictures but I publish them anyway with the © notice, can I be ordered to send them in to the Copyright Office?

Sections
407(a)(d)(1)(2)(3)
and
704 Title 44
(2901)

Yes. Under the 1978 system, the photographer will not be forced to register his pictures, but he can still be ordered to submit two copies of a published work in which a © notice appears, to the Library of Congress (the parent office of the Copyright Office). If, after being ordered to send them, the photographer does not do so *within three months,* he can be fined up to $250 (for each picture) for the first offense, plus the retail cost of acquiring the picture(s). If the photographer fails to or refuses to comply with the demand of the Copyright Office, an additional fine of $2,500 can be imposed.* All deposited pictures become the property of the Library of Congress (but you retain the copyright, since copyright is distinct from ownership of any copy). Incidentally, if you register your work, the copies sent in with the registration satisfy the deposit requirement—but the reverse is not true. Even if a work has been deposited, two additional copies must accompany any registration application.

What does "work for hire" mean?   **Section 101(1)(2)**

If you are employed by a company and take a picture for that company *as an employee,* generally speaking, that's work for hire. The company owns the picture. You have probably, somewhere along the line, signed a work-for-hire agreement with your employer, but even if you haven't, if your work was done within the scope of your employment, total ownership of your pictures belongs to your employer. If you are a freelancer and a picture is specifically commissioned or ordered by a company, and you have signed an agreement saying so, your photos may be works made for hire. However, if a magazine gives you an assignment and pays for the film and expenses, this is not working for hire unless you sign a document saying so. If you receive such an assignment, avoid signing a work-for-hire statement. Instead, agree to allow exclusive three-year rights to the client (or two-year rights). If the client insists on all rights, increase your fee. A good test for work-for-hire is to ask: "If the photographer on this assignment were to be negligent and be sued, who would be liable—the photographer or the entity commissioning the photographer?"

Are the pictures I submit to a photo editor who's listed in *Photographer's Market* or similar reference works considered work for hire?   **Sections 101(1)(2) and 201(b)**

---

*Random published photographs, under this system, are arbitrarily requested for deposit by researchers at the Copyright Office. By the way, I haven't heard of any cases where someone was fined $250, or $2,500, for not submitting the requested pictures.

No, unless you have signed a work-for-hire statement. And remember, if the pictures existed before you made contact with the editor, they were not "specifically ordered and commissioned," and cannot be works made for hire.

What if a magazine publisher   Section 201(c)
wants to reprint my picture a
second time as a reprint of the
original article, or wants to use my
picture to advertise his
publication, or wants to use my
picture a second time in an
anthology? Does the publisher have
the right?

As a stock photographer, you should assign only one-time publishing rights to a photobuyer. Unless it's stipulated in writing, the law assumes that you have assigned (or "licensed") your picture to the photobuyer only for use in the magazine, any revision of that magazine, or any subsequent edition of that magazine—which could mean more than one use, but not in another publication. In no other case may the photobuyer presume to use your pictures without your consent and/or compensation to you. If a photobuyer would like your picture for additional use, refer to the pricing guide for photo reuse in Table 8-3. Note: In the stock photo industry, we use the term *photobuyer*. This term designates that the buyer is buying certain rights (usually one-time rights), not the copyright, and not the physical black-and-white photo or slide itself. These are usually returned after the transaction. (Slides should *always* be returned.)

What penalties does infringement   Sections
(unauthorized use of a photo   412(1)(2),
illustration) call for?   205(d),
                                               411, and
                                               504

The owner of a registered copyrighted picture on which infringement has been proved may receive, in addition to the actual damages he has suffered (lost sales, for example), the amount in cash of the profits received by the infringer. If the copyright owner can prove the infringement was willful, he can receive as much as $50,000 for each infringement if he wins. But if the infringer proves that he infringed innocently, the award to the copyright owner could be as low as $100—or even zero. If the copyright is registered within three months of publication, the copyright owner can receive statutory damages, instead of lost profits. Thus, even if the infringer earned only $50, the award could be between $250 and $10,000. Legal fees may also be reimbursed, but only if the copyright was registered within three months after publication. If you do not register your picture and your picture is used without permission, you must register before you can go to court—and you may lose the right to statutory damages and attorney's fees by procrastinating in your registration.

However, other remedies, such as injunction, are available and may be worth the cost of going to court for the satisfaction. And, on occasion, the government will even prosecute an infringer—criminal penalties include fines (of which you get no share; the government gets it all) and imprisonment.

What is the statute of limitations on infringement?	**Section 507(a)(b)**

If you don't discover infringement within three years, you have no recourse for damages.

Can I take a picture of a photograph or an object that is copyrighted?	**Sections 113(c) and 107**

Yes, under the fair use doctrine, a photograph or other copyrighted work can be copied or photographed for uses such as criticism, comment, news reporting, teaching, or research. Generally speaking, if you don't intend to make a profit from the copyrighted item, the law is on your side. For example, your one-time use of a copyrighted picture in a slide program for a nonprofit lecture series or camera club demonstration does not require permission from or payment to the photographer or owner of the copyright. However, if the picture were to be used by you for self-promotion or advertising purposes, or if the picture of the copyrighted object were to be given such widespread distribution as to reduce the effective market value of the original copyrighted photograph or article, you would probably be guilty of infringement. As a stock photographer, if your pictures are used basically to educate and inform the public, taking a photograph of a copyrighted object or picture might not be infringement—but one of the criteria for fair use is the amount of the work you reproduce. A photograph of someone else's entire photo or painting might well be the equivalent of an infringement. Of course, you must keep in mind that your interpretation might be different from the court's, and consider each case in its own context.

Should I register all my best pictures?	**Sections 411(b)(2) and 412(1)(2)**

That's like asking, "What kind of boat should I buy?" It depends on whether you'll use it on a lake or an ocean, how large your family is, and your pocketbook. If you register your picture with the Copyright Office within *three months* of publication, you can claim any of the remedies for infringement that the law allows. But if you register after three months have elapsed, your legal remedies will be limited.

The cost of registering your copyright(s) must be considered a disadvantage. Most stock photographers own at least 5,000 excellent pictures; $10 x 5,000 = $50,000. Remember, registering your pictures is optional. Registered pictures do receive better protection under the law. You can, of course, save costs by group-registering your published pictures when possible.

How long can I wait to register a published picture?   Sections 104(a) 405, 406, 408(a) and 412(2)

Any length of time. Pictures registered within *three months* of first publication receive broader legal remedies than those registered later, and re-registration is the prerequisite for any suit. But copyright protection is yours whether your picture is registered or not. If for some reason your pictures were published in such a way that no notice applied to them, you have five years to register the picture(s) in order to correct the omission. If the notice was erroneous (i.e., if your name is wrong or misspelled), you may not be protected against those who rely on the information in the notice until you have registered.

If my picture is included in a magazine or book that is copyrighted, does that mean the publication owns the copyright to my picture?   Section 201(c)

No, *you* own the copyright, unless you've made and *signed* some special arrangement with the publisher. If you've leased a picture on a one-time-rights basis, then it is assumed that the publisher has only leased your picture for temporary use.

If I don't have my picture registered and it is included in a copyrighted publication without my copyright notice on it, am I protected by the blanket copyright of all the (editorial) material in the publication?   Section 201(c)

You are protected by the Copyright Law anytime your work is published in a copyrighted publication, or if your notice appears adjacent to your work in an uncopyrighted publication. The current trend for most publications is not to include a separate copyright notice in the layout alongside each published photograph. But if the publisher includes a single notice on the publication as a whole, your work is protected by that notice. In collective works (those containing the separate, identifiable works of more than one author or artist), the Copyright Law does not require a separate notice except if you choose to group-register your pictures.

Are pictures used in advertising   Section 404(a)
also covered by the blanket
copyright notice on a copyrighted
publication?

No. The publisher can claim copyright only on that material over which he has editorial authority. Therefore, if your picture is used for advertising purposes, it should be published with the copyright notice visible. Request that the advertising agency include your notice, or at least theirs.

What is the copyright status of all   Section
the pictures I published before the   408(c)(3)(c)
new law came into effect on
January 1, 1978?

Under the old law, unless you *registered* and renewed those pictures, your pictures would have copyright protection limited to twenty-eight years. Renewal would have extended the protection to fifty-six years, but, since 1978, works that are or have been renewed have their copyrights extended for a total of seventy-five years.

Prior to 1978, unless you had an agreement limiting the rights you were granting, or unless the publication reverted the rights to you after publication, copyright for the first 28 years belonged to the publication. The renewal rights were yours, though, unless you signed them away. NOTE: A monthly column on copyright, authored by attorney Ellen Kozak, is featured in *Writer's Journal* (see Bibliography). She is author of *Every Writer's Practical Guide to Copyright Law* (Inkling Publications).

Work for Hire

Although the Q & A Forum touches on work for hire, you should know more about this subject, especially if you will be accepting an occasional service assignment that could fall into a work-for-hire situation.

Before 1978, the courts generally assumed that if a freelancer did a specific photographic job for a person or company, the photographer did not own the resulting pictures; the company or client owned them. The new Copyright Law reverses this, and the courts assume the photographer owns the pictures, not the client. This alone clearly indicates the growing awareness of the resale value of stock photos.

The law now says that except for employees acting within the scope of their employment, unless there is a written agreement signed by both parties stating the assignment is work for hire, claims to ownership of the resulting pictures must be based on the rights (ranging from "one-time" to "all") that you assign to the client.

A client *could* assume ownership of your pictures under these circumstances:

1. If your client is actually your employer, and you have made no provision to transfer copyright ownership of your pictures over to yourself while under his employ. (Note: It is possible to have the copyright of your pictures transferred back to you after an agreed-upon time.)

2. The photo you produced was not actually your creation, i.e., you accepted suggestions or directions from the client or art director. In the cases *Aldon v. Spiegel* (1984) and *Peregrine v. Lauren* (1985), the courts declared service photographers to be "employees" because they accepted suggestions and directions.

At all costs, as stock photographers, we should protect and defend our rights provided by the Copyright Law. As an example, in 1985 the American Association of Advertising Agencies called for a return to the "traditional understanding" of the 1909 Copyright Law, which made the client, not the photographer, the presumed copyright owner. "Work for hire" in the present Copyright Law presumes that *you* own the copyright. Let's keep it that way.

3. If you have signed a purchase order, assignment sheet, or similar form that states (sometimes in an ambiguous or roundabout way) that you are working for hire—even though the words "work for hire" are not actually used, you may have assigned your copyright. The statement might read, "All rights to photographs covered in this contract become the sole property of the client."

4. If you have endorsed a check that has printed on it a statement that says by endorsing the check you relinquish all claims to ownership of your pictures, you may be assigning all rights: "Endorsement below constitutes release of ownership of all rights to manuscripts, photographs, illustrations, or drawings covered by this payment." A statement after the fact that the work was made for hire might have the same effect. Your recourse here would depend on various circumstances. You might cross out the offending lines and endorse the check. You might send the check back and ask the client to issue a new check minus the offending phrase. Each situation is different. If possible, consult with other photographers who have completed assignments for the same company and compare notes on how arrangements with the client have been worked out.

In some cases, the client may be testing you. Handle with care. With diplomacy, you could get full copyright ownership and remain in the client's good graces.

The Work for Hire provision of the Copyright Act of 1978 is a benefit to the stock photographer because it makes the assumption that the photographer owns the picture, not the client. If you find yourself in a game of politics with a service photography situation and your client insists on "all rights" (that is, Work for Hire) ask the client this question: "If I were to be negligent and be sued, who would be liable—me or you?" The client might back off from insisting on all rights.

Which Usage Rights Do You Sell?

The title of this book is *Sell & Re-Sell Your Photos*. It should be: *Sell & Re-Sell the Rights to Your Photos*.

You don't want to sell all usage rights, as in a work-for-hire situation. You want to *rent* your photos, selling only certain types of rights. There are different sizes, shapes, and extents of rights—but primarily you want to base your sales on *one-time-use* rights. Any other rights of use should require separate negotiation and additional payment.

Read the Fine Print

The different designations of usage rights commonly accepted in the industry are:

One-time rights. The client or publication has permission to use the picture only once. You *lease* the picture for that one use.

First rights. The same as one-time rights, except that the client or publication pays a little more for the opportunity to be the first to publish your picture(s).

Exclusive rights. The client or publication has exclusive rights to your photograph for a *specified amount of time,* such as one or two years. After that time, the rights return to you. Calendar companies often ask for exclusive rights.

Reserved rights. A client or publication may wish to pay you extra for being the only purchaser to have the privilege of using your picture in a particular manner—such as on a poster or as a bookmark—in which case you would reserve that use specifically for them.

All rights. This is the outright transfer to a client or publication of all rights of reproduction and use of your photograph. (The *title* to the photograph, however, according to the 1978 Copyright Act, remains with you, since you are the creator. After thirty-five years, if you wish the rights to the photo to return to you, or to your heirs, you or your heirs have the right to reclaim them.)

As a stock photographer, you should avoid assigning all rights to a client or publication if the picture has marketing potential as a stock photograph. If the picture, however, is timely, it may be wiser to accept the substantial payment that an all-rights arrangement commands and relinquish your rights to the picture. Examples of pictures that might soon become outdated, and therefore unsalable, are photos of sports events, festivals, and fairs.

World rights. The client or publication is granted license to use the photograph in international markets.

First edition rights. You sell rights to only the first printing of a book, etc. After that, you negotiate for other editions.

Related rights. Use of a photo for related purposes, such as advertising use.

Copyright. The transfer of the ownership rights of your photo to another party.

Specific rights. Certain rights outlined are granted.

Your standard cover letter (see Figure 9-1) can serve as an invoice to your photo editor. In some cases, however, you will come to an agreement with an editor regarding certain other rights and/or arrangements that are not covered by your standard letter. Spell out these terms in a separate letter to the editor confirming the understandings. Also send an invoice with your shipment which reiterates all of the pertinent details of the transaction, such as rights being offered, number of pictures and their ID numbers, size, color or black-and-white, date, and so on. Invoices are available at stationery stores. Professional-looking invoices are available from mail-stationers (write for a free catalog) such as New England Business Service, 500 N. Main Street, Groton, MA 01471; Grayarc, Box 227, New Hartford, CT 06057; and The Drawing Board, Box 220505, Dallas, TX 75222. For a free copy of the transmittal form we offer our *Photoletter* subscribers, send a SASE to me at the address listed in the Bibliography.

Forms to Protect Your Rights

Up to this point, we've been discussing the rights of photo usage that you sell. What about *your* rights with regard to damage, loss, or pictures being held for lengthy periods of time? Your photo-marketing endeavor necessitates submitting valuable photographic materials to persons with whom you've never had personal contact. Is this taking a risk?

Is it a risk to travel down a road at 55 mph and face the oncoming traffic? Any one of those cars could cross over into your lane. What makes you continually take this risk?

You take it because the benefits of driving your car outweigh the risks involved.

You are likewise going to have to put a lot of *faith* in the honesty of the photobuyers you're dealing with. You're continually going to have to risk damage or loss to reap the benefits of getting wide exposure for your pictures.

There are contract forms available—also called "Terms and Conditions" agreements—that a photographer can issue to a photobuyer to specify terms of compensation in the event of damage or loss of photos while in the hands of the photobuyer or his company. But newcomers (or sometimes anyone—veteran or neophyte) have little chance of getting a photobuyer to sign a "Terms and Conditions" agreement. The disadvantages to the buyer outweigh the potential benefits. In fact, he might turn the tables and ask *you* to sign an indemnification statement that will free him of any liability as a consequence of using your pictures.

Keep in mind that others you depend on to handle your prints and transparencies—the U.S. Postal Service, Federal Express, United Parcel Service, your film processor, etc.—refuse to reimburse you more than the actual film cost, in the event of damage or loss beyond their control. Also, the IRS, in assessing the depreciation of your slide inventory, sets the value not at intrinsic value, but only at actual film cost.

My advice: If you are an entry-level stock photographer, lay out your terms and conditions to a photobuyer in a friendly, easy-to-understand cover letter as shown in Figure 9-1. Once you attain stature in your stock photo operation, if you wish—or in special instances—you can test the waters by submitting a formal "Terms and Conditions" statement. This kind of statement, however, might tend to intimidate, turn off, or actually anger a publisher, unless presented by a "name" photographer. Politics, of course, is involved, and you'll have to judge how to handle each situation on an individual basis.

Even a "name" photographer will think twice before using these agreements, however. For example, such agreements usually include a provision that calls for reimbursement of $1,500 for each transparency lost or damaged. This fee has indeed been collected, but subsequent communication between photobuyer and photographer is usually not quite the same, if it exists at all. If you find yourself in a similar situation, you will probably want to weigh your loss against your relationship with the photobuyer, and determine whether you wish to press such a payment from a good client for the result of an unusual accident or an honest mistake. The photobuyers who seem to make 90 percent of the mistakes in this industry are those who are new in the field. A good rule: Don't deal with a photobuyer or publisher unless he has a track record of three years minimum.

If you wish to research these forms further, particularly as an aid in dealings with clients or companies you're not familiar with or whose track records are questionable, the following books, listed in the Bibliography, offer sound examples: *ASMP Professional Business Practices in*

Photography (includes tear-out sample forms); *Selling Photographs: Rates and Rights; Selling Your Photography: The Complete Marketing, Business and Legal Guide; Volunteer Lawyers for the Arts Model Forms; Visual Artist Legal Guide, Author Law & Strategies.*

Legal Help

If you run into a situation in which you need legal help in dealing with a photobuyer, a publisher, or the IRS, the following organizations offer assistance. To consult with just *any* attorney on a legal problem concerning the arts and publication is like offering him a blank check to finance his education in the matter. Different attorneys are well versed in some areas, less informed in others. Before you contact an attorney, make a call to one of the organizations listed below. The VLA (Volunteer Lawyers for the Arts) includes more than 800 volunteer attorneys across the nation who handle a variety of arts-related situations. For more information and a directory of nationwide VLA offices, contact the New York office, listed below. In some cases, the consultations are free. In other cases, there are the predicted fees, but at least you'll know going in that the VLA attorneys have a track record in dealing in the area of intellectual properties.

Bay Area Lawyers for the Arts
Fort Mason Center
San Francisco, CA 94123
(415) 775-7200

Lawyers for the Creative Arts
623 South Wabash Ave., Suite 300-N
Chicago, IL 60605
(312) 427-1800

Volunteer Lawyers for the Arts
1285 Avenue of Americas, 3rd Floor
New York, NY 10019
(212) 977-9270

A "Copyright Information Kit" is available free from the Library of Congress (Washington, DC 20559; (202)287-9100). It contains a copy of the law, plus forms and other updates to the law.

Model Releases

There is perhaps no area of photography more fraught with controversy and misconception among equally competent experts than the issue of when model releases are required. A recent issue of a photography magazine states, "So, at present, we are all forced by this ambiguity in the law to obtain model release forms from virtually everyone we photograph if publication is intended. It is much better to be safe than sorry, so obtain a release beforehand, regardless of the hardship, and save yourself a lot of aggravation."

The above was written by a respected columnist in a national magazine for amateur photographers. It is misleading and does a disservice to photography and impressionable newcomers to the field.

Where do great photographs come from? From great photographers who were once amateurs. What if Alfred Eisenstadt, Margaret Bourke-White, Eugene Smith, Henri-Cartier Bresson, or Irving Penn had been exposed to such misinformation as youngsters? Would it have inhibited their photography?

What about the promising photographers of today who will be photographing (for publication) topics such as poverty, agriculture, the environment, industry, our social and political institutions? Will they be influenced by what appears to be an authoritative dictum from a nationally respected industry magazine? This is only one of many admonitions from equally credible platforms that advise carrying a model release pad in your back pocket wherever you go.

Photographers are confused, and as a result, often hesitate to take or use a picture because model releases will be too difficult to obtain. This uncertainty seriously limits the photographer, and in the end it limits you and me—the public.

Freedom of the Press

"A free press stands as one of the great interpreters between government and the people. To allow it to be fettered is to fetter ourselves."

—*U.S. Supreme Court Justice
George Sutherland*

In the last decade, we as photographers have let increasing distance slip between us and a basic right conferred by our Constitution. The First Amendment affords us the right, not shared by closed societies of the world, to freedom of the press—to know what's going on about us. The First Amendment recognizes the dangers of restricting the ability of the press to report in good faith on matters of public concern. We need to be ever on guard, not only against constricting laws, but the more subtle, binding practices that the government can impose on photographers.

To wit: In years past the court has approved searches of newsrooms (*Zurcher v. Stanford Daily*) and of the minds of reporters (*Herbert v. Lando*). It has narrowed the public-figure concept in libel cases (*Hutchinson v. Proxmire; Wolston v. Reader's Digest*) and sanctioned closings of courtrooms to the press and the public (*Gannett v. DePasquale*).

As we all know, model releases are required when pictures are used for commercial purposes such as advertising and endorsement. By also requiring a model release for editorial photographs, a publication or an institution opens itself to tyranny. Who's to say what restrictions would be placed on a photographer if we didn't have the First Amendment on our side?

Camera columnists who perpetuate the model-release myth become unwitting partners in a disturbing trend that would put a muzzle—or a lens cap—on every media person, including you.

How, then, has this myth about model releases evolved? Much of the confusion arises because the information in how-to photography books is slanted to the service photographer, who definitely requires model releases for his commercial work. Little is written for the stock photographer, whose target markets are magazines and books, where editorial content slated to *inform* or *educate* does not require model releases.

Two surprising further perpetrators of the model-release myth emerge: photography magazines and prestigious film and camera companies.

Photography magazines are essentially trade magazines. In the interest of being super-safe, a growing number of corporate attorneys for trade magazines have made it a practice to advise a blanket model-release statement for all pictures published in the magazine, whether commercial or editorial. This kind of statement protects the magazine from the possibility of nuisance suits, of persons writing and saying "You used a picture of me and it put me in a bad light and I want compensation."

Timid corporate attorneys, who would advise driving to work in a tank to be safe, should not be in a position to dictate the editorial content of the magazines that influence up-and-coming photographers. The blanket model-release decree is an easy way out for corporate attorneys. But in making their own jobs easier, they diminish your freedom. If you've noticed how photography magazines have moved steadily toward abstract, soft-focus, and artificial-looking people pictures, you will understand the influences that have been at work.

Don't be intimidated by the cage-rattling of corporate attorneys—usually not photographers themselves—who are paid to protect the profit picture, not your picture.

As for film and camera companies, it is astonishing to learn of their direct role in engendering and continuing the model-release myth. They accomplish this through the annual photography contests that they sponsor. The contests attract thousands upon thousands of student photographers. Because the contests are sponsored by big names in the industry, photographers are eager to win the trophies and ribbons offered, not to mention the cash. Some of the contests have been annual traditions for decades. Photography instructors receive special literature to explain to the students the rules, one of which never fails to state: "Model releases must be available for recognizable people in any entry."

Thus photography instructors as well as students believe that, indeed, model releases are always necessary. After all, it came from The Source.

The Sponsor Is the Winner

Why are model releases required by the sponsor? Take a look at one of the other standard rules: "Winning entries become the property of the sponsor." These large companies have discovered an effective way to acquire excellent photography—cheap. The real winners in these contests are the sponsors, who find many uses for the winning entries: magazine ads, promotional brochures, flyers, billboards, TV ads, and so on. Because the winning entries are used for commercial purposes, model releases must be on file for all recognizable people in them.

So you see, your picture is no longer yours if you win. It's theirs. And since they will use the picture to promote *their* products, it is now a *commercial* photograph—which requires a model release.

Again, the distinction hasn't been made for newcomers that model releases aren't necessary in the normal course of taking pictures in the public interest. Such contests should state the difference, the reasons for the releases for contest entries, and they should also award royalties to the winning entries. (For more on contests, see Chapter 10.)

It may appear that I am belaboring this point on the myth of model releases, but the implications are far-reaching. Photography has advanced to the point where it is one of the most important communicative tools. Yet fewer "people pictures" are being taken in public because of the apprehension instilled in photographers by misinformed camera columnists and a protectionist industry. I hope that I have helped to demythologize the model release question. If you had lost part of your Bill of Rights before reading this chapter, I hope I have helped you to regain it.

You Will Rarely Need a Model Release for Editorial Use

The Constitution is brief and open to interpretation when, in the First Amendment, it affords us freedom of the press. Freedoms are sometimes abused, and court cases over the years have attempted to interpret and clarify our freedom to photograph. New York State courts have tried many cases over the years. As a consequence, many of the other forty-nine states tend to look toward New York statutes and precedents for guidance. The current spirit of the interpretation of the First Amendment is that we, the public, relinquish our right to be informed if we succumb to a requirement of blanket model releases for everything photographed. If a photograph is used to *inform* or to *educate*, a model release is not required.

What are other books saying about model-release requirements?

It has long been established that photographs reproduced in the editorial portions of a magazine, book, or newspaper do not require model releases for recognizable people. Under the First Amend-

ment of the U.S. Constitution, photographs may be used without releases if they are not libelous, if they relate to the subject they illustrate, or if the captions are related properly to the pictures, and if they are used to inform or educate. These provisions are confined to photographs used for nonadvertising and noncommercial purposes.
—from *Selling Photographs: Rates and Rights*, page 174, by Lou Jacobs, Jr. (Amphoto Books)

Can you include bystanders in the photographs of the parade when the article is published? Yes, you can, and you don't need a release. This is because the parade is newsworthy. When someone joins in a public event, he or she gives up some of the right of privacy.
—from *Selling Your Photography: The Complete Marketing, Business, and Legal Guide*, page 194, by Arie Kopelman and Tad Crawford (St. Martin's Press)

Generally speaking, news pictures that report current happenings or illustrate other items of public interest need not have the model's permission to be used. Sometimes the fine line between what is newsworthy and what is not may be difficult to draw.
—from an article by Richard H. Logan III, in *Law and the Writer*, page 111, edited by Kirk Polking and Leonard S. Meranus (Writer's Digest Books)

If the pictures are sold for editorial use such as in a nonfiction book or in a magazine in connection with an article or item that is newsworthy or of general interest, it is unlikely that he would be liable if the pictures were misused, even though no releases had been obtained.
—from *Photography and the Law*, page 35, George Chernoff and Hershel B. Sarbin (Amphoto Books)

Use of photographs in the news, educational, current illustrative areas, generally does not require a release.
—from *Photography: What's the Law?*, page 44, by Robert M. Cavallo and Stuart Kahan (Crown Publishers)

Most of your publishing markets are well aware of the fact that they seldom need to require model releases. In my own case, I started out getting model releases whenever I shot, hampering my photography in the process. Once I learned that publishers for the most part take their First Amendment rights seriously and do not require model releases (with the exception of specific instances, which I'll discuss in a moment), I stopped getting written releases and haven't gotten any for twenty-some years. (That's one of the advantages of being a stock photographer and not a service photographer.) My model-release file gathers dust in a far corner of my office, and my deposit slips continue to travel to the bank with regularity.

In the course of my photo-marketing career, I've come across publishers now and then (or photobuyers new to the job) who were unaware of their First Amendment rights or were unwittingly surrendering them. If they persist in requiring model releases when they're not necessary, I drop them from my Market List. Such was the case when the Tennessee Legislature passed a law (see page 289) requiring freelancers to submit model releases when submitting to Tennessee publishers. Until the law is repealed, I will no longer submit to publishers in Tennessee.

By and large, publishers know and protect their rights. As I've noted, some publishers depend heavily on stock photographers. A blanket model-release policy would only serve to cut them off from a major portion of their valued picture sources. They know that stopping for model releases is a disruption or intrusion contrary to the very nature of photo illustration—capturing the spontaneity and unaffected essence of the human scene.

Model Releases—When Must You Get Them?

Your photo illustrations are used to inform and to educate. That's why your photobuyers will rarely require a model release. Just when are you likely to need one?

Some gray areas have developed over the years, and these instances are the exceptions to the rule. Pictures that might shock what's defined as the normal sensibilities of ordinary people may be categorized as outside the "inform or educate" interpretation. Some other sensitive areas include mental illness, crime, family or personal strife, chemical dependency, mental retardation, medicine, religion, and sex education. Each case has to be interpreted in its own context. For example, a court case involving sex education might be treated differently in Mississippi than it would in California. Take local and regional taboos into consideration when you are publishing your photos.

A model release might be required by the publisher of an industry-sponsored magazine because of implied endorsement. If a picture of you, for example, were to appear on the cover of *Mainliner* magazine, it might imply that you, indeed, agree that the skies of United are friendly.

As mentioned earlier, model releases are usually required in service photography. If a picture of you or your son or daughter is published in a commercial way and a trade benefit is implied, you or your son or daughter should have the right to give permission for such use, on the one hand, and you should receive compensation for such use, on the other.

As for stock photo agencies—they sell pictures for both editorial and commercial use, and while they frequently do not require model releases when your pictures are submitted, they will want to know if releases are available. Being in a position to say to an agency, "MRA"—model release available—will make your pictures more salable.

If the target of your stock photography is also commercial accounts, you will want to develop a system for both obtaining and filing model releases. A free report entitled "How to Get Model Releases," is available from The Stock Solution, % Royce Bair, 6640 South 2200 West, Salt Lake City, UT 84084 (801) 569-1155. If you send a SASE, he'll send you the report and a sample "request card" designed to make the model-release experience easier for both photographer and model.

Oral Releases

Written model releases are required in New York State, but oral releases are valid in most other states. This means you can verbally ask permission for "release" from the person you photograph. This is for the purpose of avoiding later misunderstanding, even though the way your picture is used might not even require a model release. You can say, for example, "Is it OK if I include this picture in my photography files for possible use in magazines or books?"

However, if you are also a service photographer and there's a chance the picture may be used for commercial purposes, it's advisable to make your verbal request more encompassing: "If I send you a copy of this picture as payment, would you allow me to include this picture in my files for possible use in advertising and promotion?"

When you read about lawsuits involving the misuse of photographs by photographers, it's usually a service photographer who has used a photograph of a person in a manner different from what the model expected. If you are a service photographer, don't rely on a verbal model release. Get a signed release. Spell out exactly how the picture will be used. If the person is under eighteen years of age, obtain a release from his or her parent or guardian.

How do you learn if oral model releases are acceptable in your state? Most every county in the U.S.A. has a law library at the county courthouse. Consult the current volumes of state statutes for the laws on invasion of privacy. Ask the law librarian or the county attorney to assist you. For details on cases involving invasion of privacy, consult the volumes entitled "Case Index" or the equivalent. You'll be pleasantly surprised to learn that few cases are recorded.

If you are unable to visit the law library in person, try phoning them. If you are not familiar with the terms or descriptions, let the librarian know this. An expert will be more helpful if you let him or her control the conversation. They're usually flattered and will be willing to help and to refer you to additional sources of information.

Many photographers shoot the pictures that they plan to send to an agency, or that might be used from their own files for commercial purposes, within a close geographical area. They can then easily go back later and obtain a written model release, when necessary. Another route is to work with one or several neighboring families and get a blanket model release for the entire family, then barter family portraits over the years in return for the privilege of photographing family members from time to time for your stock files.

Figure 15-2 shows an example of an acceptable model release. Figure 15-3 shows a release for parents and guardians to sign for models under eighteen years old (under twenty-one in some states). These two releases have been designed to fit onto a 3x5 pad.

Can We Save Them Both? The Right of Privacy and Our First Amendment Rights

The rights safeguarded by our Constitution include the right of privacy— our individual right to decide whether we want our peace interrupted. Occasionally, a photographer violates normal courtesies, laws, and decency with his picture-taking. Such instances are of course exceptions— and all are answerable within the law.

However, we have seen instances in which leaders of political groups, individuals engaged in medical quackery, or religious cults will commit their misdeeds against society and then attempt to take refuge in our right-of-privacy laws. Usually, prominent public figures must surrender such privacy and open themselves to public scrutiny. Such is the price of glory.

One state, Tennessee, has conveniently passed a law ("The Personal Rights Protection Act of 1984") that is a bureaucrat's and politician's dream. It states that publishers in Tennessee cannot use photos featuring people if the photographer has not obtained a model release. This means freelancers cannot photograph police brutality, school system wrongdoings, highway accidents, city hall personalities, religious rites, and so on. Our First Amendment early recognized that the curtailment of information to the public gives invitation to corruption.

But what about the nonpublic figure, the person who is just going about his normal business? Invasion of privacy is not so much a question of whether you should take a picture or not, but whether the publisher should publish it or not, and in what context.

While our Constitution allows us freedom of the press, it also allows us freedom from intrusion on our privacy. Herein lies a conflict, and the

---

RELEASE

In consideration for value received,* I hereby authorize
_____ ("the photographer") and or parties designated
by the photographer (including clients, purchasers, agencies, and
periodicals or other printed matter and their editors) to use my photograph in conjunction with my name (or fictitious name) for sale to or
reproduction in any medium the photographer or his designees see fit
for purposes of advertising, display, audiovisual, exhibition, or
editorial use.
   I affirm that I am more than 18 (21) years of age.

Signature: _____

   Date: _____

Figure 15-2. Model release.

RELEASE

I, _____, parent of _____ a minor,
                         guardian
in consideration for value received,* assign to _____
its customers and representatives, the exclusive right to copy and
reproduce for the purpose of illustration, advertising, and publication
in any manner whatsoever any photograph of said minor in its possession.

                    Signed _____

                    Address _____

Witness _____

                    Date _____

Figure 15-3. Guardian's consent (for model release).

*Value received translates in everyday terms to compensation. The compensation the
model receives might be a dollar, a copy of the publication the picture appears in, etc.

courts are left to make the decision whether invasion of privacy was committed by a photographer in any individual instance.

Instances usually considered invasion of privacy would occur if you were to:

1. Trespass on a person's property and photograph him or members of his family without valid reason. (In connection with a newsworthy event would be a valid reason.)

2. Embarrass someone publicly by disclosing private facts about them through your published photographs.

3. Publish a person's picture (without permission) in a manner that implies something that is not true.

4. Use the person's picture or name (without permission) for commercial purposes.

There have been very few cases in U.S. court history involving a photographer with invasion of privacy. Except for number one above, invasion of privacy usually deals with how a picture is *used*, not the actual taking of the picture. When in doubt, rely on the Golden Rule.

A Turning Point

Privacy is important to all of us. It was an important factor in moving to our farm here in western Wisconsin, insulated by acres of rolling hills.

In my early days as a photographer, my views on privacy used to get in the way of my photographing. For example, once as a young tourist in France, I photographed two people, a man and his wife, who were so inebriated they had fallen to the ground; one was trying to help the other up. I got two pictures before bystanders began kicking me and tossing rocks at me. I had entered into that picture-taking encounter believing that I was recording insights into the problems of alcoholism in France. I exited with remorse, believing that I had invaded the privacy of two individuals and insulted their compatriots. For several years, I avoided "invading the privacy of people's lives" and took few pictures in public.

Then one day it occurred to me that the moment of life I had captured on film that day in Paris was significant. I realized that the potential impact of that minidrama on those who might view the picture outweighed any invasion of privacy I might have committed, not to mention the guilt I had imposed on myself.

From that day forward, my interpretation of *privacy* was different. Photo illustration has become a powerful communicator for all of us. If privacy is a gift we all cherish, so is the gift of *insight* photography affords us. Our lives become richer each time we move closer to understanding ourselves, our fellow creatures, and the planet we live on.

As a stock photographer, you will affect the lives of others. Closed societies are aware of this and severely limit the rights of photographers and the press. In our free society, we photographers have the responsibility of not abusing our freedom of the press. We owe it to our profession to respect the rights of our models. Your mission as stock photographer is to inform and educate, not to libel and slander. You can reassure your models with courtesy and the explanation that your photograph(s) will "be in the public interest." By making it clear how the photo will be used, and sticking to your statement, you build your reliability factor (and the reliability factor of photographers in general) in the eyes of the people you photograph.

The definition of *rights* expands and shrinks with changes in government, society, and culture. We are fortunate to live in a society that guarantees both freedom of expression and the right to privacy. Photography, at times, walks a fine line between those two rights.

Lest you be overwhelmed by all of this legalese:

"Fruity" Question

According to Robert H. Mundheim, as general counsel of the Treasury Department, when an ordinary person wants to give an orange to another, he or she would merely say, "I give you this orange." But when a lawyer does it, he or she says it this way:

"Know all men by these presents that I hereby give, grant, bargain, sell, release, convey, transfer, and quitclaim all my right, title, interest, benefit, and use whatever in, of, and concerning this chattel, otherwise known as an orange, or citrus orantium, together with all the appurtenances thereto of skin, pulp, pip, rind, seeds, and juice, to have and to hold the said orange together with its skin, pulp, pip, rind, seeds, and juice for his own use and behoof, to himself and his heirs in fee simple forever, free from all liens, encumbrances, easements, limitations, restraints, or conditions whatsoever, any and all prior deeds, transfers or other documents whatsoever, now or anywhere made to the contrary notwithstanding, with full power to bite, cut, suck, or otherwise eat the said orange or to give away the same, with or without its skin, pulp, pip, rind, seeds, or juice."

Cute animal shots are usually Track A pictures, but when people are involved with the animals in a meaningful way, the picture becomes something more than a "cute animal" picture.

16.
Your Stock Photo Business: A Mini Tax Shelter

The Great Rebate

As you read this book, if you've discovered you've missed out on a lot of selling opportunities, then I'm accomplishing my purpose. This chapter shows you another significant and far-reaching opportunity: If you work at a salaried job, you have an annual tax rebate coming to you—when you begin calling your stock photography work a *business*. Your rebate can amount to as much as $1,000 a year, depending on your salaried income, the number of dependents you claim, your photography business deductions, and a few other considerations.

What I'm going to say will enable you to buy a new camera every year, new lenses, new darkroom equipment. Listen carefully.

The System to Beat the System

I call it the "Tax Rebate System." It is legal, logical, and lovely. It is based on the fact that in our free-enterprise system, the government tries to help small businesses get off the ground. Many a flourishing business existing today started as a transfigured hobby—and made it, thanks to the initial tax allowances offered by the IRS.

If you follow a few simple IRS-approved guidelines, a tax rebate will come to you, you'll get your stock photography business off the ground, and the IRS will give you no heat. In fact, the IRS will be on your side—after all, your business will one day be in a position to pay taxes, too. Up to now you may have called your photography a hobby, but Uncle Sam will "pay" you as much as $1,000 a year or more to call it a business.

Declaring your photography as a business is easy. You simply say, "My photography is now a business." That's it. Then at income-tax time, in addition to the regular 1040 tax form, you also fill out a form called "Schedule C" (Profit or Loss From a Business or Profession).

To give airtight officiality to your business status, I suggest that you do three additional things:

1. Give a name, or title, to your business, and open a separate business checking account in this name.
2. Have some business stationery printed.
3. Ask the IRS for an employer identification number (EIN). It costs you nothing and it remains your number for as long as your stock photography business is in operation. Ask for form SS-4.

These three actions show clear-cut intention for IRS purposes, if any question arises later. Naturally, the IRS does not act kindly toward the person who fabricates a business operation and then enjoys the benefits.

Bear in mind that we are not discussing tax evasion. That's against the law. We are talking about making legitimate, legal, justified tax deductions—that's your right. And it's called *tax avoiding.**

If you are still in doubt, here's an inexpensive way to check out what I'm saying. Call the toll-free IRS number for your local area. Tax information specialists are on hand to answer questions and send you literature. Most IRS operators are knowledgeable and cooperative, but if you find one who isn't, excuse yourself, hang up, and try again. You'll usually reach a different operator, since several work the phone lines at any one time. In fact, it's sometimes a good idea to ask the same questions of two or three operators to check the consistency of the answers you get. Or, if your question doesn't have a simple answer, ask to speak to the supervisor or the *technical* person.

You can also ask your tax consultant about these guidelines, but be conscious of a need to check the thoroughness of the response. Your questions might require some research—that is, extra work—on his part. Don't open your checkbook to a tax person who has had little experience in dealing with small business in the creative field.

My own experience has been that many tax consultants concern themselves only with the routine elements of standard business situations—not the individualized self-employment questions that may take extra research and study. With this in mind, ask around your area. Speak with successful freelancers, writers, and other creative persons. Ask them, "Which tax adviser do you use?"

By establishing your business status with the IRS, in their language, you are establishing intent to make a profit. In your first five years of operation, you should be able to show a profit for any three years out of five. (In other words, you could go as long as two years before you need to show a profit.) The second five-year period, the third, and so on, are treated in the same manner by the IRS. However, the law does not say that the profit must be large (or likewise that a loss from your business must be small).

*To AVOID is LEGAL but to EVADE is ILLEGAL. U.S. Supreme Court (Gregory v. Helvering, 293 U.S. 465)

The record proves that the IRS does not come down hard on people who don't show a profit, so long as they show reasonable intent of making their business prosper. If you conduct your business in a businesslike manner—with evidence of consistent submission of your photographs, self-promotion activity, reasonable recordkeeping, and use of a business letterhead—there's little likelihood that you'll be challenged by the IRS.*

A Government Incentive to Start Up Your Business

Even though you might not make a profit the first couple years (on paper), you may have more money available to you, in terms of actual cash flow, than if you never attempted to start up your stock photography business. Here's how it works: Say you're making $20,000 a year at your regular job. Your weekly paycheck should be $384.62. But after taxes and other deductions (about 28 percent), you could take home as little as $279.12—or $105.50 less than your gross salary. Since your employer has taken taxes out of your wages in advance (withholding tax), you in effect have placed on deposit with the IRS a sum of money (about $15 a day), which, if not owed to the IRS, is returnable to you. (Maybe this is why they originally called it a "tax return"!)

Aside from your salaried job, as you are now also a small businessperson just starting up a new business, you are going to have a lot of related expenses. This is where the Schedule C (profit or loss form) and Form 4562 (depreciation and amortization) comes in, when you make out your tax forms.

Let's say that after your first year, when you have deducted the legal tax deductions listed later in this chapter (film, chemicals, car expense, stationery, travel, home office expenses, etc.), and enumerated them on your Schedule C form, you find you show a "loss" of $4,000.** On your Form 1040, you will deduct this from your regular salary of $20,000, which means your actual net for the year has been $16,000. Since taxes were taken out on $20,000 and not $16,000, you have a rebate coming back to you from the government. (Or if you are self-employed and

*The IRS could claim that your business is actually a hobby, in which case you can claim deductions only to the amount of actual gross income from your "hobby." You qualify as a bona fide business, if you claim business status and conduct your business with regularity, though as a sideline. If, after the first year, the IRS challenges your "intent" to make a profit, within sixty days after receiving an IRS notice to disallow your business deductions, you can file Form 5213, "Election to Postpone Determination," until the end of the five-year period. You can voluntarily file this form within three years after filing your first return as a business. Publication #334, available from the IRS, gives further details.

**Remember, this is an "academic loss" in that you probably would have had similar photo-, car, film, travel, heat, light expenses (deductions) whether or not you called yourself a business. Your wife's (or husband's) expenses are now also deductible if you can show that your spouse's presence on a trip (or at a dinner, seminar, etc.) had a bona fide business purpose (e.g., assisting you in some manner). By establishing yourself as a business, you can now legally deduct these as business expenses from your total income, thus reducing your taxes. When large corporations talk about taking a "paper loss," this is what they're referring to.

haven't taken advantage of all of these deductions, it will mean a lower taxable income.) The size and make of the camera you can now buy will depend on your tax bracket, exemptions, etc. You could receive back from the U.S. Treasury Department anywhere from $10 to $1,000. Nice going.

It might sound almost un-American to suggest that you come out with a loss in your business. Sometimes, however, it's more profitable not to make a profit. The popular newsstand magazine, *Money*, that advises how to handle financial matters, was launched by Time-Life in 1972. It didn't show a profit until 1981.

Your Stock Photography Business Deductions

Now that you have your own business, you can, in addition to the personal deductions you normally take, allow yourself dozens of other deductions related to your stock photo enterprise. Your film and processing expenses, magazine subscriptions, business-related seminars, office supplies, even the cost of this book, are natural business deductions as long as they aid you in your business goals. Your spouse and your children serve as models in your pictures, so a percentage of their lodging, meals, and other expenses on trips are deductible. Incidentally, photographers are the only businesspeople who have a "back-up" receipt: a photograph, which gives proof to the IRS that the photographer actually traveled to a certain location and *spent the money* (which is the main reason to collect receipts).

As an independent photographer, you are always on the lookout for stock photographs—whether you take them across town or across the country. This means your next vacation (don't use that word anymore) will actually be a business trip. You will bring back dozens of pictures of interesting mining operations in Colorado, or agricultural observations in Wisconsin, to add to your stock photography collection. You will talk an editor into giving you an assignment in one of the villages or cities along your travel route. The deductions don't occur just on your three-week summer trip, but throughout the year. Your car now becomes your "business transportation." You will keep a daily log of your travel plus gas, meals, and lodging receipts for IRS verification.**

**Generally speaking, the IRS won't question expenses for meals and lodging if they're within the limits the government allows its own traveling employees. Current rates per day: $52 (Rev. Ruling 74-433). Receipts: No receipt is required for expenditures less than $25. (Ed. note: IRS rulings change from time to time. Call your local IRS toll-free number (1-800-424-1040) to validate figures in this chapter.) A receipt is required for an expenditure of $25 or more. A receipt is required for hotel or motel, *regardless of amount*. A receipt is required for transportation only where such receipts are readily available. Check with your tax advisor on the percentage of write-off you are allowed for your meals, travel, and entertainment expense. In loss situations for example, the home office deduction is limited.

Check with your tax advisor also on new interpretations and changes, especially in the Tax Reform Act of 1986. Section 263A and 1221(3), which apply to uniform capitalization, may have undergone revision by the time you are reading this.

It continues. Since you are a photographer, everyone is a potential customer. Whenever you entertain, at home or elsewhere, keep records of your guests and define a business relationship or a potential business relationship (as a buyer of your photos; possible model; possible client). Then you can deduct those expenses too. Be sure, though, that you can show a relationship between your guests and your work to the IRS. If you travel overseas, a log will prove vital in case of an IRS audit. Your percent of business time must be 50 percent or greater, or deductions are severely limited.

A good booklet on the subject is IRS publication #463, "Travel, Entertainment, and Gift Expenses." It's free and available by phoning or writing your local IRS office.

Let's look at your new business expenses in some detail.

Office-in-the-Home

Because you may use part of your home as the headquarters for your stock photography business, the IRS allows you deductions for the portion of the house that is used to operate your business. But you cannot use your office-in-the-home expenses to create a net operating loss. If the total of your other business expenses (not including home-office expenses) is greater than your income, giving you a loss, that is allowable. But if your office-in-the-home expenses, when added to the total of your other business expenses, take you over the top to give you a loss, that is not allowable. Only that portion of your home-office expense that takes your total of expenses up to the amount of your gross business income can be deducted. If the total of your home-office expenses, added to your other business expenses, adds up to less than your gross income, the full amount of your home-office expenses is deductible.

Here's how that works. Your stock photography business, operated out of your home, has a gross income of $12,000. Your business incurs home-office expenses (such as those listed below) of $1,500. Your other normal business expenses such as office supplies, postage, travel, film, etc., total $11,500. Since your income was $12,000, you can use as a deduction only $500 of your $1,500 office-in-the-home expenses. However, the disallowed $1,000 may be carried forward to subsequent tax years. But, these carried-forward home-office expenses are subject to the same restriction each subsequent year, i.e., not allowable if the addition of their total creates a net loss from the business activity.

The room(s) in your home where you conduct your photo-marketing business must be used specifically for your photo-marketing operations. The IRS usually won't approve the room as a deduction if it's also used as a sewing room or a part-time recreation room, or if it's part of your living room. If you also have a darkroom, consider that room also as tax-deductible. Measure the square footage of your home (don't include the garage unless it's heated or air conditioned), then measure the square footage of your working space. Divide the latter by the former and you'll determine what portion of your home is used for "profit-making activity." For example, if your working area is a 14x11 room (used exclusively for your photo-marketing business), and the total square footage of your home is 1,232 square feet, you are using one-eighth of your home. "Business Use of Your Home" is the title of IRS Publication No. 587 (revised November 1986). It is a clear explanation of what you can and cannot deduct. Also check out booklet #529, "Miscellaneous Deductions." Write or phone the IRS for a free copy (1-800-424-FORM) or (1-800-424-1040).

Formerly, you were unable to use the expenditures in the following list as tax deductions. But now that you are engaged in an intent-to-make-a-profit activity, you may deduct one-eighth (or 50 percent or 100 percent—whatever your particular setup may be) of the following expenses. List these deductions on your Schedule C when you're computing your taxable income (which includes the income from your full-time employment):

Home

Home repairs	Heat	Refuse collection
Real estate insurance	Fuel	Painting
Carpentry	Depreciation	Decorating
Plumbing	Rent	Lighting
Masonry	Water	Fire losses
Electrical work	Air conditioning	Sprinkler system
Roofing	Maintenance	Burglar alarm system

Auto Use

The deductions don't end with home expenses. Your car will be used to travel on assignments, research stock photo possibilities, deliver packages to the post office. If you have two cars, designate one your business car, and use it for that purpose. Note the mileage at the beginning of the year and on December 31. No matter how many cars you have, keep a perfect record of their use (keep a diary in the glove compartment), and record trips and expenditures related to transportation for your business and professional activities.

You can also deduct a percentage of the maintenance and repair of your car equivalent to the percentage of time it is used for business. Following are some typical deductible expenses:

Insurance	Waxing	Tolls
Registration	Accessories	Parking
Gas and oil	CB radio	Repairs
Lubrication	Tires	Depreciation
Car washes	Snow tires	License
Rental	Garaging	

Travel Expenses

In order to get your stock photographs, you may have to travel far and wide—in which case these expenditures are legal tax deductions:

Bus	Airplane	Motel
Train	Taxi	Meals
Boat	Hotel	Passport fee
Equipment Luggage		Business tickets

Entertainment*

You'll have all the usual business expenses, including taking clients out to lunch. If the meal is business-related, 80 percent is deductible.

Lunches	Theater	Tickets to miscellaneous
Dinners	Nightclubs	events

Advertising/Promotion

Getting yourself known is deductible.

Design work	Leaflets	Newspapers
Graphics work	Brochures	Telephone (Yellow Pages)
Copywriting	Booklets	Radio
Typesetting	Catalogs	TV
Mailers	Business cards	Matchbooks
Flyers	Magazines	Calendars
Business gifts		Portfolio
Christmas cards		Trade shows
		Conventions
		Donations

Photo-Related Items*

Those expensive chemicals are now deductible.

Camera(s)	Processing	Darkroom equipment
Lenses	Lights	Paper
Accessories	Model fees	Chemicals
Film	Props	Instruction manuals
Printing	Costumes	

Printing

It's an important expenditure for you, and it's deductible.

(see Advertising)	Books	Announcements
Business stationery	Ads	Tearsheets
Mailers	Catalogs	Office forms

*Must be carefully documented.

Business Education, Self-Improvement, Memberships

If it's going to help you make a profit in your business, the IRS says it's deductible.

Subscriptions (business-related)	Dues to professional organizations	Cassettes
Club memberships	Seminars	Directories
Market services	Books and references	Courses
Business development		Computer networks

Office and Supplies*

The "little" expenditures in this area can add up. Be sure you keep track of them.

Insurance	Printers	Diaries
Freight charges	Independent contractors	Postage stamp envelopes
Typewriters	Paper clips, erasers	International Reply
File cabinets	Blotters, pads	Coupons
Staples, pencils, pens, ink	Mailing envelopes	Bookkeeping supplies
Paper	Rubber bands	Calendars
File folders	Return labels	Modems
Typewriter ribbon	Loose-leaf notebooks	Briefcase
Directories	Computers/software	Delivery charges
Cleaning service	Photocopier	
	Equipment lease	
	Refunds to customers	
	Computer supplies	

Extra Deductions

A sure-fire test for any business deduction is to ask yourself: "If I weren't in business, would I have this expense?"

Wages to employees	Maintenance agreements	Equipment repairs
Safe deposit box	Mail lists	Product displays
Accounting fees	Business-related tools	Professional fees
Self-publishing expenses	(X-Acto knives, etc.)	Interest
Legal fees	Postage	Bad debts/bounced checks
Babysitting (if connected with your business)	Telephone calls	Commissions
	Telegrams	Consultants
Meter-rental	Contract labor fees	
Permits and licenses	R&D (research & development)	

Keep records of your expenses. (Excellent books on personal tax records are the *Dome Notebook* and the J.K. Lasser *Tax Series*, by Julian Block (Pocket Books, New York and Simon & Schuster, New York.) Gather these together at tax time, and list them on Schedule C. These legally deductible expenses are bound to reduce your income from your regular occupation, as listed on your Form 1040. The result will be a rebate for you, or if you are self-employed, less taxable income.

*Depreciate major purchases.

Depreciation

Depreciation (in recent years called "Accelerated Capital Recovery System"—ACRS) allows businesses to replace their business equipment by offering them time-released write-offs over a period of years. For photography equipment, the time period is usually seven years. For your computer or car, it's five years. But check with your tax advisor or the IRS; these provisions change from time to time.

Investment Tax Credit is another incentive sometimes offered by our tax laws to stimulate the economy. At this writing, no ITC is available. But check with your tax advisor.

The "S" Corporation

Most stock photographers set up their business as a sole proprietorship. The numbers work out best for them. Others find advantage in setting up as an "S" corporation.

An "S" corporation may be the business structure that best fits your needs. As an "S" Corporation (formerly called a Sub Chapter S Corporation), you do not operate as a *self-employed* sole proprietor or partner. Your business income is not subject to self-employment (social security) tax. By forming an "S" Corporation, you legally change the nature of your photo-marketing income. By making the Small Business Corporation Election (on form 2553), you eliminate Corporate taxes on the Corporate income. A newly formed S Corporation never pays income tax. Instead, the net income of the corporation is reported on each stockholder's (or "owner's") individual tax return(s) as dividends (on a Schedule E). The owners pay the income tax on their corporate "S" income, but no social security tax. With this tax rate continually going up, this can represent a considerable tax savings.

Almost all forms of business have some disadvantages, and the "S" Corporation is not without its own drawbacks. Once you check with your tax advisor and gauge your financial situation in relation to the "S" Corporation, you'll know if this business form can prove to be an advantage in your own case.

Additional Tax Avoidances

Other tax avoidances you will want to consider (depending on your circumstances) are Credit for Child Care Expenses (Form 2441), Moving Expense Adjustment (Form 3903), and the tax-sheltered retirement plans such as an IRA, Keogh, or SEP (Simplified Employee Plan).

Also, two other provisions might result in the return of money to you:

1. *Earned Income Credit.* This credit is available to persons with income less than $11,000 who have a dependent child. Information on

how to apply for this is usually at the top of page 2 of your Form 1040. A rebate could be due you if your deductions reduce your income below $11,000. (*Note:* Treasury Department rulings and allowances go up and down with the times. This income figure could change.)

2. On the *state* level, about half the states offer *Homestead Tax Credit* (in Wisconsin, for example, use Schedule H, Homestead Claim). This is a rebate on your property tax if you are in a low-income bracket. If you rent, you also receive a proportionate refund.

As noted earlier, in order to be recognized as a bona fide pro in the eyes of the IRS, you have to, in good faith, be operating your business with regularity. The IRS will provide you with some excellent free booklets on operating professionally: #583 and #552 deal with recordkeeping; #587 is on using your home for your business; #917 deals with business use of a car; and #334 deals with small-business taxes. Ask for their "Your Business Tax Kit" for men or women thinking about starting up a business.

Here's some recommended reading: The Small Business Administration offers a library of how-to books, some of which are free (contact Superintendent of Documents, Government Printing Office, Washington, DC 20402); *Tax Angles* (Suite 31E, 870 7th Avenue, New York, NY 10019, Attn: Ted Cross (703) 548-2400); *Planning Your Home Business*, Kern & Wolfgram National Textbook Co., 4255 W. Touhy Avenue, Lincolnwood, IL 60646; *Julian Block's Tax Savings*, 3 Washington Square, Larchmont, NY 10538; *Home Office Magazine*, Time-Life Inc., Rockefeller Plaza, New York, NY 10020; Volunteer Lawyers for the Arts Directory, 1285 Avenue of the Americas, 3rd Floor, New York, NY 10019.

Note: The information in this chapter can be helpful to you in getting your stock photography business off the ground, because it will allow you to reinvest money into your business by keeping more of the dollars you earn.

I assume you will take this information and apply it in an honest manner. To make sure you don't put yourself in a position to get heat from the IRS, always plan your deduction activities with the IRS in mind. In other words, cover your bases *before* you go on that trip, or plan that business entertainment, or make that photo-related purchase. Ask yourself, "Can I satisfy IRS substantiation requirements?" "Does this proposed tax deduction meet current IRS guidelines?" When in doubt, give the IRS toll-free number a call (1-800-424-1040).

If you use this simple procedure, you'll encounter few problems with the IRS when they come to call (the percentages are actually heavily against your photo-marketing enterprise's ever being audited) because you have followed the rules of the IRS game. You beat the system with your own system.

How do you illustrate a cold, wintry, snowy day? Without the cat, would this picture be as effective?

17.
Computers

Makes Life Easier?

"It'll save you a day a week!" the ad in the computer magazine proclaims. Hmmmm . . . Does that mean I can spend every Friday in the hammock?

Are computers good or bad for the stock photographer? Yes, they are good or bad. They can save you time and cost you time. They can save you money and cost you money. They can save you frustration and cause you frustration.

Time savers they are. But like any new efficient tool designed to save labor, it can end up increasing labor. Remember when you switched from the push lawn mower to the riding mower? Instead of spending that extra hour in the hammock, you extended the size of your lawn. That hour you saved was spent mowing more lawn. You also put out more dollars. For the cost of the riding lawn mower, you could afford a grade school youngster trimming your lawn with nail clippers for six years. And the nail clippers don't even need gas and oil. If Parkinson would write a law for computers, he would probably say "Thanks to its efficiency, a new tool that successfully saves labor will increase labor."

What's efficiency? Golf carts are efficient, and you can finish your game a half hour sooner. But is that your attraction to the sport?

As you read this chapter, I hope it shines through that I'm all for personal computers (PCs), sometimes called *microcomputers*. I may sound like I'm condemning them, but I'm actually offering you a challenge for restraint and moderation when it comes to investing in them, utilizing them, and proselyting about them. I've had my microcomputer (Tandy) since 1979, and I've expanded my photo-business horizons to reach areas I probably wouldn't have ventured into, if it weren't for the magic of the computer. I now have four computers. If I had to do it over, yes, I would invest in a computer. But my business isn't your business. You might need one computer, or eight, or none. Keep this in mind when I, or any other person who talks about computers, starts waxing gloriously about them.

In this chapter, I'll include comments from several stock photographers who have been kind enough to give me their input through correspondence, seminars, phone calls, and a survey. I believe their thoughts and advice will help to give you a better outlook on the computer as it affects you, the stock photographer.

What Is a Computer?

Above your desk, put up a sign: A COMPUTER IS A MACHINE THAT SPEEDS UP A SYSTEM. That's all a computer does. If you didn't have a bookkeeping system before you got your computer, then you are going to have to learn all about bookkeeping in order for the computer to help you. Same goes for your system for filing your slides and negs, your Christmas card list, typing, or any business or household system. If you've heard people complain about computers, it's usually because they didn't have a working system in place beforehand for doing what they expect the computer and their programs to do now. Repeat: The computer only helps you speed up an existing system or forces you to start using a system.

Computer tasks can usually be divided into three types—words, numbers, and graphics. Typing chores (word processing), such as letters and captioning, become simplified. Recordkeeping of numbers becomes simpler, too. A combination of words and numbers, in the tech-hip vernacular, is called a *database*. A typical example of a database is a dictionary, or a telephone directory containing uniform records of names, places, or things, along with useful information about them. Graphics come in all forms: charts, graphs, and actual pictures and drawings. A computer will handily arrange all of your numbers, words, and pictures in any fashion you want them. From these lists, or *reports* as they're called, you can get a picture of your expenses vs. your income, how the stock photo business is moving along, who your clients and prospects are, which pictures are with which buyers, and what the forecast is for the future.

Which Computer to Buy?

Here are the six most popular tidbits of advice:

1. **Buy Software First.** (Software is the stuff that tells your computer what to do.) If you're a neophyte, research the software and then buy the computer that fits the software.
2. **Buy a Name-Brand Computer.** Leaders in the field at this writing

are *IBM* and its offspring look-alikes (*Leading Edge, Epson, Compaq,* and so forth). Next are *Apple* and *Tandy.* The department store computers, *Commodore* and *Atari,* follow. And there are many more personal computers.

3. **Buy What Your Friends Are Using.** After all, if you're new at this, it would be nice to know that a friend will come to the rescue.

4. **Buy the Power.** After you've done your homework, buy the most powerful machine your pocketbook can afford.

5. **Buy for Service.** If your computer breaks down, and it usually will at crucial times, where will you turn for repair?

6. **Buy Nothing.** Wait till the prices come down. What was selling for $3,000 five years ago is selling for $1,500 today.

I'll comment on these six in a minute. Buying a computer is like driving into a new community and asking the first person you see to recommend a good restaurant. If he likes Italian food, he'll probably say, "Luigi's!" The next person you ask will say, "The Fish House!" and a third person might say "McDonald's!" You are at the mercy of their tastes, not yours. And of course, if the person's brother-in-law owns the "Steak House," guess what he's going to recommend?

As photographers, most of us have learned that camera-store sales persons frequently know little about the product they're selling. You'll find the same parallel in computer retailing. The last person on the list to talk to about a computer is the computer salesperson. Tom Perrett, producer of *The Gold Book of Photography Prices,* offers further advice: "And don't listen to promises from the vendor that such-and-such software is about to be published, or such-and-such innovation in hardware will be in production next month. Very often, these promises don't materialize." This might sound like a lesson you learned when you bought your first used car. Buyer beware.

Here are comments on the six points above.

1. It sounds good to say, "Buy software first." But throw this one out. Only computer-wise people buy software first, and if you were such a person, you wouldn't be buying your first computer, nor would you be reading this chapter. Go ahead and buy your hardware first.

2. If you bought the currently (at this writing) most popular name brand, you would buy an IBM, or one of the popular IBM "clones." But according to the feedback I get at this time from other stock photographers who are familiar with the IBM and its look-alikes, the learning curve on an IBM is long and steep. Depending on what software you choose to run, you could be buying frustration and downtime spent on user's manuals. Compared to what? The computer that scored highest among our stock photographer subscribers as to ease of "getting the hang of it" is Apple's Macintosh series. The learning curve is manageable, and

its attributes are equal to IBM's. As both Macintosh and IBM introduce new machines and new software, many of which are compatible with one another, this may break down the walls between the two types of computers.

3. Should you let your friends influence your buying? Yes, if they know something about software problems and computer (minor) repair. They'll show you how things work and save you endless hours of trying to figure out the manual. As Lou Jacobs, Jr., says, "The manual writers are experts, and they assume far too much regarding the ability of the novice user."

Buy what your friends own, to be able to capitalize on their know-how. Put the law of probability on your side. For example, if ten people in your community have IBMs and no one has an Apple or Tandy, who will come to your rescue if your Apple breaks down? If you go ahead and join the ranks with an IBM, you'll probably get answers, parts, and condolences from your cohorts. A friend in need . . . But, at the same time, go cautiously . . . beware of *Technolust*, as author and photographer David Arnold calls it, a disease that afflicts many computer owners. These loyalists believe that their particular hardware is the *one and only*. It may be, for them. But if you're buying a computer, recognize that you won't get a balanced opinion from this breed.

4. Should you buy the biggest and the best? If you were a serious musician, you'd want to perform on the best musical instrument your pocketbook could afford. Look for the best that fits your budget. Keep in mind that many computer systems can easily be expanded later on down the line, as you grow in size, need, and wisdom. Buy smart. For example, it's best to buy programs that integrate with each other. An integrated system won't bypass the operating system, which will slow everything down a little, but you'll feel organized when all the pieces are integrated. Don't buy a Boeing 747 if a Piper Cub will do, and the latter *will* do if you have less than 5,000 pictures. The question comes down to how serious you are about your photo marketing. Definitely buy *big*, if you are *thinking big* about your photo marketing. But don't become computer-rich and penny-poor. You'll know where to draw the line.

5. Service to your machine is essential, yes. But unless you buy something that you have to put together yourself, or a brand that went out of production in 1978, service won't be a big problem. Most horror stories about computers being down translate to problems resulting from an act of God, or solvable human error like failing to make a backup of your data. Unlike the age we've grown up in, in which machinery equals moving parts, computers are a different animal. Except for the motor drives, there are few moving parts, hence less chance for breakdowns. Help "Hot Lines" are available for most major brand machines.

I am amazed that my original "Model II Radio Shack" (1979) still keeps up with its three newer compatriots. We clean the machines with bottled Freon and darkroom airspray, and replace the heads ourselves. We clean the heads with a rubber eraser or antistatic Bounce (a household softener for clothing). For major repairs, such as a drive that's out of alignment or a zap to the boards from a lightning strike because someone left the modem attached to the phone line, we truck it over to Minneapolis (fifty-five miles away), where it is hospitalized for three days. Knowledge of how a computer works is not necessary. Bill Pursche of *Fotofind* says, "I don't know how my car runs. I merely want it to start and get me to where I want to go."

6. Finally, don't wait. Do your homework, yes. Read *Consumer Reports*, join computer clubs, and read the computer magazines. But at some point, make the plunge. You'll make some wrong decisions, yes. But as photographer/author Fredrik Boden says, "The computerized photographers will leave you far behind if you don't make the leap." Waiting for the price to come down, or the machinery to improve, gets you "behinder and behinder." By getting your computer, what you gain in doubling your efficiency far outstrips what you might have gained in discount dollars by waiting. If you jump in now, you'll have mastered all of the basics by the time the refinements to imaging, self-publishing, cataloging and retrieving come along. Lou Jacobs, Jr., sums it up, "My computer is not a luxury, it's a necessity, even before I owned it."

Cataloging and Retrieving Your Pictures

Your photo information—descriptions, file numbers, sales history, locations can be stored in software (a *database*). You can buy "off the shelf" database programs (presently, the most popular one is dBASE III) and customize it for storing your photos. But since these programs are designed to do everything for everybody, it may take some effort to get them to do what you want. However, you can also buy custom software that is specifically designed for stock photographers. For your convenience and curiosity, I've listed several, on pages 313-316.

If you buy a catalog/retrieval program and are satisfied, please let me hear about it. But I don't want to hear about it if you've catalogued fewer than 10,000 pictures. With fewer than 10,000, you don't need a computer system. The inexpensive device between your ears can handle that amount. Twenty thousand to fifty thousand pictures is where the help is needed, and this is where the problem arises. This volume taxes the capability of current software. You also need a hard disk drive or an optical disk. A microcomputer, your personal computer, can't handle a highly specific search fast enough yet. Current software ties up your computer for hours while it searches for eight pictures of varying fields that you may want to submit in response to a photobuyer's Want Sheet. You can't survive that way.

Three-by-five file cards continue to be the stock photographer's method of choice to locate and cross-reference a picture (see Chapter 13). There's no machine to turn on, no skills involved or manual to refer to, and you don't have to wait in line until it's your turn. *National Geographic*, the Library of Congress, and your local library still use 3x5s.

If you do have a compulsion to record data regarding your slides on your computer, do it like most stock agencies do: Record basic information about each slide into a computer database, usually when the slide is initially sent out on a sale (this justifies the cost of entering the information). If the agency wants to have a caption printed out, or to track where the slide is, or to make a search for *very general* (the issue here) categories, most simple database programs will do it.

Alan Carey of The Image Works adds, "We enter only *unique* images of importance such as celebrities and historical moments. Filing via computer is not a good use of time. Retrieving pictures must be done visually."

Jane Kinne of Comstock says, "There are too many nuances to a picture to entrust them to a computer program. Sales could be lost due to wrong information entered initially, or wrong requests made of the computer. *People* are still the best searchers in the files for images."

Computer/photography author and lecturer David O. Arnold says, "To set up a system, and then key in (or pay someone to key in) data on close to 10,000 slides to save an hour or two a month, isn't worth it."

Stock photographer Jim Pickerell says, "Installation and use of a computerized system would take too much time away from more important matters, such as photographing. Besides, there's always the decision where to classify it, how to caption it. A photo one person might notate as *aviation*, another would file under *flying*. You can't give this decision to an assistant. Editorial stock photo agencies might find that a computerized system would be fine because the pictures could be filed by job. As for me, the manual system is fast enough."

Someone who is, however, a satisfied user of a computer cataloging and retrieval system is stock photographer Daniel Cox. He uses the Phototrack filing system (included in the following list) and finds it to his liking. "Requests from photobuyers are getting more and more specific nowadays," says Daniel. "Recently an editor wanted a white-tailed deer doing something specific. I set the program to search through 5,500 slides of deer on my Epson Equity 1 computer (an IBM PC equivalent). In thirty minutes, we had what we needed. In the past, finding those transparencies would have consisted of holding up over 265 slide pages and scanning them. While the computer was searching, I was doing other things. It saves on the eyesight, too. And if I upgrade my computer, the search will be much faster."

Royce Bair of the Stock Solution says, "The national average for filing stock photos comes down to a dollar an image. Keying in the images on a computerized retrieval system, or bar-coding or placing magnetic strips on the slides, only increases that filing cost."

Computers are great, but only for what they're good at. It's necessary to be selective. Refinements continually increase the capabilities of computers, and in a great many areas, their performance is dizzying. The inadequacies of a computer come to light when we attempt to ask it to perform tasks that it really can't do very well yet. Categorizing and retrieving pictures is obviously one. By the same token, by the time you read this, someone might have come up with that perfect software—user-friendly, low-priced, versatile, and speedy. Until then, it's rolling along with hunt 'n' peck.

Several programs that can be put to use by the photographer with a computer are now on the market. Most of these programs are adaptations of an existing database, have been out only a short while and have limited track records. Here's a brief description of what's available:*

1. **Photophile** is a storage and retrieval system for slides, photos, and negatives. (Peripheral Visions, Inc., 5285 N.E. Elam Young Parkway, Suite B500, Hillsboro, OR 97124.) (503) 640-1317.

2. **Darkstar** provides the darkroom photographer with exposure data such as print density magnification, lens opening, paper type, emulsion batch, contrast grade, etc. (F/22 Press, P.O. Box 141, Leonia, NJ 07605.)

3. **Fotofind** is designed to allow photographers to keep on top of cataloging, storing, finding, identifying, and tracking the history and whereabouts of their photographs. For IBM PC/XT/AT and compatibles. Source code available to dBASE owners. (Bill Pursche, Argent & Aurum, RR 1, Box 380, Sherman, CT 06784.) (203) 355-9875.

4. **Seekeasy,** although not designed specifically for photographers, is useful in storing and indexing photographs. For IBM PC and compatibles. Get a copy from a friend, your computer user group, or a computer bulletin board. If you like it and want to be a regular user, you are requested to send a registration fee to: Correlation Systems, 81 Rockinghorse Rd., Rancho Palos Verdes, CA 90274 (213) 833-3462. (If you can't find a copy, call Correlation Systems and they can supply one, or tell you where to find one.)

5. **Shooting Star Software** offers three individual programs (Photo-

---

*Write to me for a free report on which programs are currently added to this list since publication of this edition. Include a self-addressed envelope with two first-class stamps affixed. PhotoSource International, Pine Lake Farm, Dept. 200, Osceola, WI 54020. (715) 248-3800.

Star, StarTrak, and Just Labels) to keep the photographer up-to-date on where his photography is (both in-house and out), how it has been used, and how much income it has generated. In addition, the programs prepare caption lists, delivery memos, invoices, statements, and print slide labels. (Shooting Star Software, Inc., P.O. Box 2878, Alameda, CA 94501.) (415) 769-9767.

6. **Photobase Plus** is a management-information program for professional photographers. Maintains accounts receivable and payable, keeps employee and freelance records, creates an invoice and a cost estimate, maintains a client list, writes checks, shows business cash position. Cost: $1,250. Requires a hard disk and an IBM-compatible computer. (October Press Software, 200 Park Avenue South, Suite 1320C, New York, NY 10003.) (212) 477-1251. (See a similar name at #13.)

7. **Photosource Search** is designed for the stock photographer who subscribes to the marketing newsletters, *Photobulletin* and *Photomarket* (see Bibliography). The software generates compilations of photobuyers, listed variously by alphabet, payment range, and/or per the subject areas of requests each has made over a given period of time, such as Alaska, chemistry, seeds, hiking, skydivers, etc. Customized reports are also available, such as names of photobuyers in certain cities, states, or regions. The software also generates Rolodex cards, alphabetical or by buyer number, noting each photobuyer who has made photo requests in the recent months. For samples and details, send SASE. PhotoSource Search, Pine Lake Farm, Osceola, WI 54020 (715) 248-3800.

8. **The Studio Manager II** keeps track of clients, evaluates profit progress, prints estimates and invoices, keeps the books, writes checks and balances statements, prepares mailings. (PhotoSoft Company, 754 Piedmont Avenue, Suite 303, Atlanta, GA 30308.) (404) 872-0050.

9. **Gold Coast** is a program for mini stock agencies and lists names of contributors, essentials such as I.D. #, quality rating, and key-word data for later retrieval. (Gold Coast Stock Photo, 1194 Springfield Street, Feeding Hills, MA 01030.)

10. **Technet** is designed for large labs and keeps tabs on production, print quality control, and business management. (Technet Center Software, Eastman Kodak, Photographic Products Group, Building 3, 343 State Street, Rochester, NY 14650.)

11. **C-Quest** allows search for a photograph several ways: classification code, "world" number, subject description, or a combination of these. (Clif Nickerson, Image Concepts, P.O. Box 211, West Boylston, MA 01583.) (617) 835-3273.

12. **Photo SBM** (Stock Management Module) is a professional stock photo management system. Software provides retrieval of photo information, prints caption labels, maintains photo shipment history for each photo, maintains publisher list with financial information, contains

submission log and generates delivery memos, includes mail system for address labels, invoicing, generates various reports, plus much more. (Micro Software Solutions, P.O. Box 851504, Richardson, TX 75085) (214) 272-4907.

13. **Photobase** is an electronic cataloging system that allows miniature photos to be displayed in the upper-right quadrant. Text information from database records fills the rest of the screen. Photos can also be expanded to full screen. (Chorus Data Systems, Inc., 6 Continental Boulevard, P.O. Box 370, Merrimack, NH 03054.) (See a similar name at #6.)

14. **The Photo System**™ cross-files photo libraries with captions under 999 subjects. It performs high-speed computer searches, displays photo information on-line, and prints slide labels and catalogs. It runs on IBM PCs and compatibles. Full system price $139. Slide labeling alone $49. Demo $15. (Tom Mulligan The Photo System, RE, Box 472, Lewiston, NY 14092.) (416) 945-8286.

15. **Phototrack**™ for complete stock photography management, designed to run on an IBM PC/XT/AT or compatible. Generates slide labels, submittal memos, invoicing, subject lists, tracks submittals, conducts searches with up to 17 keywords in a must/any match environment, maintains client lists and history files and is usable for form letter data generation with word processors. Automates setting of printer. Has Photobar™ bar code utility as accessory program. Available in freelance ($595) or agency ($795) versions. Will hold 1 billion records with proper storage. Phototrack Software, 6392 South Yellowstone Way, Aurora, CO 80016, (303) 690-5532. Phototrack Label, a slide labeling program, is also available, for $125.

16. **Professional Photo Catalog System** allows a photographer to keep track of images on consignment or sold. A variety of reports and delivery memos can also be printed listing images given to a customer. (26058 Blossom Lane, Grosse Ile, MI 48138.) (313) 676-1327.

17. **Macstock** is a complete stock photography management database for the Macintosh. Keeps track of submissions, clients, photo and sales records. Includes word processing, invoicing, labels, searches and statistics of all kinds. For any size stock file. Price: $399. Send $5 for a demo disk. Robert Maust Photography, 148 W. Wolfe St., Harrisonburg, VA 22801 (703) 434-8283.

18. **Cymagery,** designed for stock photo collections. Files, finds, logs, edits, deletes, prints. Bar-code ready. PC-compatible. (Cymagery, 711 Kalamath Street, Denver, CO 80204.) (303) 592-1091.

19. **High-Speed,** High-speed Photographic Database Software Package for IBM; designed for photographers, by a photographer, uses the Alpha/Numeral system outlined in *Sell & Re-Sell Your Photos*. Cost: $25. Send SASE for more details. (James A. Bremner, Photographic Illustrator, 3619 Nereis Drive, La Mesa, CA 92041.)

20. **The Captionwriter** is dedicated to writing captions. Works with lap-top computers as well as IBM, Apple, Tandy, etc. A special feature is a wraparound label for slides, allowing extensive caption information. Cradoc Bagshaw, P.O. Box 25706, Albuquerque, NM 87125 (505) 881-7143.

Telecommunications: Getting in Touch

News of Lincoln's election success took six weeks by horseback to reach the hinterlands. A century later, news can reach citizens anywhere in six seconds—via computer, on-line. A modem attached to your telephone and computer can enable your computer to instantly receive information sent by other computers. Your own printer then prints the information out for you.

This speed is important to the stock photographer. The postal *information float*, the lapsed time between when a photobuyer sends a photo request list by mail and when it reaches the photographer's mailbox, amounts to three or four days. A generation ago, this meant that stock photographers who operated their business in the same city as a prime photobuyer had an advantage. The photographer was on the scene, for a phone request and same-day service. Today, a combination of telecommunications and express delivery services enables the outlying stock photographer to be just as valuable a resource to photobuyers as the stock photographer down the street. If you have a computer and invest in a modem, you're no longer at the mercy of postal information float. In addition, assignment and travel information as well as time-sensitive business tips are available to you on an instant-summons basis, giving you a substantial business edge.

Mini-electronic post offices have sprung up since the mid-seventies—CompuServe, GEnie, The Source, Newsnet, MCI Mail, and in the photography field, PhotoNet, are examples. All these offer a variety of services to the computerized stock photographer. Each service is designed slightly differently, but basically they operate in the same style as a message center or a post office, except that you need travel no farther than your telephone/computer/modem to get your mail. You pay for this convenience, though, in that a meter begins ticking once you enter this electronic post office. While there, you can read the *bulletin boards* available in your interest areas, and you can check out your own personal mail box, all at a cost, generally by the hour. And, like the post office, you can pick up on business gossip with colleagues who are on the electronic system with you, in the form of an electronic conference, generally called a round table. After 6 p.m., the hourly fee is much lower than the fee charged for this *participation time*, or *read time*, during business hours. Each service also offers gateways to major databases and specialized services, such as Dow-Jones, TELEX, and the Official Airline Guide (OAG).

Our own PhotoSource International newsletters are examples of the kinds of information available through these electronic message centers. We offer our market newsletters on several services:

NewsNet. This network provides access to more than 300 various business newsletters, and also features our monthly *Photoletter.* You can access all previous *Photoletter* issues back to August of 1982, when we inaugurated our electronic editions. This means you can search for specific names of photobuyers or certain subjects, such as wildlife or gardening, by conducting an electronic *search.* In a matter of two or three minutes, the NewsNet central computer will alert you to the specific back issues in which these subjects can be found. If you wish, you can also search for the same subjects on all of the other 300 newsletters on NewsNet.

On the *GEnie* service, sponsored by General Electric, our three newsletters are available either by subscription or on a "newsstand" basis. On the latter, for a fee (GEnie docks the fee from your monthly GEnie account), you can take a look at a current issue. Or, as with a regular subscription to a magazine, you can sign up for a year's subscription at a discounted rate. GEnie also offers an electronic meeting place for photographers, called EPHOTE. Subjects ranging from Camera Techniques to Computer Graphics are discussed between amateur and pro alike on the nightly GEnie Round Table.

MCI Mail is another twist. It is strictly a mail service, handling both electronic and paper mail. There is no central database as in NewsNet, or Bulletin Board as with GEnie. Subscribers to our newsletters via MCI receive their issues directly in their electronic mailbox. An issue remains in the mailbox until it is accessed. (With MCI Mail, there is no hourly read-time fee.) If you don't have a computer, MCI Mail will send you our newsletters by electronic paper mail, transmitted by computer to laser printing sites around the country and then delivered according to ZIP code areas to U.S. Post Offices, to be mailed, similar to the method used by the newspaper *USA Today.* A special feature of MCI Mail is its inexpensive hookup with TELEX. Alan Carey of The Image Works uses his 1,200-baud modem to communicate with photobuyers at a fraction of the cost that the usual TELEX hardware and sign-on charges require.

CompuServe is the granddaddy of electronic networks. It offers a department called the Photography Forum. Features similar to EPHOTE are available to users.

PhotoNet, on line since 1983, is designed strictly for photographers and stock photo agencies. An agency can alert its member photographers of specific needs and announcements. Photographers can inquire about equipment and get technical advice and assistance. A popular feature on PhotoNet is the "Travelers" section, where photographers can announce their travel itinerary. Photobuyers who have picture needs in that geographical area can contact the photographer and discuss assignment possibilities. The service includes a number of current photo requests, on the style of those in our market letters.

For more information about any of these electronic services, call:

Service	Number to Call	My "Call" Number on the service
NewsNet	800-334-0329	P12, P17, and P26
MCI Mail	800-424-6677	189-2053
GEnie	800-638-9636	PSI and EPHOTE
CompuServe	800-848-8199	tba
PhotoNet	800-FOTONET	PHO1300

As more and more photographers begin to access telecommunication services, prices will go down and service will go up. No longer will it be necessary to live within shouting range of the large media centers. As long as a phone line is available, whether a stock photographer is in a high mountain cabin in Wyoming or a high rise in Biloxi, he will be in touch.

Captions

Here's where the computer shines. What could be more tedious and boring than typing or writing the same caption, in neat, tiny, legible words and numerals, on twenty boxes of slides . . . not including the time that twenty captions need to be repeated because the slides are basically the same shot. It's enough to deflower a blossoming stock photo career. A computer can take over your captioning tasks.

Just as professional-looking stationery gets the attention of a photobuyer, the same holds true for neatly captioned slides. If you project the image of an efficiently run stock photo operation, a photobuyer will want to consider you as part of the team.

It's to your advantage to dress up your slides with computer-assisted captions. Here are options for using your computer in captioning.

Database generated. This approach is the most popular. If you own a computer and database software, you assign a number to each new slide. As long as that slide is part of your stock file, you can keep a record on it: who has bought it, how many times, where it is today, and so on. When you enter the slide into your system, you can also generate a caption on a small ($\frac{1}{2}$"x1$\frac{3}{4}$") slide-sized label that you affix to the slide itself. An excellent article on designing your own captioning program was featured in the June 1987 issue (p. 30) of *Outdoor Photographer*. If you don't want to spend the time testing and designing a system, you can purchase specialized software for captioning your slides, such as Phototrack, Photobase Plus, Photo Star, Macstock, Fotofind, and others mentioned above.

Bar coding is not only popular at the supermarket but among stock photographers as well. By "swiping" the codes across a reader, the photographer can enter data about the slide into a file, and at any time generate a report including such information as the slide's whereabouts and productivity. If your stock file is 20,000 or higher and you want to accurately trace the immediate whereabouts of your images, bar coding is an answer. Photographer Jim Pickerell has applied bar codes to his in-house images. "It took eight hours a day for eight weeks for a staff member to code 30,000 in-house slides," Jim says.

A supplier of bar code labels is Watson Label Products, 3684 Forest Park Boulevard, Building D, St. Louis, MO 63108 (314)652-6715. The bar-coding hardware, which plugs into a computer keyboard, costs about $650 (available from Barcode Industries, 17 Barstow Rd., Great Neck, L.I., NY 11020 (516) 466-5770).

Turnkey Software such as the Cradoc Captionwriter (Stockware, Box 25706, Albuquerque NM 87125. (505) 884-7143) is designed solely for captioning slides. The software will drive most computers and printers. Assignment and stock photographers often use the Captionwriter with a portable computer, such as a Radio Shack 100, to accomplish their captioning right at the light table, in a motel room, or in the office. Captions can be affixed immediately or printed out at a later time. The Captionwriter has the ability to get twice the usual amount of words into a caption by featuring a *wrap-around label*. The cost ranges from $60 to $89.95, depending on your brand of computer.

Direct Printing can be done right on the caption mount with the *DiaMind* (Elden Enterprises, Box 3201, Charleston, WV 25332), a unit that will print up to 60 characters of caption information—20 characters per line—onto the wide edge of a mount, or two lines on either narrow edge. It costs just under $1,300.

Magnetic Strips are for large collections of slides. The original information is typed into a portable (NEC) computer, transferred to an encoder, which then electronically fixes it onto a magnetic self-apply label, which is affixed to the base of the slide. A duplicate label can be put on a 3x5 file card for cross-referencing. The user can later generate a printout by swiping the slides through the encoder. Because the format of the slide input always remains the same, the information can be entered into a computer database at a later time. The SlideScribe™ is available from DRT Corporation, 690 Mendelssohn Avenue, Building 12, Minneapolis, MN 55427. 800-345-4118. The cost for the complete system is just under $4,000. For just the label maker, without the magnetic encoder, it's $1,800.

Of course, if none of the above systems are in your future, you can always use the time-tested manual method of typing or handwriting the label or slide.

If someone were to invent a riding vacuum cleaner, we can agree that it wouldn't save time, because most housewives/husbands would discover

Figure 17-1. The Cradoc Captionwriter software can turn your computer and dot-matrix printer into a slide captioning tool. It features a ½"x3½" label that wraps around both sides of a 35mm slide.

Figure 17-3. The SlideScribe system produces both a caption label and a magnetic stripe that contains identical caption information. The magnetic stripe can be used to print out the caption text on a separate report, or to enter the information into a computer database.

Figure 17-2. Computer-generated slide captions add a professional touch to your stock photo operation. In this illustration, the Phototrack software produces three-line labels using a 22 cpi printer. The software allows you to use your existing numbering system.

Figure 17-4. When a group of slides require the same repetitive information, the computer can generate duplicate caption labels.

Illustration 17-1. *Captioning your slides is the "Main Event" when it comes to computers and photography. Well-captioned slides increase sales. The SlideScribe, pictured above, generates labels not only for the slide itself, but also for a 3x5 file card. The information can be entered into a computer database at a later time, thanks to an encoded magnetic stripe (similar to a charge card), which can be affixed to the lower half of the slide.*

more places to clean. Captioning your slides offers the same enticing trap. A word of advice from Photobase Plus software producer Mark Iocolano: "Put the photographs into the system as they are used, and convert gradually. When new photographs are taken or added to the file, put them into the computer that day. If you try to start from scratch, you'll never catch up."

Word Processing

Word processing, the ability to produce professional business or form letters, is probably the computer's greatest advantage to the stock photographer. It's a real time-saver. Stand-alone word processors are available, but because their capacity for storing letters for later use is limited, they have not been popular with the stock photographer. The computer not only stores all your letters or other documents, but also stores and merges address lists.

Some photographers who have added a second computer to their office arsenal have discovered how helpful it is to "dedicate the old computer to strictly one major task, such as all the word processing," says Royce Bair, "which frees the new computer to handle the general workload of everything else" (accounts receivable/payable, payroll, and general ledger).

If you are a speedy thinker and typist, you'll want to match your style with appropriate software. For example, "The program WordStar 2000 is slower than Kodachrome II in a Retina reflex," says photographer Dave Arnold. As I type this manuscript, I'm using the most antiquated of all word-processing software, Electric Pencil. But it is light-years faster than a quill pen.

Word processing becomes a necessity for your promotional efforts. You will build a list of present buyers and potential buyers, along with individualized information about them, such as when was the last/first time they bought a picture, who they replaced at the ad agency or publishing house, what is the most convenient time to contact them, etc. When you're ready to announce an upcoming trip, or a picture of yours that appears on the cover of *National Wildlife*, word processing is an efficient method to get a personalized notice in a letter or on a postcard out to persons on your list.

Word processing also provides a bypass around one of the major roadblocks of writing: "I just don't like to do second and third drafts of my letters or manuscripts." No rewrites and convoluted insertions are necessary with word processing; corrections, changes, and additions are simple to incorporate. You'll find that writing becomes far less of a chore. I've seen no guarantee that a word processor is a sure-fire route to a Pulitzer Prize, but there's no doubt it gives you the edge over the competition who happen to be still tussling with the now-antiquated typewriter. Like buying the best musical instrument won't guarantee that you'll produce heavenly sounds every time, with a word processor, the end results are still up to you. But having the right equipment can give you confidence as you develop and refine your expertise.

Spread Sheets

Before computers came along, accountants would use the stub of a pencil and a large sheet of graph paper to combine available figures about a business in order to produce a forecast or present-day picture. Spread-sheet software does the same, but can do it bigger, better, and faster. A stadium full of accountants with their pencils might not even accomplish the same results as a modern-day spread-sheet program.

The charts on pages 254 and 255 are good examples of what can be entered into a spread sheet. Since information on your photobuyers and sales is already included in your computer's database, you'll be able to engage in "what if" projects. Spread sheets supply you with facts to hang on to, as well as show you what's in store for you if you want to take up the challenge.

For example, if you wanted to increase your stock photo sales next year from $10,000 to $12,000, a 20 percent increase, a spread-sheet program could let you know the percent of increase in sales you'd have to engineer with each of your photobuyer clients. It would also indicate how many new photobuyers you'd have to add to your roster. Of course, you could crank that figure up to a 30 percent or even a 50 percent increase. The results can tell you the work you have to perform in order to accomplish your goal.

Computerizing gives other benefits, too: photographer Harvey Phillips lauds the ability of a computer "to give my business a professional look when I submit a computerized invoice." Software is available also for standard business needs such as accounts receivable, accounts payable, payroll, and a general ledger. As Colorado photographer Bill Ellzey says, "If nothing else, the computer gives me the feeling I'm getting organized."

Graphics

Some day in the future, stock photographers are going to look back on the present-day system we use to market our stock photographs and shake their heads. As you read this, we are on the edge of a momentous revolution in picture retrieval.

As you know, both you and the photobuyer are limited to the pigeonhole retrieval method of locating pictures. You file them away in a slot and pull them out to view them. It's the same system our U.S. Postal Service uses to sort and find envelopes. The system was invented by our first postmaster, Benjamin Franklin.

Optical disks, similar in technique to the video disks used for full-length movies, will eventually come into price ranges affordable to photobuyers and stock photographers. Optical disks can store 10,000 to 50,000 full-color pictures and more, depending on the technology. In essence, the application is simple: You will be able to transfer your stock photo file of original transparencies and black-and-whites to disk and send an optical disk copy to a photobuyer or stock agency. The images will be transferred to the client's main source disk, along with pertinent details about you and each picture.

When the system operator needs a specific picture, he or she enters a description into the computer, which locates a dozen or two dozen choices. The pictures can be viewed on screen, printed out in hardcopy, or transmitted via phone lines or satellite elsewhere to another computer. Large corporations and the military are now using this method. Eventually, the technology will be available to all of us.

Right now, graphic illustrations of photographs are available on your computer. Dan Tidwell, stock photographer from Folsom, California, uses his Apple computer and File Maker Plus to produce examples of available photographs. Rather than submit originals, he matches a photobuyer's current photo needs with a minicatalog of digital illustrations of what's currently available from him. (See Figure 17-5.) Another Apple program that will produce similar results is Microsoft File. (For use with IBM and compatible machines: Chorus Data Systems has a similar program.) In addition to a computer and software, the stock photographer would use a video camera to copy the photo, and an electronic scanner and special printing head on the printer to digitize the photo, inserted like a piece of paper into the printer.

The Microtek MS-300A can scan a photograph and transfer the information into tiny dots, which can then be transferred either to a disk for storage or to hardcopy for a layout in a newsletter, or transmitted elsewhere. An example of this process is the digited version of the cover photo on my book. (See page 327.) Digitizing pictures takes a lot of room in a computer's memory, but as the technology is improving and the prices are coming down, the scanner will soon be as common in a stock photographer's office as a telephone.

One more bit of magic is computer photographics. Because optical disk pictures are broken down into digital pixels (tiny dots), a system operator can manipulate the design, color, texture, and tones of the picture, and even add parts of other pictures. This approach would not be useful in photojournalism, where all of us expect unretouched documentary photography, but it offers great possibilities in the field of photo illustration. Computer photographics is no longer pure photography, but like a century ago, when etchings gave way to photography, the day is coming when photography will give way to computer photographics. This

Dan Tidwell
P. O. Box 384
Folsom, CA 95630-0384
(916)361-4283   October 7,1985

Kearney Reitmann
Editor

555 De Haro Street
San Francisco, CA   94107

Article Suggestion:

Mr. Reitmann:

    I am proposing an article for the REVIEW section that will cover these
points.

    I hope you are interested, may I hear from you soon, please.

    Sincerely,

    Dan Tidwell

Figure 17-5. Computer-generated line drawings aid the photobuyer in assessing
the impact of a photo. Photographer Dan Tidwell uses his Macintosh to provide
a catalog of selections for a potential buyer.

doesn't make etchings or photography any less valuable as mediums. It offers exciting horizons for the stock photographer.

Where To from Here?

Computers offer stock photographers an excellent springboard to the automated business office of the future. Is the noncomputerized stock photography operation now a relic of the past?

The good ol' days for the stock photographer of the past, generally translates to hand-printed captions on slides, carbon paper copies of transmittal letters, typewritten correspondence, partyline telephone calls, Rolodex and 3x5 file cards, all handled by the U.S. Postal Service. If you made mistakes in the good ol' days, you couldn't blame it on a computer. But this doesn't mean that your office nowadays has to look like something out of *Star Wars* in order to compete.

At a time when leading agricultural economists have declared the small commercial dairy farm a has-been, many farm families from Pennsylvania to here in Wisconsin are proving that pronouncement decidedly wrong. These families, with a conservative approach to farm technology, with diversification and with tireless manual labor, children included, have, with wise management and planning, largely escaped the high debt that has accelerated the demise of the small, family farmer. The get-big-or-get-out theory that has dominated American farming for the past few decades may no longer be valid.

In like manner, an "addiction to computer technology," as photographer Mike Fuger calls it, can lead to high debt for the stock photographer.

"Whether you're using a postal meter or licking postage stamps, the package still has to contain good stock photography," says Alan Carey of The Image Works.

Photographer Dave Strickler of Newville, Pennsylvania, doesn't plan to invest in a computer, ever. "I can wait the extra days to receive market information," he says. "I leave the scrambling to other photographers. Not all stock photography needs to be delivered yesterday." Dave has been selling his own stock photography successfully for twenty years.

For the new generation of stock photographers, it's going to be a different story. Changing technology will have a great impact on not only stock photography but also the other areas that affect it—publishing, printing, package delivery, communications, and travel.

We've been treated so far to only a tiny portion of the computer's potential. We are all going to take a ride on a massive technological wave that will have some of us riding the crest, others swept into the broiling undercurrents. Computers and computer technology will increase the speed of that wave. But in the end, good management, good photo illustrations, and wise business decisions, as usual, will be the key to moving forward in your stock photography business.

Appendix A
Third-Choice
Markets

Paper Product Companies

For want of a better name, I've grouped calendars, greeting cards, posters, postcards, and the like under the heading *Paper Products*. This segment of the marketplace produces millions of products but pays very little. And why not? There are millions of standard excellent pictures available to them from thousands of photographers—all scrambling to sell their silhouettes of a seagull against the setting sun. As you learned in Chapter 2, you can't expect dependable sales from standard excellent shots because of the overwhelming competition.

Moreover, the *large* calendar and greeting card houses do not welcome freelance submissions. Their photographic needs are filled by either staff people or their freelance regulars who are proficient with 4x5- and 8x10-format cameras.

The middle-size and smaller calendar and card markets do rely on freelance submissions, but they also rely on your vanity to fill their photographic needs cheaply. Not only are their rates low, but they attempt to acquire three- to five-year exclusive rights and sometimes all rights (see Chapter 15 to define the difference) to your photograph. They may even ask you to transfer copyright of your picture over to them. Such terms, which take a photo out of circulation, are contrary to your working methods and diminish the resale and income potential of your stock photographs. Remember this when you're thinking of dealing with a calendar or greeting card house: The stock photo agencies seldom deal with them. When they do, they negotiate for a high fee and a two- or three-year limit for *one-time* picture use, and they allow North American rights only. (Otherwise, a greeting card or calendar company will resell your picture

Employ the 360 degrees available to you when you select a subject for photo illustration. A straight-on view would have had less impact.

overseas for added profit—to them, not to you.)

Stock photo agencies know they can get better mileage and better return elsewhere for their pictures, so why shouldn't you? Most newcomers to stock photography start out with the paper products field and then graduate to the more lucrative and dependable markets outlined in Chapters 1 and 3. Why waste your time and talent in the paper products field when markets with lucrative photography budgets are waiting for your talent and know-how at this moment?

The one redeeming feature of greeting cards, posters, and calendars is that they can offer a showcase for newcomers to the field. If you feel this exposure would be advantageous to you, then deal with the well-established companies. Check an early edition of *Photographer's Market* against a current edition to see if a firm is still listed and the address is the same. I strongly advise you not to deal with paper products firms that have been in business less than three years, unless they come well recommended. If you are doubtful about a certain company, ask for a list of other stock photographers whom they deal with.

Here are the markets for paper products:

Postcards. You can sell and resell your travel pictures more often at higher fees elsewhere, so why bother with the low-paying picture postcard companies? If you nevertheless want to pursue this field, look on the back of current postcards in gift shops and stationery stores in the state or country you're visiting to find addresses of the companies that produce the cards. Also consult the Yellow Pages of the local telephone directory (under "Printers," "Publishers," "Postcards") for companies and addresses. The same goes for souvenir color transparencies—the kind you buy in a gift shop at the airport. Send the companies color photocopies of your work, with a request for their photographer's guidelines. If you find the right company and can provide them with the right photographs, monthly royalties from a "bestseller" can provide you with a tidy stipend.

Calendars. Calendar markets prefer large-format but will look at 35mm. They buy exclusive rights. They use staff or established service photographers who shoot in 4x5 or 8x10. Sometimes they will use freelancers, especially the smaller companies.

Calendar companies usually accept the standard scenic clichés; however, some houses have become innovative in their photographic tastes. Every now and then a calendar company will produce a line of calendars featuring abstracts or art photography. However, the experienced (and financially successful) calendar houses have learned to stick with the standards that appeal to the general public.

Greeting cards. Trends change more quickly here; visit a stationery store to see what's selling now. They buy exclusive rights (see Chapter 15); the pay is low and competition is high.

Posters. These are usually produced by calendar and greeting card houses; however, some are produced by independents. Nevertheless, the constraints mentioned previously hold true for the poster markets. They rely on freelancers, but they also usually require exclusive rights.

Puzzles, placemats, gift wraps. Again, you can sell your pictures at higher rates to other markets. Unless you are doing a favor for an in-law, stay clear of these markets. Your time and talent are worth more than they can offer.

If you wish to try your luck at calendar, greeting card, poster, and placemat sales, you'll find the following of some help: the market reference guides listed in Table 3-1 and in the Bibliography. You can also write to the National Association of Greeting Card Publishers and Gift Wrappings, 600 Pennsylvania Avenue, Washington, DC 20003, and ask for the *Artists and Writers Market List.* This brochure lists several dozen possible markets.

Paper product art directors historically buy more large-format pictures than 35mm. However, you can circumvent this problem by having enlarged reproduction-quality duplicates made of your choice 35mm slides. Consult the Yellow Pages, or Creative Color or Compcor, mentioned in the Bibliography.

Contact markets for calendars, greeting cards, and posters by using the mail techniques outlined in Chapter 9. Table 8-2 tells you how much to charge for sales to these markets.

Commercial Accounts

Commercial markets are concentrated in metropolitan areas. They attract service photographers. Many books and most how-to courses are devoted to some phase of commercial photography.

Commercial markets prefer to deal with photographers in person. They can afford to. The pay is high. So is the competition. It is *possible* to sell stock pictures to commercial accounts; it's also possible to win the Irish Sweepstakes. Commercial accounts do use stock photography, and they'll pay a good price if *you* want to pay the price—huge investments in time, prints, transparencies, shoe leather, travel fees, postage and UPS costs, phone bills, and mental frustration—for *each* sale.

You might make sales of your stock photography to commercial outlets if you can answer yes to the following five questions:

1. Do you live conveniently close to the commercial account so that you can make periodic (at least monthly) visits to keep yourself and your work in the photobuyer's mind? (Commercial accounts "buy" the photographer as well as his photographs.) Commercial accounts rarely deal by mail with photographers. They figure the stakes are too high to risk dealing long distance.

2. Are you prepared to provide *rush* service to your clients?

3. Are you willing to shoot to a client's specifications, not your own? Commercial accounts have rigid photographic requirements: "I want a red background, a 1961 Dodge convertible, two blond males."

4. Can you provide model releases for all recognizable people in your pictures?

5. Are you willing to relinquish ownership of your pictures? Ordinarily if you are dealing with commercial accounts, you would be doing so on a service-photography basis. (See the discussion of work-for-hire in Chapter 15.)

Some commercial markets do use stock photography regularly, but they usually obtain their stock pictures from a stock photo agency they're familiar with, where they know they can get (1) speedy service, (2) immense volume to choose from, (3) a variety of styles to choose from, (4) the work of established service photographers, (5) the going rates, and (6) an established and easy line of communication.

The only advantage you have as an independent stock photographer breaking into the commercial markets is that you can charge a lower fee. But that isn't even an advantage at ad agencies or PR firms, where the fee *they* earn from their client is a percentage of the fees the agency pays for the components of the account, including the photography. They could actually lose money if they bought *your* picture at a low fee.

Commercial accounts listed here prefer dealing in person with service photographers. Some even have policies against dealing long distance, unless it's with a top-ranking pro (or his rep), who contacts the accounts through a market listing service such as Photonet or *Photobulletin*.

If breaking into the commercial accounts is a challenge you just can't turn down, here are four books that will be helpful in breaking into the commercial side of stock photography: *Selling Your Photography*, by Kopelman and Crawford (St. Martin's Press); *Sell Your Photographs*, by Canavor (Madrona Publishers); *Stock Photography*, by Herwig (Amphoto); and *You Can Sell Your Photos*, by Scanlon (Harper & Row). Here are your commercial targets:

Ad agencies. Ad agencies rely heavily on photography for their visuals. The smaller the agency, the more apt they are to take time to look at you and your photography. The reality: Ad pictures are usually created and shot to order by an established service photographer. If ad agencies want stock photos, they historically go to a stock agency or to the established local pros first. Since ad agencies want to deal in person with their photographers, contact the agencies closest to you (see the Yellow Pages).

Graphic design studios. The smaller studios do buy from freelancers.

The pay is good, and if you love knocking on doors, wearing out shoe leather, and showing off a portfolio, these folks will entice you with the carrot on a string. They may like you, but you'll find that they still like dealing with a large stock agency better. They figure they will get better value by dealing through overnight express services with a large New York agency.

Record covers. If you know the industry backwards and forwards, you might score here with stock photography. But it's rare. They prefer dealing with local service photographers or massive stock agencies. If you deal with record companies, it is more likely to be as a service photographer supplying photography for promotional and advertising use, rather than the record covers themselves.

AV: Filmstrips, motion pictures, video discs. These audiovisual markets rarely buy stock photography off the street. They turn to stock photo agencies or have a staff photographer shoot it. The prospective AV photographer must be prepared to adapt to rapid change. Time spent cultivating this market is usually fruitless because the AV field lends itself best to the service photographer, who routinely visits clients.

Business and industry. Since businesses of any size (and these are the only ones who have volume photo needs) have staff photographers and on-tap independent service photographers, your pictures won't carry much weight with them, even if your pictures are outstanding. When these people need a stock picture, they go to a stock agency. Business and industry are not worth developing as a market for your stock photos; selling stock photography to business and industry is usually a some-time thing. If you rely on a rep or a market service, they will usually find you business leads, such as annual reports or corporate in-house publications.

Fashion. Don't confuse fashion with *glamour*, which sells well to the publishing industry. The fashion industry sometimes has use for stock shots for backgrounds, but they consistently go to stock agencies for the selections. Unless you live in New York, your chances of scoring are about zero. Fashion photography is service photography, and unless you can answer yes to the five questions posed earlier, fashion photography will be lost motion for you.

Product photography. Forget it. They don't buy stock pictures—it's all "to order."

(See Table 8-2 for prices to charge for audiovisual, record cover, and other commercial-market sales.)

Other Third-Choice Markets

The following are included in third-choice markets because they rate an A in "Exposure Value," C-minus in pay and resale potential.

Newspapers. Sunday newspaper feature supplements sometimes buy stock photography (see Chapter 1). Daily and weekly papers (a good starting place for the beginner) will occasionally buy a single photograph. The pay is low, but the exposure is helpful. It's like free advertising. Contact the photo editor of your nearest metropolitan newspaper for guidelines and payment information for picture stories, photo essays, and single picture sales. Your human-interest pictures and local scenics will sell newspapers.

Government agencies. Although the government is this country's largest publisher, it is also its smallest, since each unit deals on its own local specialized level. Government photobuyers come with a variety of titles: art director, editor, promotion manager, etc. They buy pictures for their publications in a variety of fields: agriculture, transportation, commerce, health, education, and so on.

They publish pamphlets, manuals, books, posters—the works. Finding the buyers is like entering a maze. It's said that it takes seven phone calls (don't give up) to locate the federal employee you're looking for. I know photographers who have persisted and found a market in the government for their photo illustrations, but they live in cities where there is a large federal center, such as Washington, D.C., Kansas City, or Atlanta. Caution: Government publications are often not copyrighted, which means your pictures could become public domain if a valid copyright notice is not included with your picture.

Art photography. A definition of art photography, of course, is elusive. Generally speaking, when photographers refer to it, they have in mind the photographs seen in magazines such as *American Photographer, Popular Photography,* and *Print,* and in salons and exhibitions.

Art (or artful) photography is salable. Collectors will purchase it in much the same way as paintings, and for the same reason: the investment value is ultimately dependent on the renown of the painter or photographer.

Except for a few specialized, low-paying magazines, art photography is not marketable in the publishing world. Photobuyers hang them on their office walls, but rarely buy them for publication in their books or magazines.

Do single art pictures bring in money? Witness a Ben Shahn or a George Silk going for $1,000, a Eugene Smith for $500. Once you become famous, your pictures will sell for prices like these and higher. So don't give up your Sunday photography. In the meantime, keep shooting those marketable pictures I discuss in Chapter 2. Your family and your accountant will thank you.

If art photography is an area of great interest to you, here are two excellent publications to check into: *The Photograph Collector,* Robert Persky, publisher, The Photographic Arts Center, 127 East 59th Street, New York, NY 10022; and *Strategies,* Harold Simon, publisher, SGPL Arts, Box 383, Montclair, NJ 07043.

Appendix B
Choosing
Your
Equipment

Big Camera or Little Camera?

Camera columnists usually advise their readers that *versatility* is the key to pro photography. The photographer is counseled to be prepared with both the experience and the equipment to handle whatever the occasion may demand, from 35mm natural light situations to 4x5 industrial-photography setups. *Basic equipment* is defined by them as including not only wide-angle and telephoto lenses with filters, but several different sizes of cameras (each with back-up bodies).

These recommendations are valid if you are a service photographer. But the stock photographer doesn't need to invest in so extensive an arsenal. You will probably be able to get started with one 35mm (top quality) single-lens reflex camera. Stock photography requires no studio, no lights, no multiple array of cameras, and rarely any special-effects lenses.

The type and style of camera equipment you'll need will be determined by your PMS/A and your Market List. For example, if your photographic strengths are in the areas of people pictures, indoor situations, and natural light, you'll have little use for a 4x5 camera and artificial light. If you own such equipment, you might consider selling it and buying back-up equipment for your 35mm system.

On the other hand, if your strong areas center on wildlife pictures, for example, a long lens or larger format may be appropriate. You might want to trade off your 35mm equipment for 120-size. In the 120 format, you'll want to be aware that Hasselblad-type cameras with *through-the-lens viewing* are noisy when you trip the shutter, and they can be distracting in situations in which you do not want to be obtrusive. The twin-lens type of camera, such as the Rolleiflex or the Mamiya, is generally much quieter. But, again, much depends on you and your PMS/A.

The 120 and the 4x5 format are the sizes of choice if or when you take Track A pictures (scenics and standard excellent pictures). You can successfully use 35mm for these areas, though, and quality 4x5 reproduction dupes can be made from your 35mm.

Though your equipment for making stock photos needn't be elaborate or extensive, you will want it to be complete for your needs, that is, capable of producing the kind of photos you want to deliver to your particular spectrum of markets. A good 35mm or 120-size camera with top-quality wide-angle, normal, and telephoto lenses, is basic. If your financial situation won't allow the auxiliary lenses, rent or borrow them to test their suitability to your PMS/A and Market List. These and other lenses will quickly pay for themselves if you've planned your marketing strategy wisely.

If you've done any reading in how-to photography books and magazines, you've encountered admonitions against black-and-white grain. The question of grain, however, is one that technicians enjoy debating—photobuyers have a different viewpoint and aren't so concerned about it. Graininess in black-and-white may be a concern when talking about salon prints. Photo illustrations, however, are judged on their illustrative, not their technical, quality.

The late Ed Wallowitch, a pioneer in the field of photo illustration, once was asked why he shot with a used Pentax instead of a Nikon. "Because I can own *two* of them and have a back-up, for the price of one Nikon," was Ed's reply. Grain, however, is rarely acceptable in color transparencies, especially if it's the result of poor exposure, a cheap lens, or camera movement. Bargain-basement lenses have no place in stock photography, but quality optics do—and at any price.

Before buying any equipment, compare prices. An easy way to do this is to check mail-order catalogs, such as Unity's, Sears, or J.C. Penney's. Check the ads in the photography magazines. Check also the sale ads or the classified ads in a Sunday newspaper for used equipment. Comparing prices can save you dollars. And by comparing the features of each camera or lens, you can decide for yourself what you need, rather than letting a camera department salesperson influence your purchase.

What other equipment is essential for the stock photographer?

Your Accessories

Lens shade. Buy one for each of your lenses. The screw-on or stretch-rubber kind works better than the snap kind.

Lens cap. Caps are necessary to protect your lenses when they aren't being used. Dust, oil, or scratches on your lens will affect picture quality.

Meter. If your camera doesn't have a reliable light meter built in, use a hand-held one, preferably the spot meter type. Rarely will you want to use the incident and reflective types of light meter, which require getting right up to your focus of interest. This breaks the mood or atmosphere of the situation you're photographing.

Carrying case. Make it yourself. Buy four slabs of one- to two-inch thick foam rubber. Glue or rubber-cement one slab in the top and one in the bottom section of a small suitcase. (Find a good durable suitcase at a secondhand store. A well-worn suitcase works best. It doesn't announce that you're a photographer, and your bag in the luggage rack doesn't look like a camera case to airport thieves.) Use the other two pieces of foam rubber to nest your equipment in. Using a marker, outline on these pieces the shape of each piece of equipment, plus a few slots for film cartons. Cut the shapes out to the size of each piece of equipment. Glue these two cut pieces of foam rubber onto the first two pieces, in the top and bottom of the suitcase. Your equipment will fit snugly in these slots, and the two pieces in the top section of your suitcase will hold the equipment in firmly.

Tripod. Since your photo-equipment needs as a stock photographer will be minimal, invest in a sturdy tripod—the kind with several knobs for tilting and raising. It will prove handy for scenes with inadequate lighting, and especially for slow color film, such as Fujichrome or Kodachrome.

Extra body. To preclude any disaster while photographing a special situation or an assignment, purchase an extra body that can also be used for color film if you're shooting in black-and-white. If your primary camera body needs repair or preventive maintenance, you'll still be in operation with the back-up body.

Belt. An ammunition carrier, that is, a canvas belt with pockets in it, the kind available in surplus stores (or the commercial vest available in photo stores), is a good accessory to have for carrying lenses to keep them handy for quick changes. Such a carrying vest or belt can also be made on a sewing machine using denim or heavy-duty sailcloth.

Appendix C
Spotting
Your
Black-and-Whites

You can easily eliminate the tiny spots on your prints with a #0 water-color brush and a product such as Marshall's Neutral Black or Spotone's #3. Sometimes a #1 pencil will do a good job, if your print is a J or similar matte surface.

If you've never spotted a print before, use a few of your reject prints to practice on. The idea is to dab in tiny dots; don't "paint." After a few tries, you'll soon become an expert.

Since stock photographers often print several of the same picture to distribute to several buyers, the question often comes up: How well should I spot each print?

After looking at the same print for several minutes as you're spotting it, dozens of flecks become apparent—and you might find yourself spending an undue amount of time spotting. When you first pick up a print to examine it, scan it for a few seconds and note in your mind the most obvious flecks that need your attention. The photobuyer scans your pictures just as quickly. Also, 90 percent of your pictures will be used in the layout in a much reduced size—thus reducing (or eliminating) the problem.

Appendix D
The
Darkroom

Developing and Printing: Do It Yourself or Farm It Out?

Should you set up your own darkroom or send your negatives off to a film lab to make up your prints? Again, your PMS/A and your Market List will be the best guides for your particular situation. If most of your stock photos will be color transparencies, a darkroom may be of little use to you, since color processing is complex, risky, and expensive to set up on your own. You'll fare better sending your color out.

Photobuyers rarely use color prints. Only about 10 percent of your Market List will accept color prints, and then only if they are 8x10 and technically perfect. And most of these markets will be in the lower-paying ranges. On the other hand, 90 percent of the photography budget at many publishing houses goes for black-and-white prints. If your Market List includes many photobuyers who use primarily black-and-white, you may want to consider your own darkroom. Even with black-and-white, however, it's possible to farm out your developing and printing and still come out ahead.

Here are some elements to think about in making your decision. Your personal darkroom time is valued at X dollars. (For the sake of illustration, use the minimum-wage figure.) Add to that darkroom equipment and operating costs (paper, chemicals, etc.). Include interest and depreciation. Set these costs against what developing and printing charges would be at a processing lab in the nearest city (you can do all your communication with the lab by mail). If you have tailored your Market List wisely and score frequently with your submissions to photobuyers, it could turn out that farming out your developing and printing could actually cost you less than investing the time and dollars into having your own darkroom. A typical custom printer is Robert Meier at Photo Marketing Labs, Rt. 5, Box 42, Menominee, WI 54751. We have found his prices to be fair, and he also includes photo illustration tips and comments if you ask for his critique.

You may wish to have a darkroom, though, for the enjoyment, flexibility, immediacy, and complete control it gives you.

Darkroom Equipment

If you do plan to set up a darkroom, the following list will ensure that your system will be complete:

To Develop Film

Magnifying glass*
Developing tank(s)*
Developing reel(s)*
Developer*
Stop bath*
Fixer*
Hypo clearing agent*
Photo flo*

Chemical bottles*
Graduate*
Funnel and filter*
Thermometer*
Timer*
Film washer*
Film squeegee*
Film clips*

Film dryer
Negative filing system
B&W darkroom data guide
Sponge
Changing bag
Water filter system
Water temperature controls

To Print

Enlarger*
Enlarging lens*
Negative carriers*
Lensboard*
Enlarging bulb*
Safelight and bulb*
Safelight filter*
Enlarging easel*
Polycontrast filter kit*
Canned air*
Photographic paper*

Print tongs*
Trays*
Chemicals*
Chemical bottles*
Developer*
Enlarging meter
Contact printer
Focus lens
Projection print scale
Negative brush*
Paper cutter

Paper safe
Darkroom apron
Toners
Print flattening solution
Photo chamois
Gloves
Dry mounting tissue
Mounting board
Print washer
Print dryer
Ferrotype plate and polish

*The necessities.

Combine the Options

If you can't afford to build and equip a darkroom just now, all is not lost. Search for a neighbor or contact a friend who may have a darkroom you could rent or trade time for with family portraits, etc. High school, local community college, or vocational school students who enjoy darkroom work might serve as apprentices to you in trade for your marketing of their pictures. *Caution:* Photobuyers expect professional quality from you. Train your apprentice(s) to meet your print quality standards.

In my case, I started out by borrowing the lab of a nearby college, trading my photographic services in return. Once I learned the mechanics of darkroom work and paired this knowledge with my PMS/A, I set up a small darkroom of my own in one of our closets.

Today I have a large darkroom in the office area of my barn, where I produce a master copy of each print. I send my black-and-white master prints to a lab in Minneapolis to have twenty duplicate file copies, plus an 8x10 negative, made of each master. You'll find a similar volume processor in your local Yellow Pages. Most theater people and politicians use these houses for their volume black-and-white printing.

If a darkroom is in your future, make your decision as to size and content, based on a thorough examination of your PMS/A and your Market List.

A newsletter in the field: *Practical Darkroom Newsletter*, Roger Ferris, Editor, P.O. Box 628A, West Redding, CT 06896.

Appendix E
Tips
for
Nonwriters

Photobuyers sometimes pay more for your pictures when they are accompanied by a text or story. As a photo illustrator, you will sometimes be called upon to supply words with your pictures. Don't freeze. Here are a few tips.

Instead of attacking that blank sheet of paper in your typewriter as though you were preparing a technically perfect, erudite report, consider it a letter you are writing to a friend. As in a letter, keep the tone, the mood, friendly. You can even go as far as to type in a fictitious salutation at the top of your "letter." Some writing textbooks suggest that you write "like you talk." One caution about that technique: Too often, trite phrases and overworked clichés will creep into your text. They might sound clever when you say them, but they look god-awful when you read them.

Don't attempt to be cute in your writing. If something you've written strikes you as extremely nifty, or clever: *Danger!* Strike it out. It might sound that way to you, your grandmother, or your son, but not to your readers. Keep it simple.

That's easy to say, but not easy to do. Keep to your subject, and *only* that subject. Don't try to tell the history of the world. If a secondary thought or idea comes along, write it down, yes, but on a separate sheet of paper, and develop that idea later.

Try to entertain, not to educate. Your readers come to you *not* to be educated, but to be entertained. Don't attempt to inflict a message on your readers. To paraphrase an old Hollywood homily: If your readers want a message, they'll go to Zap Mail.

In cases where a caption or a copy block of a hundred or so words is needed, the editor might ask you just to supply the raw details. The editor will tailor them to his needs. If you decide to move into more extensive picture stories and articles, there are two ways you can go: You can explore teaming up with a writer friend or acquaintance, which often works fruitfully for both partners, but takes cooperation and logistics, such as who does what, how the proceeds will be d or you can handle both copy and photos yourself. If you prod photos yourself, ask the photo editor of the publication what their pugᵤ *rate* is. This rate can be a *guide* to what your share of the package should be.

If you decide to be the producer of the whole package, the best course of action is to start right in with on-the-job self-training. I hesitate to recommend that you take a writing course through your local adult-education system. Most of these courses (I used to teach one) are aimed at creative writing. They're for a broad audience of writers and are too generalized in their content for your specific needs.

Writing is too vast a subject to treat in a weekend writing course or in a few pages of this book. Let your personal Market List be your guide. Do your editors like to see short features, news reports, extended captions, full-length features, or short copy blocks? Master the writing of these in whatever happens to be the preferred style of your editor(s). Give yourself assignments to produce articles similar to those in the magazines on your Market List.

There are many writing books available that cover these different formats. Here are some books that will help you teach yourself to write for your particular markets.

Beginning Writer's Answer Book. Polking, Chimsky, and Adkins, eds. Writer's Digest Books.
The Elements of Style. William Strunk, Jr., and E.B. White. Macmillan.
How to Write, Speak and Think More Effectively. Rudolf Flesch. Harper & Row.
Make Every Word Count. Gary Provost. Writer's Digest Books.
A Treasury of Tips for Writers. Marvin Weisbord, ed. Writer's Digest Books.

In the Bibliography, I've listed additional books, seminars, and newsletters for part-time writers.

Bibliography

Note: All of the books listed are in my personal library, and each has its own strengths and degree of usefulness. Ask your librarian or bookstore for a copy and examine each for its application to your own photo-marketing operation.

Selling Your Pictures

Freelance Photography: Advice From The Pros. Curtis Casewit. Collier Books. Conversations with service photographers in the field reveal some helpful advice for stock photographers as well.

How You Can Make $25,000 a Year with Your Camera: No Matter Where You Live. Larry Cribb. Writer's Digest Books. Service photography at its most accessible.

Outdoor Photography: How to Shoot It, How to Sell It. Robert McQuilkin. MCI Publishing. P.O. Box 162, Winfield, IL 60190. A specialized area treated in an easy-to-read style by a pro who knows this select field.

Photographer's Market. Connie Eidenier, Ed., Writer's Digest Books. A favorite desk-top reference for locating names, addresses, and categories for your Market List.

Selling Photographs: Rates and Rights. Lou Jacobs, Jr., Amphoto Books. (Revised 1987.) The author is both a writer and a working photographer. Clear and concise.

Selling Your Photography: The Complete Marketing, Business and Legal Guide. Arie Kopelman and Tad Crawford. St. Martin's Press. The marketing section is aimed more toward the New York service photographer than the non-New York photo illustrator, but the legal and business pointers are useful.

Sell Your Photographs: The Complete Marketing Strategy for the Freelancer. Natalie Canavor. Madrona Publishers. Good hints for the photographer who lives in a large metropolitan area, especially New York, and expects to make personal contact with editors and commercial accounts.

Stock Photo and Assignment Source Book. Fred W. McDarrah. Photographic Resource Center lists the names of photographers who are available for assignments, plus their specialties. Even if you don't get yourself listed, you'll find this book a useful lead to sources who use a lot of photography.

Stock Photography: How to Shoot It, How to Sell It. Ellis Herwig. Amphoto Books. Written by a knowledgeable pro.

The Foreign Syndication Handbook—A Guide to Selling Stock Photos All Over the World. Vicki Comiskey. Haberman Press. How to deal with stock agencies abroad.

Where and How to Sell Your Photographs. Arvel Ahlers. Amphoto Books. An old favorite, first published in 1952. Some of the marketing methods suggested are not in use today.

How to Produce & Mass Market Your Creative Photography, Ken Townend. Photographic Publisher's Guild (Nevada City, CA). A former ad agency executive shows how to sell by volume to boutiques and gift shops.

How to Make $50,000 a Year as a Nature Photojournalist. Bill Thomas. Writer's Digest Books.

You Can Sell Your Photos. Henry Scanlon. Harper & Row. Authored by the head of Comstock (a photo agency) and founding member of PACA (Picture Agency Council of America). An excellent treatise on how to sell your Track A pictures.

The Business Side

ASMP Professional Business Practices in Photography. American Society of Magazine Photographers, 205 Lexington Ave., New York, NY 10016.

Gold Book of Photography Prices. Thomas Perrett. Photography Research Institute, Carson Endowment, Carson, California.

Freelance Photographer's Handbook, Fredrik Bodin. Focal Press, 5 Wiley St., Gloucester, MA 01930.

The Complete Handbook for Freelance Writers. Kay Cassill. Writer's Digest Books, Cincinnati.

Do-It-Yourself Marketing Research. George Edward Breen, McGraw-Hill, New York.

The Basic Darkroom Book: A Complete Guide to Processing and Printing Color and Black-and-White Photographs, Tom Grimm. New American Library, 1633 Broadway, New York, NY 10019.

The Entrepreneurial Woman. Sandra Winston. Newsweek Books, New York.

How to Get Organized. Stephanie Culp. Writer's Digest Books, Cincinnati.

Pictures for Organizations. Phil Douglis. Ragan Communications, Chicago.

How to Do Your Own Accounting for a Small Business. Roger R. Milliron. Enterprise Publishing, Wilmington.

How to Organize a Small Business. Clifford M. Baumback, Kenneth Lawyer, and Pearce C. Kelley. Prentice-Hall, Englewood Cliffs, New Jersey.

National Photo Calendar, P.O. Box 3768, Costa Mesa, CA 92628.

How to Win the Battle against Inflation with a Small Business. Murray Miller, M.D., and Franz Serdahely. Enterprise Publishing, Wilmington, Delaware.

Travel Photo Source Book, SATW, 1120 Connecticut Ave., Washington DC 20036.

The Expert Witness Handbook, Dan Poynter. PARA Publishing, Santa Barbara.

Photographing for Publication. Norman Sanders. R.R. Bowker & Co. An examination of the best methods for achieving print excellence for publication.

How to Cut Photo Costs. Robert McQuilkin, MCI Publishing, P.O. Box 162 A, Winfield, IL 60190.

The Dr. Jeffrey Lant Catalog, Suite 507 B, 50 Follen St., Cambridge MA 02138.

(Includes self-promotion manuals for the entrepreneur.)

Peak Performers. Charles Garfield. Avon Books, New York.

Procedure Manual for Cataloging Photographs, Center for Creative Photography, 843 East University, Tucson, AZ 85719.

Organizing Your Photographs. Ernest Robl, Watson-Guptill Publications.

Penny-Pinching Postal Pointers for Everyone. Edmund J. Gross. Halls of Ivy Press.

Photography Magazine Index. Stu Berger. Paragon Publishing.

Professional's Guide to Publicity. Richard Weiner. Weiner Publishing.

Successful Business. Arthur Liebers. Key Publishing.

The Successful Promoter. Ted Schwarz. Contemporary Books, Chicago.

The Writer's Resource Guide. Bernadine Clark, Ed., Writer's Digest Books, Cincinnati.

Tax Angles, 901 N. Washington St., Alexandria VA 22314.

Legal Questions and the Photographer

Author Law & Strategies. Brad Bunnin. Nolo Press.

"Copyright Information Kit," Library of Congress.

Fear of Filing. Volunteer Lawyers for the Arts.

How to Pay Less Tax. Consumer Guide Publishing.

Legal Guide for the Visual Artist. Tad Crawford. Madison Square.

Photography: What's the Law? How the Photographer and the User of Photographs can Protect Themselves. Roger M. Cavallo and Stuart Kahan. Crown Publishers.

Strategies for the Harassed Bill Payer: The Bill Collector—and How to Cope with Him. George Belden. Grosset & Dunlap.

U.S. Master Tax Guide. Commerce Clearing House, Inc.

Visual Artists Legal Guide, The Professional's Handbook. Tad Crawford. Graphic Artists Guild.

What Everyone Needs to Know about Law. U.S. News & World Report Money Management Library, U.S. News & World Report Books.

Your Income Tax. J.K. Lasser. Prentice-Hall.

Newsletters

APIdea, 22231 Mulholland Highway, Suite 119, P.O. Box 4055, Woodland Hills, CA 91365. How-to tips for the service photographer.

Journal of the Photographic Society International, Venice, CA 90291. Includes a monthly column on marketing.

Guilfoyle Report, AG Editions, 142 Bank St., New York, NY 10014. Especially for the nature photographer. Includes trends, how-to business tips, market leads.

Photoflash, Box 7946, Colorado Springs, CO 80933. How-to tips.

Partyline, PR Aids, 330 West 34th St., New York, NY 10001. Market leads of freelancers and photobuyers searching for pictures.

PhoTak Newsletter, P.O. Box 2104, Neenah, WI 54956. Focus is on the indoor and outdoor photo equipment and supplies of the stock photographer.

Photography Today, Route 2, West Highway 46, Box 197, Templeton, CA 93465. About the business side.

The Photoletter, PhotoSource International, Suite 5, Pine Lake Farm, Osceola, WI 54020. Pairs picture buyers with photographers; lists current photo needs of specific editors and photobuyers.

ASMP Bulletin, Stuart Kahan, Editor-in-Chief, 205 Lexington Avenue, New York, NY 10016.

Photographic Resource Center Newsletter, 1019 Commonwealth Ave., Boston, MA 02215.

Photograph Collectors Newsletter, Bob Persky, 127 East 59th St., New York, NY 10022.

PSI Journal, Albert Moldvay, 1380 Morningside Way, Venice, CA 90291.

Scuba Chrome Journal, Burton McNeely, P.O. Box 338, Land O'Lakes, FL 33539.

Western Photographer, John Cates, Editor/Publisher, P.O. Box 19269, San Diego, CA 92119-0269.

ASPP Newsletter, P.O. Box 167, Redding, CT 06896.

SPAR Newsletter, 1123 Broadway, Rm. 914, New York, NY 10010.

PAI Newsletter, P.O. Box 167, Redding, CT 06896.

Practical Darkroom Newsletter, P.O. Box 628, West Redding, CT 06896.

Strategies, Harold Simon, P.O. Box 838, Montclair, NJ 07042.

National Photo Traveler, Nadine Orabona, 3008 Petite Court, Los Angeles, CA 90039.

Markets Abroad, Michael Sedge, Strawberry Media, 2460 Lexington Drive, Owosso, MI 48867.

Photo travel newsletters, Picture This Press, P.O. Box 3768, Costa Mesa, CA 92628.

Aperture, Michael Hoffman, Elm St., Millerton, NY 12546.

Light Impressions Review, Light Impressions Corporation, Box 940, Rochester, NY 14603.

Nikon World, Nikon, Inc., 623 Stewart Ave., Garden City, NY 11530.

Mind Your Business, P.O. Box 14850, Chicago, IL 60614.

National Home Business Report, Betterway Publications, Inc., White Hall, VA 22987.

For Photojournalists and Writers with a Camera

Authorship, 1450 S. Havana, Suite 620A, Aurora, CO 80012.

Contacts, Larimi Communication Associates, 151 E. Fiftieth St., New York, NY 10022. Pairs editors with PR people.

Copyright Management, 1505 Commonwealth Ave., #32, Boston, MA 02135. Copyright updates and case histories.

Directions, Travel Information Center, Woodstock, VT 05091. News and trend updates in the travel field.

Published! Platen Publishing, Suite #137A, 132 Shaker Rd., East Longmeadow, MA 01028. Articles on the craft of writing, researching tips, markets for photojournalists.

Every Writer's Practical Guide to Copyright Law, Ellen Kozak, Inkling Publications, P.O. Box 65798, St. Paul, MN 55165.

Freelance West, Box 601, Edmonds, WA 98020. Leads and tips for the freelancer; regional.

Freelance Writing. Curtis Casewit. Collier-Macmillan. Advice from several dozen pros.

American Writer, National Writers Union, 3818 Van Ness Street NW, Washington, DC 20016.

Ragan Report, 407 S. Dearborn St., Chicago, IL 60605. For public relations people and copywriters.

Towers Club Newsletter, Box 20308, Vancouver, WA 98661. For independent writers who self-publish; tips and how-to information.

The Travelwriter Marketletter, Room 1723, The Plaza Hotel, New York, NY 10019. For writers who also sell their travel pictures.

Writer's Digest, 1507 Dana Ave., Cincinnati, OH 45207. For writers; includes a monthly column on photography.

Writer's Journal, Inkling Publications, P.O. Box 65798, St. Paul, MN 55165.

Special Reports

The following publications and others relating to photo marketing are available from PhotoSource International. For prices and additional titles, write to me at PhotoSource International, Station 5, Osceola, WI 54020.

"Stock Photo Agency Strategies." A lengthy report on how to match your collection of stock photos with the right agency. Includes sample contract as well as a computer printout of agencies that deal in your category of pictures.

"Fine-Tuning Your Photo-Marketing Techniques." For the veteran photo illustrator. An advanced how-to report.

"Pre-Travel Planning Kit." List three countries, provinces, or states you plan on visiting, and you'll receive a computer printout of possible market contacts with names and sample cover letters.

The 4-weekend "Get Started ACTION Kit." Shows you how to get moving on your stock photography business in one month (4 weekends).

PhotoSource Search is a computerized search of back issues of *Photobulletin* and *Photomarket*. The reports list buyers, subject matter, geographical breakdown, etc. Photobuyer addresses are supplied in report form or on Rolodex cards.

Seminars and Workshops

A seminar will more than pay for itself if you shop wisely. Most of the seminars listed here offer helpful insights into publishing and graphics, and information directly related to running your own photo-marketing business. I've included a few of the many Track-A-oriented seminars available for readers who pursue the secondary and third-choice markets. New seminars on marketing your photos are often presented locally. For a list send SASE for a free copy of our current list of seminars in your area. Ask for "Seminar List."

"Autumn Eye," P.O. Box 1171, Telluride CO 81435. How to market outdoor photos.

The Bill Thomas Touch of Success Photo Seminars, Box 51532, Indianapolis, IN 46251 (317)271-7423. How to take and sell outdoor pictures.

Business Guide, Professional Workshop for the Visual Artist. The Graphic Artists Guild, Room 405, 30 E. Twentieth St., New York, NY 10003. How to keep more of what you earn.

Communicating with Pictures. The Douglis Visual Workshops, 212 South Chester Rd., Swarthmore, PA 19081. How to make and how to use pictures as editorial communication.

Elaine Sorel Workshop. Elaine Sorel, 640 West End Ave., New York, NY 10024. Teaches artists how to be good businesspersons.

Phillips Photo Illustrators, Harvey Phillips Seminars, 4 New St., Colts Neck, NJ 07722.

Matula Photography High Profit Seminars, Franklin Matula, 1101 Richland Dr., Waco, TX 76710.

Photo Illustration Seminars, Ron Sanford, 599 Oregon St., Gridley, CA 95948.

Focus, Mike Fuger Seminars, Box 11651, Kansas City, MO 64138.

Travel/Stock Photography Seminars, Fredrik Bodin, 5 Wiley St., Gloucester, MA 01930.

Outdoor Photography Seminars, Jeff March, 1922 South Oswego Way, Aurora, CO 80014.

Motivating the Reader and Selling the Graphic Arts Buyer. Dynamic Graphics Inc., Box 416, Peoria, IL 61614. How to deal with photobuyers.

New England Photographic Workshops, 30 Bridge St., New Milford, CT 06776. Marketing your photos.

Owens Valley Photography Workshops, P.O. Box 114, Somis, CA 93066. General photographic training.

Summer Photography Workshops, Rochester Institute of Technology, Technical & Education Center, One Lomb Memorial Dr., Rochester, NY 14623. How to upgrade skills and enhance techniques in photojournalism.

Rohn Engh's Annual Photo-Marketing "Fall Color" Workshop. Held last weekend in September in Osceola, Wisconsin. Pine Lake Farm, Osceola, WI 54020. The workshop is three days and covers the elements in this book plus Q-and-A feedback and personal critiques on students' pictures. Other Rohn Engh marketing workshops are held: third week in August: New Milford, CT; second week in September: Telluride, CO; second week in November: Hawaii.

Tom Stack Stock Photography Seminars, Suite 212A, 3645 Jeannine Drive, Colorado Springs, CO 80907 (303)570-1000. How-to instruction on how to break into the field of stock photography. Presented by a long-time stock photo agent.

Western Photo Workshops. P.O. Box 1171, Telluride, CO 81435 (303)728-4584. Marketing as well as general how-to photographic training.

Wilderness Photography Seminars, Robert McQuilkin, P.O. Box 162, Winfield, IL 60190. How to live in the wild and take photos and picture stories that sell.

Writer's Digest Saturday Seminars, Writer's Digest Seminars, 1507 Dana Ave., Cincinnati, OH 45207. How to write and photograph for your markets, and how to sell to them.

"How to Attract More Clients Without Advertising." 21 no-cost, low-cost marketing techniques and strategies to get "them" to call you—instead of your having to locate and call "them." Pete Silver, P.O. Box 5002, Woodbridge, CT 06525. Available on audio tape only.

"Jeffers Marketing Breakthroughs Course." Jeffers Corporation, 2570 San Ramon Valley Blvd., Suite 203A, P.O. Box 5600, San Ramon, CA 94583. (415)830-2700. How to promote and market your product or service. Available on audio tape.

Travel Workshops by Lisl Dennis, Box 2847, Santa Fe, NM, 87501.

Additional Workshop Sources

National Press Photographers Association, Inc., Suite 306A, 3200 Croasdaile Drive, Durham, NC 27705.

Professional Photographers of America, 1090 Executive Way, Des Plaines, IL 60018.

Photographic Society of America Regional Conventions, 2005 Walnut St., Philadelphia, PA 19041.

Local camera stores often sponsor half-day workshops. Consult the Yellow Pages.

Photography magazines (for the pro and amateur) often list current seminars and workshops.

Universities, colleges and technical schools conduct seminars and workshops. Consult your telephone directory.

Associations

Association of Electronic Cottagers, 677 Canyon Crest Drive, Sierra Madre, CA 91024.

Homebased Businesswoman's Network, 5 Cedar Hill Rd., Salem MA 01970.

Biological Photographic Association, 115 Stoneridge Dr., Chapel Hill, NC 27541.

International Association for Home Businesses, P.O. Box 14850, Chicago, IL 60614.

National Alliance of Homebased Businesswomen, P.O. Box 95PL, Norwood, NJ 07648.

National Association of Women Business Owners, 2000 P St. NW, Washington DC 20036.

National Federation of Independent Businesses, 150 West 20th Ave., San Mateo, CA 94403.

Rural American Women, Suite 700A, 1522 K Street, Washington, DC 20005.

Women's Owner Network, 1664 Siesta Drive, Sarasota, FL 33579.

Association for Multi-Image, Suite 401, 8019 North Hines Ave., Tampa, FL 33614.

National Association for the Self-Employed, Suite 17450, 1999 Bryan, Dallas, TX 17450.

National Press Photographers Association, Inc., Suite 306A, 3200 Croasdaile Drive, Durham, NC 27705.

Advertising Photographers of America, 823 N. La Brea, Los Angeles, CA 90038.

American Society of Magazine Photographers, Station 7, 205 Lexington Ave., New York, NY 10016.

American Society of Picture Professionals, Box 5283, Grand Central Station, New York, NY 10163.

Professional Photographers of America, 1090 Executive Way, Des Plaines, IL 60018.

Associated Photographers International, Suite 119, 22231 Mulholland Highway, P.O. Box 4055, Woodland Hills, CA 91365.

Photographic Society of America, 2005 Walnut St., Philadelphia, PA 19041.

Professional Photographers of Canada, Building 5, 1811 McKenzie Rd., Abbotsford, B.C. V23 3Z2, Canada.

Professional Women Photographers, % Photographics Unlimited, #14, 17 West 17th Street, New York, NY 10011.

Picture Agency Council of America, Attn.: Comstock, 32 East Thirty-first St., New York, NY 10016.

Volunteer Lawyers for the Arts Association, 3rd Floor, 1285 Avenue of the Americas, New York, NY 10019.

Directories That Will List Your Stock Photography

The Creative Black Book, 401 Park Avenue, South, New York, NY 10016.

Stock Photo and Assignment Source Book, The Photographic Arts Center, 127 East 59th St., New York, NY 10022.

Beautiful Pictures II, Creative Color, Burton McNeely, 4911 Grace Street, Tampa, FL 33607.

Editors Guide to Freelance Photographers, Publishers Network, Rich Kutner, 828 Charcot Ave., San Jose, CA 95131.

Stock Workbook, 940 North Highland Ave., Los Angeles, CA 90038 (800)547-2688.

The American Photographer, American References Publishing, Les Krantz, 919 North Michigan Avenue, Dept. PSI, Chicago, IL 60611.

ASMP Stock Photo Handbook, 205 Lexington Avenue, New York, NY 10016.

American Society of Picture Professionals, Annual Directory of Members, Box 5283, Grand Central Station, New York, NY 10017.

Chicago Talent Sourcebook, 212 West Superior, Chicago, IL 60610.

Working Press of the Nation, Volume V, National Research Bureau, 424 North Third Street, Burlington, IA 52601.

Society of American Travel Writers Annual Directory of Members, 1120 Connecticut Avenue, Washington DC 20036.

Picture Sources V, Special Libraries Assn., 1700 18th Street, NW, Washington DC 20009.

RSVP, Lebenson/Creighton Publishing, P.O. Box 314, Brooklyn, NY 11205.

Magazine Industry Market Place, R.R. Bowker Inc., 245 West 17th Street, New York, NY 10011.

Madison Avenue Handbook, Peter Glenn Publications, 17 East 48th Street, New York, NY 10011.

Note: A signed copy (8x10) of any of the photographs in this book is available for $25 by writing the author: Pine Lake Farm, Route 2, Box 93, Osceola, WI 54020. (715)248-3800.

Index

Accessories, 336-37
"Additional rights available," 267
Address labels, 146
Advertising agencies, 11, 111, 134, 332
Advertising expenses as tax deductions, 301
Advertising by stock photographers, 185-87, 301
Advertising use of photos, 25, 134, 268, 274, 283, 332; and copyright, 277
Adweek Creative Services Directory, 186
After-the-trip contact letter, 206
Agfachrome film 80, 85
Agreements, terms, and conditions, 281
Air-drying of prints, 83
All rights, 8, 196, 204, 270, 274, 279
Alphabet/number ID system, 144, 239, 243
American Passage, 91
American Photographer, 334
American Photographers Directory, 186, 350
American Society of Journalists and Authors Directory, 57
American Society of Magazine Photographers (ASMP), 57, 197; Guide to Professional Business Practices in Photography, 136, 137, 166, 186, 194, 226, 281, 345, 346, 350, 351
American Society of Picture Professionals, 57, 185, 226, 347, 351
Ampersand Inc., 185
Amphoto Books, 58, 166
Animal Pictures, 229, 292
APA (Advertising Photographers of America), 57, 226, 350
Apple Computer, 309
ARC Books, 228, 303
Arnold, David O., 310, 312, 322
Art director, 6, 111
Art fairs, 226
Art librarian, 122
Art photography, 11, 334
Art Photography Directory, 227
Art shows, 188, 226
Art of Winning Foundation Grants, The, 261
Artists and Writers Market List, 331
ASA, 80, 91
Assignments, commercial, 79, 100, 101, 102; fees for, 194-96; invoice for, 166; by mail, 193; query letter for, 206; self-, 199-204; side pictures during, 197
Associated Photographers International (API), 101, 231, 346, 350
Associated Press, 220
Association of Advertising Agencies, 278

Association Publications, 11
Atkinson/Stedko, 89
Audiovisual Marketplace Directory, 57
Audiovisual (AV) markets, 11, 333
Auxiliary lenses, 336
Available light, 80, 292

Background, 22-23, 26, 29, 30; lighting of, 105; as symbol, 25
Bacon's Publicity Checker, 57
Bagshaw, Cradoc, 315, 320
Bair, Royce, 312, 322
Bar Coders, 318
Bardes, 143
Basic Darkroom Book, 105
Basic Education Grants, 260
Bay Area Lawyers for the Arts, 282
Beautiful Photography, 230, 350
Benjamin Film Laboratories, 88
Berkey K&L Custom Services, 88
Black-and-white, 20, 79, 339; cataloging of, 236-41; conversion to from color, 83-84; cost of, 79, 80; decor photos in, 230; filing of, 242-45; film for, 80; marketable prints in, 81-82; preparation of, 142; quality of, 167-69; size of prints for, 81, 82, 83; spotting of, 83, 142, 338
Blue Book of Photography Prices, The, 136, 137-38
Bodin, Fredrik, 210, 311, 345, 348
Book publishers, 16, 203
Bowens Illumitran Model 3-C, 89
Broadcast Interview Source, Inc., 183
Brochures, for self-promotion, 177, 178; use of photos in, 127-28, 134
Budgets for photography, 3, 7, 11, 121, 126, 134
Business cards, 174, 175, 176
Business deductions, 298-302
Business letters, 115
Business outlets, 333
Business Practices in Photography, 166

Calendars, 10, 134, 190, 251, 279, 329, 330
Calumet Carton, 145
Camera Arts, 334
Capital gains, 303
Captions, 144, 163, 210, 223, 318, 320
Captionwriter Software, 315, 319, 320
Carey, Alan, 312, 317
Casewit, Curtis W., 42, 344, 347
Cataloging your photos, 236-43, 311-16
Catalogs, for self-promotion, 178-80; use of photos in, 134

Cavallo, Robert, 1, 166, 286
Central art libraries in publishing houses, 120, 121-22, 135
Changing Times Magazine, 187
Checklist, 24-point, 167
Checks with conditions on back, 279
Chiaroscuro, 23
Chicago Talent Sourcebook, 351
Cibachrome, 89, 121
Circulation of magazines, 69, 126, 130
Classified advertising, 185, 186
Clichéd pictures, 95
Closed markets, 251, 329
Close-up views, 22
Color, 79, 84, 339; black-and-white, conversion to, 83-84; cost of, 79, 80; decor photos in, 230; filing of, 244; film for, 80-81, 84-85; negatives vs. transparencies, 86; photocopies in, 90, 143; quality of, 167, 169; questions most often asked about, 84-90
Color coding, of categories on *Market List*, 59; of mailing list, 175
Color Film Corp., 89
Color negatives, 85; transparency enlargements from, 87
Color prints, 80, 85, 86
Columbian Safeway Mailer, 145
Columbia University Press, 261
Comiskey, Vicki, 155, 345
Commercial Markets, 331-33
Commercial use of photos, 8, 11, 23, 79, 100, 101, 102, 111, 120, 134, 268, 283, 285, 287, 288, 331
Compcorps, 88
Compensation, for lost pictures, 164
Competing agencies, 214
Competition, 21, 30, 53, 59, 119, 125, 138, 164, 174, 195, 203, 204, 213, 214, 252, 329, 331
Complaints, stock agency, 221
Composition, 22, 23, 28, 249
Compu/Pix/Rental (C/P/R), 219-20
CompuServe, 316, 317
Computer, 307-27
Computer graphics, 324
Computerized cataloging, 219, 235, 239; printout for fee negotiation, 197
Comstock, 217, 312, 350
Concessions in negotiations, 196
Contact Press Images, 220
Contact prints, 83, 142, 239
Contacts, 116, 183, 347
Contacts: with photo buyers, 280; with stock agencies, 220-21
Contest, 187, 189; copyright loss in, 189, 285
Contract forms, 281
Contrast, 82, 105
Conversion, 83
Cooperative (co-op) stock agency, 225
Copying others, 23, 199
Copyright, 189, 263; group registration of, 264, 271, 272; information kit, 282; length of, 270; notice of, 144, 167, 263, 264, 266, 269, 270, 272; ownership, 263, 270; questions about, 269-77; registration, 263, 264, 266, 269, 275, 276; transfer of, 329; on unpublished pictures, 271. *See also* Ownership; Rights
Copyright Act of 1976, 263-64
Copyright infringement, 121, 263-64, 268-69; penalty for, 273-75; statute of limitations on, 275
Copyright Law, 55, 263, 265, 266, 270-77
Copyright Management, 347
Copyright Office, 263, 264-65, 266, 267, 271, 272
Copyright Public Information Office, 265
Copyright, Revision of 1976, 263
Corporate markets, 333
Corporation, "S," 303

Costs: of black-and-white vs. color, 79, 80; of brochures, 175; of darkroom time, 339; of duping slides, 88; of letter writing, 115; of mail, 146; of mailers, 175; of reps, 222-23; of sales calls, 114; of telephoning, 116
Cover letters, 3, 115, 136, 148-49, 167, 207, 279, 280
Cover photos, 23, 127, 134, 268
C-Quest, 314
Cradoc Captionwriter, 319, 320
Craft shows, 226
Crawford, Tad, 166, 286, 344
Creative Black Book, 128, 350
Creative Color, 88, 230
Creative Directory of the Sun Belt, The, 186
Credit lines, 138, 163, 180-81, 216
Cross-reference system, 237, 241, 242-44
Cuardra Associates, 58
Curtis 1000, 145
Custom Color Laboratory, 88
Cut Your Photo Costs, 91, 345
Cymagery, 315

Dale Color Inc., 88, 231
Dale Laboratories, 91
Damage to photos, 280-81
Darkroom, 80, 105, 339-41; newsletter, 341
Darkroom equipment, 340
Darkroom Photography, 105, 185
Darkroom, Practical Newsletter, 347
Darkroom Techniques, 105
Darkstar, 313
Database, 308, 311, 318
Dated Pictures, 160, 266
Dating System, 144, 240, 265-67
Day rate, 194, 197
Decorating with Photographic Art, 231
Decor photography, 10, 11, 53, 189, 226-32
Dennis, Lisl, 210, 349
Denominational publishers, 8, 122; *Yearbook of American and Canadian Churches*, 59
Depreciation, 281
DiaMind, 319
Digital pictures, 121, 133, 224
Directories, 55, 57-58, 130
Display dupes, 88, 89
Display Fixture Co., 241
Display prints of transparencies, 89
Documentary photography, 93, 94, 261
Documentary Photography Grants, 261
Dome notebook, 302
Dramatic landscapes, 229
Dramatic-lighting formula, 105-07
Drawing Board, The, 280
Duplication, by extra exposures, 87; of prints, 142, 161, 167; at stock agencies, 221; of transparencies, 86, 87-89, 123, 157, 161
Duplicator, 89
Dynamic Graphics, 349

Earned income credit, 303, 304
Eastman 5247 movie film, 83, 87, 90-91
Eastman, William R. III, 228
Editorial assignments, 111
Editorial content of magazines, 127
Editor's Guide to Freelance Photographers, 186, 350
Edmund Scientific Co., 103
Educational Marketer Yellow Pages, The, 186
Educational publishers, 8
Ektachrome film, 80, 85, 89, 91
Ektacolor Print Film No. 4109, 87
Electric Pencil, 322
Electronic cottage, 350
Electronic paper mail, 317
Ellzey, Bill, 37, 46, 229, 323
Encyclopedias, 26

Endorsement, use of photos, 283
Energy tax credit, 304
Engh principle for marketable pictures, 22-26, 107-09, 199, 257
Engh, Rohn, annual workshop, 349
Enlargement from color negatives, 87
Envelopes, 145, 174
EPHOTE, 317
Epson computer, 312
Equipment, 10, 84, 335-37; insurance on, 250
Erotic photos, 229
Ethics: of photobuyers, 123; in photography, 94, 289-91
Every Writer's Guide to Copyright Law, 277
Exclusive rights, 279, 329; and stock agencies, 220
Exclusivity with stock agencies, 220
Exhibitions, 188, 226
Expenses: on assignments, 197; form for, 198; as tax deductions, 301
Experimental photography, 51

Fair use doctrine of copyright law, 55, 269, 275
Family of Children, 17
Family portraits, 101
Famous file, 61, 334
Fashion photography, 333
Fast films, 80
Federal Express, 165, 225, 281
Fees, corporate photography, advertising photography, 194; assignment photo illustration, 194-97
Fellowships, 260-61
Ferrotype-drying, 83
File folders, 235
File Maker Plus, 324
Filing system, 235-45, 312, 324
Film, 80-81; black-and-white, 80; color, 84-85; technical quality of, 84-85; types of, 83
Film holders, 83, 84
Filmstrip companies, 88
Financial aids, 260-61
First Amendment, 283, 285, 286, 289, 292
First-Class Mail, 147
First rights, 120, 279
Flyers, 175-76
Folio Magazine, 186
Foreign markets, 155
Foreign Syndication Handbook, 155, 345
For Sale or for Soul, 61
Form letters, 148-50, 204-10; categories, 117-19
Fotofind, 311, 313
Foundation Center, The, 261
Foundation Grants Index, 261
Four-Weekend Action Plan, 73-77, 215, 348
Fox Professional Color Labs, 259
Free Business Planning Guide, 304
Freedom of the press, 283, 289, 291, 292
Freelance Photographer's Handbook, 345
Freestyle Mailers, 146
F-surface paper, 83
Fujichrome film, 80, 85
Fujicolor film, 86

Gadney's Guide to Contests, Festivals & Grants, 227, 261
Galleries, 234
Gamma-Liaison, 220
Gamma Photo Labs, 88
Gannett v. DePasquale, 283
Gebbie's All-In-One Directory, 57
General-interest magazines, 8, 151
GEnie, 316, 317
Getting a Grant, 261
Getting started, 73
Gift wholesalers and manufacturers, 227

Gift wraps, 331
Glass mounts, 142
Glossy prints, 82
Goals, 135; setting of, 247-48; timing of, 249; written, 249, 252-53
Gold Book, 137, 309, 345
Good marketable pictures, 22-23, 31
Government agencies: as clients, 11, 333-34; toll-free numbers for, 260
Gradations of contrast, 81, 82, 105, 167
Graininess, 85, 91, 191, 336
Grants, 260-61
Grants and Aid to Individuals in the Arts, 261
Grants in Photography—How to Get Them, 261
Grants Register, 261
Graphics, 308, 323
Graphic design studios, 11, 332
Greeting cards, 10, 190, 251, 329, 330
Group registration of copyright, 264, 271
Guide to Copyright Law, 347
Guide to Successful Exhibitions, 227
Guidelines from publishers, 60, 129, 154
Guilfoyle Report, 228, 346

Herbert v. Lando, 283
Herwig, Ellis, 208, 214, 345
High contrast, 105
Highlights for Children, 156
High-risk marketing, 51
High Speed Software, 315
Holding fee, 158-61
Holding time for pictures, 157-61, 281
Hollywood Film Enterprises, 89
Homebusiness associations, 350
Home deductions, 299
Home Office Guide, The, 304
Homestead tax credit, 304
Horizontal format, 25, 85
Hot Line, 310
How to Cut Your Photo Costs, 345
How to Cut Your Taxes in Half by Incorporating Your Job or Business, 304
How to Produce and Market Your Own Limited Edition Photographs, 228
How to Produce and Mass Market Your Creative Photography, 228
Humidity and storing pictures, 244
Hutchinson v. Proxmire, 283

IBM computer, 309
Identification systems, 3, 143-44, 239, 320
Illford film, 80
Image Works, 312, 317
IMS Directory of Publications, 57
In-camera dupes, 89, 142
Individual Retirement Plan (IRA), 304
Indoor shots, 80, 85, 91
Industrial photos, 230, 333
Industry magazines, 11
Information USA Directory, 57
Inkling Publications, 277
In/out ledger, 253
Inside editorial uses of photos, 127, 130, 268
Insights from photos, 94, 96, 291
Insurance, 162, 258-59
Insuring packages, 146-47, 163
Interlibrary Loan Service, 55
Internal Publications Directory, 57, 210
International Reply Coupons, 147
Internegatives, 83, 163
Interpretive photography, 93, 94, 96
Invasion of privacy, 289-91
Investment Tax Credit, 303
Invoices, 165, 178, 280
IRS, 224, 280, 296, 297, 299, 304; toll-free number, 296, 298, 304

Jackson Marketing Products, 144
Jacobs, Lou, Jr., 44, 249, 286, 310, 311
Jeffers Marketing Course, 349
J.K. Lasser Tax Diary, 302
J-surface paper, 83

K-25 film, 85, 91. *See also* Kodachrome
Kalt Corp., 143
K & K Color Lab, 89
Keogh retirement plan, 303
Kiwanis Magazine, 251
Kleer-Vu Plastics, 143
Kodachrome film, 80, 85
Kodacolor II film, 86
Kodak, 87, 183, 231; F-surface paper, 83; J-surface
    paper, 83; Plux-X film, 80; T-Max film, 80; Tri-
    X film, 80; VPS film, 86. *See also* specific
    films
Kopelman, Arie, 166, 286, 344
Kozak, Ellen, 277, 347

Labels, 167, 224, 318, 319
Ladies' Home Journal, 120
Large-format internegative, 83
Larimi Communications Associates, 58, 184
Law and the Writer, 165, 286
Law libraries, 288
Law of 125, 258
Lawyers for the Creative Arts, 282
Leasing of photos, 210-11, 231, 267-69
Legal help, 282
Lens cap, 336
Lenses, 10, 336; auxiliary, 336; long 99; telephoto,
    99, 336; wide-angle, 336
Lens shade, 336
Letterhead, 174
Letters: after the trip, 200; magic query letter, 151;
    to photobuyers, 148-49; to stock agency, 218
Liability stipulation, 163, 165, 166
Libel cases, 283
Library of Congress, 236, 264
Life Magazine, 8, 94, 151
Lifestyle, 1-2, 7, 51, 54, 128, 129, 331
Light Impressions, 143, 347
Lighting, 105-07
Light meters, 105, 336
Light ratios, 107
Line conversions, 103
Literary Market Place, 58, 226
Loans, 260-61
Local newspapers, 128
Logo, 173
Look Magazine, 8, 151
Loss of pictures, 147, 161-66, 280
Loupe, 167

Macintosh computer, 309, 325
Macstock Software, 315
Madison Avenue Handbook, 58, 186, 351
Magazine Industry Market Place (MIMP), 58, 128,
    186, 210, 351
Magazines, 11-16, 24; circulation of, 126, 130;
    and color, 79; editorial content of, 127; gener-
    al-interest, 8, 151; industry, 11; nonprofit, 11,
    126-27, 128; photography, 284, 346; regional,
    8; revenue sources for, 11; sample issues of,
    154; special-interest, 8, 10; top, 8; trade, 184,
    199, 284; weekly, 8
Magic query letters, 115, 152-55
Magnetic strips, 319, 320, 321
Mail, 2, 112, 114, 115, 141, 161, 331, 332; assign-
    ments through, 193
Mailers, 175, 177
Mailing cartons, 146
Mailing list, 175
MAIL SAFE, 145

Mainliner Magazine, 282
Maintenance charge from stock agencies, 220
Malpractice suits, 163
Manila-file-folder system, 240
Market directories, 55, 57-58
Marketing: as a business, 247; directories on, 130;
    vs. selling, 125; strategy, 125; strengths and
    weaknesses in, 51; "sweepstakes," 8, 9, 22,
    60, 129, 331; by telephone, 177-80; zero-price,
    138. *See also* Personal photographic market-
    ing strength areas (PMS/A)
Market List, 3, 55-60, 62, 73, 79, 83, 84, 102, 115,
    119, 128, 129, 135, 138, 152, 161, 174, 181,
    193, 201, 216, 251, 252, 261, 265, 282, 335,
    336, 339, 340, 343
Markets abroad, 155, 347
Markets: breaking-in, 251; "closed," 251, 252;
    commercial, 331-33; prime, 10, 12-15, 16; sec-
    ondary, 10; target, 10-18; third-choice, 10-11,
    329-34; total number of, 6; travel, 210; trends
    in, 6-7
Marshall's Neutral Black, 338
Maust, Robert, 44, 178, 315
MCI Mail, 316
McNeely, Burton, 42, 88, 347
McQuilkin, Robert, 91, 178, 183, 344, 345, 349
Measuring your sales strengths, 253-55
Meisel Photochrome Corp., 89
Meranus, Leonard, 166, 286
Meters, 105, 336
Microfiche card, 90, 224
Microtek, 324
Midtown Foto, 259
Mind Your Business, 347
Minorities, 191
Mishandling of pictures, 161
Missing elements in marketable picture princi-
    ple, 26, 28, 30-31
Misunderstandings with photobuyers, 113
Model release, 25, 100-02, 165, 219, 282-83, 287-
    88, 331, 284, 285; available (MRA), 288; blan-
    ket, 101, 274; examples, 290; form for, 101;
    oral, 288-89; possible (MRP), 219; when re-
    quired, 283, 287, 288
Models 23, management of, 97-100; payment to,
    100; professional, 97; shyness of, 99; sources
    for, 101
Modem, 311, 316
Modernage Photo Services, 89
MONEY Magazine, 187
Mood in photographs, 24, 30, 32, 107-09
Mounted slides, 142, 143
Movie camera film, 83
Multiplecolor System, Inc., 91
Multiple copies, 142
Multiple sales of decor photos, 227-28
Multiple submissions, 119, 120, 126, 142, 157,
    161, 299

National Association of Greeting Card Publishers
    and Gift Wrappings, 331
National Endowment for the Arts, 261
National Geographic, 8, 31, 36, 93, 251, 312
National Home Business Report, 347
National Photo Calendar, 345
National Photo Traveler, 347
National Press Photographers, 349, 350
National Research Bureau, 210
National Textbook Company, 304
National Wildlife, 322
NEBS, 224
NEC Computer, 319
Negatives, 142
Negotiating fees, 134, 194-96
New England Business Service, 218, 224, 280
New England Photographic Workshops, 348

News features, for self-promotion, 185
Newsletters, 61
NewsNet, 316, 317
Newspapers, 11, 26, 128, 334
News pictures, 220, 282
Newsstand magazines, 6, 19
Nonexclusive arrangement, 221
Nonpaying markets, 138-39
Nonprofit magazines, 11, 126-27, 128
No-risk marketing, 55
North American rights, 329
Northwest Color Lab, 89

October Press Software, 314
O'Dwyer's Directories, 58
One-person agency, 223-25
One-time rights, 121, 125, 126, 135, 268, 274, 279
On-target pictures, 167
Optical disc, 324
Orabona, Nadine, 210, 347
Organization, 235, 244-45, 248-49
Organizing your photographs, 346, 237
Outdoor Photographer, 318
Outdoor shots, 80, 85, 91
Overexposed slides, 88
Owens, Bill, 185, 261
Owens Valley Workshops, 348
Ownership of photos, 263, 270; in contests, 189.
    See also Copyright; Rights

P = B + P + S + I (marketable picture principle),
    23-31, 107-09, 168, 199, 257
Packaging, 3, 144-46, 167, 254
PACK-A-LOPE, 145
PAI Newsletter, 347
Paper product companies, 10, 329-31
Paragon Publishing, 346
Parents Magazine, 5
Parkwood Camera Stores, 259
PARTYLINE, 116, 184, 346
Payment, on acceptance, 161; for assignments,
    194-95; of models, 100; ranges of, 126-27
People Magazine, 5, 121, 251
People in photos, 24, 25, 30, 31, 257; as distrac-
    tions, 27; missing, 27, 30
Peripheral Visions, 313
Permanent-file system, 122-23
Permission to photograph, 102
Perrett, Thomas I., 136, 137, 309, 345
Persky, Robt., 334, 347
Personal photographic marketing strength areas
    (PMS/A), 3, 37, 38, 53-55, 62, 73, 79, 83, 84,
    102, 116, 117, 125, 135, 161, 177, 181, 201,
    215, 251, 252, 261, 265, 282, 335, 336, 339,
    340
Personal visits to photobuyers, 114-115, 231; to
    stock agencies, 217
Phillips, Harvey, 46, 323, 348
Photo acquisition director, 6, 111
Photobulletin, 36, 128, 150, 202, 213, 219
Photo contests, 189, 285
Photocopying, 120-21, 143; of slides, 90; for spe-
    cial effects, 104
PhotoDataBank, 219-20
Photo Decor, an Idea Book, 231
Photo District News, 186
Photo editors, 6, 60-61, 111-23
Photo essay, 200-01
Photoflash, 346
PhotoGenesis, 89
Photograph Collector's Newsletter, 334, 347
Photographer's Market, 55, 58, 148, 154, 161, 210,
    216, 251, 273, 330, 334
Photographic Arts Center, 58, 334
Photographic Publisher's Guild, 228, 345
Photographic Resource Center, 347
Photographic Society International, 346

Photographic Society of America, 349
Photographing for publication, 87
Photography and the Law, 166, 287
Photography budgets, 3, 7, 11, 121, 126, 134
Photography Galleries and Selected Museums,
    226
Photography magazines, 284
Photography Magazine Index, 346
Photography Research Institute, 136
Photography Today, 346
Photography, What's the Law, 166, 282
Photo guidelines, 160, 129, 154
Photo illustration, 93-98, 100, 101, 103-09
Photojournalism, 94, 220
Photoletter, 1, 25, 56, 113, 119, 141, 150, 161, 172,
    189, 219, 221, 346
Photomarket, 128, 150
Photo Marketing Labs, 91
Photophile, 313
Photobase Plus, 314, 322
Photonet, 150, 316, 317, 332
Photo researchers, 6, 213, 215
PhotoSource International, 25, 84, 313, 314, 346
PhotoSource Search software, 314, 348
PHOTOTIX, 143
Photo Traveler Newsletter, 203
PhotoTrack, 312, 319, 320
Picture Agency Council of America (PACA), 217,
    350
Picture pirates, 123
Picture Sources V, 58, 351
Picture This Press, 347
Pine Lake Farm, 320
Plastican Corp., 143
Plastic sleeves, 142, 143
Plus-X film, 80
Polaroid positive/negative film, 83
Polking, Kirk, 166, 286
Polyvinylchloride, 143
Portfolios, 114, 115, 187-88
Portraits, 26, 101, 229
Positive-stat method, 89
Postage, 146-48, 167
Postal scale, 147
Postcard markets, 10, 134, 206, 329, 330
Postcards, included with submissions, 158; for
    self-promotion, 178
Posterization, 103
Posters, 10, 190, 251, 329, 330, 331
Preparation of photos for market, 142-44
Press cards, 103
Press freedom, 283, 289, 291
Press kit, for self-promotion, 190
Press releases, 184-85
Previsualizing, 37
Pricing, photo illustration, 126-27, 129-35, 138-
    39
Pricing the service photo, 136-138
Prime markets, 10, 11, 12-15, 16
Prime travel markets, 210
Principle, production, 23
Printcrafters, 177
Printing equipment, 85; custom printing, 339,
    340
Print magazine, 334
Prints, color, 85; glossy, 82; quality of, 81-82; size
    of, 81, 82-83
Priority mail, 146
Privacy rights, 289-93
Privilege fee, 136
Pro, looking like a, 148, 167, 171-74
Pro Color, 89
Product photography, 234, 333
Professional business practices in photography,
    194
Professional Photographers of America, 349
Promoter, The Successful, 346

Promotional literature, 115; tools, 190
Promotional use of photos, 25, 134, 231, 332
Protection, of files, 244; of rights, 281-82
Protective sleeves for photos, 142, 143
Public domain, 266, 271
Public figures, 289
Public Relations Basics for Community Organizations, 184
Public relations firms, 11, 111, 203, 204, 332; travel assistance for photographers by, 202, 209
Publisher's copyright notice, 264, 276, 277
Publishers Weekly, 186
Purcell, Carl, 39, 88, 210

Quality, of film, 84-85; of photos, 81-82, 144, 167-68, 256, 336
Quantity of photos to send, 144, 167
Query letters, 3, 115, 151-55; for assignments, 204-09

Radio Shack, 310, 319
Reader's Digest, 5, 283
Record covers, 11, 134, 333
Recordkeeping, 59, 235-45, 301
Redbook, 5
Red Tag Photo, 91
Reference guides, 55, 130
Regional magazines, 8, 180
Registered mail, 147
Registration, of copyright, 263, 264, 266, 269, 271, 272, 275, 276
Rejection reasons, 256-58
Reliability factor, 112, 126, 128, 146, 148, 150, 197, 217, 291
Renting of pictures, 8, 120, 125, 126, 135
Reports, special, 348
Representatives (reps), 222-23
Reprinting of photos, 274
Reproduction dupes, 88, 157
Research, on pricing, 130; your article, 200; on stock agencies, 216-17
Reselling photos, 126
Reserved rights, 279
Resin-coated (RC) papers, 83, 144, 231, 241
Resolution, 80
Retrieving pictures, 243-44, 311-16
Reuse of photos, 122, 135, 274
"Rifle" method of submissions, 151
Right of privacy, 289-91
Rights, 279-80; all, 8, 196, 204, 270, 271, 279; on assignments, 197; in contests, 189; exclusive, 220, 279, 329; first, 120, 279; inside editorial, 127, 130, 268; North American, 329; one-time, 120, 125, 126, 135, 268, 274; protection of, 280-82; reserved, 279; stating of, 148; world, 280. See also Copyright; Ownership
Risks, 161, 280
Ritz Camera, 260
Rolodex, 117, 177
Rotarian Magazine, 251
Royalties, 285
Rubber stamp for identification of photos, 143, 144, 241, 267

"S" Corporation, 303
Sales tax, 160
Salon prints, 336
Salons, 188
Sanders, Norman, 87, 345
Sandwiching of slides, 88
Sanford, Ron, 42, 348
Santa Fe Photography Workshop, 210, 349
Sarbin, Herschel B., 165, 286
SASE, 146-47, 167, 256
Saturday Evening Post, 5, 151
Schedule C tax form, 295, 297, 300, 302

Scholarships, 260-61
Scubachrome, Journal, 347
Seasonality of photo purchasing, 155
Seasonal pictures, 157
Secondary markets, 10
Sedge, Michael, 155, 347
Seekeasy, 313
Self-assignments, 199-204
Self-evaluation, 253, 254
Self-knowledge, 49
Self-promotion, 171-90; effectiveness of, 187; literature for, 115
Selling, 125
Selling Photographs: Rates and Rights, 282, 286
Selling Your Photography: The Complete Marketing, Business and Legal Guide, 282, 286
Sell Prints for Profit, 231
Seminars, 178, 348-49
Sepia tones, 227, 230
Service photography, 2, 9, 79, 81, 97, 101, 111, 114, 120, 123, 126, 134, 137, 138, 158, 164, 187, 199, 220, 263, 287, 288, 331, 332, 335; assignments for, 269; pricing in, 136-38
Sharing Ideas, 183
Shooting Star Software, 313
"Shotgun" method of submissions, 151
Shrink wrap, 231
Shutter speed, 80
Silhouettes, 51
Silk-finish prints, 231
Simon, Harold, 334, 347
Single-lens reflex camera, 335
Single sales of decor photos, 226
Size: of decor photos, 230-31; of prints, 81, 82-83
Ski Magazine, 251
Sleeves for protection of pictures, 142, 143, 239
Slide cabinet, 240
Slide mounts, 142, 143
Slides: copyright notice on, 272; duplication of, 87-89; improvement of during duplication, 88; photocopies of, 90. See also Transparencies
SlideScribe, 319, 320
Slow film, 80
Small Business Administration (SBA), 247, 304
Small Press Review, 186
Smith, W. Eugene, 82, 94, 283, 334
Smolan, Rick, 40, 220
Society of American Travel Writers, 58, 204, 351
Society of Photographer's and Artist's Representatives (SPAR), 222, 347
Software, 308, 313-15
Source, The, 316
Special effects, 103-05
Specialization: in book publishing, 10; in magazines, 8, 10; in publishing houses, 10; in small agencies, 225; in society, 8, 59; in stock agencies, 214-15, 225; in subject areas, 51, 59-60, 217, 252
Speculation, assignments on, 202
Sports Illustrated, 8
Sports photos, 229
Spot meters, 105, 336
Spotting, 83, 142, 168, 338
Spread sheet, 323
Stabilization process, 83
Standard cover letter, 115
Standard excellent pictures, 18, 31, 125, 213, 329
Standard Periodical Directory, 58
Star Trak Software, 314
Stating fees, 136, 148
Stationery, 3, 129, 148, 149, 152, 172, 173, 174, 296, 318
Stats, 89, 90
Statute of limitations on copyright infringement, 275

Stock photo agencies, 3, 11, 18, 22, 60, 79, 88, 89, 97, 203, 213, 329; competing, 214; contacting, 217-19; finding the right one, 215-17, individuals, 223, limitations of, 214-15; mini-stock agency, 223-25; model releases for, 287; problems in dealing with, 220-222; research on, 216-18; Track A shots to, 53
Stock Photo Assignment & Source Book, 58, 226
Stock Photo Darkroom, 89
Stock Photo Handbook (ASMP), 351
Stock Photo Source Book, 58, 350
Stock photography, 2, 9, 10, 31, 126; history of, 93; number of photos published per day, 22
Stock Photo Submission Sheet, 164
Stock Pictures Invoice, 164
Stock Solution, 312
Stock Workbook, 186, 350
Stolen pictures, 161-62
Strategies Newsletter, 347
Strickler, David S., 41, 180, 326
Studio manager, 314
Style, 144, 167, 256
Submissions, unsolicited, 150, 167
Successful Promoter, The, 185
Sunday newspaper feature supplements, 333
Supply/demand ratio, 251
Sweepstakes marketing, 8, 9, 21, 60, 129, 331
Symbol, 22, 26, 28, 30; background as, 26; missing, 30

Talent, 112, 129, 249
Talk Show Guest Directory, 58, 183
Tandy Computer, 307, 309, 316
Target markets, 10-18
Tax Angles, 304
Tax avoiding, 296
Tax benefits, 202. See Chapter 16
Tax deductions, 295-305
Tax form, Schedule C, 295, 297, 300, 302
Tax identification number, 296
Tax incentives. See Chapter 16
Tax kit, 304
Tax Rebate System, 295-98
Tax Reliever, The, 304
Tax, sales, 160
Tax write-offs, 202
Technical quality, of film, 84-85; of photos, 81-82, 256, 336
Technolust, 310
Telecommunications, 316
Telephone, cost of, 116; fear of, 117, 180; marketing by, 116-17, 180; toll-free numbers, 260-61
Telephoto lenses, 99, 336
Television contacts, 58
Telex, 316, 317
Tennessee Model Release Law, 287, 289
Terms and Conditions Agreements, 165, 281
Terms of Submission and Leasing, 165
Textbooks, 8, 26, 79, 156, 180
Trademark, 174-74
Trade shows, 181-82
Transparencies, 79, 80, 84, 85, 339; cataloging of, 241-42; display prints of, 89; duplication of, 86, 87, 157; identification of, 143-44; loss of, 167; vs. negatives, 86; preparation of for market, 142-43. *See also* Slides
Travel assignments, 202, 204, 205
Travel expenses as deductions, 301
Travel markets, 209, 210
Travel Photo Source Book, 345
Travel pictures, 202-04
Travel requirements for top markets, 5
Traveler, Photo, 203
Travelwriter Marketletter, 116, 202, 210, 347
Travel Writer's Market Directory, 58
Trimming black & whites, 168
Tripods, 337

Tri-X film, 80
Twentieth Century Plastics, 143
Twin-lens cameras, 335
Textured finish, 26
Third-choice markets, 10-11, 329-34
Thomas, Bill, 228, 345
Tidwell, Dan, 324, 325
Timely stock agencies, 220
Time Magazine, 187, 251
Titles for photobuyers, 111
Toll-free numbers, 259-60; IRS, 296, 298, 304
T-Max film, 80
Tonal completeness, 82
Tonal gradation, 81, 82, 105
Top markets, 5, 6, 8
Towers Club Newsletter, 347
Townend, Ken, 227, 345
Track A pictures, 49, 51, 53, 59, 60-62, 89, 117, 125, 199, 202, 215, 216, 226, 231, 336; outlets for, 213-14
Track B pictures, 31, 49, 51, 53-54, 59, 60, 62-63, 93, 117, 119, 128, 213, 215, 216
Trade magazines, 184, 199, 284

Ulrich's International Periodical Directory, 58
Underwater Photography Directory, 58
Unicolor, 143
United Press International, 220
Unmounted transparencies, 143
Unsolicited submissions, 150
UPS, 146, 147, 165, 219, 225, 281
USA TODAY, 187
Usage rights, 279-80
U.S. Department of Economic Development, 203
U.S. Department of Tourism, 203
U.S. Envelope Co., 146, 206
U.S. News & World Report, 5
U.S. Postal Service, 141, 146, 165, 206, 281
USTS Travel Information, 206

Vericolor Slide Film 5072, 86
Video discs, 134
Vinyl sleeves, 142-44
Visible Spectrum, 227
Visits, to photobuyers, 114-15, 331; to stock agencies, 217
Visual Artist's Legal Guide, 346
Visualizing picture-taking possibilities, 97
Volunteer Lawyers for the Arts (VLA), 282, 304, 350

Washington International Arts Letter, 261
Western Photo Workshops, 349
Western Photographer, 347
Wet darkroom procedures, 83
Where & How To Sell Your Photographs, 58
White mailers, 145, 146, 167
Wide-angle lenses, 336
Wildlife, 222
Wolston v. Reader's Digest, 283
Work-for-hire, 7, 8, 120, 190, 265, 267, 273, 274, 277-79
Working Press of the Nation, 58, 351
Workshops, 348
World in Color, 89
World Travel Directory, 58
Writer's Digest, 61, 348
Writer's Digest Saturday Seminars, 349
Writer's Journal, 277
Writer's Market, 59
Writing, 115-16, 342-43
Written goals, 249, 252-53

"Your Programs from Kodak," 182

Zellemat Co., 231
Zero-price marketing, 138
Zurcher v. Stanford Daily, 283